Communications

and Political Development

STUDIES IN
POLITICAL DEVELOPMENT

1. *Communications and Political Development*

Edited by Lucian W. Pye

❖

Sponsored by the Committee on
Comparative Politics of the Social
Science Research Council

Communications
and
Political Development

Edited by Lucian W. Pye

———•◆•———

CONTRIBUTORS

FREDERICK W. FREY   HERBERT PASSIN

HERBERT HYMAN   ITHIEL DE SOLA POOL

DANIEL LERNER   WILBUR SCHRAMM

DAVID C. MC CLELLAND   EDWARD SHILS

JAMES N. MOSEL   FREDERICK T. C. YU

PRINCETON, NEW JERSEY

PRINCETON UNIVERSITY PRESS

FOREWORD

This volume is the first in a series of Studies in Political Development sponsored by the Committee on Comparative Politics of the Social Science Research Council under a grant from the Ford Foundation for the period 1960-1963. In turning to the theme of political change and modernization, the Committee hopes to make a contribution to political theory as well as to enhance our understanding of the national and political "explosion" of our time. The distinctive phenomenon of contemporary politics is the new or rapidly changing nation, testing out political forms, processes, and policies in its efforts to find its place in the modern world. The Committee's program seeks to develop concepts, insights, and theories which will improve our capacity to understand these experiments and to evaluate their prospects.

In furthering these aims, the Committee has sponsored a series of conferences and research institutes in which the insights of American and foreign social scientists, educators, journalists, political leaders, and government officials have been brought to bear on the problems of modernization and democratization in the developing areas. The projected series will publish the results of these conferences, institutes, and individual scholarly efforts. Other volumes scheduled for early publication include *Bureaucracy and Political Development*, edited by Joseph LaPalombara; *Education and Political Development*, edited by James S. Coleman; and *Political Development in Turkey and Japan*, edited by Robert Ward and Dankwart Rustow. The volumes based on the Committee's two summer institutes, and individual scholarly efforts, will deal more directly with the theory of political change—with political typologies conceived in developmental terms, and with the factors that affect the direction, pattern, and tempo of political change.

The papers which appear in this volume were prepared for the Conference on Communication and Political Development which was held on September 11-14, 1961, at Gould House, Dobbs Ferry, New York, under the direction of Lucian W. Pye. The papers have undergone substantial revision since that time, and the editor has provided continuity and coherence by placing the papers in the framework of theories of political change and by drawing attention to significant findings which have a bearing on these processes.

The conference was attended by members of the Committee on

Comparative Politics and by the authors of the papers published in this volume. Others who participated included: Te Cheng Chiang, *Ta Hua Evening News*, Taipei; W. Phillips Davison, Council on Foreign Relations; Yukio Ichinose, Kyodo News Service, Tokyo; Keval Ratanmal Malkani, *Organiser*, Delhi; Robert E. Scott, University of Illinois; Clarence E. Thurber, Ford Foundation; W. Howard Wriggins, Department of State; and Pendleton Herring and Bryce Wood of the Social Science Research Council.

GABRIEL A. ALMOND

PREFACE AND ACKNOWLEDGMENTS

THIS is an experiment in intellectual stock-taking and in the application of new concepts to novel situations. For numerous reasons the Committee on Comparative Politics felt compelled to explore the relationships between social communications and political development and to discover the possible relevance of knowledge recently gained in communications research for understanding and influencing the prospects of political modernization in the new states. As political scientists we were attracted by the prospect that communications research might significantly contribute to the development of theory for comparative politics. We speculated that the communications process might be a critical variable governing the different possible patterns of political development. As members of the community of social scientists we were anxious to enlist the assistance of specialists in communications research in attacking the complex problems of political development and social modernization. As citizens we sensed an urgent need to uncover the various ways in which communications might facilitate the quest of leaders in the new states for democratic development. Our intellectual impulses were thus reinforced by our concern over the fundamental issue of the prospects for freedom in societies now anxiously striving to become a part of the modern world.

Hence the decision of the Committee on Comparative Politics to sponsor this study, to invite outstanding scholars to appraise the implications of different aspects of communications research for political development, and to call a conference to examine the problems of the new states in terms of the communications process and in the light of communications research.

Intellectually, neither communications nor political development represents a unified or compact field of knowledge. Communications research consists of a multitude of approaches and perspectives, ranging from the analysis of mass communications to the study of the complex processes by which cultural values are transmitted, from the study of the roles of writers and artists to that of the subtle ways in which each generation is taught the culture of its people. Therefore, to judge the utility of communications research for dealing with the host of problems associated with political development we needed the assistance of a wide range of specialists, including students of the mass media, psychologists, sociologists, anthropologists, and political scientists. Out of the variety of approaches of these scholars has come a rich array of insights and an ever deeper appreciation of the multiple dimensions of communications in human society. We have also learned that whether the focus is upon the mass media or the individual communicator, upon the gross political aspect of communications or the subtle transmissions of basic social values, almost all aspects of communications have a relevance for understanding the complex processes of social change and political development.

Our experiment has also revealed that the time is not ripe for finding an overarching order in the relationships between communications and political development. Innovation and tidiness rarely go together; and the same is true of new fields of knowledge and the formulation of coherent general theories. The boundaries of a dynamic field of knowledge cannot be described by smooth configurations, and in rapidly expanding fields there are certain to be sharp discontinuities and as yet unchartable borders. In reflecting our current state of knowledge in new fields of research, this study inevitably bears these characteristics of intellectual innovation. At the same time a first measure in seeking intellectual order is to survey and appraise existing knowledge, and this has been a prime purpose behind our experiment.

In presenting the results of our experiment to a wider audience we are aware that, although the separate contributions can stand quite adequately alone, it would be impossible to relate them to each other through the customary device of a single introduction. It has therefore seemed wise for the editor to accompany the reader throughout most of the volume, introducing the individual contributions, filling certain more conspicuous gaps, and providing as much of a unifying framework as is appropriate at our current stage of knowledge.

This volume was inspired by the leadership of Gabriel A. Almond, the chairman of the Committee on Comparative Politics of the Social Science Research Council, and it was advanced by the collective efforts of the entire membership of the Committee. This study is also heavily indebted to all the participants in the planning conference, who in contributing to the stimulating discussions inspired us in writing new materials and in revising the initial papers.

It is a great pleasure to acknowledge our indebtedness to the friendly assistance and wise advice of Pendleton Herring, who participated in all the decisions which made this study possible. In countless ways Bryce Wood supported our enterprise with a unique combination of enthusiasm and sensitivity.

Richard W. Hatch of the Center for International Studies, Massachusetts Institute of Technology, with great care helped to edit the work of all the authors and to transform the separate chapters into a book. Finally, we owe a special debt of appreciation to Alice Preston, who helped to arrange the conference and who transcribed our discussions, typed and retyped the manuscript, and finally read the proof and made the index.

LUCIAN W. PYE

CONTENTS

*Communications
and Political Development*

PEOPLE in three-quarters of the globe are now engaged in the baffling process of searching out new relationships with their fellow men and in striving to find their appropriate places in new societies, the dimensions of which they cannot yet fully grasp. Those whose sense of the universe was long bounded by the world of the village and the tribe are now being compelled to picture themselves as members of a nation which in turn belongs to a wider world of modern nations. The relationship between citizen and polity is never static even in the most well-established country; for individuals are constantly engaged in adjusting and re-evaluating, either restlessly and erratically or gradually and persistently, their sentiments, emotions, and judgments about their collective identities: there is always the pulse of life in any nation and the spirit of nationhood is always changing. But in the new countries of Asia, Africa, and the Middle East the thrust of change is different, and the issue is that of whether the essence of nationhood is to be realized.

In recent years a host of societies have been dramatically elevated to the status of sovereign independence, and consequently the family of nations has undergone a radical change in both size and composition. The creation of a nation, however, is a slow and complex process. The sudden and even violent changes in the lives of countless people have often been enough to ignite the spark of nationalism, but greater changes are needed to establish the realities of viable nationhood. Clearly the equanimity of the age is challenged in a multitude of ways by the problems of nation building in transitional societies. Thus a central problem of our day which should tax the full ingenuity of scholarship and of policy imagination is that of comprehending the many facets of political development and of influencing the dynamic processes of nation building.

It was the pressure of communications which brought about the downfall of traditional societies. And in the future it will be the creation of new channels of communication and the ready acceptance of new content of communications which will be decisive in determining the prospects of nation building. Throughout the transitional world the hopes and the fears about a new kind of life are ceaselessly stimulated by communications from abroad, which in turn become

mixed with memories of the old traditions. The pattern of development is inevitably governed in each particular setting by whether
the modern world has been communicated as being friendly and
sympathetic or hostile and foreign, as being benign and comforting
or harsh and intractable. Similarly, the process of recreating a coherent
modern society rests upon the ways in which people come to accept
and to utilize new dimensions of social communications. Thus the
turmoil of life in these disrupted and emerging societies flows from
the passage of communications.

Communication is the web of human society. The structure of a
communications system with its more or less well-defined channels
is in a sense the skeleton of the social body which envelops it. The
content of communications is of course the very substance of human
intercourse. The flow of communications determines the direction
and the pace of dynamic social development. Hence it is possible to
analyze all social processes in terms of the structure, content, and flow
of communications.

The term communications encompasses the bulk of social behavior,
for the vital force of human relations is man's capacity to send and
receive in countless ways both intended and unintended messages.[1]
In this sense communications permeate the social environment and are
to be found in every aspect of social life. This means that the analysis
of processes of communication is one way of studying social life. The
term communications, however, is also applied to a particular institution or industry, that of the mass media, the press, the radio, journalism, and to some extent the popular arts. The nature and the state
of the specific structures specializing in the communications function
invariably affect profoundly all processes of communications in the
society, but these special institutions never have a monopoly of communications. In this study of communications and political development in the new states our prime approach will be in terms of the
broader concept of communications as an all-pervading aspect of social
life. We shall, however, be constantly concerned with the relationship between the institutions of mass communications and the patterns
of political change basic to the problems of contemporary nation
building. Although our emphasis will be mainly analytical and

[1] For a useful introduction to the non-linguistic dimensions of social communications see Edward T. Hall, *The Silent Language*, Garden City, N.Y., Doubleday,
1959. See also Ithiel de Sola Pool, "The Role of Communications in the Process
of Modernization and Technical Change," UNESCO Document SS/NAC/1960/18.

not institutional, we shall be interested at every turn in learning about the best ways for developing modern and free institutions.
We shall therefore be equally concerned with both the theoretical
problems which emerge from viewing political development in terms
of communications processes and the practical policy problems of how
governments in transitional societies can best manage the communications media to facilitate modernization.

An assumption underlying this study is that by singling out the communications dimensions of social action we can gain a new perspective
for seeking insight into even the most well-recognized and institutionalized social processes. In recent years, for example, we have come to
a deeper understanding of some problems of national defense by
thinking of such acts as the development of different weapons systems
or the adjustment of defense budgets as in some measure acts of communication designed to deter the other side in the cold war.[2] As another example, the fields of administration and organization theory
have been greatly enriched by the insights which have come from viewing bureaucracies and industrial firms as essentially communications
processes in which influence and decisions are governed by the flow of
information and the control of messages. In many respects the communications approach has provided a more ·dynamic view of organizational behavior than can be readily derived from the more conventional concepts of status, hierarchical position or post, and of role,
which have usually been used in analyzing bureaucratic structures.[3]
Even such a well-established field as economics has benefited from
conceptualizing some of its central problems in terms of communica-

[2] For analysis of defense problems in terms of communications, see Thomas C.
Schelling, *The Strategy of Conflict*, Cambridge, Mass., Harvard University Press,
1960; Herman Kahn, *On Thermonuclear War*, Princeton, Princeton University
Press, 1960; Glenn H. Snyder, *Deterrence and Defense*, Princeton, Princeton University Press, 1961; Wilbur Schramm, "Psychological Implications of Military Posture
in Peacetime," Smithsonian Social Science Series, mimeographed.

A significant example of the degree to which defense problems have come to be
thought of in communications terms is the recent debate over fallout shelters, and
the issue of whether the construction of such shelters would "communicate" to the
Russians a provocative and threatening message.

[3] Compare the fundamental concept of bureaucracy in Max Weber's *The Theory of
Social and Economic Organization* (trans., A. M. Henderson and Talcott Parsons,
New York, Oxford University Press, 1947) with such examples of the application
of the communications approach to organization theory as Chester Barnard, *The
Functions of the Executive*, Cambridge, Mass., Harvard University Press, 1938;
James G. March and Herbert A. Simon, *Organizations*, New York, John Wiley and
Sons, 1958; and Robert K. Merton, "Manifest and Latent Functions," *Social Theory
and Social Structure*, rev. ed., Glencoe, Ill., The Free Press, 1957, pp. 19-84.

tions processes. This is true not only for studies about consumer preferences but also for understanding better the dynamics of investment and production decision making.

Above all, however, the communications approach has been most rewarding in providing deeper and more subtle insights into political behavior. There is a peculiarly intimate relationship between the political process and the communications process. For within the domain of politics the communications process has a fundamental function. Few people can observe at first hand the sequence of acts which constitute even a small segment of the political process; men must depend instead upon a communication system to provide them with a comprehension of the substance of politics at any particular time. It is through the organization of the communications process that the host of random actions which represent the pursuit of power by people throughout a society are placed in some form of relationship with each other; that order is established in the sphere of power considerations and a society finds that it has a polity.

The communications process also performs an amplifying function by magnifying some of the actions of individuals to the point that they can be felt throughout the society, in a sense transforming mere "man-sized" acts into "society-sized" acts. To a remarkable degree the difference between private and public affairs is determined by the extent to which acts of individuals are either amplified or ignored by the communications process. Without a network capable of enlarging and magnifying the words and choices of individuals there could be no politics capable of spanning a nation.

Another function of the communications process is to provide the essential basis for rationality in mass politics. A people can sensibly debate their collective actions only if they share a common fund of knowledge and information. And only if they have some minimum appreciation of how others have been informed about the state of affairs can citizens decide upon the wisdom and the validity of the reasoning behind the actions of their leaders.

All forms of political action are based on trying to fathom the unknowable which always shrouds the moves of individuals in a collective context. Thus politics calls for calculations about the nature of others, predictions about the likely behavior of men in different contingencies, and interpretations about the significance of apparently random events. To an important degree the communications process informs the members of a community of the extent to which they can and should legitimately question the motives and intentions of those initiating political actions. The communications process establishes standards which can keep a people from becoming unduly naive or excessively suspicious about what men are likely to do when they have great power at their command. In short, with an effective communications process people can more readily gain a realistic sense of the domain of the relevant in comprehending political motives.

Similarly, the communications process establishes a common framework of considerations as people strive to see into the future. Those who deal in political power are expected to have some of the qualities of the prophet and the soothsayer, for political power always has a dynamic dimension involving the issue of control over future developments. The communications process informs people as to how farsighted or nearsighted their leaders are.[4]

In proceeding along this line of analysis it becomes apparent that the communications process helps a society establish its rules of political causality and define its domain of the plausible. In large part, politics is made up of attributing relationships to all manner of occurrences in a society, and it is the politician who is presumed to be peculiarly sensitive to understanding and interpreting interconnections among events. In its simplest and crudest form this process involves those in power identifying a connection between their policies and all that is good that has befallen the society, and those out of power interpreting all that is evil to have followed inexorably from the same policies. The communications process provides a basis for limiting and making explicit the legitimate scope of political causality so that leaders and citizens can all be compelled to accept the same sense of the plausible. At the same time, by identifying the appropriate rules of responsibility, it can hold the political actors tightly in a web of causality. The communications process thus gives form and struc-

---

[4] It is a commonplace to observe that democracies are generally excessively preoccupied with short-run matters of the moment; therefore the question is frequently raised as to whether the democratic process is capable of coping with the long-run problems which lie at the heart of the process of nation building. It is less commonly recognized that one of the virtues of democracy is precisely that it reduces the time horizon of a people to the limits of sound predictions, and thus it protects a people from the fraudulent claims of omnipotence on the part of pretentious would-be leaders. In a sense, a democracy protects itself from insufferable nonsense by treating as political cranks all who make exaggerated claims of seeing further into the future than is possible on the basis of the common reasoning ability of man. Thus the concern in a democracy for matters which are immediately at hand is in part a reflection of a distrust for all that is falsely clever in the assertions of the prophet, the soothsayer, and the astrologer.

ture to the political process by surrounding the politicians on the one side with the constant reminder that political acts have consequences and that people can have insatiable expectations of politics, and on the other side with the warning that illusions of omnipotence are always dangerous even among people who have a casual understanding of causality.

These observations about the relationship between politics and communications have been historically appreciated by those concerned with improving the conditions of government. Indeed, political activists have customarily revealed in countless ways their instinctive sensitivity to the fact that the state of politics is a function of the communications process. Whether the inclination is for controlling the press or encouraging the freedom of the press—a fundamental basis for differentiating among political leaders—there is no questioning that all politicians must react to the realities of the communications process. Likewise, the citizens of established polities have repeatedly demonstrated their elementary appreciation of the communications process by readily permitting their judgments of its integrity to determine the degree to which they either have faith in or are cynical about their political system.

In the development of the American society, for example, the very concept of democracy has been inexorably linked to a belief in the need for the freedom and integrity of the press and the mass media. In the American view a free, independent, autonomous, and preferably non-partisan press is an essential prerequisite for democratic government. The vitality of American democracy has been frequently seen as threatened by the dangers of a one-party press or by any sign that the television industry has not been exactly equal in its treatment of political parties and candidates.

In view of this tradition of explicit concern, both in theory and in practice, for the relationship between politics and communications it is fully within the evolving tradition of political science to ask: "What is the role of communications in the political development of the new countries?"

A scanning of any list of the most elementary problems common to the new states readily suggests the conclusion that the basic processes of political modernization and national development can be advantageously conceived of as problems in communication. For example, the generally recognized gap between the Westernized, more urbanized leaders and the more tradition-bound, village-based masses, which is the hallmark of transitional societies, represents a flaw in the structure of the national communications and a fundamental problem in personal communications among people with grossly different life experiences. Similarly, the process by which the modern world has impinged upon traditional societies, producing both cosmopolitan leaders and xenophobic nationalists, is in essence a communications process. At both the domestic and the international levels the process of modernization depends upon people receiving new messages, new pictures and images of what life can be, and learning new responses to new stimuli. The emotional responses and the psychological reactions to this profound process of cultural change can all be analyzed as part of the communications process which lies at the heart of a contemporary and nearly worldwide movement in which all traditional societies in varying degrees are responding to the modern world.

In this collective study a focus on communication processes has been used to illuminate other dimensions of the complex relationships between elite and mass in transitional societies. We shall be exploring in depth, for example, the delicate balance between the need for quality cadres of intellectuals possessing modernizing skills and the need for the masses to have a sense of popular involvement, and indeed emotional identification, with the national life. The radical disruption of the old order and the persistent infusion of emotions into public affairs can blind a people to the overriding need for standards of excellence if great developments are to be realized. Indeed, the need to cast away old standards can leave a society with the urgent requirement that it find new and possibly even more demanding standards. At the same time, at the mass level the need for a popular basis of politics calls for more than atavistic appeals. There must be leadership for both those who will set the standards of the emerging societies and those who will become the responding citizenry of the new states. Attention must be given to building both a quality press and a system of mass communications; to ignore the first at the expense of the second is to court the evils of demagogic politics.

Other authors in this study have been able to use the communications approach to explore the basic problem of the relationship between the introduction of modern technology and the role of fundamental social processes in transitional societies. It is apparent, for example, that some governments in the new countries once placed excessive faith in the potentialities of modern means of mass communications. Deeper analysis shows that the press and radio can have a profound influence in changing the ways of people only if they are fully supported by the informal, social channels of communications which are intimately related to basic social processes. Rapid national development calls for the coordinated and reinforcing use of both the impersonal mass media and the more personal, face-to-face pattern of social communications.

At the same time, the communications approach readily brings to light the basis for the apparent successes the Communists frequently seem to have in mobilizing support for nation building, while also suggesting reasons why their achievements may not be enduring in the long run. As we shall be observing in some detail, the Communist technique is largely one of controlling and standardizing what are usually the more informal and random channels of communications, and thus turning these face-to-face processes of communications into essential mass media communications without in any substantial respect raising the level of communications technology.

These are only a few of the general hypotheses which have emerged from this collective study and which have justified our expectations of the value of analyzing the problems of political development in terms of communications. Above all, at this stage we note that a peculiar advantage of the communications approach is that it provides a common basis for analyzing both the most manifest structural problems and the most subtle questions of attitudes and values in the total process of political change and nation building. In a sense the communications function both cuts across and provides a link between the objective sociological and economic problems basic to macroanalysis and the subjective psychological problems of microanalysis which must be combined in any complete study of political modernization. In highlighting the problems of both the society and the individual, and even more important, by stressing precisely the manner in which these two dimensions of human life impinge upon each other, the communications approach provides a means for coming to grips with all of the most fundamental problems in political development.

For example, the widely recognized problem of creating political consensus in most of the new states is in part one of building new and more universal means of national communications, of establishing more effective channels of communication and transportation so that all segments of the society can become more closely involved with each other. In part, however, the problem of political consensus is related to the deeply held attitudes and sentiments of the separate individuals which emerge out of their accumulative communications experiences. Thus from a communications point of view it is possible to relate the problems of the development of the mass media, the organization of political articulation and the expression of interests, and the formation of collective opinions with the individual's reactions to the challenge of new ideas, his groping with conflicting values, and his search for new perspectives—and to demonstrate that all these complex problems underlie the general problem of political consensus.

This particular way of relating macro- and micro-analysis opens the way to the possibility of extensive and fruitful cooperation among several of the social sciences in working on the problem of political modernization in transitional societies. Indeed, an explicit consideration which underlay the organization of this study was the feeling that, if the problems of political development were conceived of in terms of communication, people trained in such diverse fields as journalism and the study of the mass media, sociology, social psychology, and even clinical psychology, might possibly be readily and usefully recruited to the task of working on the massive problems of the new countries. This exploration of such an approach constitutes in a sense an invitation to all such students to contribute their insights, theories, and techniques of analysis to the general effort to understand and assist the process of nation building. In addition it is to be hoped that since there is an inherently close relationship between the communications process and the political process this particular basis for welcoming the assistance of all relevant social sciences will also ensure that the resulting contributions are likely to be significant for understanding the political dimensions of development.

Communications and Public Policy for Development

It is not necessary here to elaborate on the great need for social scientists to collaborate in providing greater understanding of the problem of political development in the transitional societies. The process of modernization is manifestly multi-dimensional, involving all aspects of human society, and hence a problem which calls for contributions from all the social science disciplines. The advantages of collaboration based on the communications approach, however, go beyond the peculiarly close functional relations between politics and communications. Another significant consideration is the fact that the field of communications studies has already proved itself a remarkably effective bridge between the world of theoretical social science and the world of public policy.

This leads us to the fact that, in spite of the accelerating interest of political scientists in the problems of the underdeveloped areas, we have not as yet accumulated the necessary insights and generalized knowledge to provide the basis for a sound doctrine for political development which in turn might be of value for the policy makers in the new countries.

To a disturbing degree Western political theory has ignored the problems of nation building as a systematic goal of public policy. By and large Western thinkers have assumed that the "nation" and the "state" are natural phenomena which are reflections of the essential character of the particular societies which gave rise to them and which continue to provide them with their fundamental dynamism. Western thinking about the process of nation building has at best been guided by a faith in spontaneity: a faith that a people will naturally, if not prevented by outside controls—e.g., colonial authorities—create for themselves national institutions which will represent their distinct cultures and their true genius. In this view the institutions of a society reflect the basic character of a people.

This belief in the "natural" quality of the polity has contributed to a strange perversion of the scientific spirit, for it has encouraged scholars to feel that they should seek only to understand the actual operations of all political systems and not pass judgment on the shortcomings of any. Unfortunately the realities of political life for the vast majority of the peoples of the underdeveloped countries— which means the majority of mankind—do not permit of any such comfortable 19th century view. Faith in spontaneity died soon after the first ex-colonial people began to experience frustrations and disappointment in their efforts to become modern nations. It is not likely to be revived as long as so many of the people of the new countries have profound feelings of insecurity and remain unsure of their own abilities.

Western scholarship in the meantime has become increasingly aware that people in the new countries aspire to have things which are in no way consistent with their fundamental cultural patterns; that, politically, they want their societies quickly to possess all the attributes of the modern nation-state. The time has clearly arrived for those who value free institutions to face up to the very real problems of the appropriate strategies and doctrines which might facilitate the process of nation building in the transitional countries.

Significantly, the field of communications research emerged out of a comparable situation when free institutions were under attack and there was a compelling problem of public policy. The prime thrust behind the development of modern communications studies was the challenge of Nazi propaganda and the need for a major effort in psychological warfare in support of the democracies during the Second World War. In response to that national crisis, social scientists soon learned that they could make significant contributions to the field of public affairs. After the war the growing field of communications research continued to be delicately balanced between the scholars' world and that of government officials and private industry. Thus within the field there has always been a unique respect for practical policy problems and a high degree of understanding of how scholarship may be turned to policy ends without damaging the growth of knowledge.

Most of the policy-oriented work in communications has dealt with the problems of changing the attitudes and behavior of others and of communicating across the barrier of differing cultures. These two problems are both crucial in the process of political development. In most of the new countries there is the massive problem of trying to awaken the bulk of the people to new ideas and to the potentialities of new techniques, without at the same time producing crippling tension and deep psychological frustrations and anxieties. Unless the masses of the people are exposed to new ways of thinking and led to adopt new attitudes, there can be little hope of any steady progress toward economic development, social modernization, and political maturity. Since the gap in outlook between the innovators of change within many of the governments of the new countries and the bulk of their rural population is as great as that between different national cultures, the leaders are in a sense confronted with much the same kind of problems in communications as have interested students of international communications. Just from this consideration alone it would seem that communications research should be in a peculiarly favorable position in assisting the process of political development.

A strong case could indeed be made that the two most general and most fundamental problems in political modernization are precisely these two of changing attitudes and reducing the gap between the ruling elites and the less modernized masses. It would follow that if students of international communications were to shift their emphasis from, say, the problems of communicating the policies and the image of the United States to the emerging countries to the problems of domestic communications within these countries, they could readily make a substantial contribution in the effort to deal with one of the most demanding problems of world politics.

The Concepts of Modernization and Political Development

If the students of communications, along with other social scientists, are to assist the peoples of the transitional societies, there is a need for general agreement as to what is meant by modernization and political development. Therefore in introducing this study a few comments may be in order here so as to avoid semantic difficulties and some common misconceptions.

In recent years there has been a conspicuous and uneasy search for satisfactory words to identify and describe the non-industrialized societies of the world which have now become or are shortly to become sovereign nations. We have sought to use, but with only varying degrees of satisfaction, such terms as "backward," "non-Western," "underdeveloped," "developing," and "emerging." In large measure the problem, of course, stems from our concern over possibly offending those being identified. But it also arises from our own uncertainty as to the nature of these societies, their future prospects, and the appropriateness of our even suggesting that possibly they should change their character to be more in accord with the industrially advanced societies. A generation of instruction in cultural relativism has had its influence, and social thinkers are no longer comfortable with any concept which might suggest a belief in "progress" or "stages of civilization." In the meantime, however, as the West has gradually learned to appreciate and sympathize with cultural differences, many of the spokesmen for the non-Western world have become increasingly impatient with their own traditions and have insisted that it is their right and duty to change their societies to make them more like the industrial world. Yet there is a note of qualification in even the most insistent of these calls for change, for there is the realization that more respect is to be gained from being distinctive than from being an inferior version of a foreign culture. Everyone seems to sense that some forms of difference are acceptable while others are not.

Thus confusion exists in both the West and in the new countries over the desirability and propriety of encouraging the spread of modern but foreign ways. There are few people indeed who do not have some mixed feelings about the meaning and the value of change in transitional societies. Hopes and anxieties seem to merge and create an unstable basis for commitment and for expectations. When national leaders in the new countries express concern over the possibility that their countries will lose their unique character to the leveling qualities of the modern world, they often reflect a mixture of longing for the old and of fearing that they may fail in gaining the new. The tendency toward rationalization in the new states and toward a patronizing spirit in the advanced countries is encouraged by the fundamental uncertainty over the likelihood that any particular country can realize the amount of change necessary for it to achieve membership in the modern world.

If discussion is restricted to the economic realm, many of these uncertainties seem to disappear. Both laymen and scholars find it relatively easy to explain what is meant by economic progress, and there is usually near unanimity about the desirability of such progress. Thus for the last decade people have been able to champion enthusiastically the cause of economic development while remaining confused and uncertain about other aspects of social change. During this decade people have sought in numerous ways to isolate the concept of economic development and treat it as a problem apart from all other problems of development. This tendency has been reflected in government policies, both in American aid programs and in the development plans of the new countries. Even in social science research there has been this same tendency to separate the economic aspect of development from the other dimensions of social change.

Recently, however, it has become increasingly clear that the problems of economic development are inexorably linked to all phases of life in transitional societies. We have learned that very few of the essential prerequisites for economic growth are related to purely economic matters. The habits of mind, the values and world views, the social conditions of life, and the stability and effectiveness of government are all clearly crucial factors determining the prospects of economic growth. Thus for both policy maker and scholar what began as relatively uncontroversial and presumably narrowly technical problems have increasingly become entangled in the most complex of social and political issues.

The inescapable conclusion seems to be that the concept of development cannot be reserved for the economic sphere alone. But what should be the meaning or even the index of "development" in the other aspects of society, and particularly in the political realm? One can easily become skeptical about the appropriateness of applying the concept of "modernization" to politics and of classifying as "developed" the political practices of industrial societies. Indeed, it might be argued that the political in even the most economically and socially advanced societies is the preserve of the more traditional features of the society, and that all political systems must represent a blending of the historical and the contemporary.

The difficulty with the concepts of political modernization and development is that there are so many legitimate ways of judging and evaluating a political system. For example, to some extent a political system must deal with the solving of problems, and hence it might be possible to judge various systems according to the extent to which they produce rational policies. Yet a political system is expected to do more than merely solve problems; it must cope with insoluble issues, and it must provide people with a sense of identity and of fundamental membership in a larger community. Clearly the multifunctional character of politics and the fact that a political system cannot be thought of as producing a single "product" means that no single scale can be used for measuring the degree of political development.

If we were to isolate all these various functions of politics we would find that most of them could be readily related to a pair of fundamental problems. First, the realm of politics, as generally thought of, consists of two rather different forms of activities, involving different structures. These are, on the one hand, the domain of administration and formal government and, on the other hand, the political processes of the society which permeate in a diffuse fashion the entire society and provide the fundamental framework of the polity. Thus political development must involve both the strengthening of formal government and the establishment of mechanisms for giving coherence to the polity as a whole.

The second fundamental problem lies in the fact that there is a basic tension in contemporary politics between the universal characteristics of the nation-state which arise from the functional requirements of being a member of the nation-state system and the particularistic character of each nation as it reflects its cultural and social history. The very concept of nationhood has meaning only in terms of a general system of nation-states; for any people to feel that they represent a nation they must believe that they possess most of the institutions and governmental forms which modern states are expected to have. Countries must follow the international styles if they are to be considered sovereign states. On the other hand, the essence of nationhood is also to give expression to the uniqueness of a people and to differentiate the self from all others. The nation-state must rest upon a sense of national identity, and in human affairs a sense of identity always requires a feeling of continuity, of stability over time, and a capacity not to yield always to the demands of the outside and foreign world. Political development thus requires a recognition of the tension between meeting the universal standards of the nation-state and adhering to the particularistic standards of a cultural tradition.

To return to the first of these problems: it is relatively easy to identify the qualities of modern administration. Indeed, within the realm of formal government it would be possible to specify in considerable detail the qualities of organization and the patterns of routinized behavior which might appropriately be classified as either "modern" or "traditional." Within the domain of governmental rule and authority, modernization is clearly associated with the degree of specificity of function, the extent of universalistic norms of conduct, and the prevalence of achievement considerations. Since there is little question as to what constitutes development in this dimension of the political sphere, it is not strange that almost all conscious attempts to further political development have focused on strengthening the formal organs of government. Under colonialism the common test of political development centered on precisely the advancement of administrative rule; and since the end of the colonial period American foreign aid assistance has also largely concentrated on this same aspect of political development.

It is by contrast considerably more difficult to characterize the modernization of the process of politics in the society at large. Yet it is in this domain that the ultimate test of political development must be met. It is possible, however, to identify certain minimum considerations as to what should constitute development in the purely political sense. With the modernization of a polity should go an increase in the capabilities of the society to mobilize its people for national efforts. Modernization also implies a widening of participation in ways which affect the decision-making process. Also in a developed polity there should be a wide range of interests, all freely represented and well rooted in the social and economic life of the society as a whole. A modern polity is thus one that contains conflicts and that seeks to manage controversy so that no significant interest is arbitrarily suppressed while at the same time the collective interest is guarded.

We might further characterize a modern political process as one capable of coping with change in the sense of being able to purpose-fully direct change and not just be buffeted by social forces. There are also such matters as stability, orderly transfer of power, respect for constituted authority, adherence to legal procedures, and a clear recognition of the rights and duties of citizens.

In dealing with these central problems of the political process it is clearly not possible to rely solely upon the distinctions between "modern" and "traditional," urban and rural, *Gemeinschaft* and *Gesellschaft*, which the social theorists have found useful in categor-izing social and economic systems. The processes by which interests and values are expressed and then combined to give form and sub-stance to political life represent in all cases a fusion of those traits of behavior customarily identified as both "modern" and "traditional." Similarly, the processes by which people learn about the nature of political life in their country and come to participate with skill and effectiveness are much too complex to be usefully categorized accord-ing to such an elementary dichotomous scheme.

The process of organizing sentiments, articulating and aggregating interests, and the orderly extension of participation always entails a combining or fusing of many elements in a people's cultural tra-ditions. It involves considerations which follow from the sociological and economic realities of the society, and also from the psychological and cultural character of a people. It involves thus both macro- and micro-analysis. This suggests that possibly a fuller understanding of the essentials of political development can be uniquely gained by studying the political process in terms of the communications process. This was one of the lines of thought which led us to this particular study of the relationship between communications and political development.

The second basic problem which complicates the concept of political development—that of the tension between the universal standards of the nation-state and the particularistic qualities of national identity—is also one which can be usefully studied in terms of communications processes. In this case we are compelled to deal with the interactions which stem, on the one hand, from the diffusion throughout the world of all aspects of modern life and, on the other hand, from the needs of every particular culture constantly to reassert its unique identity. The problem involves the flow of ideas, the clash of values, and the creation of new images and new expectations. These are all matters which are central to a communications approach to social and political analysis.

The problem of political development can thus also be thought of as one of cultural diffusion, and of adapting, fusing, and adjusting old patterns of life to new demands. From an historical perspective it is possible to conceive of the evolution of the nation-state system as a basic element supporting the gradual diffusion throughout all societies of what we might call a world culture.

This world culture is of course the essence of what we think of as modern life. It is based on a scientific and rational outlook and the application in all phases of life of ever higher levels of technology. It is a reflection of urban and industrial society in which human relations are premised on secular rather than sacred considerations. It embraces the spirit of enlightenment, at least a formal acknowledgment of humane values, and the acceptance of rational-legal norms for governmental behavior. Also within the realm of government, it implies a strong need to pay deference to democratic values and practices, at least in the minimum sense of encouraging mass involvement in political activities.[5]

The pattern of diffusion of this world culture and the consequences for subsequent political life in different societies constitute fundamental problems in communications research in which the crucial variables include the manner in which the new culture was communicated, the particular agents of acculturation, the intensity and the duration of the communications, and the ways in which affected peoples initially reacted and resisted communications. Whether the process of introducing new ideas and practices is highly disruptive to existing patterns of social life or whether the transition will be relatively smooth depends in each society upon factors inherent in the communications process. Communications studies can bring to light the essential dynamics of the original traditional society, which are

[5] The stress on mass movements in Communist and totalitarian countries has often made them seem in world opinion to be less anti-democratic polities than they are because of this assumption in the world culture that mass participation is somehow related to progressive and modern societies.

most important in determining the ability of the society to accept and reject specific qualities of the world culture. For it is the communications process which gives form, structure, and meaning to a society, and the ways in which this process is disruptive will be crucial in determining the capacity of the society to preserve and reshape its identity.

Political development from this point of view can thus be thought of as involving rapid social and cultural change while preserving a sense of community. In adjusting between the demands of the cosmopolitan and the parochial, the political system must constantly strive to provide a people with what they will accept as a satisfactory balance between the universal standards of the modern world and the particular interests of specific elements of society. By viewing this problem in terms of acts of communication, we may hope to discover the various ways in which different societies have grappled with this basic issue and note the ways in which some societies have satisfactorily solved the problem and others have not. This was the other line of thought which lay behind the planning of this study of the relationship between communications and political development.

The Many Aspects of the Communications Approach

We have been speaking as though there were a single well-established communications approach. In recent years there has been considerable interest in applying in the social sciences the concepts and techniques of analysis which were developed in the field of cybernetics and information theory and which are frequently referred to as communications theory. Indeed, Karl W. Deutsch, in pioneering in the application of the methods of communications engineers to social science, focused precisely upon the relationship of communications to nationalism.[6] In the light of these developments we should make it clear at the beginning that although we are happy to acknowledge our indebtedness to those who have worked to build up these rigorous theories of information and communications, our approach will be highly eclectic.

Those involved in this study will be looking at the relationship between communications and political development from several different perspectives, and they will concentrate on different aspects

[6] See his *Nationalism and Social Communications: An Inquiry into the Foundations of Nationality*, The Technology Press of M.I.T. and John Wiley and Sons, New York, 1953.

of the problem. Our purpose is to explore many facets of a common problem, to search in many ways for new insights; it is not that of striving to formulate a single coherent theory. Our expectation is that we shall be able to advance basic hypotheses which will have to be considered in the development of more general theories of political development. Since this study is not guided by a single set of assumptions nor a uniform perspective, its organization and structure is somewhat complex. It may therefore be helpful as we close this introduction to present a brief over-view of the order of topics.

Our discussion begins with an examination of the fundamental structure of the communications processes in societies at different levels of development. The stage is thus prepared for analyzing how investments can be made in the institutions of communications, and how communications as a distinctive industry can be advanced as a part of national development.

After this initial examination of the basic institutions of mass communications, we can proceed to the problem of relating the communications process to the sphere of politics. The logical opening for us to take in so entering the domain of politics is that which leads into an examination of the ways in which political issues can get a wider hearing throughout a polity. This link between communications and the need for political articulation involves largely the uses politicians can make of the mass media. There is thus a direct connection between the structure of communications and the character of political articulation in the society. At this point in our study Edward Shils presents us with an analysis of the dangers of demagogues and the need for the responsible few who can be the quality cadres in establishing for the emerging polity a constructive spirit of politics.

In modern societies both the institutions of mass communications and the processes of political articulation depend upon the existence of professionalized communicators, the journalists and reporters, writers and artists. How do such classes emerge, and what role do they play in giving a people a sense of nationhood and in disseminating a wider understanding of the potentialities of collective political action? At this turn in our study we gain enlightenment by following Herbert Passin's description of the history of writers and journalists in the making of modern Japan and his interpretation of similar problems in the currently emerging states of Africa and the rest of Asia.

In these first chapters we deal with the prime communicators who build and use the institutions of mass communications. Once we have explored these salient problems which in a sense lie at the heart of the total communications process, we will be prepared to turn to the more general problems of how the institutions and processes of communications, in reaching out to a people as a whole, can influence their capacities for citizenship and for participating in the modern world. At the more strictly political level Herbert Hyman deals with the role that the mass media and the basic patterns of communications play in the political socialization of the new citizen of transitional societies. More specifically Hyman focuses on the ways in which the less directly political aspects of mass communications, including particularly the material which surrounds explicitly political information, can influence the orientations of people who have already been politically socialized by more traditional institutions. In this analysis he takes us into the realm of political re-socialization, and thus opens the discussion of the complex questions about the changing of fundamental human values in the modernization process. The stage is set in this way for a deeper look into the psychological dimensions of cultural change. David McClelland confronts the fundamental aspects of this problem by demonstrating, through the use of content analysis of communications to children, how it is possible to measure the degree to which a people are being instilled with the motivations essential for effective performance in the modern world.

After we travel from the analysis of mass institutions to the dynamics of individual psychology, it is helpful to pause to survey the various ways in which the relationship between communications and politics may fit together in the total nation building process. The problem calls for a case study within the context of a national society, and James N. Mosel fulfills our need with a survey analysis of the communications pattern and processes in transitional Thailand.

Throughout the volume we are interested in the policy implications of our various findings and insights, but after the case study we shall be ready to turn explicitly to policy matters and to the possible uses of communications as an instrument in furthering political and social development. The rational application of communications for social objectives calls for an understanding of the relationships between the mass media, the informal channels of communications, and the potentialities of political organizations and parties in the total communications process. Ithiel de Sola Pool deals with these problems and also directs our attention to some of the critical differences between Communist and non-Communist use of communications for political development. The stage is thus set for case studies of these two alternative patterns of development, with Frederick T. C. Yu examining the experiences of Communist China and Frederick W. Frey analyzing the ways in which Turkish leaders have applied their policies for rapid national development. Our study closes with a general conclusion by Daniel Lerner, who outlines some of the main considerations that will have to be incorporated in any general communication theory of modernization.

With this agenda in mind we may turn to our analysis, first, of the general models of communications systems, and, then, of the prime institutions of mass communications in transitional societies.

CHAPTER 1

MODELS OF TRADITIONAL, TRANSITIONAL, AND MODERN COMMUNICATIONS SYSTEMS

~.~

ALTHOUGH we shall be concerned with all aspects of social communications, we should begin with an examination of the institutions and the organization of the media specifically designed for mass communications. As a first step we shall seek to describe very briefly the essential characteristics of the communications systems typical of traditional, modern, and transitional societies.

We would note at the outset that to a large degree there are constant elements in the nature of all communications processes; the universal qualities of both individual man and human society allow for only limited variations. Thus our three categories of society share much in common, and their differences are only relative, not absolute. With this qualification in mind we may begin our comparison by outlining the differences in the structure and organization of the communications system in each of the three types of societies.

The most striking characteristic of the communications process in traditional societies was that it was not organized as a distinct system sharply differentiated from other social processes. Traditional systems lacked professional communicators, and those who participated in the process did so on the basis of their social or political position in the community or merely according to their personal ties of association. Information usually flowed along the lines of the social hierarchy or according to the particularistic patterns of social relations in each community. Thus the process in traditional societies was not independent of either the ordering of social relationships or the content of the communication.

Since the communications process was generally so intimately related to the basic structure of the traditional society, the acts of evaluating, interpreting, and responding to all communications were usually strongly colored by considerations directly related to the status relationships between communicator and recipient. At present among many transitional people there is still a strong tendency to appraise the reliability of various media mainly on the basis of the strength of their personal relationship with the source of information.

A modern communications system involves two stages or levels. The first is that of the highly organized, explicitly structured mass media, and the second is that of the informal opinion leaders who communicate on a face-to-face basis, much as communicators did in traditional systems. The mass media part of the communications process is both industrialized and professionalized, and it is comparatively independent of both the governing and the basic social processes of the country. Both as an industry and as a profession the modern field of communications is self-consciously guided by a distinctive and universalistic set of standards. In particular the mass media system is operated under the assumption that objective and unbiased reporting of events is possible, and that politics can best be viewed from a neutral and non-partisan perspective. Thus even the partisan press tends to strive to appear to be objective.

A modern communications system involves, however, far more than just the mass media; the complex interrelationships between general and specialized informal opinion leaders, and between attentive and more passive publics, are integral parts of the whole communications system. Indeed, in modern industrial societies, with the ever-increasing ease of mechanical communications and physical travel and the increasingly effective organization of specialization and discipline, there tends to be—paradoxically— an increasing reliance upon direct word-of-mouth communication.[1]

The critical feature of the modern communications system is that orderly relationships exist between the two levels so that the total process of communications has been aptly characterized as involving a "two-step flow."[2] Political communications in particular do not rest solely upon the operations of the mass media; rather, there is a sensitive interaction between professional communicators and those in influential positions in the networks of personal and face-to-face communications channels. Above all, the

---

[1] *Ithiel de Sola Pool's forthcoming study of acquaintanceship networks confirms the impression that in modern life the world becomes considerably smaller and the individual in any specialized profession sees more of more people in his field than was common in earlier periods.*

[2] *Elihu Katz and Paul F. Lazarsfeld,* Personal Influence: the Part Played by People in the Flow of Mass Communications, *Glencoe, Ill., The Free Press, 1955; Elihu Katz, "The Two-Step Flow of Communications: An Up-to-Date Report on the Hypothesis,"* Public Opinion Quarterly, *21, Spring 1957.*

interactions between the two levels take the form of establishing "feedback" mechanisms which produce adjustments in the content and the flow of different forms of messages. Those responsible for the mass media are constantly on the alert to discover how their communications are being received and "consumed" by those who control the informal patterns of communications. Similarly, those who give life to the informal patterns are constantly adjusting their actions to ways in which the mass media may be interpreting the temper of "public opinion" at any time.

In short, a modern communications systems consists of a fusion of high technology and special professionalized processes of communications with informal, society-based, and non-specialized processes of person-to-person communications. This suggests to us that the measurement of modernization of the communications system should not be related solely or even primarily to the degree to which a society obtains an advanced technology, mass media system; instead, the real test of modernization is the extent to which there is effective "feedback" between the mass media systems and the informal, face-to-face systems. Modernization thus hinges upon the integration of the formal institutions of communications and the social processes of communications to the point that each must respond with sensitivity to the other.

With these considerations in mind let us now characterize in gross terms the essential characteristics of the transitional communications process. Structurally the key consideration is its bifurcated and fragmented nature, for it usually involves in varying degrees one system which is based upon modern technology, is urban-centered, and reaches the more Westernized segments of the population, and also a separate complex system which conforms in varying degrees to traditional systems in that it depends upon face-to-face relations and tends to follow the patterns of social and communal life. The essential characteristic is that the two levels and separate parts are not closely integrated but each represents a more or less autonomous communications system.

In the transitional society only in an erratic form does the urban-based communications process penetrate into the separate village-based systems. There is usually no systematic pattern of linkage in even a single country, and idiosyncratic considerations are often decisive in determining in any community the individual who plays the role of transmitting and interpreting the communications of the mass media to the participants of the local system. Differences in the particular social and economic status of these transmitters from community to community can have decisive consequences on how the different sub-systems are related to the mass media system.

In addition to this fundamental division between the urban and the elite level and the village or mass level, there is a further fragmentation in terms of the isolated sub-systems. Indeed, in most transitional societies villages in different parts of the country tend to have less communication with each other than they separately have with the urban centers. The pattern is like the spokes of a wheel all connecting to a hub, but without any outer rim or any direct connections among any of the spokes.

Most of the problems of political development can be thought of in terms of the ways in which such fragmented communications systems can become more effectively integrated into a national system while still preserving the integrity of the informal patterns of human association. Development thus involves the increasingly effective penetration of the mass media system into all the separate communal dimensions of the nation; while at the same time the informal systems must develop the capacity to interact with the mass media system, benefiting from the greater flow of communications but also maintaining a sense of community among their participants. In the chapters to follow we shall be dealing with the numerous facets of this general problem of the interrelationship between a mass media system and the plurality of face-to-face, social-based systems. It is only necessary at this point to make it clear that the process of development is less dependent upon increased investment in the modernized, urbanized, or mass media system than it is upon the adjusting of the informal, rural systems to each other and to the mass media system. Indeed, excessive investment in the modern sector may create an even greater imbalance and thus exaggerate more than ever the bifurcated nature of the transitional system as a whole.

Although these structural differences appear to be the critical factors in differentiating the three types of communications systems, we must round out this brief characterization by suggesting some further differences which follow directly from these structural considerations.

There are, for example, certain fundamental differences in the volume, speed, and accuracy with which information is transmitted in the three systems. A modern communications system is capable of transmitting a massive flow of uniform messages to a wide audience. In contrast a traditional system handles only a very limited volume of messages, at very uneven rates of speed—some factual news might be spread very rapidly while more complete information might be disseminated at a much slower pace—and with great variety in repetition.

The sheer volume of communications possible in a mass media system means that much of the function of the informal, person-to-person level of communications in a modern system centers on screening out specialized information from the mass flow for the consumption of particular audiences. The role of opinion leaders is thus one of investing time and energy in "keeping up" with particular matters and insuring those who are dependent upon them that they are "fully informed" and "up to date" on the special subject. The tremendous volume of communications also means that single messages can easily be lost in the flood, and that the attention of a mass audience can be guaranteed only by repetition.

In a traditional system the prime problem besetting the active participant in the communications process was generally the inadequate volume of information to provide a complete picture. People turned to opinion leaders to learn what could be made out of the limited scraps of information received in the community. The skill of opinion leaders was not one of sorting out specialized information but of piecing together clues and elaborating, if not embroidering, upon the scant information shared possibly by all present. Thus the traditional system depended upon the role of the wise man and the imaginative story-teller who needed few words in order to sense truth and who could expand upon the limited flow of messages.

A transitional system, in combining features of both the modern and the traditional, usually does not have the necessary mechanism for controlling and keeping in proportion the volume, speed, and consistency of the flow of communications. The mass media sector of the communications process of the transitional societies generally relies heavily upon foreign and international systems of communication for the information it disseminates; but there are no ready criteria for selecting what should be retransmitted, and consequently there is a random element as to the relevance and appropriateness of what is communicated. An even more serious problem is the lack of specialized opinion leaders capable of sifting the messages of the mass media system and drawing attention to matters of special interest to particular audiences. Instead those in key positions in the face-to-face systems usually are more like the activists in the traditional systems, and hence their special skills lie in expanding upon limited information rather than in selecting from a voluminous flow of communication.

This difference in the skills stressed by informal opinion leaders in the modern and in the transitional systems tends to aggravate the consequences of the very unequal speed of communications at the two levels in the latter system. The mass media sector of the transitional system, with its inadequately staffed and poorly financed organizations, although it greatly exceeds the capacity of the more tradition-bound systems to retransmit their communications, may not be able to keep pace fully with the international flow of communications.

The limited rate at which the sub-systems can reflect accurately the flow of the mass media system creates one of the most basic tensions common to transitional societies. For it becomes apparent now that these societies do not have just the problem of relating or fusing elements of the international or world culture with parochial practices and sentiments, but they must usually operate with incomplete or inaccurate images of modernity and partly frustrated expressions of the parochial.

With this general outline of the gross differences among the modern, traditional, and transitional systems in mind we may now turn to a detailed consideration of the problems inherent in building up the more modernized sector of transitional communications systems.

CHAPTER 2

COMMUNICATION DEVELOPMENT AND THE DEVELOPMENT PROCESS

WILBUR SCHRAMM

As NATIONS move from the patterns of traditional society toward the patterns of modern industrial society, spectacular developments take place in their communication. From one point of view, developments in communication are brought about by the economic, social, and political evolution which is part of the national growth. From another viewpoint, however, they are among the chief makers and movers of that evolution. The purpose of this paper is to explore this interaction and seek a basis for understanding it.

I. Communication in National Systems

In the following pages we shall be speaking often about national systems and occasionally about communication systems. Therefore, let us say at the beginning precisely what we mean by "system."

When we refer to a system, we mean a boundary-maintaining set of interdependent particles.[1] The key words are *boundary* and *interdependent*. By interdependence we mean a relationship of parts in which anything happening to one component of a system affects, no matter how slightly, the balance and relationship of the whole system. By boundary-maintaining we mean a state in which the components are so related that it is possible to tell where the system ends and its environment begins. Both individual human beings and organized groups are therefore systems, as indeed are all living things. Organizations achieve the status of a system when their various component roles are widely recognized and encouraged to persist even though the individuals in these roles can, in theory at least, be replaced; when the lines of communication tieing the roles together are established and generally recognized; and when aspects of the organization are

[1] For some of the concepts on these first pages the author is indebted to discussions with his colleague Robert C. North, who was co-author with him of a recent memorandum, "International Relations as a Behavioral System." The deeper debt to Kurt Lewin's field theory, to Talcott Parsons, Robert Merton, and Harold Lasswell, will be easily recognized.

to some degree internalized by the members. In this form the organization becomes more than a framework and more than lines of hierarchy drawn on a chart. It becomes somewhat analogous to an "organism," with input and output, an energy transformer, a steady state, and the other characteristics of a behavioral system. Furthermore, it develops a characteristic way of behaving, which we learn to recognize.

We have chosen to plug into the systemic structure at the level of national systems. It is apparent, however, that the national system is made up of component systems and itself belongs to a partly developed world system. Thus in order to deal effectively with a system of any magnitude it is sometimes necessary to shift the level of analysis from one level to another—up and down the scale—without losing track of what units are interacting on the particular level which is being examined. It is necessary to keep clearly in mind whether at any given moment we are looking at a given entity as a system of component parts or as one of many units in some larger system. When our focus rests upon the state as a system, we view the member units—groups and individuals—as undifferentiated; that is, as though they were not systems in themselves but mere particles operating in the larger entity. When our focus rests upon some smaller component unit, we view it as a discrete organism differentiated in turn by a highly complex arrangement of member particles. Thus we may view the behavior of a decision maker as, in effect, the state making up its mind or as the behavior of an individual with needs, values, and other behavioral characteristics of its own. We may view the behavior of a newspaper as part of the nation's communication behavior or as the behavior of a sub-system with needs, values, and behavioral characteristics of its own. The ability to examine the same behavior on several different levels lends a certain flexibility and power to this type of analysis, and it would be surprising if illuminating analogies were not found in the behavior of systems at different levels of complexity.

In very general terms all behavioral systems, of whatever complexity, appear to behave in the same way. That is, they try to maximize their level of desired functioning and minimize the associated stress and strain. Their desired functioning reflects needs, goals, values. Their levels of stress and strain reflect the difficulties, the frustrations, the effort associated with behaving in a particular way. A very simple closed system—"closed" meaning that it has no significant input or output relationships with its environment—can probably reach an equilibrium between needs and functioning and continue to operate at a relatively strainless level. An "open" system—all human beings and social organizations are open systems—is subject to pressures from outside that must be reconciled with internal pressures. Any relatively complex system has many desired activities; good management requires some compromise among them. Any relatively complex system will put special strain at any given time on certain of its components; good management requires that strain be distributed as equitably as possible and so far as possible be kept everywhere below the level where it might do serious harm. Therefore, since even the best management can hardly be expected to eliminate strain entirely, the goal of leadership is to operate within a tolerable level of strain. This is akin to what we call the "steady state" of a biological system, and we can say, without stretching the term too much, that a social system, too, learns to operate within a steady state. Just as the healthy body maintains its temperature within the limits of a degree or two, so does the healthy social system appear to try to keep strain within certain limits, satisfying as many of its needs and goals as possible, varying strain up and down, but trying to keep the peaks of variation within tolerable extremes.

Almost any system can withstand high levels of strain for a brief period. Some systems can apparently endure higher strain than others; for example, it is probably true that the tightly controlled system represented by a Communist state can exist at higher average levels of strain than a system like our own. And it should be emphasized that the state of optimum health of a system is not a complete absence of strain but, rather, "just enough" strain. Since an absence of strain would probably result in stagnation, lack of alertness, lack of adaptive change, a certain amount of continuing strain is probably necessary for survival in society.

We are going to focus on the cognitive elements of a behavioral system. In a human individual, therefore, we should be concerned primarily with the behaviors of the sensory and nervous "systems." These behaviors include the gathering of information from different parts of the environment and different parts of the body, the storage and retrieval of information, the arranging, processing, and evaluation which takes place in decision making, the circulation of information to the action centers, and especially the preparation of orders which result in the sending out of messages into the environment.

Now let us, for a moment, think of the kinds of communication which a small organized group such as a primitive tribe would be compelled to engage in. It would have to post watchmen to inform it of threats and opportunities (an enemy tribe approaching, a herd of buffalo within range of hunters). There would be a tribal council to decide what to do about the needs, goals, and policy. If all members of the tribe were not close together, there would doubtless be couriers to carry information and orders from the council. When necessary, someone would be appointed to carry a message to a neighboring tribe or negotiate or barter. The elders of the tribe would have to serve as custodians of the history, the customs, and the skills, and the elders or the parents would have to pass appropriate parts of such knowledge on to the young members of the group. The tribe would probably have a bard or other entertainer. In other words, the primitive tribe would *institutionalize* most of the communication behaviors of the individual.

In a South Asia village at the present time these functions are all being performed, and many of the same institutions will be found to exist. The chief differences come from the intrusion of higher systems and more developed communications. That is to say, the representatives of the state and national governments take part in the life of the village; the national goals become in part a determinant of local decisions; the national radio, the regional newspaper, the national information program, a bit of the national school system, the national and state roads, the bus, and travelers, all enter the village. The village is thus a more completely "open" system than the tribe would have been; and it is open to the forces of change which seep down from the national policy.

In the industrial state these relatively simple roles have been taken over for the most part by complex organizations—the news gathering machinery, scientific research, and other sophisticated sources of intelligence; the printed media, broadcasting, and film; the complex of schools, libraries, computers, and other devices for storing, retrieving, and imparting information; the machinery of government and public opinion; the apparatus for international communication through diplomacy, mass media, trade, and personal contact; the provisions for extending interpersonal communication through such multipliers as telephone, telegraph, recording, and postal service; and all the provision for entertainment through the mass media and the large-scale organization of spectator sports. The rate and amount of communication are enormously increased, and the area of inter-connection is greatly widened.

Yet if visitors from the region of Alpha Centauri are looking down on us from their space ships, they may see less difference between the early and the late patterns of social communication than we do. They will doubtless notice that communication bears a peculiarly organic relation to society. It is not anything separate from the rest of society: it is really *society communicating*. Therefore its function varies more in degree than in kind. At a later stage it is faster, more complex, more extensive, but essentially it does about the same thing. Whether in a modern state or a traditional one, that is, it handles the cognitive business of society. It passes back and forth the danger signals of rising strain, the need signals, the opportunity signals of ways to satisfy needs, the decision signals by which the organism tries to maximize its desired functioning, minimize the associated stress and strain, and maintain a satisfactory working balance inside and outside. At any moment in the history of society the function of communication is to do whatever of this is required by society.

Thus the structure of social communication reflects the structure and development of society. The *size* of the communication activity—the development of the mass media and their audiences, the transfer of the individual communication roles of traditional society to organizations, the stretching out and multiplying of communication chains—reflects the economic development of society. The *ownership* of communication facilities, the purposeful *use* of communication, the *controls* upon communication—these reflect the political development and philosophy of society. The *content* of communication at any given time reflects the value pattern of society. The patterns of communication *networks*, which determine where information flows and who shares it with whom, reflect the homogeneity of culture and geography within a society. Of course there are also personalities and idiosyncrasies in any communication system—for example, the fact that the *New York Times* is what it is partly because there was Adolph Ochs; the Columbia Broadcasting System is what it is partly because there were William Paley, Frank Stanton, and Ed Murrow; and American schools are what they are partly because Charles William Eliot and John Dewey lived. But if one considers that it takes a certain kind of society to produce an Adolph Ochs, a William Paley, a Frank Stanton, an Ed Murrow, a Charles W. Eliot, and a John

Dewey, then even this aspect of communication can be considered a reflection of the larger patterns of society.

Only by the most brutal surgery, therefore, can social communication be separated from society, and when the operation is completed both parts of the organism are dead. For the facilities of communication are part of the living structure of society, and the act of communication is part of the living function of society. Communication grows and changes with society because it is something society does. It is a way society lives.

It might be assumed from what has just been said that to speak of the *interaction* of economic development and communication development would be no more realistic than to try to solve the chicken and the egg problem. But this is not strictly true. Although economics and communication are both organic to society, and neither can develop to any great extent without a corresponding development in the other, still they act powerfully on one another. Organic development does not necessarily mean completely simultaneous development; nor does it mean development in which one component does not affect another. Recall the far-reaching personality, behavioral, and physical changes that result from the increasing control over sight and musculature which enable a child to learn "coordination"; and the equally broad changes that come from the circulation of sex hormones at the onset of adolescence. Recall how a change in one human communication channel—for example, the destruction of the optic nerve—can result in adaptive behavior in the use of other communication channels, such as the auditory and tactical senses. This same effect of one component on another can be illustrated on the level of the social group by the different play of all the members of a football team which suddenly acquires a star quarterback, or by the different behavior of a platoon when it is given an inspirational leader. In each of these cases we have the same result: changing behavior on the part of the larger organism which can be traced back to interactions and adaptive behavior on the part of the components.

By the same token, society makes certain economic arrangements before it can do certain things with communication, and it must do certain things with communication before it can do certain things with economics. For example, it must provide a basis of financial support before it can maintain a newspaper, and it must advertise or otherwise spread the news of goods for sale before it can build a wide market for its manufacturers. A development in one line stimulates developments in the other. A more efficient communication system makes industrial development easier, and industrial development makes communication development easier. More and better newspapers provide more reason to learn to read, and higher literacy provides reason for having more and better newspapers. The more that people feel able to take part in political activities, the more they feel the need of education and information. The more information they get, the more they are interested in political developments. The more education they have, the more they seek information. The typical history of communication development in countries where it is farthest advanced is a chain of interactions in which education, industry, urbanization, national income, political participation, and the mass media have all gone forward together, stimulating each other.

In the social change we call "economic" development, development in one line can never get far in advance of development in the others. Just as a physician can alter the well-being of a patient by changing his food supply, injecting something into his veins, resting or exercising his muscles, giving him oxygen rather than air to breathe, or reducing or raising his anxiety, so can a society minister to itself by changing its educational system, its industrial system, its distribution of political power, or its news carrying system. But if any of these lags far behind—if the patient does not get enough to eat or breathe, or if society has inadequate productivity or information—then the whole system will fall ill, and there will be no advance along any line.

This is the nature of the interaction we are considering.

II. Communication as Mover

Essentially what happens in national economic development is that a more active national system is created. Relations that have been dormant are awakened. Components that are largely self-centered become interrelated. There is an enormous increase in activity and productivity throughout the system.

This makes inevitable a very large increase in the amount of strain felt within the system. One of the most common formulas for systemic strain is a discrepancy between the level of functioning prescribed by the goals and the needs of the organism and the actual level of functioning. To bring about the conditions for national development, there must be a great heightening of national goals.

Because these are widely discrepant from existing national behavior, there results a painful amount of strain. Just as communication has been employed to raise the goals, spread the news of them, and widen their acceptance, so now it is employed to raise the level of national accomplishment toward the goals. It is employed, with all the skill available to the leaders of national development, to manipulate and even out the level of strain. Strain must be painful enough to encourage activity, but not painful enough to *dis*courage activity. Therefore, strain must be built up, it must be reduced by national activity, it must be relaxed temporarily as a reward, it must be built up again. This is, of course, what goes on in connection with "five-year" plans and other subsidiary campaigns within the grand effort.

In contributing to this manipulation of goals and strain, social communication does not work as the exclusive servant of any particular political philosophy. In a state that is developing along Marxist-Leninist lines, communication takes a form somewhat different from its form in a non-Leninist state, but this is because the *entire society* takes different form. Efficient communication is just as essential to communication in China as in India, in Cuba as in Brazil, in Guinea as in Pakistan. There are surprisingly few differences among the ways it is used to speed development in these different states. Because of the intense development of mass media in the Western countries we sometimes think of highly developed communication as a Western phenomenon, but, if anything, the Communists have given more attention than non-Communists in the last few decades to ensuring an adequate development of national communication. They place different controls upon social communication and use it for somewhat different political goals, but essentially they use it to perform the same varieties of tasks as do other countries.

Walt W. Rostow[2] has listed the developments he considers necessary "pre-conditions" to what he calls economic "take-off." These are, he says, "the building of a new generation of men and women trained appropriately and motivated to operate a modern society; . . . a productivity revolution in agriculture; . . . a massive buildup of transport facilities and sources of energy; and . . . the development of a capacity to earn more foreign exchange." Daniel Lerner[3] has

[2] See W. W. Rostow, *The Stages of Economic Growth*, Cambridge, England, Cambridge University Press, 1960.

[3] See Daniel Lerner, *The Passing of Traditional Society*, Glencoe, Ill., The Free Press, 1958.

developed more fully one "pre-condition" which Mr. Rostow, the economic historian, subsumes under others but which a sociologist like Mr. Lerner prefers to set off in a more important position. He speaks of a "national empathy" which must develop as the people of a developing country acquire a feeling of nation-ness and a capacity for working together.

Now if we ask, "To which of these 'preconditions' must communication contribute?" the answer is, "*All* of ·them.*" Communication must be so developed as to make for a greater effort in every way. Let me cite six of its essential functions.

I. COMMUNICATION MUST BE USED TO CONTRIBUTE TO THE FEELING OF NATION-NESS

Without this feeling no nation can pierce the economic barrier. There must be a growth of national loyalties and awareness, supplementing local loyalties and local awareness. Peoples of different cultures, different languages, different political and religious beliefs must come to realize their common interest and the usefulness of working together toward goals.

This realization involves a gradual widening of horizons, a gradual change in focus of attention from local matters and local concerns to national ones, a tremendous speeding up of information from distant places. In the traditional society a village is self-contained. Its news is the gossip of the neighborhood. Its concerns are those of the families that live there. In the process of economic development the news becomes national news. The neighborhood interest persists, but now must be related to the national interest. The man who had been chiefly a citizen of the village is now self-consciously a citizen of the nation.

But the citizen cannot extend his environment unless the communication system extends its environment. In the oral, traditional society the provisions for wide-horizon communication are inefficient: the traveler and the ballad singer come too seldom and know too little. A modernizing of society requires mass media, some of which must be national. The radio and a few newspapers must carry the news and viewpoint of the nation, and they must come into the village. When they do so, people will learn to read the print and acquire receivers for the radio. And when this happens, the local communication systems—the coffee house, the bazaar, the casual conversation, the local government, the local newspaper if there is one—will also concern themselves with national matters, and if there is adequate leadership the sense of nation-ness will grow.

2. COMMUNICATION MUST BE USED AS THE VOICE
OF NATIONAL PLANNING

An enormous effort is required of the people of a developing nation. They must learn new skills, new ways of living. Their labor must help provide the necessary capital. They must be willing to defer gratifications until the nation as a whole can afford them. Above all, they must understand why they are making this effort and feel that they have a part in determining what shall be done.

In part this requires only what we have already specified—efficient national media to feed the local communication systems. These media must carry the information, the discussions, by which the nation arrives at an understanding of need and consensus upon plans. They must communicate widely to the entire country the agreed-upon goals, the national decisions, and the reports of progress. *Speed is of the essence.* An efficient national effort is impossible without it.

But more than that is required. Increasingly, to maintain a sense of nation-ness, a sense of participating, there must be *two-way* communication. There must be a channel by which the needs and concerns and achievements of a local community can be communicated upward and outward. This does not happen by accident. The political system, if it is to carry such information, must make efforts to get reports from its local representatives. The newspapers, if they are to carry local materials, must have an arrangement for local correspondents. Ultimately there must be a national news service to gather news systematically and to share it with the rest of the country. There must be avenues for criticism of policies and practices, both locally and nationally. This means meetings, officials to act on complaints, opportunities to "write to the editor," opportunities to have discussion and debate. In a nation going through the process of development the amount of communication enormously increases, and much of it is this kind of communication.

3. COMMUNICATION MUST BE USED TO HELP TEACH
THE NECESSARY SKILLS

It must do so on a very broad front. It must help teach literacy so that citizens can broadly and efficiently participate. It must help teach technical specialties of all sorts so that technology can go forward. In particular, it must help teach the skills needed for agricultural production so that a sufficient proportion of the population may be freed from agriculture to live in the cities and work in industry, and so that hunger can be banished as an enemy of national progress.

This is perhaps the point at which communication can make its greatest contribution to national growth. All forms, all channels of communication are required. There must be textbooks for schools; films, radio, and print for community education; organized group and individual instruction to supplement the media. There must be facilities to produce these materials, and a program to put them into use.

The basic skill to be taught is literacy. Without this no nation can expect to have sufficiently wide political participation or a sufficient number of technically trained workers. A crash program in teaching adults to read and an expansion of schools until every child has a school to attend are necessary parts of economic development. But so versatile are the audio-visual media that they can leap over the barrier of illiteracy and, even before the adults learn to read, teach some of the technical knowledge and political awareness they must have. A tough battery radio selling in the neighborhood of five dollars would open the doors of millions of homes in developing countries to news and information long before the literacy program reaches those same homes. A workable sunlight projector would carry technical information into many communities where neither electricity nor literacy have penetrated. Educational television and films can teach, without the aid of print, if they can reach into a community. It is not necessary, therefore, to wait on the extension of literacy before elementary technical skills, and in particular, agricultural skills and hygienic practices, are shared with non-literates.

Thus the development of education, the teaching of literacy, and community instruction can go forward together. It will be found that one helps the other. In particular, the new readers can practice on the subject matter they most need as citizens and can help teach non-readers.

While training in technical skills, the developing nation must not forget the skills of communication. More about these later. For a short time many of the necessary communications personnel can be trained in more advanced countries, but as soon as possible the training must be done in the country itself.

4. COMMUNICATION MUST BE USED TO HELP EXTEND THE EFFECTIVE MARKET

If most people are to live and work in the cities, if there is to be national industry, if the country is to build its foreign trade, obviously there must be communication directed to these ends.

The nature of such communication will depend on the importance of private enterprise in the nation's plans. If most industry and commerce is to be nationalized, then most such information will be carried by the channels of management and will consist chiefly of price and availability facts. On the other hand, if private enterprise is to be encouraged, then private ownership of the communication media will also be encouraged, and there will be opportunity for advertising to play a large part in extending the markets. Here too the developing countries have much to learn from the more fully developed ones. They can avoid some of the mistakes the latter have made and adapt some of their more effective procedures in commercial communication. In any case, this phase of the development must include widespread extension of telephones and telegraph, adequate postal service, and transportation.

5. AS THE PLAN DEVELOPS, COMMUNICATION MUST BE USED TO HELP PREPARE PEOPLE TO PLAY THEIR NEW PARTS

In a developing country the eyes of communication are forever on the future. In fact, this is one of the significant differences between traditional society, where attention is on the past, and modernizing society, where it is overwhelmingly on what is to come. Future orientation has two very important effects. For one thing, it stimulates people to greater efforts and strengthens them to endure hardships—which are seen as temporary but necessary preludes to a better day. In the second place, it actually prepares them for new roles, new responsibilities, and new problems. This it does by reporting constantly on national plans and national achievements, on the experiences of other states that are industrializing, and on the national "heroes" who are to be emulated.

A large proportion of mass media time and space in developing countries is therefore used for such a combination of reporting and exhorting. Many developing countries—notably the Sino-Soviet bloc—have found it desirable also to develop a large corps of trained agitators for the same purpose. Even where a developing country has no need of such close control over its people as the Sino-Soviet countries feel they have, the mobilization of national effort and the informing of the people on national plans and needs is usually a major purpose of the national information program, and this requires some managerial and planning skill in the government's information office.

6. COMMUNICATION MUST BE USED TO PREPARE THE PEOPLE TO PLAY THEIR ROLE AS A NATION AMONG NATIONS

The process of economic development inevitably requires that horizons be widened from local to national and thence to international events. Partly, this is a consequence of expanding trade and growing national importance. Partly, and all too often, it is because the developing country finds it convenient to stimulate loyalties and work efforts; to excuse deprivations, and to displace hostilities by finding an international scapegoat. Thus the Soviet Union found it helpful during the years of Soviet development to fear the Western countries, Poland finds it convenient to fear Germany, Egypt to fear Israel, Cuba to fear the United States, and so on.

In any case, the media are required to report on the rest of the world, which in turn usually requires arrangements with one or more international news agencies. The implications of this change should not be underestimated. In one generation, during the time of swift development, the eyes of the common man must be lifted from his village to the world. This change must be mirrored in the school system, the newspapers, and the daily conversations.

TABLE 1: THE DISTANCE OF NATIONAL
ECONOMIC DEVELOPMENT

POPULATION	NIGERIA 32 million	PAKISTAN 80 million	ITALY 45 million	UNITED KINGDOM 52 million
Per capita national income (dollars)	68	60	409	1,144
Per cent of adults literate	11	14	85	99
Per capita annual consumption of newsprint (kgs.)	.1	.1	3.6	19
Circulation of daily newspapers per 1,000 persons	7	9	107	573
Number of cinemas	52	284	7,414	4,325
Radio receivers per 1,000 persons	2.1	2.7	140	284

Figures furnished by UNESCO.

III. Economics as Mover

As economic activity spreads throughout the system, the act of balancing and sharing the strain becomes more delicate; it requires quicker reports from farther away and quicker orders to more scattered centers. Components must be in touch. The same kind of understandings, the same bases for cooperation, which have existed among a few must be made to exist among many. Knowledge must be gathered more broadly and shared more widely. Information must be transmitted more swiftly, not only for the period of the five-year plan or even for the period of great economic development, but permanently—because the national system is moving toward a level of functioning that will always require wide and swift communication. Thus the developing nation must be prepared to support an enormous increase in the day-to-day communication within the system.

A considerable amount of the system's capital must therefore be devoted to maintaining the growth rate of communication at no less than the growth rate envisioned for the whole system. New and longer channels of communication must be created. New and more efficient devices must be developed to gather information, store it, and share it. New skills must be developed among communicators and among users of communication. Such growth obviously requires substantial support and organization.

At a minimum, economic modernization requires a widespread system of mass communication; schools available to most, if not all, of the nation's children; that the majority of citizens, teenage and beyond, be taught to read; a widespread plan of community adult education and technical training.

The requirement of a mass communication system, of course, does not necessarily mean that every home must have a radio and be reached by a daily newspaper, or that television must blanket the country. These are later goals. For the transitional period the UNESCO standards of 10 newspaper copies and 5 radio receivers per 100 people are not too low. Home television can wait, although television as a multiplier of schools and teachers makes a great deal of sense. UNESCO also suggests two cinema seats per 100 people, but in the transitional period the use of films for teaching and community information makes more sense than the extension of cinemas for entertainment.

In any case, widespread mass media developments require such large-scale supporting developments as the following:

Printing machinery—typesetting equipment, presses, photo-engravers, and all the other equipment of the composing and printing rooms.

Broadcasting equipment—transmitters, studio equipment, recorders, towers and antennas, and all the other necessities of modern broadcasting.

Projectors, cameras, and studios where films can be made.

A supply of electrical power.

A supply of newsprint, which is usually scarce and expensive in underdeveloped countries.

A supply of film, which must usually be imported.

A source of foreign news and a means of exchanging news within the nation.

A source of programs and another of films.

A book and magazine publishing capability.

At least the rudiments of a telecommunications network whereby to exchange programs and point-to-point communication.

A supply of receiving sets, and either the facilities to build them or a feasible way of importing them.

Expert managerial personnel for all the media.

Trained professional personnel—editors and news handlers, producers and script writers, film makers, and the like.

Trained technical workers—printers, compositors, pressmen, engineers, broadcast and film technicians, and projector operators.

Personnel trained to repair and maintain all this equipment.

The schools, the literacy training, and the community education, no matter how modest they may be in physical appearance, will require supporting activity of an even higher order. For example:

School buildings, which may at first be makeshift but soon will require a great deal of new construction.

Textbooks, together with people to write them and facilities to print them.

Teaching and laboratory equipment, which will range from slates and blackboards in the early grades to elaborate mechanical and electronic equipment in the technical training program.

Supporting media: reading material for new literates and technical trainees, teaching films, film strips, and projectors, sound recordings, ultimately programmed self-instruction and television. The fewer the skilled teachers, the more necessary these become.

A high degree of organization, including the equivalent of a large agricultural extension service, a nation-wide literacy teaching program, and a technical training program that makes use whenever possible of on-the-job training.

Skilled managerial personnel, including school administrators, adult education administrators, and generalists able to co-ordinate the several branches of the program.

Trained teachers for the schools, the colleges, the literacy program, and the community and technical training programs; and, consequently,

Schools or programs for training teachers.

Maintenance and repair personnel for buildings and equipment.

A large number of volunteers and semi-professionals to augment the short supply of trained teachers.

These lists are suggestive rather than exhaustive. No attempt has been made to put a monetary figure opposite any of the items, although it is obvious that they represent a very large outlay. Obviously, to take, in a few decades, the steps in communication required of a developing country requires national sacrifice, a willingness to allocate scarce commodities to communication rather than elsewhere, and a major national effort in self-improvement. Let us inquire what are the conditions of society necessary to nurture such a development.

It goes without saying that the basic requirement is a national commitment to swift advance. Another requirement is the ability to put together the capital, in labor or resources, needed to build industry. Beyond those, however, the requirements vary with the political system and with the kind of development.

The task of paying for a new communication system is somewhat easier for socialist or communist countries than for countries where private ownership is more highly valued and where the decision-making power is more widely distributed, notably because the centralized government in the socialist country has greater control over the planning of the system. Anyone who has looked hard at Soviet mass communication has been impressed by the *orderliness* of the system.[4] In contrast to our own mass media, which "just grew" in

---

[4] See Alex Inkeles, *Public Opinion in Soviet Russia*, Cambridge, Mass., Harvard University Press, 1953; and Wilbur Schramm, *One Day in the World's Press*, Stanford, Stanford University Press, 1959, pp. 7-8.

response to the pressures and opportunities of free enterprise, the Soviet media show the signs of having been planned purposefully to do a job for the state. Competition is, for all practical purposes, eliminated. Newsprint and machinery are allocated, not on the basis of ability to pay, but on the basis of where they are needed to do the state's job. A newspaper is permitted to exist, not merely where it can be supported by advertising and subscriptions, but where it is felt, by the government or the party, to be needed. Thus allocation of funds and materials for needed developments in communication is as simple as allocation for any other part of the state's operation.

For example, if China decides to raise its literacy rate from 10 to 50 per cent and quadruple its attendance in higher education, as it is supposed to have done in the last ten years, the allocation of materials, personnel, and effort to those tasks is relatively easier than it would be in a country like India. China is in a better position than India to enforce strain on its system. If the Soviet Union decides, as it did some years ago, that a certain number of newspapers of certain kinds are needed in Kazakhstan, it is relatively easy to make sure that there are exactly that number of newspapers and of the specified kinds. It is less possible in a system like India's or our own.

In a state which supports its communications by private enterprise it is necessary to consider certain basic requirements for introducing one or more of the media—for example, potential audience, potential advertising support, availability of technical skills and equipment. Thus in South Asia, at the present time, it is estimated that a city of 50,000 is about the smallest that could possibly support a daily newspaper, because advertising support, literacy, and individual income are all low. The availability of technical skills and equipment, of course, is a hurdle that a controlled country as well as a democratic one must leap. But the economic requirement of support does not exist in exactly the same degree for a controlled country. If the Soviet Union or China, or any other controlled state, decides that a newspaper or a radio station should be located at a given point, it need not consider the problem of advertising support, or even very seriously consider whether an eager audience awaits the new medium. It can make a decision in terms of desirable development rather than free enterprise support.

A controlled country is in position, if it so wishes, to hurry any of its communities ahead, communication-wise, fifty years overnight—

in short, to graft communication onto the system without an organic development. Since that experiment has never been tried seriously, the result is still conjectural. But what would happen if, for example, a nation suddenly introduced television in a part of the country where development otherwise had barely begun? Would this make a broad and general change in the village? Would it speed up development in a healthful way? Would it destroy old values and raise frustrations which the nation would be unable to relieve? We do not know. The best evidence we have is what happened in villages like Tepotzlan, when the main road to the capital came in. Here the results were by no means all desirable.[5]

For the controlled state, as for the more democratic one, the costs of building a mass communication system and a school system are enormous. But in the controlled state operators can often be spared some of the struggles and uncertainties which democratic countries have in starting new media. In South Asia, for example, all except the most successful vernacular newspapers barely hang on to life. They cannot afford good printing equipment. They cannot afford to hire the reporters whom the new departments of journalism train for them. They usually cannot afford a news wire. They cannot afford to make a contract for newsprint, and because they cannot sign a contract they may pay double the price on the odd lots market.

Mr. A. R. Bhat, president of the Association of Indian Language Newspapers, has given us a representative budget and outlook for a new daily newspaper in an Indian city of 50,000 which previously had no newspaper.[6] The paper might expect a circulation of 1,500 the first year, 5,000 by the third year. Working capital of at least 150,000 rupees would be required to last through the first three years, by which time the paper would be very nearly self-supporting although far from making a profit. All the expenses would have to be on the very lowest side. The press would be hand fed. The editorial staff would be paid on the average about 200 rupees (just under 45 dollars) a month.

The most interesting aspect of Mr. Bhat's financial prognosis is that he estimates that it would take a monopoly market in a city of

[5] See Robert Redfield, *Tepotzlan—A Mexican Village*, University of Chicago Press, 1930; and Oscar Lewis, *Life in a Mexican Village—Tepotzlan Restudied*, Urbana, Ill., University of Illinois Press, 1951.
[6] A. R. Bhat, *Problems of the Vernacular Language Press of India*, prepared for the UNESCO Asian Conference in Bangkok, January 15-30, 1960; Paris, November 30, 1959; duplicated by UNESCO.

50,000 people to support one such four-page daily newspaper on a starvation budget. In the United States, of course, a city of that size would support a daily of 24 to 48 pages, grossing four or five million dollars a year. But in a new country or a developing country there is no comparable base of business and industry (to advertise) or of literates (to subscribe). The private resources for supporting the media are unbelievably low. The average Indian family, for example, feels able to spend one rupee per year (about 21 cents) on newspapers. The average total annual income of a Burmese or an Indonesian is sufficient to pay for subscriptions to about four magazines.[7]

Therefore, to the extent that a developing country chooses to develop its media by private enterprise, it must accept considerable restriction on its ability to locate and start new media. Until productivity and income build up, there will be little advertising support. Until literacy and income build up, there will be a small market for subscriptions. It is not contended that there are no advantages in having privately supported media, or that privately supported media may not have a special claim on the people and hence a special effectiveness, even during the period of development, but merely that there are certain special difficulties about starting privately supported media in a developing country.

The nature and degree of these difficulties vary with the media as well as with the political system. Printed media require literacy and urbanization. Radio and movies skip the requirement of literacy, and radio, at least, avoids the requirement of urbanization. All the media require skilled personnel, but different kinds. Print requires writers, editors, and printers. Radio requires a small number of program and managerial personnel, station engineers and technicians, and a widespread capability for maintenance of receiving sets. Schools require a very large number of skilled teachers.

We have chosen to talk about the schools along with the mass media for a specific reason. Whereas the problems of education and information tend to be separated in an advanced country, in a developing nation they are connected. The mass media must carry the main burden of informing and teaching the public for a long time before an adequate school system can do its part. The planning

---

[7] See S. Marbangun, "The Magazine Press in South East Asia," paper presented to UNESCO Bangkok conference, January 1960.

TABLE 2: FINANCIAL PROJECTION OF A NEW DAILY
IN AN INDIAN CITY OF 50,000 PERSONS

I. CAPITAL REQUIREMENT

1. Initial investment

Printing machinery and equipment	27,000 rupees	
Composing room equipment	6,500	
Office and other furniture	1,500	
Library	5,000	

2. Working capital 45,000

3. Provision for initial losses until paper is
   self-supporting 65,000

	Total	150,000

II. MONTHLY EXPENSES

1. Salaries and wages

Editorial staff (9)	1,805	
Managerial staff (9)	1,200	
Factory staff (35)	2,740	
Menial staff (7)	440	
Gratuity and provident fund	1,031	

2. Other working expenses 5,195

3. Variable expenses

Newsprint	4,488	
Ink, stores, etc.	350	

	Total Monthly Expenses	17,249

III. MONTHLY INCOME (AT BEGINNING OF 4TH YEAR)

Sales	7,650	
Advertising	8,160	
Sundry receipts	300	

	Total Monthly Income	16,110

Figures by A. R. Bhat, President of the Indian Languages Newspapers Association.

for mass media therefore gears into the planning for schools and technical training. In a developing country the use of mass media as teacher multipliers assumes an importance it does not have in an advanced nation. Thus the economic strategy of communication development in a developing nation is not separable into a strategy for education and a strategy for information; it must be one strategy.

Ideally the strategy is to depend on the different channels at the stage of national development where they provide the largest returns in proportion to their cost and to other capabilities. When literacy is low, radio recommends itself. For a few dollars a radio can be put into a village and that village connected, in a way it has never been, to the national effort. For a few tens of thousands of dollars a radio station can be erected to serve thousands of villages. When literacy begins to rise, a foresighted government will encourage the growth of printed media to supply the new literates and keep them in the reading audience. When teachers are in short supply, a wise government will use teacher multipliers, such as teaching films, educational television, and the newest and in some respects most promising of all the multipliers: programmed self-instruction.

It will do these things, that is to say, if it can. The typical country entering into a transitional stage of development feels itself caught up in a circle of needs it has no way to break out of. For a million dollars it could do a considerable job with radio, but the million is needed for schools, and only one-third of it is available because industrial and agriculture training are needed more. If newspapers were plentiful and people could read them, much of the agriculture information might be carried by them; but newspapers are few and starving, and literates are few and poor. We shall not box the compass of needs and frustrations. The point is that there is no single action by which a developing country can break out of this trap. A new teacher training college will not do it, nor will a television station, nor subsidized newsprint, nor any other single action. The economics of development requires that a nation pull itself up painfully, inch by inch, by its own bootstraps. It is the organic nature of a national system that communication development cannot far outstrip other developments.

Some strategies are better than others, as we have indicated. It is safe to say that the optimum strategy has not yet been tried. What would happen, for example, if a developing country were to stop trying to build to an old blueprint and look at the media and educational channels with new eyes?

Each of these countries has a great shortage of teachers. Each of them has an extremely broad educational task—children to be put into schools, adults to be taught to read and count, farmers to be taught how to produce more from the soil, housewives to be taught better hygienic practices, workers to be taught the skills of technology, public servants to be taught the duties and responsibilities of public service, everyone to be taught the responsibilities and privileges of citizenship at a critical time for their country. But in almost none of the countries is there much development along these lines.

In other words, the coast is clear. The planning can begin fresh. The new countries can consider the whole range of communication possibilities without being much constrained by what they have done before. Thus, for example, they do not have to consider the problem of introducing educational television or programmed learning into an already fully developed and staffed educational system; they have only to ask, "How can we use these devices?" They do not have to consider how to expand or improve a service of community education; they have only to consider what kind of community education they want.

There is no reason why these new countries should go through all the steps which older countries have taken, or make the mistakes which older countries have made. Just as some nations have gone from the ox cart directly to the airplane, so can the new countries skip over great periods in the history of education and communication. They can consider freely whether they should introduce some version of the phototypesetter into their printing plants rather than going through the stage of hot metal. They can consider freely whether they have to go through the stage of Mark Hopkins on one end of a log, or Abelard, a book of Aristotle, and six students, before jumping at once into a program of teacher multipliers.

Each country obviously has to find teacher multipliers. It takes a long time to train an adequate corps of teachers in a developing country. A high official of an African state was recently discussing United States requirements for teachers' certificates and noted that some teachers must have five years of college. "Do you know what job a teacher in my country would have if he had five years of college?" the African said. "He would be minister of education!" These countries cannot wait until they have trained enough teachers well enough. But they have several kinds of multipliers available. One of these is educational television. In our own country ETV constitutes "enrichment." In a developing country a television set in each village could constitute a whole school. A second multiplier is programmed self-instruction. In our country this is only an excitingly promising tool, something to be tested and examined thoroughly before we decide exactly where we need it. In a developing country it might well save years in the process of economic development by giving the people a device by which to teach themselves the skills and information they most need. Finally, there is the teacher multiplier we know as volunteer or semi-skilled help. The Communist countries have shown how to use this kind of help; China is supposed to have between five and ten million volunteers of this kind. There is no reason why people who have learned to read should not— with the help of television or radio or films—help others learn to read; or why, with the help of programmed self-instruction, laymen should not help other laymen learn skills; or why, with the help of these new devices, persons who have a little education should not shoulder much of the burden of teaching the very young. Personal communication represents the wheel or star network pattern, whereas the mass media represent chiefly the chain pattern, and we know some of the advantages of the first two patterns.[8]

There is another multiplier of teaching efforts that seems promising. Inasmuch as a developing country has an educational task that is village-wide, could it not so organize its program? Is there really anything to be gained by fragmenting the activity: one organization to teach the children, another to teach adults to read, another to instruct the farmers, and so on? Why not, in the period of rapid development, consider the possibilities of planning the program for the whole village so that one part of it helps another, and so that the responsibility is centered?

It is exciting to think what one of these countries might do if it would thus consider this problem anew.

Even so, it would not be easy to break out of the restraining circle previously mentioned. At best, the task of building a communication system is a heavy economic burden, slow and dependent on the general economic growth of the nation. All the more reason, then, to apply some imaginative strategy, using the new teaching devices and a maximum of lay helpers, in whatever organization will best do the job.

IV. Some Political Implications

Let us look at some of the political implications of the interaction of economics with communication.

For one thing, *power lies with control*. It is hardly necessary to remind a political scientist or a politician of this fact, but in a developing country, where the channels of communication are mostly short and personal, the control of the long channels becomes dramatically important. In a village which has but one radio the ownership of that radio is both a symbol and a tool of power. The owner is in a position to know what is happening in the capital, or in foreign capitals, or in the market, before others know it. Furthermore, he is in position

[8] See Alex Bavelas, "Communication Patterns in Task-Oriented Groups," *Journal of the Acoustical Society of America*, 22, 1950, pp. 725-730. Also Harold Leavitt, "Some Effects of Certain Communication Patterns on Group Performance," *Journal of Abnormal and Social Psychology*, 46, 1951, pp. 38-50.

to share the experience of using the radio, or the information derived from the radio, with whomever he wishes. Anyone who has gone into a Middle Eastern village where the headman had the only radio can hardly fail to have been impressed with the contribution of that radio to the status of the owner and his ability to grant favors. Similarly, the ownership of a newspaper by a political advocate in a developing country is an altogether more potent fact than such ownership by a political advocate in a country like the United States. Governments developing along Marxist-Leninist lines have underscored this by maintaining ownership of all communications. In non-Leninist developing countries there is a long history of press seizures, press censorship, and other actions reflecting respect for the power of any widespread communication in a volatile and changing situation.

In the second place, *Mass communication confers status*. We see this in our own country, where television entertainers become widely known with a sort of pseudo-intimacy and where impressive voices are often mistaken for the voices of wise men. This phenomenon is also seen in some developing countries to an exaggerated degree. In many countries, therefore, there has been an apparently conscious effort to determine what personalities would be permitted to break out of anonymity on the radio, and what personalities would be mentioned in the news. In an advanced country the world close at hand blends almost imperceptibly into the distant world; the problems of one's home blend into those of one's community, and the latter into the problems of the state and the nation and the international community. There is a time when a country is developing, however, when the world one can see with his own eyes and experience at firsthand is sharply separated from the world at a distance. During this period of high systemic strain there is often a political conflict between local loyalties and wider loyalties, and a considerable uncertainty about national policy and national leadership. It is during this period, when literacy is growing and radios are becoming more widely available, that the power of mass communication to confer status becomes particularly important, for the media represent almost the only direct contacts of the villager with high status figures on the national level, and almost the only map of environment that is any real alternative to the map projected from local experience.

In the third place, it must be obvious that *communication can be used either as national stimulant or tranquilizer*. The general belief is that the powerful entertainment media in this country have a certain tranquilizing, escapistic effect on our citizens, but on the other hand the President can use the media in a most effective and immediate way to engage public attention and rally public support around a national policy. The point is, therefore, that the mere presence of a communication system does not necessarily contribute to national development. It is possible to conceive of a national television network carrying only fantasy and entertainment, using valuable time that might otherwise be given to the national effort, and directing attention *away from* national problems. It is possible to conceive of a national school system so directed as to lead people to live apart from world problems, and therefore to place little importance on and give little aid to a program of national economic development. The content and the use of communication channels, rather than their mere presence, are therefore determining. This ability to serve either as stimulant or tranquilizer is useful to a government which recognizes that strain can be manipulated, and that it needs at times to be raised, at times lowered.

Fourth, the question arises *whether communication development per se contributes to wider and more democratic control of national government, and whether national economic development per se contributes to the wider and more democratic control of communication.*

The second of these positions is upheld by Nixon,[9] who shows that among economically developed countries there is over-all a greater amount of press freedom than among less well developed countries. This is, however, a rather unsatisfactory use of simple statistics to prove an extremely complicated point. For one thing, the Communist countries show no such development toward press freedom as Nixon's conclusion implies. So far as his measure goes, there is as much control over the press in the Soviet Union, which is a highly developed country, as in Albania, which is a poor and little developed country. Measuring more subtle behavior, one observes a few signs of increasing press freedom in the Soviet Union: a bit more criticism, somewhat wider coverage of foreign events, a slight leavening of the deadly seriousness and purposefulness of the press. Certainly in other ways—for example, in contacts with foreigners—greater communication freedom has recently been permitted in the Soviet Union.

[9] R. B. Nixon, "Factors Related to Freedom in National Press Systems," *Journalism Quarterly*, 37, 1950, pp. 13-28.

The best conclusion we can draw at the present time is that national economic development *need not* bring about greater communication freedom. It is entirely possible for a nation to develop from traditional society to industrial society (as, indeed, the Soviet Union did) without changing its degree of control over the press and without relaxing its paternal control over the communication input of its people. On the other hand, it seems altogether reasonable to believe that economic development, with consequent greater political stability and a lower rate of social change, provides the conditions under which greater press freedom is feasible, and, other things being equal, that controls will probably be relaxed.

There is another way to say this. Whereas it is easier for a developed country to have a completely free press and free communication, it is much harder for a country in the early stages of development to do so. The amount of freedom which India permits is quite unusual among developing countries. Indeed, it is probably wrong for us to expect a country which is trying to gather together its resources and mobilize its population for a great transitional effort to permit the same kind of free, competitive, and sometimes confusing communication to which we have become accustomed in this country. This is a luxury which we can now afford. We could afford it during our own period of economic development because we moved slowly and had the resources of a wonderfully rich continent behind us. A comparatively poor country, trying to do in a few years what we did in a century, feels that it can hardly afford such a luxury. It can hardly afford to have its energies divided in any way. We must be prepared to sympathize with this point of view, and to expect that as these countries grow toward economic strength and political stability, they will be more likely to encourage communication freedom.

About the other half of the question—whether communication development per se contributes to wider and more democratic control of national government—we must say, as before, *not necessarily*. It is possible, apparently, to use a more efficient communication system more effectively for tight controls over political action. It is clearly possible to use a more efficient school system to indoctrinate a generation with a desired political viewpoint. Efficient communication works as well for a dictator as for a democrat—probably better, in fact, for the dictator because he is more likely to seize a monopoly over communication. But on the other hand, it is clear that communication development *provides the conditions for* wider participation **if** the political philosophy permits it.

Does communication development make for more democracy *regardless* of the governing political philosophy? This is a very interesting question, which we are now in position to examine with such countries as the Soviet Union serving as our laboratories. Is there any sign, for example, that the creation of a professional corps of newsmen has created any greater skepticism about official news in the Soviet Union, any greater likelihood of objective news handling, less "teaching" through the news? If such signs exist, they are hard to see. It is true that there are signs of change in the Soviet press. Professional newsmen like Adjubei have been active in making, first, *Komsolskaya Pravda*, and now *Izvestia* more interesting to look at and read. "Human interest" items are now permitted. The viewpoints of Western nations are more frequently presented than they were ten years ago. It may be that the professionalization of the news corps, along with the generally greater stability of the country, have an effect. In any case, this sort of development should provide one condition for such an effect—*ceteribus paribus*. The news corps of the Soviet Union is still a long way from being a "third estate"— an active influence on policy and an active critic of government. But this is the direction in which communication development moves, and its effect should be easier to see in countries where control is less efficient than in the Soviet Union.

We can also profitably ask whether the great increase in foreign news and foreign contacts do not contribute to greater democratization of government and wider political participation. In countries which are developing along non-Leninist lines there are dramatic signs that this is happening. Women are coming out from behind their walls and their veils. Men whose horizons were a few miles wide, whose political decisions were usually made for them, are moving intellectually beyond their villages into the area of national problems and endeavoring to decide for themselves. The children of these men, in the new primary schools, are thinking of world geography and world politics. There is no doubt that in these countries both interest in political questions and confidence in one's own knowledge are being built.

But is a similar thing happening in the Communist countries? Here again we have difficulty in answering because the Communist countries are not open to the kind of research we should need before we could answer with confidence. The Soviet schools and media are still teaching the same world demonology. But certain interesting things are happening. There is impressive evidence in the Soviet Union of interest in the Western world. The number of contacts between Eastern Europeans and the citizens of Western countries has been greatly increased. Scientists in particular have had many occasions to talk frankly with their opposite numbers. In the Soviet Union opinion and audience research have recently been instituted, though divorced from any theoretical or political interpretation. I think we can suppose that learning is a contagious thing wherever it is engaged in, and that a broadening of focus of attention is likely to throw near-at-hand things into sharper perspective, whether under Khrushchev, Castro, Nasser, or Nehru.

As the system emerges from its period of rapid growth and high strain, and launches into a pattern of high metabolism and lower strain, these indications are at least hopeful.

CHAPTER 3

COMMUNICATIONS AND POLITICAL ARTICULATION

∿∿∿∿∿∿∿∿∿∿∿∿∿∿∿∿∿∿∿∿∿∿∿

A DIRECT relationship exists in all societies between the structure and organization of communications and the character, tone, and, even to a degree, content of political expression. The politician's role both as articulator of the collective identity and as champion of specific interests is invariably conditioned and limited by the media of communications available to him. No leader can rise above the restrictions of the specific communications networks to which he has access, and at the same time none can escape the consequences of being surrounded by a communications system.

At the simplest level the technology of communications at any time can affect the style of elite communications. Irrespective of cultural differences there appears to have been a pattern of congruent changes as political orators have first been given the assistance of public address systems and then have had to adapt to the use of radio and then television. These changes have all contributed to changes in the public image of the politician, to say nothing of changes in the nature of the profession itself.[1]

In a broader sense the political process as a whole is influenced by access to the means of communications. Questions about the ease of access and the existence of limitations to the use of mass media touch upon some of the most important issues determining the character and the stability of political life in any society. Indeed, an examination of the conditions for obtaining access to various forms of communication usually is a highly rewarding way of comparing political systems, for such an approach can not only reveal how control and power are distributed in different systems but also can provide information about the very character of power itself in each society. From such an approach we can readily perceive fundamental differences between totalitarian and authoritarian systems;

[1] *For analyses of the effects of radio and television on American political campaigns, see such studies as Ithiel de Sola Pool, "TV: A New Dimension in Politics," in* American Voting Behavior, *ed. Eugene Burdick and Arthur J. Brodbeck, Glencoe, Ill., The Free Press, 1959, pp. 236-261; Leo Bogart,* The Age of Television, *New York, Frederick Ungar, 1956; Angus Campbell et al.,* The American Voter, *New York, John Wiley and Son, 1960.*

in the former, control extends to an attempt to monopolize nearly all existing communications processes in the society, while in authoritarian systems control of access is limited to only certain critical aspects of the total communications process.

The level of technology and the issue of access constitute two fundamental parameters of any political culture. The basic character of a political culture is determined, however, primarily by the more complex interrelationships between the structure of the communications systems and the processes by which political interests are given expression and are combined and related to form political programs or policies. In an earlier study of the Committee on Comparative Politics a theory of the political process was developed in which three of the eight universal functions common to all political systems were communications, interest articulation, and interest aggregation.[2] It was postulated in that study that these functions can be found in all political systems and thus provide a fundamental basis for comparing and categorizing systems. Continued experimentation with the functional approach suggests that definite and discernible relationships exist between the manner in which a function is performed, say the communications function, and the way others, say the interest articulation and interest aggregation, are performed.

It appears that in transitional systems there is a particularly close interrelationship among precisely these three functions. In most transitional countries the processes of modernization and industrial growth have not as yet proceeded to the stage in which the social structure is sufficiently differentiated and the population adequately specialized to create a wide range of specific interests with quite definite but still limited political objectives. At the early stages of national development the most common groupings still tend to be of a communal nature, with each representing a way of life and a diffuse and unlimited set of interests. Under these conditions specific, concrete political interests tend to appear as either the highly personal demands of individuals or the uncompromising and unnegotiable assertions of distinctive ethnic, religious, or other communal groups. This lack of effective mechanisms for formulating and advancing functionally specific interests tends to highlight

[2] *Gabriel A. Almond and James S. Coleman, eds.,* The Politics of the Developing Areas, *Princeton, Princeton University Press, 1960.*

and indeed further exaggerate the fragmented and unintegrated character of the communications process which we have already noted in describing the transitional communications structure. That is to say, the informal, face-to-face processes of communications are not able to present to those with access to the mass media a clear sense of the concrete and specific interests of different elements of the population.

Conversely, the national leaders in such situations are compelled to speak to an essentially undifferentiated audience. Without ready means at hand for measuring the distribution of any specific interests, such leaders may feel that they have no alternative but that of striving to appeal to all by reaching for the broadest common denominator. Hence the propensity to avoid in public discussions the specific treatment of concrete issues and to indulge in emotional and more diffusely nationalistic appeals.

The sum effect of the inadequate processes for articulating particular interests is to weaken the possibilities for a rationally based system of interest aggregation. When leaders are unsure of the distribution of particular interests they cannot follow strategies of systematically calculating the relative appeal of different policies in support of different combinations of very specific concerns. Under such conditions public discussion tends to drift away from the hard realities of social conflicts and to become mired in vague generalities.

This tendency may not have serious consequences for the development of a modern democratic polity if there is open competition among all who might wish to engage in such forms of political articulation. Indeed, the continuous exposure of a citizenry to the exaggerated language, the substanceless promises, and the emotion-tapping appeals of politicians who are avoiding hard realities and disciplined reasoning can produce the widespread sense of skepticism about the potentialities of politics which is a first requirement of a responsible and democratic electorate. Once a people have learned to discount and distrust the pie-in-the-sky language of shallow politicians and to see through the superficial idealism of easy prophets they have entered the world of modern, sober politics. It is this possibility of immunity through exposure which caused the philosopher T. V. Smith to observe, "They also serve who only articulate."

In most transitional societies the public experience in learning to discount the exaggerated language of politics fails to take place because there is little open competition among politicians. Instead of different themes and different combinations of policies competing for public attention, those engaged in political articulation tend to present a common front. Political skill in articulation in such circumstances is not related to sensitivity and artistry in isolating and then aggregating values and issues. Once again the consequence is a propensity to avoid the demands of problem solving in terms of real issues and to stress skill in tapping public emotions. The lack of competition means that for the public the trend is not toward choosing and selecting with a skeptical mind but the more extreme consequence of either becoming completely distrustful and contemptuous of the realm of politics or abandoning any attempt at rational judgment and seeking satisfactions from emotionally identifying with the only ones who speak with power.

The purpose of political articulation is, of course, not just the training of a critical and questioning electorate. For transitional societies it might be argued that a more basic purpose of political articulation is that of instilling in people new values and new outlooks. Modernization calls for the transformation of popular tastes and fashions, the creation of novel devices and demands, and the welding together of new loyalties. These are all tasks for the popular politicians, and it might seem that if the politicians all present a common front in articulating the new values the process of modernization may be facilitated more effectively than if there are conflicting and confusing voices.

This problem touches on a wide range of issues which lie at the core of political development and modernization. We shall in subsequent chapters examine in greater detail the relationships between communications and the changing of basic values and attitudes in a people who are still close to the world of tradition. We need only note here that there is a legitimate place for the charismatic leader, the prophet who would give a people a new sense of direction, and certainly development may at times be greatly assisted by the entire political class of a country all pushing in the same direction and all presenting the same promises for a new future.

The test, however, must be a pragmatic one. For the nationalist leader there is always the danger of failing to achieve the full stature of the charismatic leader and appearing instead as a false prophet. Similarly, if the leaders of a country are united against all aspiring leaders but the country does not seem to be realizing its objectives, it is likely that a sense of demoralization will spread among precisely that class of responsible citizens who are likely to have the critical skills necessary for modernizing the society. When politicians talk about radical programs of change but fail to produce substantive results, the consequence can only be a general debasement of standards throughout the society.

The dilemma of the modernizing politician is that he must strive to bring about in a people a fusion of emotions and skills, a desire for the novel but also a respect for the self. The articulating politician must call both for change according to the ways of the modern and hence foreign world, and loyalty to the sense of historical identity of a people. He must ask people to turn their backs on the ways of their forefathers while still preserving their sense of uniqueness. As we shall repeatedly observe in this study, the process of political development calls for a fusion of the general and the parochial, of that which is foreign and universal in the modern world culture and that which is distinctive and unique in the particular culture.

The process of political articulation must achieve a satisfying, and also a satisfactory, blend of the universal and the parochial. The popular politician must endlessly grapple with this problem. In many transitional societies he finds it peculiarly difficult to achieve an effective blending because he has so little guidance on what are in fact the real interests of the different groups in the society. In many transitional societies what tends to happen is that the articulating politician must generalize his discussion of the parochial and parochialize his treatment of the universal. Unsure of what are the parochial interests in his society, he is driven to creating an idealized and abstracted version of a traditional pattern. At the same time he must present the universal which is at the heart of the modern culture as being merely the values and interests of one apparently parochial segment of the society, albeit that this is usually the elite segment. In short, the modernizing politician can easily appear to be cast in the role of wanting to advance only the particular interests of a small elite when he speaks of the goals of modernization, and not being able to understand the values of the specific interests when he talks of the traditional and the unique in his society.

These problems, combined with numerous others, tend to weaken the sense of assurance of political leaders. The very concepts of political representation and of responsible leadership are confused as those with power become anxious about their capability to manage a modern political system. Traditional concerns about status and hierarchy mix with memories of authoritarian administration during the colonial period to produce a need to be assertive and uncompromising in proclaiming personal identity with the national interests.

The sum effect of these various difficulties is confusion over expected standards of performance throughout the society. The process of modernization demands an ever-increasing degree of self-discipline and a widening commitment to the ideals of excellence in all fields of life. The responsibility of the popular politician is to facilitate the transformation of an inchoate political community into a civil society. There is thus a direct link between the ways in which leaders perform the function of political articulation and the possibilities for the emergence of critical elements throughout the societies who have a sense of competence and who are dedicated to raising the level of society.

We must turn now to a full analysis of this relationship between the dangers of demagogy and the need for such key groups of intellectuals who can foster a sense of modern standards in transitional societies.

CHAPTER 4

DEMAGOGUES AND CADRES IN THE POLITICAL DEVELOPMENT OF THE NEW STATES

EDWARD SHILS

~.

I

THE first condition of the establishment of a modern political order is the creation of an effective administration, stable institutions of public opinion, modern educational systems, public liberties, and representative, deliberative, legislative institutions. These are the prerequisites of the growth of a polity, of an order to which the inhabitants of the sovereign territory will feel they belong and to whose authorities they will attribute legitimacy. Demagogy, or rhetorical charisma, which used to be called "rabble-rousing" and is now called "mobilization of the masses," sometimes appears to be a short cut to this objective. But in its attempt, by flamboyant oratory and the display of a radiating personality, to incorporate the mass of the population into a great national effort, it almost always arouses the more clamorous among them to demands and expectations which far exceed the possibility of fulfilment. It tends to encourage the "masses" to believe that the occasion of their persistently or momentarily felt grievances results from the deliberate action of the demagogue's opponents. Thus it causes commotion; it produces changes which are only of the moment; it generates conflicts which impede the growth of a progressive, modern political order. Far from being a short cut, demagogy is one of the greatest menaces to the political development of the new states. Let us look at its workings.

Poverty of natural resources, insufficient capital to develop what resources they possess, insufficient organizational skill and discipline—these are but a few of the deficiencies which stand in the way of the creation of stable modern polities in Africa and Asia. Except for the deficiency of natural resources—and technological development may modify even that—none of these obstacles is insuperable. But not one of them is removable by "crash programs," and certainly not by "crash programs" which consist largely of the resounding reiteration of irrelevant clichés reinforced by the coercion of the laggardly and the dissident. The menace of demagogy lies partly in the fact that it bases its appeal on advocacy of just such programs.

The development of a modern polity calls for a redefinition of the image of the self, a redirection of the cognitive categories, new capacities in relation to time and task. These constitute opinion of a deeper sort. They must first be firmly developed in the minority on whose initiative and persistent action national development depends in the first instance. The development of integrity and skill in administrative judgment; the development of cadres of reasonably punctual, reasonably honest, reasonably dutiful persons; and the growth within a small circle of people of a standpoint which regards the entire national community as the first object of its public solicitude—all these take time. They take time because they depend on the formation of fundamental dispositions and of traditions of institutions, of traditions within families, educational bodies, business enterprises, and government departments. Even though they do not have to be created in the majority of the population, they cannot be created quickly, for they are formed only through study, practice, and personal interaction, processes which require years. Another danger in demagogy is that what it so quickly creates—other than religious or quasi-religious attitudes formed by conversion—does not go deeply into the dispositional structure, and it does not last. It is merely enthusiasm, and it is in the nature of enthusiasm not to last in most people. It is also in the nature of enthusiasm to generate expectations for large and basic transformations in the order which it confronts, and the situation of the new states is not such as to satisfy such expectations.

It is not the flash of enthusiasm but persistently sustained exertion that is the prerequisite of national development—not just because such exertion may be a moral virtue in itself, but because it is required by the complex undertakings which are on the program of modernization. Persistently sustained exertion is a function of attachment to a task, to the norms which govern its performance, and to the role in which those norms are embodied. Demagogy cannot create such an attachment. It can help along the zealous hatred of one's opponents and paranoid beliefs in the incessant efforts of one's opponents to undo one. Obdurate fanaticism, at the peak of the political pyramid, may succeed in giving the impression that it is the ideological orientation which modernizes a political regime. Ideological fanatics can intimidate their immediate subordinates and bring them to obedience;

ideological fanaticism can even infect them and cause them to share the beliefs and the affective intensity which characterize its espousal by the elites. Thus, with the kind of coercion that accompanies demagogy, something may be accomplished in the way of modernizing a society. People *can* be forced to perform particular roles, even up to a fairly low level of proficiency. If they see their colleagues beaten on the scene or taken away to torment and misery, they are likely to exert themselves and do something like the job that is expected of them. They will not be very adaptive; their efficiency will be low; they will break the tools they are given to do the job; but they will do things like routine manual and clerical work. However, the more complex the task, the less effective coercion will be; and the roles involved in political modernization are not of the order of routine manual labor. The coercion that accompanies demagogy, insofar as it results in the creation of a surplus of wealth or the attainment of a higher gross national product, may contribute to political development—but only indirectly and not weightily.

Moreover, the impression of *ideological* orientation conveyed by demagogy is a false one. Hostility toward the West or toward whites, and belief in Pan-Africanism, does not have enough intellectual content to constitute an ideology. Such slogans as Pan-Arabism, Pan-Africanism, and the African personality are often vigorously, even vehemently, expressed; but they are not yet ideologies in the sense of having a differentiated and compelling intellectual content.

Lastly, since demagogy, although ostensibly addressed to the ordinary people, is in fact addressed to the most volatile, it may be appropriate in times of national danger from an external enemy. With respect to domestic problems, however, its chief function and its frequent intent are to divide a people by rallying those who respond to it against some presumed internal enemy. Thus in the new states, where traditionally received identifications already work to separate rather than unite the people, the hunger of the demagogue for approbation leads him to exploit loyalties of division. When he attempts to arouse the counter-loyalty to national symbols, it is usually through allegations of danger to the national community arising from the machinations of "imperialists" and "colonialists."

II

It is in the context of the foregoing that we have to set the fact that there seem to be few politicians in the new states who, addressing large audiences of the poor and uneducated, are able to speak on behalf of the whole society without attempting to arouse hostilities which are irrelevant to the tasks of modernization. (Nehru and Nyerere are, perhaps, the only ones. Whatever the deficiencies of the Pakistan and Sudanese presidents and of the Malayan and Nigerian prime ministers, they are not demagogues—they are too soldierly or aristocratic in their bearing to be demagogues.)

Demagogy is nearly inescapable in the new states, just as it is a constant presence in the advanced ones. Where political competition for the vote and assent of a society-wide electorate exists, it receives a tremendous impetus; and the impetus is all the stronger where there is a strong populistic element in the culture of the political profession. The availability of the media of mass communication is an invitation to their demagogic use—even more pronouncedly so where the populace is illiterate and scattered in many not easily accessible villages, and where there is the belief that the members of this populace must be "mobilized" for the progress of the country. There is something in the views of the forgotten Le Bon. The mere contemplation of a large audience dilapidates even a rational mind. The structure of political discourse—the length of the communication, the absence of dialogue, and the belief that the audience is on a lower level than one's self—promotes the need to exaggerate and to have recourse to raucous clichés.

Demagogy must be accepted as a fact of life that will be amplified by the use of wireless broadcasting. Its contribution to modernization is not likely to be great except in unusual instances—as, apparently, in Tunisia—where the demagogue is also the kind of charismatic person who impresses by the obvious sincerity of his concern for the public good and by the resonance of his executive effectiveness. Max Weber thought that a country with as much particularism as Germany would stand to benefit from a plebiscitary presidential election—he drew some of his inspiration from the consideration of the United States—and Prime Minister Nehru obviously believes that India's centrifugal potentialities can be held in check by his appearance all over India as the symbol of India. It is likely that this proposition is supported by the experience of President Bourguiba in Tunisia. It is also possible that the renowned oratorical capacities of President Sukarno give Indonesia such unity as it possesses. But the unity which the speeches of Sukarno give is probably not a very deep one and contributes little to the political modernization of Indonesia as long as practically everything else is neglected. The reinforcement of the fragile unity of India contributed by Nehru's indefatigable speech-making is only a reinforcement of the much more important factor of the administrative unity of India, embodied in the coherence of the Indian Civil and Administrative Services, the (hitherto) apolitical coherence of the Indian Armed Forces, and the corps of Indian journalists (mainly in the English-language press) who, whatever their deficiencies, are "all-Indian" in their outlook on most things.

The Indian case is instructive. Unity is a necessity of political modernization. The transcendence of territorial parochiality and of ethnic, tribal, and religious particularism must yield to some measure of consensual acceptance of membership in the larger national community as a basic component in each man's and woman's self-image. But is this sense of membership in the national community as much a product of direct discourse from the center as it is of a belief in the effectiveness of authority, of the good sense of authority, of the fact that it seems "to mean business"? Coherence at the center, strength—not just verbal symbols of strength—will legitimize the elite and the system in which it operates.

The mass of the population is fairly docile in most of the new states; it is likely to comply with most authority which does not demand fundamental reorientations of its routines—and it will even accept some of these, if those who recommend them seem legitimate. The mass of the population will move slowly into the national society if the center of the society is sound. It will not move into the national society if it is agitated and divided.

James Mill said that there was no need to worry about the vote of the working classes as long as they had before them the model of a respectable, hard-working middle class. *Mutatis mutandis*, this principle finds application in the new states. The intellectual centers of the middle class—the intellectuals as the bearers of sober opinion—must be built up to offset the disadvantages and to gather the advantages of such demagogic, charismatic iridescence as exists in the political elite. The building up of these centers will establish standards of technical performance, professional integrity, and genuineness of bearing. From these centers they will flow laterally into newcomers, upward into the political elite, downward into the mass of the population.

These qualities are qualities of stable, humdrum dutifulness, of sticking to a task through thick and thin out of conviction as to its imperious necessity. They are the qualities of what we could call *Berufsstolz* and *Berufsethos*. They are part and parcel of a culture in which occupational and professional roles and performances are important. Such roles and performances are not yet firmly established parts of the cultures of the old societies which are going into the making of the new states of Africa and Asia. They are also not entirely incompatible with those cultures, as numerous individual instances so well demonstrate. Such qualities can be selected from and nurtured in the new states—as the mere existence of so many civil servants and of a no less impressive, though much smaller, number of hard-headed professional journalists, business-like technologists, and serious and· sometimes creative scholarly and scientific intellectuals testifies.

III

The formation of this sober, task-oriented, professionally responsible stratum of the population is, perhaps, the most important precondition of the political development of the new states. Its formation is a necessity not just because their technical skills are required to implement the great ambitions of the elite but, rather, because their prosaic matter-of-factness is essential as a matrix which can absorb the shocks of demagogy, temper its winds, and perhaps even moderate its resonance.

In nearly all the new countries the initiative has passed from the notables to the demagogues and their "verandah-boy" clientele, and the towns have become the most important theaters of political life. It is imperative that a sobering counterpoise be constructed in the opinion of the intellectuals which provides the culture in which the politicians move. They are, after all, urban men—at least, urbanized men—and they are sensitive to what those who are *educated*, and *near at hand*, or *close to their minds* think of them.

The carriers of this *Sachlichkeit* come to it through various paths. They come to it largely through the discipline of advanced modern education and the discipline of the practice of professions in which oratory is not a major determinant of success. They are medical doctors, engineers, and technologists, university teachers and research workers, higher civil servants, and some secondary-school teachers and administrators. Overlapping them is a circle of journalists, editors, and broadcasting technicians, producers, and announcers. These are all people with fairly specific jobs to do, jobs about which there are fairly specific expectations and which are the objects of fairly clear standards of performance. Most of their practitioners have acquired their training in the metropolis, in institutions such as universities, hospitals, research institutes, and large business enterprises where it is conventional to expect punctuality, diligence, and reliability, and where most of the professional staff approximate these standards in their performance.

These people are relatively few in number, and they are often isolated from each other by distance, by professional specialization, and by the nature of their cocktail conviviality. The question is: How can they be brought together to form a community sufficiently solidary, sufficiently self-confident, sufficiently well grounded in its opinion, that it can make itself felt among the politicians and even, in the course of time, penetrate into the back country, into the lower ranks of leadership, and into the younger generation?

The establishment of loose communities of professional persons, bound together by a mutual respect for role and proficiency and supported by a parallel conviviality, will help form a body of skilled business-like persons, prosaic and hard-working. These are necessary for economic and social development, but their importance for political development is no less great. They will provide the anchor for a matter-of-fact opinion which will be capable of judging policies on their merits and which will be less manipulable into enthusiastic flights of political fantasy.

This culture, which is now beginning to come into existence—it has already done so in India—is not likely to be a technocratic culture. It will not be the "Soviet of technicians" toward which Thorstein Veblen looked for the salvation of Western society. In India there is no sign that these people wish to take over political power as a unitary body. There are various reasons for this. For one thing, although these professional persons do interest themselves in their national progress and in the policies which affect it, they are not highly politicized. They render judgments, express opinions, comment on affairs which they feel are their concern; but they do not preoccupy themselves with politics to the exclusion of nearly everything else. Their own jobs are their center of gravity.

IV

Is it not likely that the professional matter-of-factness which has begun to emerge in the educated classes of the new states will become a narrow specialization concentrating exclusively on the technical tasks for which the profession has been trained? Has this not already happened to some extent in America? And, if this happens, will this not undermine the incipient formation of a pluralistic system of civil opinion or prevent its emergence? I think not.

My reasons are as follows: Persons in a new state with foreign training or with advanced modern training acquired in their own country are set apart into a class which includes all others with similar training. This kind of training, quite apart from its specific substantive content, is characterized by a common uniqueness vis-à-vis the culture of most of the rest of the population. It is *modern* culture, which distinguishes its bearers from all those who do not have it. It confers status on its bearers and enters into their self-consciousness. In each individual it makes for a certain measure of solidarity with those other individuals who have a no less modern culture, even though its specific and technical content is very different from that of one's own modern culture. The boundaries of technical specialization are transcended, not by an integration of the various spheres of knowledge into a unitary body of knowledge, but by the integration of the individual bearers of the various specialized spheres of modern knowledge into a single class, bound together by their high evaluation of the possession of some segment of modern culture.

This formation of a single class of those with advanced modern education gives rise to a culture of its own. It is a culture which rotates to a considerable extent about convivial things, such as standard of living, eminence of associates, and the like. But it has a certain substance too—namely, professional reputation, respect for accomplishment, diligence, professional integrity.

Despite the attractions of majesty, there is a tendency in this class to be somewhat removed from politics. Disillusionment, an oppositional disposition, the embitterment of frustrated aspirations, snobbery, and dismay provide some fraction of the motivation for standing at some remove from politics and for taking a detached view of them. These motives alone would lead to an anti-political attitude if they were not tempered by a number of other factors such as moderation of affect, relative success in life, a multiplicity of interests, and an acceptance of the new order of life brought about by the first steps of modernization. This new class, without being fanatically nationalistic, has a sense of a "stake in the country." Its members have come to feel that the country is theirs as much as it is the politicians' who declaim about it so volubly. They think that they are its custodians as much as are the politicians even though they do not clamor and orate about their custodianship.

Not everyone in the educated classes has this attitude. The oppositional mentality dies hard; the fantasies nurtured by the movement for independence leave a residue of sadness when it is seen that reality has not come forward to match them. Poverty and unemployment alienate intellectuals; a belief in their own superfluousness and ineffectiveness alienates them. The company of other self-designated "failures" aggravates the sense of alienation. These are all phenomena which we notice in India especially; but there are parallel tendencies in all new states. The tendencies seldom go so far outside India because the rate of development and, more particularly, the capacity of the economy to incorporate the intellectuals remuneratively are, for the time being, greater than the capacity of the intellectual institutions of the countries concerned and the overseas institutions which supplement or provide the main supply to produce aspirants to such incorporation. The simple certainty of employment on the completion of the course of studies, whatever it might do to the intensity of exertion, does much to offset the common inclination toward an anti-political alienation.

I do not wish to be misunderstood. This class of the educated are not perfect beings. They are not necessarily solidary in their devotion to transcendent values of scientific and scholarly truth, literary and artistic expression, professional proficiency, or civility in matters of public concern. Vanity, sloth, inefficiency will certainly be found among them. There will certainly be unconscionable toadies and place-holders among them, and superior Pococurantes for whom nothing, above all in their own countries, is good enough. And, of course, there will be many who are simply second- or third-rate, who have allowed their skills to gather dust behind the screen of an indolent complacency.

These tarnished ones of the educated class are the victims of their own personal deficiencies, the inadequacy of their training, and their poor environment. They are the victims of the insufficient development of intellectual and professional institutions in their own countries, of the one-sidedness of their ties with the metropolis, or of the rupture of their ties with the metropolis. They are the victims of their scanty numbers, which make for insufficient stimulation in an intellectually impoverished environment.

V

They are, all this notwithstanding, both the executants and the spirit of any modernization which their countries will undergo. The modernization of their countries cannot proceed without their active and energetic participation. They know they are needed, and this makes possible their self-confidence. Where, in addition to being needed, they actually accomplish something which they regard as significant, their outlook becomes more positive and more stable.

The effective performance of persons in these roles is a function not only of their training but also of the professional culture in which they live. In complete isolation only the strongest character, only the most powerfully creative individual, can perform up to the level of his capacities. Most persons need the buttressing of other more or less like-minded persons who share their standards, exemplify them, and provide a resonance for their expression and accomplishment. Without this they relapse into slipshodness and indifference, into a sense of isolation and neglect. They become alienated from their successful contemporaries, more easily tempted by the prospective rewards of judicious subservience to the political elite. This is a winding path on which it is difficult to turn back and from which it is accordingly difficult to return.

The condition of the creation of an independent center of opinion which can withstand, partly counteract, and even moderate the virulent emptiness of demagogy is a coherent, relatively unified, professional stratum in the capital. This is a condition which is not easily attained. The absolute numbers are quite small in most of the new states. They are often widely dispersed within the boundaries of their country. Where the university is not in the capital, an important component of educated opinion is withdrawn from frequent intercourse and there are other pressures among the university teachers which make for an unrealistic and deeply alienated opposition. Journalists too are torn between the sensational exposure of scandals and the deferential consideration of the claims of majesty. Those who work for foreign-owned newspapers are under further constraints, not always moving in a single direction. Civil servants must watch their steps and hold their tongues. Those employed by foreign firms must also be on the lookout lest they lay themselves open to charges of disservice to the national interest—from either journalists or politicians.

Each faces these distracting, disuniting forces and feels them working within himself. Then there are the differences between the American-returned and the English-returned, the Western-returned and the Moscow-returned, the been-to and the never-been-to. There are gradations of status among these, and struggles to modify the balance of status.

There are also the differences of special competence, the differences between the humanistically and juristically educated and the scientifically and technologically educated, and all the other tendencies toward differentiation and segregation imported from the metropolis and also in some measure inherent in the various specialties.

It is most necessary for the strength of the educated class, for its contribution to cultural life as well as to economic and social development, that these patterns of specialized expertise should not be allowed to moulder. They must be fostered by strengthening the solidarity of those who possess them: on a local scale, through professional organization; regionally (e.g., on a West African or on a Southeast Asian scale), through congresses, associations, and collaboration; and internationally, by the maintenance of bilateral, recurrent, and more intense communications with the metropolis. In the course of time, as numbers increase, this type of professional development will threaten to dissolve such unity of the educated class as now exists.

Further professional specialization may make for a narrower and even less continuous political concern. In the advanced states a better civil tradition and a stronger body of institutions of public opinion have enabled their societies to resist the effects of a gratifying and preoccupying specialization in the professions. The weaker civil traditions of the new states may not be able to do so. A critical point may be reached before the moment when independent institutions of opinion are strong enough to dispense with the participation and support of the technologists and other specialists.

It would be especially injurious to the strength of the independent institutions of opinion in most of the new states because the technologists usually, with the civil service, embody the major practical experiences of the modernized sector of the society. The civil service at its higher reaches can be an important component in the formation of instructed opinion through its participation in convivial circles; but it cannot give any publicly visible manifestation of its outlook. University and higher school teachers lack the practical experience and the authority of speaking on the basis of that experience; and their tradition, not diminished by independence, is toward political alienation. Journalists, by their traditions acquired at home or imported from abroad, tend toward an anti-political attitude; in the new states this is often combined with the necessity of "adjustment" to the regnant authorities and their own factual ignorance and lack of direct reportorial experience of the situations they write about.

Thus the technologists, in which we include educated managers of the larger commercial and industrial enterprises, have a very central position in the promulgation of a practical, level-headed opinion about the course of events in their own society. Specialization and increasing numbers, which will enable them to enjoy more exclusively the conviviality of their professional colleagues, would mean the weakening of a central section of the bearers of public opinion.

What are the protections which exist or can be created in the new states against this withdrawal of the technologists and business managers? The demarcation of the boundaries of those who have received an advanced modern education; their small numbers, which prevent the technologists and managers from being convivially self-sufficient; and the common culture of modernity—these are the present guarantees against this withdrawal. But this bulwark will not survive. Numbers will increase, and the growth of secondary education will erode the sharp demarcation which at present separates those with higher education from those without it. The factors which at present keep the technologist-managers inside the circle of the educated, which make them into intellectuals, will not endure indefinitely; and the centrifugal forces will gain in strength.

VI

What kinds of new centripetal forces can be generated in the new states to keep the technologists and, to some extent, the managers from falling away from the "intellectual class"? One solution lies in the syllabus of the course of technological study, and this applies equally to the advanced as well as to the underdeveloped states. There should be a greater component of a humanistic social science, a component of sociological self-understanding, introduced into the curriculum of the engineering and scientific courses in British, American, and French technological training institutions and in the cor responding institutions in the new states.

The solution which is put forward by Sir Charles Snow seems to me to misstate the problem. It is not a question of a gap between the humanistic and the scientific-technological cultures; this formulation presupposes that these two cultures exhaust the possibilities of cultural variety. It is, rather, a matter of creating and establishing a third culture, a culture of a deeper civil understanding, of a self-understanding which is social self-understanding and not just individual self-understanding. This third culture is already in incipiency in certain parts of the present-day social sciences, and enough exists to become a worthy part of the culture of the new states.

It is, therefore—to pursue Sir Charles' formulation a bit further—not an integration of the humanistic and natural science cultures of which they stand in need but an integration of the professional and civil culture. The professional culture will root in them the pluralistic orientation necessary for the development of a modern polity; and the civil culture will give them a standpoint to juxtapose alongside the ideological political culture of the demagogic politician. Neither of these alone will be adequate to the tasks of political development.

The civil culture alone might be very feeble in its impact, certainly in its power, in conflict with the demagogic culture. Those at the center of the demagogic culture control the purse strings, and in some ways they have an ascendancy over the conscience of the intellectual class. The intellectual class is reluctant to oppose the demagogic politician, partly for considerations of prudence and concern for their own skins, physical and economic. They are also reluctant to oppose the politicians even where they disagree, because the politicians have arrogated to themselves the symbols of national existence and of anti-colonialism, before both of which the intellectuals are cautious to avoid acts or thoughts which might be considered disloyal. Being an intellectual of integrity in an underdeveloped country is even more difficult than it is in the advanced countries. Many will become time-servers, and others will withdraw.

The withdrawal is by no means an unqualified disadvantage as long as it is a withdrawal into the professional sphere. It is true that this constitutes an enfeeblement of the civil sphere, but only apparently and immediately. Indirectly, the building up of the professional sphere, the formation of a professional community or of professional sub-communities, will contribute to the establishment of civility. It will contribute to the subsequent growth of civility by creating alternative modern objects of attachment, and will thus provide an alternative to the hyper-politicization, which the demagogue practices and which he wrongly regards as the ideal. It will contribute to the civil culture through providing a field of sober, realistic, and responsible judgment.

A Supplementary Note Addressed to Social Scientists

To speak in the idiom of the present discussion: It is to the communications network of the highly educated that social scientists should turn their attention. They should consider the conditions of the intellectual institutions of the new states: newspapers, periodicals, clubs, wireless stations, colleges, universities, technological institutions, research institutes, and the convivial circles of those who people them. Attention should be paid to the factors which determine the maintenance of standards of proficiency, and to the influence of eminence in adherence to these standards on the position of those who reach the heights. The solidarity and cleavages of the highly educated, and the significance of each of these in strengthening or weakening the influence of the educated among the political elite and among the less educated form another problem of concern to social scientists. Radio broadcasting should be considered not only as a channel which links the elite to the mass but also as a mode of communication within the educated class and, above all, as one of the intellectual institutions within which financial support can be found for intellectual work.

The economics of communication—problems of production costs, circulation, outlets, etc.—should be examined for newspapers, book publishing, and periodicals; the machinery of book circulation through bookshops, libraries, etc. should be gone into. Likewise, the position of authors in the new states should be studied.

At the flanks of these subjects there should be studied (a) the images and responses of the less educated to the more highly educated; and (b) the images and responses of the political elite toward the highly educated who are not engaged professionally in politics. The latter should include the willingness of the politician to listen to the opinions of the educated, both informally and in formal advisory capacities.

CHAPTER 5

THE EMERGENCE OF PROFESSIONAL COMMUNICATORS

T H E problems of political articulation are not those of the politicians alone. In any society only a small fraction of political communications originates from the political actors themselves, and this proportion tends to decrease with modernization as increasing numbers of participants without power join the communications process. In a fundamental sense modernization involves the emergence of a professional class of communicators.

In initially outlining the salient characteristics of the three types of communications structures we observed that in the traditional system there were at best only a very few specialized communicators. The process of communications depended upon people who were performing other social roles. By contrast, we noted that the mass media dimension of the modern communications process not only is comparatively independent of other social and political processes but also constitutes a distinctive industry in both an economic and social sense. Both as an industry and as a profession the modern field of communications tends to generate an ethos and a relatively distinct set of norms for guiding its functions.

There are many qualities of mind and of social class associated with the communications profession. In modern societies journalists, radio and television commentators, and political reporters tend to have a commonly agreed upon standard of excellence by which they can judge each other's performance. There may be much confusion and lack of precision in this concept of profession, but there is one central assumption upon which the entire modern communications industry is built. This is the assumption that objective and unbiased reporting of events is possible and desirable and that the sphere of politics in any society can be best observed from a neutral or non-partisan perspective. Traditional communications processes on the other hand tended in general to be so closely wedded to social and political processes that the very act of receiving and transmitting messages called for some display of agreement and acceptance. Hence in traditional systems the essential structure of the communications process encouraged the expectation that all communications tended to reflect a partisan view, and that there could be no neutral or non-partisan point of view for judging, evaluating, and discussing political events.

The emergence of professionalized communicators is thus related to the development of an objective, analytical, and non-partisan view of politics. As the professional communicators perform their distinctive role as men who understand politics but are not of politics, they are likely to influence their publics to believe that there can be politically neutral institutions at the very heart of public affairs. The evolution of stable, creative politics requires that a citizenry come to believe that in their political system there are certain fundamental institutions which stand apart from immediate partisan conflict, which can be fully trusted and respected, and which can limit but also give meaning to the entire realm of politics. This is to say that there is a direct connection between the integrity of the communications industry and constitutional government.

In transitional systems those who would be the journalists and the reporters of public affairs generally do not have a strong sense of independent professional standards. In large part the economic poverty of the mass media makes it impossible for the society to support a full community of professional communicators. Journalists in most of the new states tend to be so underpaid that they can hardly feel that they represent an independent force capable of criticizing and judging those holding political power. In many of the new countries the journalistic profession has little opportunity for independent development because the most rewarding careers with the mass media tend to be with essentially propaganda agencies for either the government itself or for the dominating political party or movement. Under these conditions writers and communicators may be able to play a constructive role in facilitating the nation-building process but they cannot assume the lead in training the citizenry to appreciate the virtues and the possibilities of non-partisan, and hence essentially constitutional, institutions.

For these and other reasons the small groups of would-be professional journalists in most of the new countries have a variety of tensions and problems which tend to reduce their effectiveness. On the one hand they are close to all the realities of politics in their countries; they can observe the inner politics of personal relationships so common to transitional systems; they know the seamy side of life and hear all the rumors of corruption; and they are constantly aware of the gap of hypocrisy which always exists in any political system between public pronouncements and inner cal-culations. On the other hand the journalists tend to be people anxious to become a part of the modern world; they are usually attuned to international developments and the latest fashions and fads in the industrial countries; and above all they tend often to have at least an exaggerated if not romanticized view of the per-formance of modern political systems. Many of these journalists, sensitive to their own difficulties in meeting the professional stand-ards of their counterparts in the more developed societies, become cynical about the performance gap between the politicians in their country and their idealized notions of what leaders should be able to do in a modern society.

The sum effect of these tensions often undermines the ability of the mass media in the new states to educate the citizenry in the basic standards essential for a civil society. The press and radio in such situations are not likely to be inspired to communicate an ob-jective, realistic, and compassionate view of the problems of politi-cal life. In recognizing these difficulties of the journalists it is also essential to acknowledge that in a few of the new states some seg-ments of the mass media have heroically overcome the handicaps and have performed truly impressive community and civic services. In recent years there have been many moving examples of isolated newspapers gallantly adhering to the highest ideals of journalistic integrity even when threatened by extreme political reprisals. In other new countries the press has often been the only effective loyal opposition to the domination of a one-party nationalist movement. In these countries where the political class has not been able to establish the effective basis of a competitive party system but in which there has been considerable sympathy for democratic ideals the press has indeed been able to perform a uniquely constructive function by adhering to its professional standards and serving as a temperate critic and oppositional force.

The problems of the emerging journalists in the new states stem not only from the side of the politicians; they are also related to the process of disengagement from the traditions of the writer. In the early stages of modernization journalists and writers are usually close together, and it is often difficult to distinguish be-tween the two roles. Indeed, in most of the new countries it is cus-tomary for the leading authors periodically to perform journalistic tasks and to engage in political reporting and criticism.

Under these conditions the development of a professional journalistic ethos becomes deeply enmeshed in the general problems of the writers' emergence from a traditional role. Viewed from this perspective it becomes readily apparent that the establishment of an objective and politically non-partisan community of specialized communicators is complicated by a host of extremely subtle problems. There is, for example, the tension between the writer's tradition of involvement in life, of commitment to ideas, and of passion for causes and principles and the journalist's standards of detachment and non-partisanship. There are also those problems which the writers and journalists of the new states must share in common: such problems as the relationship of the indigenous languages and the world languages, the difficulties of expressing modern concepts in local languages, and the issues about using European languages and the problems of translating world literature into local tongues. Indeed, these problems of the relationship between local languages and the major Western languages represent a peculiarly intense form of the general problem of transitional societies in achieving a satisfactory fusion between the world culture and the indigenous tradition, between the universal and the parochial, a problem which we have already observed to be at the heart of the modernization process.

Leaving aside the problems of the journalist, we should recognize that in the relationship between communications and modernization writers as creative artists have a vital role. Historically in nearly every case in which a society has experienced a significant movement toward modernization the initiation of the process has been signalled by a literary awakening, by a renaissance in literature. The novel is not only a modern form of communications; it has also been in many transitional societies one of the most effective agents for giving people an understanding of modern life and of new values and new concepts.

In order to appreciate all the nuances in the complex interrelationships between journalists and writers, and to perceive the subtle ways in which questions about language and the creative forms of communications can influence political modernization, it is necessary to explore in considerable depth some particular historical experiences. Therefore with these considerations in mind we may now turn to an analysis of these and other related problems as they appeared in Japan's transition to the modern world.

CHAPTER 6

WRITER AND JOURNALIST
IN THE TRANSITIONAL SOCIETY

HERBERT PASSIN

EACH nation that enters the cycle of modernization must at some point break through in three fields: political and social reform, language, and journalism. The break-throughs may take place simultaneously or at separate times within a broad historical period. In China the May 4th movement of 1919 was a simultaneous climax of literary, philosophical, and political ideas seeking to burst free of the restraints of the half-emancipation of the 1911 Revolution. But in India the Bengal renaissance of the late 19th and early 20th century—that outpouring of creative energy in literature, the arts, music, and philosophy led by Tagore—came first; the modern developments in politics led by Gandhi followed by several decades. The Japanese cultural renaissance, insofar as this is the correct label, started about twenty years after the Meiji Restoration in 1868, when political and administrative reforms were well under way.

The relations among these three elements are governed not only by the stage of development of the society but also by its traditions and its specific historic experiences. Underdeveloped countries are not *tabulae rasae* waiting virginally for Western ideas to be inscribed. Each has a long history, a set of predispositions which select out, under specific historic conditions, the particular Western influences to which they will respond. There is obviously a great difference between a country like Japan, which enters the modern world with an already established tradition of secular literature, a well-developed script, a relatively well-educated population, and a differentiated class of writers, scribes, scholars, publicists, and users of the written word,[1]

---

[1] Almost two hundred years before the opening of Japan there was a distinctively modern flavor in her literary life. The Genroku period (1688-1704) saw a modest renaissance in literature and the popular arts based upon the rising strength of the cities and the urban classes. (This was the period of the *ukiyo-e*, the "pictures of the floating world," perhaps the form of Japanese art best known in the Western world.) From Genroku on, a lively publishing industry developed, with large commercial publishing houses and professional writers and book illustrators. Large editions, running into the thousands, were published, using an improved version of the traditional wood-block prints, to satisfy the vastly increased audiences created by the

and a country like the Congo, with no unified national language, a multiplicity of tongues, high illiteracy, and only an indigenous oral literary tradition. The problem of the writer in the advanced non-Western civilizations, like Japan, China, Korea, India, and the Arab states, is therefore fundamentally different from what it is in countries without a powerful secular literary tradition. When the former enter the modernization process, they bring with them a literary tradition and a model of the writer as artist. The problem we have to explore with them is how an older pre-existent literary tradition is gradually transformed in response to new needs, ideas, and literary models. With the societies lacking this literate tradition the problem must start at a more primitive level: how does literature itself, as a creative pursuit and as a profession, emerge?

The relations among these elements also vary with the particular historical situation that is being faced. By now Japan is into her fifth modern generation since the Meiji Restoration. Most of the new French African states are only at the start of their pioneer modernizing generation. It is not only that the particular problems faced are different, but also that each country faces the challenge posed by the West at different times. In effect it is a different challenge and in some senses even a different West. Japan first faced these problems in an age of expansive imperialism and capitalism, when the literary models immediately available to her in the English language were those current in late Victorian England. A flood of novels in the early Meiji period took their inspiration from such secondary literary figures as Bulwer-Lytton and Disraeli. It was only at a later point that real contact was made with the great models of West European and Russian literature. The French African writers, who have given birth to a remarkable, if somewhat limited, literature, had their point of departure in later phases of French literature, so that the influence

growing prosperity and aggressiveness of the urban population. Commercial lending libraries distributed these to even larger audiences. Sansom describes a publisher's party of the early 19th century that has the solid ring of Madison Avenue: ". . . over eight hundred guests, including the elegant and the vulgar . . . more than two hundred who had not been invited. Meals were served for 1,284 persons." Among the guests were "Confucian scholars; academic painters . . . ; three renowned calligraphers; leading colour-print men . . . ; comic prose writers and poets . . . ; and distinguished officials and scholars as well as a number of publishers, book sellers, paper-merchants and wood block makers. Glamour was added to the occasion by the presence of important military personages from the shogun's court." (*The Western World and Japan*, London, The Cresset Press, 1950, pp. 232-233.) The best account of the Genroku renaissance will be found in Howard Hibbett, *The Floating World in Japanese Fiction*, New York, Oxford University Press, 1959.

of symbolism and other modern literary trends has entrenched itself centrally among them. A distinguished Japanese composer, whose son, still in his twenties, is also a composer, once said to me: "I am the Shostakovich of Japan [actually he was much more like César Franck], and my son is the Schoenberg." The father, who was educated in the early 1920's, encountered Western music largely in its late 19th-century romantic form; his models were the late classical tradition. His son, on the other hand, came into musical consciousness of the West in the period of neo-classical and atonalist ascendance, the age of Schoenberg, Bartok (almost passé), Webern, and Berg. "Western music" meant something different to each one.

Moreover, each generation in the course of ongoing modernization faces different problems, and the accumulation of its experience gives the succeeding generation a new starting point. The "struggle generation," with its heroes and renaissance men, gives way to the bureaucrats, engineers, and politicians. In India, which is still only midway through its independence generation, there are already long and loud complaints that the post-independence bureaucrats are betraying the ideals of the Gandhi generation. But in Japan, which is still "modernizing" and "Westernizing," the fifth modern generation is so far from its heroic forebears that the Meiji Era has now entered the realm of historical study and romance. At this point the changes going on in Japan are to be described more accurately as the development of a Japanese version of advanced industrial civilization than as "modernization." Each generation, then, creates a new tradition for its successor. The first modernizing generation faces Western literature from an immediate background of the traditional literature. But for the next generation the past, or tradition, already includes a considerable admixture of Western literature. Contemporary Japanese literature today therefore takes its point of departure not from the pure Japanese past, nor in direct response to Western influences, but from its own tradition, which by now is a melding of both elements that has gone through several stages of achieving its own form.

In this chapter I shall analyze the relations between writers and journalists in the transitional societies. My examples will be drawn mainly from Asia, but occasional reference will be made to other areas as seems appropriate. Inevitably I draw heavily on the Japanese experience, in spite of her uniqueness in certain respects, not only because it is the case I know best but also because I am persuaded it has unique illustrative value.

On the surface there would appear to be no greater contrast than between modern Japan, with her highly developed industrial economy, her near-universal literacy, her 700,000 university students whose number grows yearly, her newspapers reaching millions of readers, her thousands of professional writers, and some newly launched French African state with near-universal illiteracy, an overwhelmingly primitive economy, and a limited intellectual class that is too busy to deal with anything except politics and that has still to establish a regular newspaper. Yet to some extent the difference is one only of degree. Japan, having started on the road of resolute modernization first, has already in one form or another had to face up to the problems others have faced or still have to face. Her history, then, provides us with a preview, as it were, of the choice points, the problems, and the alternatives that lie along the way. The outcomes will very likely be different, but there is much to learn from seeing how different peoples with their own particular traditions and historical experiences have dealt with these problems.

It would be as well at the outset to make clear what we mean by the "writer" and the "journalist." If we look to the extremes, we can define them fairly clearly. At one pole we have the creative artist with a vision, a *vocation*, represented, let us say, by someone like Henry James. At the other we have the technician of words, the scribbler preoccupied with the immediate, the evanescent, the surface; the image that comes to mind is the hot-shot police reporter on the big city daily. But the reality is much more like a continuum. The moment we leave the extremes, the distinctions become blurred. At the higher ranges of journalism the journalist stops being a mere reporter and becomes a commentator, essayist, propagandist—a "writer." The writer who leaves pure fiction becomes a commentator or essayist, thus meeting the journalist moving in the other direction. Even at lower journalistic levels the writer and journalist meet: the human interest or feature reporter is often not clearly distinguishable from the light essayist or short-story writer. If we take the full range of periodical publications, we shall find daily journalism at one end and the literary journal at the other. Yet even these extremes may not be absolutely pure. The press may be an important outlet for creative writing, essays, commentary, and criticism (social, literary, and artistic); and in these activities the professional journalist may take as much part as the professional writer. Between these extremes we find a whole range of weeklies, monthlies, and specialized journals that combine news, commentary, philosophy, politics, literature, aesthetic theory, and literary criticism. Here the journalist becomes a writer, even if not a creative writer, and the writer, as commentator with views on philosophy, aesthetics, politics, and social reform, becomes a journalist. In fact, in the central areas it is hard to separate them out.

I. Language and Modernization

By now even the casual student of the underdeveloped countries knows about economic growth, political modernization, and national unity. But for some reason the problem of language, which is so central to the development of a modern outlook, has received very little attention.[2] This problem has two principal aspects: first, the need for a modern language capable of expressing new ideas; second, the relation of language to the unified nation-state. The first will be discussed in Part I of this chapter, and the second, more briefly, in Part II.

In the course of its transition to modernity every non-Western country finds itself at one time or another confronting the problem of language. One reason is simply that in the early stages the content of modernity comes to them in some foreign language, usually a European one. (In Korea, Japanese was the "metropolitan language.") Modern educated people must often therefore actually think their modern thoughts and express their modern sensibilities in a foreign language. Just recently, for example, an Indian friend of mine, a professor of philosophy, commented that he has never, to the best of his recollection, thought in Hindi about philosophical problems. My friend was not educated abroad, and he speaks and writes Hindi very well; but when it comes to the modern philosophical problems that preoccupy him, which he has studied only in English, he feels at a loss to formulate them in Hindi.

This will not surprise us as it applies in the advanced ranges of Western thought that have no counterpart in the traditional languages. For many decades the Japanese medical student was required to write his thesis in German, with the result that he could properly express his medical ideas only in that language; today the vocabulary of Japanese medicine has developed to the point where it is possible

[2] One of the few full-length treatments of language problems in a transitional society is John De Francis' interesting, if somewhat biassed, analysis of the language issue in China, *Nationalism and Language Reform in China*, Princeton, Princeton University Press, 1950.

to write textbooks and to carry on medical education in Japanese. Nor should we be surprised to discover an African physicist working in some European language rather than in his native dialect. This is quite common in culture contact that involves much borrowing. When the Japanese started to take over Chinese Buddhism, from the 6th century on, they had in the first instance to take it over entirely in the Chinese language. Their own relatively simple language and religion had no counterparts for the complex elaborated *corpus* of Buddhist theology, metaphysics, and philosophy. For several centuries the Japanese sat on this indigestible heap, expressing Buddhist thoughts in mispronounced Chinese, and only gradually domesticating the vocabulary. Some words and ideas became sufficiently current so that they could pass as perfectly good Japanese; others had to be encapsulated and swallowed whole (just as, for example, the Greek word "hubris" becomes a standard part of the vocabulary of philosophers and literary critics; we know that it is not English, but it occupies a place in thought that cannot be exactly filled by any English word); for still others, Japanese equivalents were found or invented. But even after 1,200 years a proper reading of Buddhist texts in Japanese requires special training; the vocabulary has still not been completely digested.

Thus technical language, whether of science, philosophy, or religion, may, we can well understand, have to be expressed for a period at least in a foreign language. But the modern sensibility goes much farther. A good example is the Japanese difficulty in finding a satisfactory generic term for "the people." There are of course many Japanese terms that refer to people in particular capacities or statuses or as biological organisms. But none of these can quite convey the modern notion of people as "citizens," endowed with "rights." Traditionally the people, or the common people (*shomin*), were subjects (*tami*) bearing obligations to their superiors. A wise ruler was enjoined to treat them well and look out for their needs, but this was not a matter of right. Therefore the development of a modern political vocabulary presented unique problems. In the earliest documents of Meiji Japan the term *heimin* (ordinary people) was used, but this had the sense of the "lower orders" as distinguished from the "higher orders." Later words were equally unsatisfactory in one way or another. *Kokumin*, one of the most commonly used, is made up of two elements: *koku*—which means country, or nation, but rather in the sense of state or government; and *min*—which has the sense of subject, rather than people. *Minzoku* (*min* = subject, or people; *zoku* = family, group), which is often used in the Japanese word for "nationalism" (*minzoku-shugi*), emphasizes the national or ethnic group character of the people. *Minshu* (*min* = subject, people; *shu* = type) implies the notion of the people as a racial group. Attempts have been made to use the term *shimin* (*shi* = city; *min* = subject, people), but this cannot have the same connotation as in the West, where the word "citizen" has come from the specific experience of the mediaeval city, with its corporate rights as against the king or the feudal power. More recently Japanese left-wingers have turned to the word *jinmin* (*jin* = person, human; *min* = subject, person) as a closer approximation to their concept as it is used in the "people's democracies."[3]

The problem therefore is not simply one of substantive words but of concepts, notions of process, inherent perceptions of logic and order—the expression of ideas and sensibilities perhaps never before expressed in the language.[4] A recent court case in Japan illustrates this dramatically. A prominent politician, Arita Hachiro, has sued the novelist Mishima Yukio[5] for "invasion of privacy." Now, apart from the novelty this presents in Japanese law, the interesting thing is that there is no word in Japanese for "privacy";[6] the legal brief must use the English word (pronounced *puraibashii*). Arita is charging Mishima with a violation, that cannot be formulated in traditional Japanese, of a law that does not clearly exist on the Japanese

[3] This term is used in the official name of Communist China, as translated into Japanese, *Chūgoku Jinmin Kyowakoku* (Chinese People's Republic).

[4] See Edward Sapir (chapter on "Language," in *Culture, Language and Personality*, selected essays edited by David G. Mandelbaum, Berkeley, University of California Press, 1958): "It would be difficult in some languages, for instance, to express the distinction which we feel between 'to kill' and 'to murder,' for the simple reason that the underlying legal philosophy which determines our use of these words does not seem natural to all societies. Abstract terms, which are so necessary to our thinking, may be infrequent in a language whose speakers formulate their behaviour on more pragmatic lines. On the other hand, the question of presence or absence of abstract nouns may be bound up with the fundamental form of the language; and there exist a large number of primitive languages whose structure allows of the very ready creation and use of abstract nouns of quality or action" (p. 36).

[5] The reader may recognize him from some of his novels translated into English: *Five Noh Plays, Temple of the Golden Pavilion, Confessions of a Mask*, and *The Sound of Waves*.

[6] Other languages also seem to lack a generic word for "privacy." The reader might have an interesting time trying to formulate a sentence using the word in French, Spanish, or Italian. In Spanish one can use *privado* as an adjective, but there is no noun counterpart; all the possible words imply solitude, retirement, isolation, secrecy, reserve, etc. The same is true in French. What this implies for "national character," I would not presume to say.

lawbooks. The result is the type of anomaly familiar to all observers of the underdeveloped countries.

Here are a few other examples that come to my mind (I am sure that others will have their own pet examples): a group of Korean professors, huddled around a fireless pot-belly stove one freezing February day in 1947 at the University of Seoul, who confessed that they could express themselves much more accurately and freely in Japanese than in Korean; an Indian couple, the wife from the north, the husband from the south, who carry on their ordinary communication in Hindi but in their tender moments express their feelings to each other only in English; or Gabriel D'Arboussier, one of French West Africa's greatest political leaders, energetically campaigning in his elegant French in Kaolack, a Woloff-speaking back district of Senegal, through an interpreter.

These are not, in my view, idle paradoxes. They point to the problem of the modern educated classes, particularly of the writer and the user of words, and to major national problems. How uncomfortable it is to live in an uncertain language medium we perhaps cannot even comprehend. For many modern educated people there is often a sharp separation between the language of thought and the language of emotion or of daily life. An Indian may be raised at home speaking Malayalam and then have his education in English. This means that his early experiences, emotions, and affective relations are carried on in one language and his contact with ideas, modern life, and modern institutions in another. If he then has a traditional family life after he is married, the discontinuity can become very extreme indeed. Or take the case of a Filipino who may have been raised at home speaking Ilocano, then started his education in Spanish and finished it in English; now that Tagalog is being made the national language, in what language will he be able to express himself well?[7] In many countries we find that writers are uncertain of themselves in whatever language they use.

Their uncertainty may not be entirely a disadvantage. At its best it brings a differentiated sensitivity. The writer's words and experiences have a different echo, which may give a shadow and a perspective that the unilingual writer cannot achieve. Thus the non-Westerner

---

[7] "One cannot write completely in a language in which one does not think," Leopoldo Yabes reminds us in his "Fifty Years of Filipino Writing in English," *Literary Apprentice*, 1951, p. 97. "The earlier writers thought in Spanish or perhaps in the vernacular; while the younger writers, at least the more able among them, think in English."

writing in a Western language often brings to it a distinctive flavor, as we can see in the poetry of Senghor and other French Africans or in some contemporary Filipino writing. By knowing words in a slightly different way, or by knowing other words for the same experience or for part of the same experience, the experience itself becomes something different. The Indian writer Raja Rao has even argued that this situation offers the possibilities of a new and fresh language. "Indian English," he holds, is not simply an imperfect form of standard English but a distinct language or dialect of its own.[8] In the same vein, a Filipino critic argues that a distinctive Filipino-English, just like Irish, Australian, or American (as distinct from British) English, is in the making: "It is a living language . . . on the lips and minds of an ever growing number of users, with a modified vocabulary and diction, idiom, and sentence structure, and a new cadence. . . . (It) has all the promise of a new way of thought and talk. Upon this new, or rather newest, English, Filipino writers will 'erect' the literary language."[9]

But apart from its implications for the quality of writing and the plight of the writer this linguistic schizophrenia accentuates the separation of the modern educated person from his fellow-nationals who still live a more or less traditional life and carry on their daily existence and thoughts in the traditional language. The alienation of the modern elite from "the masses" has one of its sources right here. The modern educated person often finds that he cannot discuss with the "masses" many of the problems that preoccupy him because they present themselves to him in a foreign language or in words for which the popular language has no counterpart. In some instances he may not even speak the indigenous language well. And since he may be strongly motivated by nationalist and populist-democratic sentiments, his inability to feel himself in real communication with "the people" produces guilt and frustration. In the colonial countries this split between the traditional and the modern sensibility becomes institutionalized in the social structure, and the language becomes one of the important defining elements in the distinction between the traditional elite and the modern elite, between the elite and the masses.

[8] In the preface to his collection of short stories, *The Cow on the Barricades*, Bombay, Oxford University Press.

[9] Cristino Jamías, "Our Literature in English," *Literary Apprentice*, 1951, p. 107.

The form in which the modernizing elite takes shape is decisive for this general process. Japan, for example, had the good fortune to be able to carry on her modern development in her own language. She had, of course, to absorb other languages, but these could be taken as objects of study rather than as the languages of thought itself. Undoubtedly she started out with certain advantages, not the least of which—by comparison with many other new states—were a compact geographic area whose borders were more or less clearly defined both by the sea and by virtually unchallenged historical sanction;[10] a population relatively homogeneous in race, language, religion, and custom; and a centralized national state, although not of a modern type. She already had, in spite of dialectical variations, a single well-developed national language that was adaptable to new ideas, or from which new ideas could be constructed. A standardized version of the Tokyo dialect was made the national language and diffused through the schools and all national institutions.[11] Since Japan had resolved on universal compulsory education as early as 1872—well before many Western countries—the national language soon became very nearly universal. Therefore it was completely usable for much of the work of modernization. By 1886[12] the form of the solution to the colloquial-classical problem became clear, and the new *gembun-itchi* (unification of the spoken and the literary style) provided the basis for the development of a modern literary style based upon a refined and elaborated colloquial. There was always of course a contact with foreign languages, but Japanese were by and large able to think and write in their own language. Foreign languages played an important role in the early stages of the modern educational system through foreign teachers and professors[13] and through foreign-sponsored (usually missionary) schools, but it was not long before the main bulk of foreign teachers were replaced by nationals and the foreign-sponsored schools turned to Japanese. Textbooks were written in Japanese, scientific vocabularies were developed and domesticated, and, although new ideas and concepts continue to come from foreign languages, Japanese is able to absorb them in

[10] There were marginal problems with the Russians in the north and with the Chinese over the Ryukyu Islands.

[11] This was done energetically from 1882, with the publication of a plan by Yatabe Ryōkichi.

[12] With the publication of Mozume Takami's *Gembun Itchi* in that year.

[13] At the peak of foreign influence, in the late 1870's, there were over 5,000 foreign teachers in Japanese schools, particularly in the sciences and technology. (Hugh Borton, *Japan's Modern Century*, New York, Ronald Press, 1955, p. 176.)

its own idiom and at its own pace. It is therefore possible for a Japanese to acquire a complete modern, even Western, education in his own language. There is no currently underdeveloped country of which this can be said.

One unique advantage of Japanese—as of several other languages—is its possession of a "classical" language. Japanese has an open-channel relationship with Chinese, drawing upon it for new concepts and vocabulary, much as we do with Latin and Greek, or the Indians with Sanskrit, or the Arabs with classical Arabic. Not all classical languages are equally usable, of course, but most of them have such a long tradition of literature and speculative philosophy, as in the case of Sanskrit, that they offer at least the same resources as Latin for the construction of new words. The question is a highly technical one, but we may put it very briefly: confronted with new ideas and objects, a language has fundamentally two alternatives—to generate new words from its own resources, or to incorporate foreign words *in toto*. The Japanese, for example, when trying to express the notion of a "motor" could create a neo-Japanese term derived from Chinese root-words, *hatsudōki* (generating-motion-machine), or simply take over the foreign word, which they pronounced as *mōtā*. All languages do both—and in the example given the Japanese did both at the same time—but there is a great variation in their inherent capacity to generate a modern vocabulary and style from their own resources. Fashion, and the vagaries of nationalistic sensitivity, may also have something to do with the final decision. Many new nations seem to be wasting an inordinate amount of time trying to create words for Western objects and ideas when they might more conveniently take over a Western word. During the war, for example, Japanese ultranationalism required the purging of the language of Anglicisms, so that *beisubōru* (baseball), a perfectly acceptable and understandable word for Japan's national sport, had to be rendered in a Sino-Japanese neologism as *yakyū* (field ball). (It has now become *beisubōru* again.)

A Japanese type of development seems possible to some extent for certain other countries that have either escaped colonialism or have an adequate linguistic basis for the growth of a modern language. It would take us too far afield to discuss them in detail here, but we might mention Hebrew, Korean, Thai, Chinese, Vietnamese, Burmese, Arabic, and Bahasa Indonesian. Whether they will in fact succeed, and how long they will take, is quite another matter. All we can say is that they show the possibility of developing into a modern unified national language.

How different is the situation in countries that have experienced a long period of colonial domination, or that have either no usable literate language or no single language with an unambiguous claim to priority, we can see in India, the Philippines and most of Africa. None of these were historically nations in the Western sense, and in none had there ever been a sovereign political state which covered exactly the same territory as the present governments. In India, for example, there are dozens of separate "national" groups speaking fourteen major languages and hundreds of dialects. Under British rule English became the common language of the educated classes, and even of the semi-educated, since it was the language of adminis-stration and of education. The attempt to make Hindi the national language runs into the opposition of entrenched institutions and also of the other language groups, jealous of their status and convinced that Hindi is inferior to their own languages. The Bengali and Marathi are able to argue with some justice that they have a much more developed literature than Hindi. The speakers of the southern, Dravidian languages, which are not even genetically related to Hindi, have additional objections. The establishment of Hindi, they feel, will impose an enormous burden on them. Every person will have to speak his native language at home and in his own province, and in addition he will have to learn the national language. Beyond that, however, educated southerners feel that they will have to know English as an international language, so that at the very least they will have to know three languages, all of them unrelated. If in addition the speaker comes from some dialect area in the south, he may very well have to dominate a minimum of four languages in order to operate: his native dialect, the standard language of his region, Hindi, and English. The Philippines have similar and perhaps even more difficult problems; because the indigenous languages all lack an important literate tradition,[14] there is serious question whether they provide within the foreseeable future a sufficient basis for a modern language. The many tribes of which the Philippines are made up speak dozens of distinct languages, such as Tagalog,

[14] I am aware that there were some pre-Spanish scripts in the Philippines, perhaps syllabaries related to those of Malay. But these completely disappeared under Spanish rule to the point that no effective indigenous literate tradition remains for modern Filipinos. The effective starting point of their own literate tradition is Spanish and English.

Visayan, Ilocano, Bicol, Pampango, and Moro. None has an un-
challengeable claim to priority; Tagalog, which has become the
national language, apparently provides the best groundwork for
a national language, but Visayan can claim more indigenous speakers.[15] The problem is complicated by the fact that the first national
modern language was Spanish. Although it is slowly dying out, it
still lives on, especially among the upper classes and older educated
people. Since the American occupation, English has become the true
national language of the educated and administrative classes. Whether
it can really be displaced by Tagalog is a major cultural and political
problem.[16] In most of the new African states the situation is even
more difficult; there is no language for which even the slightest claim
to status as a national language can be made. The result is that all
of the new African nations must carry on the business of modernization—administration, economic development, public enlightenment,
education, and intellectual development—in the metropolitan language, either English or French.

In all of these cases the problem has not been the "recovery" of
independence, or the "restoration" of a previously existing sovereign
nationhood, but rather the creation *de novo* of a common national
sentiment among all the people living in a given geographic area: in
other words, the creation of a nation where none existed before. If
we allow ourselves to speculate on the future, there would appear
to be three models to which these new nations can approximate: first,
a strictly federated form, such as the Swiss, where each local language would remain in full force and with no single national language. Many people, however, would be likely to learn at least one
of the other regional languages. Second, the complete dominance
of one national language and the reduction of the others to dialect
status for purely domestic or local use, as in the case of a number of
European countries. In France, for example, Provençal, Breton,

[15] According to the 1939 *Census of the Philippines*, the three divisions of Visayan
(Cebuan, Hiligaynon, and Samar-Leyte together) tallied 6,491,699 speakers, while
Tagalog tallied 4,068,565. For the considerations that went into the selection of
Tagalog as the national language, see Ernest J. Frei, "The Historical Development
of the Philippine National Language—III," *Philippine Social Sciences and Humanities
Review*, Vol. xv, No. 2, June 1950.

[16] The rancorous debate on this issue in Filipino intellectual life is linked with a
new wave of Filipino nationalism, part of the search for disengagement from American "cultural domination" and for a new "Asian personality" for the Filipinos. For
the feeling of this argument, see the recent article by Jose Villa Panganiban, Director
of the Institute of the National Language, "Language and Nationalism," *Comment*,
Second Quarter, 1960.

and Basque carry on a feeble local existence while French is the effective language of national communication, literature, thought, administration, and education. A less extreme case might be Spain, where Catalan, Basque, and Gallego still manage to carry on a minor literature in spite of the overwhelming domination of Spanish. The third possible model is that of the Soviet Union: the vigorous existence of certain local languages along with the complete penetration of Russian as the national language. In most of the new African states the "national" language is most likely to be foreign, either English or French.

II. Language and Politics

Let us now look at the relations of language to politics in the narrower sense. Most of the new states come into existence without that unity of sentiment, geography, administrative organization, language, and cultural tradition that is taken for granted as the basis of nationhood in the more settled states. Japan and Korea, with their relatively homogeneous populations sharing the same language, culture, and tradition, come closest to the Western conception of the nation-state. But even an enduring historic entity like China was not so much a nation-state in the modern sense as a multi-national empire with a central core of Han people and a periphery of tributary states. The rest, as we have seen, are to a great extent creations of the colonial powers. Their geographical limits have been determined by extremely complex historical considerations, and when we come to the newly formed African states it is apparent that the present limits cannot be assumed to be permanently fixed. A common national language becomes an urgent necessity for the promotion of the sense of nationhood and, therewith, national unity.

It is not surprising therefore that in many of the new states the problem of language penetrates into the very heart of national politics in a way that it no longer does, except peripherally, in the more settled states.[17] A few examples will illustrate this linkage of language and politics. The reform of the Turkish script was, we may recall, a basic part of Ataturk's political program. In India the attempt to establish Hindi as the national language presents the country with some of its most pressing current issues. It has aroused the provincial nationalism of the non-Hindi language groups; stirred deep regional, communal, and cultural divisions; and forced the

[17] In Spain, for example, where Basque, Catalan, and Galician separatism still remain latent political issues.

reorganization of state boundaries to the accompaniment of vast civil violence running into tens of thousands of deaths.[18] The ramifications of the language problem reach into the inmost problems of the country—in literature, the arts, journalism, education, and public life. In Ceylon the problems of the national language, of the recognition of the minority language, and of the relations between the speakers of Sinhalese and Tamil are central to an understanding of what is happening today. The very basis of pan-Arab nationalism, Albert Hourani has argued eloquently, lies in the community bounded by a common language rather than by religion or by traditional law. ". . . [language] emerged as the common good of the Near-Eastern people, just as law had been their common good in the past."[19] In China language reform is an old political issue; the struggle for the ascendance of *pai-hua*—the vernacular, spoken language—as against the stilted classical, official language, which played such an important part in the May 4th Movement, has been well won, but the Chinese Communists have raised new issues by their radical plan of replacing the traditional system of ideographic writing with a fully alphabetic script. For thirty-five years the Japanese virtually suppressed the use of Korean as a public language,[20] much as the Russians did with Polish; the result is that the Koreans today have among their most urgent tasks to bring their language up to

[18] At the moment of writing (August 1961), India is going through another language struggle. Master Tara Singh, leader of the Sikh community, is in the midst of a fast "unto the death" to force the establishment of Sikh as the official language of the Punjab. Sikh is already, it should be noted, one of the two official languages, along with Hindi. Moreover, the only difference between Sikh and Punjabi—the vernacular of the Punjab State—is the script: Punjabi is written in the Devanagari script, as is Hindi, while Sikh is written in Gurumukhi; otherwise the two "languages" are identical. This is a good example of how passionately people feel about language allegiances. For the first time in Indian history, however, a political fast has been challenged: two Hindi leaders have concurrently entered a fast "unto the death" to prevent the government from giving in to Master Tara Singh's demands.

[19] Albert Hourani, "The Regulative Principle of Society," in *Democracy in the New States—Rhodes Seminar Papers*, New Delhi, Office for Asian Affairs, Congress for Cultural Freedom, 1959.

[20] The use of Korean was not forbidden outright, but it was discouraged, and Japanese was deeply entrenched as the official, public language. Immediately after the annexation of Korea in 1910, the Korean language was permitted in the inferior schools for Koreans but not in the superior institutions. All Korean language newspapers were abolished except for one, the *Mei Ilbo*, which was under government control. After the independence demonstrations of 1919, the policy was eased somewhat, so that two vernacular newspapers as well as magazines could be published. In higher education, although the main channel for advance, the Keijō (Seoul) Imperial University, carried on in Japanese, several mission colleges were allowed to offer Korean as an elective. But in 1940, with the intensification of the war crisis, the use of Korean was almost completely prohibited.

date and to develop a body of materials that can be used for study in the schools and universities. At the end of World War II, when Korea became independent, Seoul National University (formerly the Japanese Keijō Imperial University) had a library of several hundred thousand volumes in Japanese but virtually none in Korean except for some of the classics. A whole modern literature and journalism, not to speak of textbooks, had to be developed in the Korean language, and to a great extent by a generation whose modern education and modern sensibilities were expressed in Japanese, just as so many Indians today can properly express their (modern)[21] ideas only in English. In black Africa there is virtually no new or prospective state (with the possible exception of Somalia) that does not have built into the very center of its problems that of language; their modern development must be carried on in the metropolitan language they have inherited in their schools, public institutions, and administrative structure. Some of the more ardent pan-Africans of the Présence Africaine have proposed the development of Swahili as a pan-African language, but so far none of the African languages has a realistic and enforceable claim to the status of national language. The tenuous and fragile unity of the new states, most explosively illustrated in the Congo, is constantly menaced by divisive groups based primarily on linguistic allegiance.

Since writers and journalists are by definition professional users of language, we can expect a priori that their work, even without explicit intent, is often more political in implication than it would be in countries with a more settled relation between language and politics.

III. The Press

The rise of journalism in the underdeveloped countries is almost exclusively the result of Western influence. It is true, as Shils has pointed out, that there is some antecedent for "nearly every section of the modern intellectual class,"[22] at least in what Bertrand Russell called the "economically but not culturally backward" countries.[23] In the advanced pre-modern societies, such as Japan, China, India, Korea, and the Arab states, we find well-developed intellectual activ-

[21] There is a Yoruba proverb, which seems appropriate here: "Modern traps are extremely good for catching modern rabbits."
[22] Edward Shils, "The Intellectual Between Tradition and Modernity: The Indian Situation," in *Comparative Studies in Society and History, Supplement I*, The Hague, Mouton and Co., 1961, p. 9.
[23] Bertrand Russell, *The Problem of China*, London, 1922.

ity in the arts, literature, philosophy, religion, scholarship, and even science, with their corresponding practitioners. But one group that has no real precedent in the traditional societies is the journalists. An exception might possibly be made in the case of Japan, where broadsheets and timely ballads, very reminiscent of Elizabethan England, were in wide use from the 17th century on. These were usually reports, commentaries, and illustrations of striking current events run up hastily on wood-block prints and hawked in the streets to the public.[24] In spite of the primitive methods of production and distribution, we learn that in December 1701 a popular print reporting the successful conclusion of the vendetta of the 47 Ronin was on the streets within one day of the event. But this was still not real journalism nor was it the real ancestor of the modern Japanese press. Journalism in the sense of a continuing attempt to reach a public audience is entirely a Western idea even in Japan. Its minimum prerequisite is the very idea that the news is important.

In all of the transitional societies journalism develops almost simultaneously with the new awareness of the outside world and a new nationalist self-consciousness. In part it is based on the simple need for information about world and national developments. Even before the opening of Japan the Tokugawa Shogunate was already publishing a kind of journal, with items culled from the Batavia press brought up by the Dutch from the Indies, in order to keep up with what was going on in the world.[25]

In the early stages of journalism in the transitional societies direct foreign influence was very important. In some cases the colonial government itself published journals, sometimes to encourage modernization and the acquisition of the metropolitan civilization, sometimes to forestall an opposition press, and sometimes simply for purposes of public information. In others resident foreigners opened the way or carried on an important part of the national journalism. In Japan, for example, resident foreigners very early began to publish

[24] These included the so-called *yomiuri* (news-hawking), *ezoshiuri* (hawking of illustrations), *fure-uri* (announcements), *seki-ban* (stone impression), and *kawaraban* (slate impression). As early as 1615 a slate impression illustration of the siege of the Osaka castle by the Tokugawa forces was widely distributed in central Japan, presumably with the encouragement of the Shogun Ieyasu himself, in order to impress reluctant feudal lords into greater cooperation.

[25] This was the *Batavia Shimbun* (Batavia Newspaper), published for internal use by the *Bansho Torishirabe-dokoro* (Institute for the Investigation of Barbarian Writings) from January 1862. Another journal of the same kind, the *Kaigai Shimbun Besshu* (Overseas News), started in August of the same year. However, an earlier effort along these lines had started in December 1860.

English-language newspapers which provided both models and materials for the Japanese press. Some even undertook the publication of Japanese-language newspapers, among which the most notable was the *Nisshin Shinjishi* (Reliable Daily News), published by the Scottish journalist J. D. Black between 1872 and 1875. The same was true in India, where the very earliest newspapers were published by resident Englishmen, some of them, for one reason or another, not in full sympathy with official government policy. The first newspaper in India, the *Bengal Gazette*, was started in 1780 (eighty years after the first daily newspaper was started in England) by James Augustus Hickey. Most of the leading English-language newspapers, which played a major role in India's political and intellectual development, were started by Englishmen and have gone into Indian control only since independence. In French West Africa, until quite recently, the only important newspapers were those run by foreigners: *Paris-Dakar*, published in Paris and flown to Dakar; the *Abidjan-Matin*; and the weekly *L'Afrique Nouvelle*, a brilliant journal of news and comment, published by the White Fathers in Dakar.[26] Similarly, in British West Africa, although there has been a much larger national press, the leading newspapers in Sierra Leone, Nigeria, and Ghana have been and remain those associated with the *Daily Mirror* of London. In still other cases the foreign press, usually that of the metropolitan country or of journalists near at hand, provided the models for the national press. In fact, many of the characteristics of the press in various countries can be understood only by reference to the foreign models with which they were in contact.

But more important was the development of the new ideas of the nationalist modernists. For them a press was essential for public enlightenment and for political action. We find therefore at the very outset of the modernization process a close union between political and social reform and journalism. It would not be far wrong to say that virtually all the early journals in Asian countries were related to the reform movements. People with new ideas created journals to express their political views, trying through them both to win public support and to clarify their ideas. The journals were not only instruments of propaganda; they also served organizational purposes,

---

[26] For the best account of the history and current status of the African press, see Committee on Inter-African Relations, *Report on the Press in West Africa* (mimeographed), distributed by the Director of Extra-Mural Studies, University College, Ibadan.

strengthened internal unity, exerted leverage on the government, and provided a coherent interpretation of events for the faithful: "The earliest press corps in India—Krishnalal Shridharani writes—consisted of either nationalists or social reformers. The pioneers of journalism did not so much want to satisfy the natural curiosity of man concerning his fellow men, as to use the power of the printed word to fight an alien authority and to combat the evils of Indian society. . . . News was incidental; the cause was the main thing. . . . No truly great leader or social reformer could do without being an editor. Raja Ram Mohan Roy . . . used journalism for the abolition of Sati and the introduction of widow remarriage. Tilak started a powerful Marathi daily; Ranade, Gokhale, Aurobindo Ghosh, C. R. Das, Motilal Nehru, Abul Kalam Azad, Subhas Bose—all were journalists at one time or another."[27] Gandhi too, we might add, with his *Harijan*.

The same story, with suitable modifications for local historical and political conditions, can be told of almost every transitional state. The early newspapers of Japan were not so much newspapers in the modern sense as organs of groups or individuals with their own political and cultural views to advance. Every newspaper had its own team, or coterie, which included important politicians, writers, and public figures holding a roughly common point of view. Although Japan had no colonial power to oppose, the early press was oppositional; most of the newspapers supported the liberalizing tendencies against the relatively conservative government. In self-defense, and also in respectful awareness of the great power of the press, government leaders or persons closely associated with the government felt obliged to publish their own organs; these were always a minority, however. It is also significant that K'ang Yu-wei, who attempted the ill-fated 100 Days of Reform in China in the summer of 1898, included the "encouragement of newspapers" as one of the main planks in his program.

In the colonial countries the early press was characteristically in the language of the metropolitan country, with the vernacular presses developing later. The principal organ of the Filipino national renaissance, led by Rizal, was a Spanish-language journal, *El Solidaridad*, actually published in Madrid. The attempt by nationalists to use

[27] Krishnala Shridharani (in collaboration with Prakash C. Jain), "The Journalist in India—a Study of the Press Corps," Center for International Studies, MIT, 1956, Communications Program B/56-3, pp. 3-4.

Tagalog came only in the next stage.[28] The nationalist press of
British West Africa, which carried on the struggle for independence—
Zik's *West African Pilot* is the best example—was also an English-
language press. Moreover, even when a vernacular press came into
being it was usually much inferior to the metropolitan-language press.
This still remains true in India, the Philippines, Africa, and Burma.[29]
In some cases even the beginnings of a vernacular press may be
traced to foreigners, particularly missionaries. Where the vernacular
languages already had a script and a literary tradition this could
be done fairly easily. But in the case of non-literate languages, or
of languages in need of considerable reform, the process was more
difficult. A script had to be developed, a modicum of literacy in that
script had to be created, and only then could a press start. But the
creation of a vernacular press often meant a deliberate limitation of
its audience. A Hindi press, for example, excluded Marathi, Bengali,
Tamil, and other language readers. Since in many cases only the
metropolitan language provided a true national platform, publication in the vernacular—which is very much in the spirit of nationalist sentiment—harmed that very sentiment by promoting provincial
and separatist loyalties as against the larger national loyalty sought
by the nationalists.

With some reservations, it would not be wrong to say that the
press in the transitional countries has been on the whole an important force for modernization. In Japan the early newspapers quite
self-consciously performed an educational role. In addition to their
news function they often published stories and novels, translations
of Western works embodying scientific and philosophical ideas, and
articles on Western life and thought. But even without deliberate
intent the modernizing nationalism that inspired much of the journalistic enterprise inevitably communicated itself in myriad forms
to the readers, oozing out of the words themselves, as it were. The
new vocabulary of modern politics was brought into public attention, an ever-increasing public was kept in regular awareness of political issues, and the great national debates were reflected, even if

[28] English-language journals still represent three-fourths of the circulation of
daily newspapers in the Philippines, Tagalog less than one-tenth. See *The Philippines*,
Vol. III, Table XI-3, p. 1,015 (subcontractor's monograph, HRAF-16, Chicago, 5,
New Haven, Human Relations Area Files, Inc.), where figures for the year 1954
are given. In non-daily periodicals Tagalog has a somewhat better showing in
relation to English, and in "Fortnightlies" it has a clear plurality (p. 1,016).
[29] The best newspapers in Burma are the English-language ones, particularly *The
Nation* of Rangoon.

in a partisan mirror, in the press. How far these influences penetrated depended of course both on the management of the press
and on the degree of literacy. In Japan the influences on the broad
public were extremely effective because near-universal literacy developed quickly. In India and other countries with very high illiteracy the degree of penetration among the masses was very much
less. However, the literate and articulate parts of the population
were continuously affected in a modern direction.

Related to the reform bias of the early nationalist press is its strong
oppositional character. In colonial countries this is entirely understandable because the general burden of the nationalist movement was
the struggle for independence. Almost always the government in
power, the *status quo*, and the forces that supported the *status quo*
were the principal targets. But this same oppositional tendency, growing out of particular national conditions, was prevalent even in
countries that went through their nationalist development without
direct colonial rule. In Japan the early newspapers usually took the
liberal, anti-government side. A considerable majority of the newspapers in the 1870's and the 1880's supported the "People's Rights"
(*Minken*) movement, the political parties, and the movements for
a democratically responsible parliamentary system and constitution.
In the early 1920's, at a much more advanced stage in Japan's development, once again the newspapers played a major role in forcing
the adoption of universal manhood suffrage in 1925. For slightly
different particular reasons the early Chinese press was also oppositional. It was strongly modernizing, opposing the forces and ideologies based on Confucianism and tradition, and it also opposed the
political reality of the country: disunity, warlord control, the delay
in the establishment of a modern state system based upon representative government. In Thailand, although the press has always been
much less anti-government, it was in general somewhat more pro-
modernist than the government, so that at least in its social criticism
and commentary it lent its weight to the modernizing element within
the elite rather than to the more conservative element.

The result of the historical journalistic bias is that as the transitional states emerge into independence, or into a greater control of
their own destiny, they have an oppositional, partisan press which
finds it difficult to transform itself into the kind of responsible, non-
partisan press that the new situation requires. There are, of course,
many material difficulties. Except in Japan the non-Western press

remains in a rather primitive stage of development. It is only in India and the Philippines that we can see clearly the development of a few newspapers of truly modern, comprehensive, non-partisan type that may eventually be comparable to the mass Western press. In Shridharani's words, "Political independence having been achieved, newspapers are no longer run as a mission, but have become mainly commercial ventures."[30] In one way or another most of the newly independent states are entering this stage.

Equally important, Japan is the only non-Western country that has a true mass press. Virtually everyone in Japan is touched by newspapers or journals of some kind. Statistics show an average circulation of about 2.2 newspapers per family, not to mention the thousands of journals that reach a comparable intensity. By contrast, all other Asian countries are still very far indeed from reaching their potential mass audiences; their newspapers circulate mainly among the elite. In French Africa very few countries even have daily newspapers, their development being discouraged by illiteracy (running higher than 80 per cent in many cases), poverty, the fact that large elements of the population still remain outside the modern sector, and the complication of numerous languages. Often the only national language is that of the metropolitan country, which means that only a small proportion of the people can use it. Therefore, although the vernacular journals may be potentially capable of reaching larger audiences, they cannot be truly national; and the national journals in the metropolitan language cannot circulate widely among the masses.

In its earlier phases Japanese journalism went through many of the stages still found in varying degrees in the rest of the non-Western world. But Japan was able to go beyond this and achieve a degree of specialization and professionalization of a mass press that compares favorably with, if it does not actually outrank, that in the most advanced Western countries. This new development can be dated from about the time of the Sino-Japanese War (1894-1895). By the time of the Russo-Japanese War (1904-1905) the Japanese press was able to rival the Western press in its corps of war reporters and the speed and ingenuity of its transmissions.[31] The preconditions

---

[30] *Op.cit.*, p. 13.
[31] "All the newspapers . . . took the chance to test their power and ability and sent a number of correspondents to the front. . . . Among those sent by these papers (The *Asahi* and the *Osaka Mainichi*) as war correspondents were many who became famous journalists afterwards . . . competition among papers was the strongest

for a modern non-party press—widespread literacy, a writing tradition, a corps of literary specialists, an advanced economy, the technical ability to handle press and production methods, the managerial capacity to establish efficient systems of distribution—developed very quickly in Japan. Rapid economic growth, coupled with the huge literate population and facilitated by a single national language and its literary tradition, brought into being the same, if not a greater, range of differentiation as in the West. Today Japanese newspapers are enormous enterprises which play a major role in public life.[32] The *Asahi* and *Mainichi* newspapers have perhaps the largest daily circulations in the world, between three and four million, and the rate of newspaper readership is the highest in the world, over two newspapers per family. In Japan journalism may be said to have reached a fully modern status by the early part of the 20th century. The rest of the non-Western world still remains in the condition of Japan of the 1870's and 1880's.

The Communist and the strongly autocratic states have attempted a different solution: a wholly, or at least largely, party or governmental press. In China the entire press is controlled by the party and government, as in Russia. This permits, through controlled distribu-

imaginable. The *Osaka Mainichi* attached one of its members as a coolie to the Eleventh Division of the Imperial Army and 'scooped' the news of the battle in Nanshan. The paper was also careful to instruct some of his [sic!] war correspondents to send their telegrams through Chinese telegraph offices. The *Asahi*, which until that time was superior to the *Osaka Mainichi* in funds, chartered a fast ship for the transport of mail reports. The *Asahi*, the *Osaka Mainichi* and the *Jiji* issued extras as soon as big war news was received. This was done irrespective of expense, from their ambition to increase their circulation and also from their consciousness of the mission of papers. . . . During the war, the *Asahi* and the *Mainichi* issued about five hundred extras. . . . An American correspondent who was engaged by the *Osaka Mainichi* . . . was a friend of Col. Roosevelt's. He was sent to Russia as a special correspondent when the war broke out. His reports from the Russian capital of the real condition of Russia were splendid. . . . He gave the editors of the *Mainichi* tips of [sic!] the peace conference which was being held in Portsmouth. To compete with the *Mainichi*, the *Asahi*, the former's rival, engaged Mr. Dillon, a correspondent of the *Daily Telegraph* . . . and got him to report . . . from America." Kanesada Hanazono, *The Development of Japanese Journalism*, Tokyo, The Tokyo Nichi-Nichi, 1934, pp. 50-51.

[32] Japanese newspapers have from a very early date carried on a wide range of activities not usually associated with a newspaper. They are, for example, the most important supporters of international cultural exchange activities, bringing over, or cooperating in bringing over, symphony orchestras, concert artists, art exhibitions, etc. They support a wide range of public educational activities, and their awards to writers, artists, and public figures play a very important part in cultural development. Leading newspapers also support scientific expeditions, especially of the more dramatic types, such as the climbing of Himalayan mountains, explorations of the South Pole or of archaeological remains in Iran, and so on. In fact, they come rather close in many of their activities to the work of an American foundation.

tion and massive government investment, large circulations and targeted coverage of all sectors of the population. Some of the "guided democracies," such as the U.A.R., Guinée, Ghana, and Mali, have also moved in a similar direction, although by no means so completely.[33] Guinée, which in effect had no press of its own before independence, has established a completely government-controlled press.[34] In Ghana, where the main newspaper still remains largely foreign-controlled and the rest of the national press has been very feeble, the government has attempted to establish its own press through government subsidy, the privileged import of modern equipment, and party-supported distribution. So far the success of this venture remains unsettled. In any event, although these countries may solve some of the problems of a backward press through massive government support and control, they will by the same token have foreclosed the possibility of an independent, non-partisan press.

A modern nation needs not only daily newspapers but also an infrastructure of all kinds of specialized journals, which may be weekly, fortnightly, monthly, or even quarterly. In a well-developed journalism we find mass journals aimed at general or specific audiences (such as farmers, women, children, teenagers, young girls) as well as special journals aimed at select and limited audiences (intellectual, political, professional, scientific, academic, literary, economic). It is here that the great weakness of journalism in the underdeveloped countries shows up most strongly. Once again, it is only in Japan that such journals exist on a scale adequate to the needs of a modern society. In India, which is somewhat farther along than most of the

[33] Indonesia, which falls in the same general category and has given the term "guided democracy" to the world, has gone rather far in the suppression of an independent press, but still cannot be compared to the others. I would exclude autocratic states of the type of Pakistan and Korea for the reason that their suppression of the press is along more traditional lines; they do not have the positive aim of creating their own controlled mass audience so much as the purely negative one of eliminating criticism. The few Pakistan moves in the direction of a government-controlled press have evoked very considerable protest. In Korea the various governments have exerted a largely negative censorship control. In Burma, during the brief period of military rule, no serious attempt was made to control the press; in fact, a good part of the press supported General Ne Win. In other words, we must distinguish between "positive guidance" and "censorship."

[34] Guinée had no newspaper at all until 1946. In 1954, *La Presse de Guinée*, published in Dakar, was started by a Frenchman, and a few weeks before independence it became a daily. In December 1958, however, it was suppressed. Since then, the only newspaper permitted is *La Liberté*, the organ of the official party which is still not, as of the time of writing (August 1961) a daily. (See J. de Benoist: "The Position of the Press in French-Speaking West Africa," *Report on the Press in West Africa, op.cit.*)

other new states, there is an extensive specialized periodical list, but it is poor in quality and financially insecure. For the rest, with the exception of a few notable journals here and there, the picture is much bleaker. The development of this kind of journalism depends upon an intricate joining together of such apparently divergent factors as the growth of literacy, professional standards and attitudes in journalism, managerial and business skills, and available capital.

IV. Literature, Journalism, and Politics

We can see that the writer is peculiarly affected by the new ideas that modernity brings to his society and also by the language problems they entail. But in this he is no different from other intellectuals, particularly other users of the word. His uniqueness lies in his self-conscious attention to questions of language and of literary form. Once he has developed a new modern sensibility, he is often literally incapable of expressing it in traditional forms. For many writers in early modern Japan, for example, the traditional literature, which leaned towards extreme allusiveness and a preoccupation with surface and texture, no longer seemed adequate to express their new needs for psychological depth or character portrayal. In many non-Western societies the didactic, moralizing mode—Horace's *utile*: "the end (of literature) is to implant into the reader's mind a moral lesson which the author desires to be emulated"—becomes a straitjacket for the writer's new sensibilities as well as for his new philosophical or political outlook. The problem is peculiarly important not only in the Confucian societies of China, Japan, and Korea but also in societies with a great hieratic tradition. Islam, for example, discouraged a secular literature as it did a representational art. In the non-literate societies the indigenous oral traditions provided an even less satisfactory model for modern writers. The very forms themselves have to be taken from the outside. For example, "the short story in Tagalog . . . is still a new art. . . . It was an alien seed brought by the American occupation during the first decade of the twentieth century."[85] Speaking of the pre-1941 theater, one writer says flatly: "There was no Filipino theater. There were moro-moro plays, and there were the *zarzuelas*."[86]

In poetry the problem is even more delicate. The traditional short

[85] Florlinda F. Soto, "The Short Story in Tagalog," *Diliman Review*, October 1953, p. 37.
[86] Daisy Hontiveros-Avellana, "The Filipino Theater," *Literary Apprentice*, 1955, p. 100.

Japanese poem might be suitable to express a sudden insight or feeling, or to capture the moment on the wing, but it certainly did not allow space for the development and elaboration of ideas. Poetry is, of course, neither all idea nor all emotion, but insofar as the poet felt the need for a larger form of expression, the traditional form was often insufficient. The difficulty is that poetic forms and rhythms emerge from the most intimate layers of a nation's experience. They are therefore the hardest to imitate and absorb, as translators know well from their labors. Although the general conception of a poem can be understood, its special characteristics of meter, rhyme, and tone simply cannot be transplanted, especially from such fundamentally dissimilar languages as English and Japanese. Poetic form in English depends upon sentence rhythm and rhyme. In Japanese, rhyme makes no sense, and the basic rhythmic device is quantity, with alternations of five and seven syllable lines recommending themselves as the inherent poetic forms. Therefore, although some poets found the traditional forms entirely satisfactory, and others could use them to express certain of their sensibilities, the very awareness of other forms inevitably made an uncritical acceptance impossible. This did not mean that the traditional poetry had to be entirely abandoned. In fact, it was not. But a new poetry arose side by side with it, and the older traditions had to go through the critical sieve of the new consciousness.

But even if the poet is able to work out new forms more suitable to the expression of his sensibilities, he cannot be sure that his audiences, who have been raised in traditional forms, will be able to follow him. The modern Western composer of electronic music, *musique concrète*, and other "advanced" forms has the same problem of the relation of the modern consciousness and traditional forms. In order to be modern and fully to express his modern self, does the artist have to throw out the old entirely, or can he retain it and yet go on to something new? More fundamentally, do not the traditional and modern modes conflict in some essential way as, for example, in the very different sensibilities required by traditional musical modes and modern modes? If you are trying to think musically in the diatonic scale, then the indeterminacy of traditional scales may very well interfere. A sensitivity to the linear character of traditional music makes it difficult to acquire a proper "ear" for harmonic depth.

Yet there is no doubt that both can coexist. In Japan, although a modern-style literature has developed, essentially a transformation of Western literary influences by the Japanese "spirit," traditional forms still remain, and remain very popular. There are over one hundred journals entirely devoted to traditional poetry, with millions of readers and countless thousands of practitioners.[37] The thrust of modernity does not necessarily eliminate all of the traditional sensibility; even the fully modern person has one side of his personality that can be satisfied only by traditional forms. One of the leading figures of the new naturalistic movement of the early 20th century in Japan, Natsume Sōseki, gave himself over to Chinese-style poetry in his later years. Similarly, many Japanese writers have started out fiercely "Western" in their early years, only to mellow into more "Japanese" modes in later years. But what very often happens is that although there is coexistence—say between traditional and modern musicians—there may be little contact between them. Different possible lines of development suggest themselves: the traditional forms may be embalmed and left as museum pieces while a modern style grows up alongside. This is what is done to some extent in Japan, where the *noh*, *kabuki*, puppet theater, and classical verse forms are carried on without change at the same time that a fully modern theater, poetry, and literature are pursued. Or the traditional forms may be used as the basis for a modern literature in the light of new ideas and experiences. E. Sarathchandra, for example, is trying to create a modern Ceylonese theater on the basis of the traditional drama; similar experiments can be found in India and in Africa.[38] Another possibility is to drop the old entirely and to experiment exclusively with the new forms. A final possibility is to create entirely new forms based upon both traditional and modern elements. In the various arts we can find all of these processes at work.

LITERARY MOVEMENTS AND THE SPIRIT OF MODERNIZATION

But the writer in transitional societies is also a member of his intellectual generation. Like them he is usually an ardent advocate of

[37] Harold Henderson has made the interesting calculation that at least 1,000,000 *haiku* are published every year and about half that number of *tanka* (*An Introduction to Haiku*, New York, Doubleday, 1958, pp. 1-2). This does not, of course, take into consideration the countless millions written but not published.

[38] Sometimes, it should be noted, this leads to the vulgarization of traditional forms, particularly in music, as in Indian movie music or "Oriental modern" music that cannibalizes traditional themes rendered in modern popular harmonies and rhythms.

reform, modernization, and enlightenment; whatever particular position he may take on the political spectrum, he is, at the very least, involved in public issues. For a modernizing politics no less than for literature a new language is needed, one that is capable of expressing new ideas and sensibilities and also one that can involve the people in the modernization process. This is where politics, literature, and journalism come together. To the extent that writers take as one part of their vocation the work of public enlightenment, there is not too much difference between their conception of themselves as writers or journalists, or even as politicians.

Tagore, for example, certainly did so. But he would probably not have liked to think of himself as a "journalist," at least in the narrow sense of the scribbler, preoccupied with the immediate, the trivial, and the superficial. Yet, as the Bengali poet Buddhadeva Bose has observed, Tagore was a "super-journalist in prose; this wizard in rhymes and harmonies was also a great commentator. He discussed all questions of his times, big or small, abstruse or mundane, and always his exposition was full, his insight pure, and his language rich and moving. . . . The elder statesman needed him as much as the apprentice in verse."[39] Insofar as Tagore, or any other writer in the transitional societies, uses his writing as a form of criticism of society—its political condition, its social problems, its quality, its standards, its aspirations, its hypocrisies, shortcomings, needs, hopes— he does in fact write journalism. He is journalist and commentator as well as pure "writer."

The term "literary movement" usually refers not only to literary change in the narrow sense but also to reform and the development of a vernacular national language as well. The language must be changed and a new literature developed not only for the benefit of writers but also on behalf of the people to provide a better medium of communication, of leading and modernizing the people, or of carrying through reforms. In the countries with an important literate tradition the modernizing elements, who favor as part of their populist democratic outlook the participation of the people in politics, usually favor the vernacular over the classical language. Conservatives usually try to retain the classical language as the container of the classical and traditional values, institutions, ethical ideas, and atti-

[39] Buddhadeva Bose, review of Bhabani Bhattacharya, ed., *Towards Universal Man: Rabindranath Tagore*, and Amiya Chakravarty, ed., *A Tagore Reader*, in *Saturday Review*, May 13, 1961.

tudes towards authority. Therefore this debate becomes part of the political debate within the country.

Nowhere is this clearer than in the famous May 4th Movement in China.[40] The "literary movement," which was presumably concerned with purely literary questions such as the development of the vernacular, the struggle against the classical language, anti-Confucianism, and the development of new literary forms, was an organic element of the political struggle. Literary reform, in the view of the reformers, was part of the political task of sweeping away the old and preparing the ground for a new, democratic (or at least populist), modern China. Therefore the "writers" were all journalists and politicians, or at least publicists, at the same time. Their views were promulgated to the public and to other intellectuals in coterie journals, where like-minded writers, politicians, journalists, and intellectuals joined together to express their new ideas in editorial, commentary, essay, and analysis, as well as in creative literature. Lu Hsun's fiction was not only an important new literature but a "weapon" in the struggle against reaction and authority. In the same way, Hu Shih's famous experiments in the new poetry were both an exemplification of the new ideas and a political gesture. Therefore there could be no clear separation of the roles of writers and journalists in this great national crisis. Both were taking part in their own ways—and often in identical ways—in the movement which was against traditionalism, autocracy, warlordism, and foreign control, and for students' rights, nationalism, and increased popular participation in government.

This close relation of literature, politics, and journalism is one of the striking features of the intense phases of the transitional process. Jose Rizal, the great Filipino national hero, the leader of the anti-Spanish nationalist movement of the late 1890's, was both a novelist and a journalist (as well as a physician). Burma's U Nu set out to become a writer, and even after he became Prime Minister he wrote a play.[41]

In Japan during the early modern period this relation was extremely intimate. The press played an important role in the publication and encouragement of literature, and literary men often took active

[40] See T. T. Chow, *The May Fourth Movement*, Cambridge, Mass., Harvard University Press, 1960. The movement started with great demonstrations by students in Peking on May 4, 1919 and spread throughout the rest of the country. It was strongly supported by intellectuals, professors, teachers, writers, and reformists.

[41] *The People Win Through.*

part in journalism. Many of the early journalists themselves were publicists on behalf of political ideas and groups, or writers won over to journalism as an outlet for their work or ideas. Most of the writers were on the side of the opposition to the Meiji oligarchy and supported the more modernizing and democratic positions in the political disputes raging in the country. One group of successful writers was identified very closely with the Liberal Party, which advocated responsible parliamentary government and a democratic constitution. Stimulated by this success, several members of the rival Progressive Party, which was also, although more moderately, oppositionalist, then turned to literature in the hope of thereby expanding their own party's influence. But aside from these direct political connections, literature and journalism performed an essential role in Japan's modernization by diffusing new ideas, supporting the vernacular, and creating a national audience. While the newspapers published long novels and translations, a host of specialized journals grew up to provide an outlet for poetry, the short story, and literary criticism. Some of these were pure literary journals, based upon the ideas of a particular school or faction, but others were the organs of political-intellectual groups, for whom the literature they published was simply the exemplification of their ideas.

THE WRITER AS RENAISSANCE MAN
IN TRANSITIONAL SOCIETIES

In the early stages of the development of a modern culture and nation, when the past still remains vividly present and the new beckons onward to its yet unrevealed mysteries, a new type of "renaissance man" makes his appearance. Anyone who has been privileged to observe these early stages of awakening has been struck by the appearance of men who are equally at home in politics, literature, journalism, and the arts; soldiers who write poetry; writers who become prime ministers. It is not yet Plato's age of philosopher-kings, but rather a period when a still undifferentiated sensitivity and talent have many different directions to choose from and choice is not necessarily a foreclosure of other possibilities. In India the classical example is Tagore, great lyric poet, novelist, writer, and at the same time, in Buddhadeva Bose's phrase, "super-journalist," who had a deep influence on the development of political thought. Tagore also composed music (his songs still occupy an important place in India), took an active part in international relations, particularly in bringing East and West together, and created a great modern university in Shantiniketan. In his later years he began to study painting, although in this he never attained the proficiency he attained in music. In Japan there were the great men of the "Enlightenment," such as Fukuzawa Yukichi. Although Fukuzawa did not take part in politics directly—in the conviction that some leaders should stay independent of government—he was an important political influence on the public and on the politicians both through his advocacy of such Western ideas as individual rights, individual dignity, self-reliance, and liberty and through his promotion of simple and direct language. In the course of his fruitful life he created the greatest of Japan's private universities, Keijo, and also one of the first modern-style, liberal newspapers, the *Jiji Shimpo*. "There are now few editors who can write novels or plays and at the same time discuss politics and the diplomacy of the day"—a Japanese historian of journalism tells us. "However, in the early days of journalism there were not a few editors who had literary talent. Osamu Watanabe, who was the editor of the *Osaka Mainichi*, wrote novels; Fumio Yano, who was the editor of the *Hochi*, is the author of the famous story 'Fujo-Monogatari'; Tetcho Suyehiro, who was managing editor of the *Akebono Shimbun*, wrote 'The Setchu-Bai' (Plum Blossoms in the Snow) and other famous novels; Ryuhoku Narushima, who was the editor of the *Choya Shimbun*, was not only a noted editor but one of the best poets in those days."[42]

Many of China's great modern figures showed this same versatility. K'ang Yu-wei, known for his brave but unsuccessful "100 Days of Reform" in 1898, was also a distinguished poet, an astronomer, a philosopher, and a world traveller. Hu Shih, who had the distinction of being the main intellectual target of the Communist regime, was the leader of the "literary movement" which was one of the elements in the explosive mixture of the May 4th Movement; but he was also a poet, a philosopher—the introducer of Deweyan pragmatism into the intellectual ferment of post-1911 China—a distinguished historian of Chinese literature and philosophy, a poet, an editor of a political journal, a politician, and an educator.

In every one of the new states one finds these many-sided men, some who have already made their mark, others much less well known. An Indonesian friend once explained to me his problem: whether to continue as editor of one of Indonesia's leading news-

[42] Hanazono, *op.cit.*, p. 33.

papers or to become a novelist, politician, movie actor, or diplomat. The African examples that come to mind are legion: Léopold Senghor, poet and President of Senegal; the poet, impresario, and politician Keita Fodeiba in Guinée; medical doctor, novelist, administrator, and educator Davidson Nicol in Sierra Leone; and the hosts of lesser figures who in former French Africa combine poetry with politics or in other places devote themselves with equal zeal to teaching, research, politics, administration, literature, public enlightenment, journalism, and support of the arts. During a parallel period in Spain, the modern "Renaissance" of the Generation of 1898, which included Unamuno, Machado, Valle-Inclán, and Baroja, a similar catholicity is evident. All of these Renaissance figures were active not only in literature but also in the revitalization of science and scholarship, in the development of political thought, and in journalism. The new prestige and popularity of the intellectuals, Julian Marías tells us, "derived partly from the fact that the major writers usually published articles in the daily newspapers."[43]

THE MERGING ROLES OF WRITER AND JOURNALIST

The differentiation of writer and journalist is therefore not so sharp in the early stages of modernization. Writers of modern sensibilities, particularly if they have political interests, take part in journalism. Since journalists are often men of strong political views, their journalism is conceived as part of their general political activities.

Two considerations are important here. First, in the early stages the intellectual elite is very small in number, and the preconditions for a well-developed modern literature and journalism are not fully established. Very few countries can afford the luxury of an extreme differentiation of elite function. Poets, writers, and artists must take part in politics, administration, and education. Qualified people are at a premium and must at least to some extent be open to a wide range of functions. Moreover, the modern literate sector is not sufficiently developed to provide the basis for a vigorous literature and journalism. There are not enough journals, whether daily or periodical, nor enough readers, publishing houses, bookshops, and publishing outlets. Where per capita income is extremely low, books are too expensive for ordinary people, and often for the educated classes as well. It is with the expansion of literacy, the growth of a literate audience,

[43] Julian Marías, "The Situation of the Intelligentsia in Spain Today," in Richard Pipes, ed., *The Russian Intelligentsia*, New York, Columbia University Press, 1961, p. 183.

the increase in the numbers of educated people, and the specialization and commercialization of journalism and publishing, that the writer and journalist begin to separate out. How far this separation goes depends upon the traditions of the particular country. Very few countries, even in Europe, reach the American extreme of almost complete professionalization of journalism and the relegation of letters to their own separate domain.

Second, in each society and at each stage of development the "life of the writer" is defined in a different way. There are very few societies in the world where the writer is able to live entirely on his "creative writing." But he does not consider it inconsistent with his life as a writer to supplement his income in other ways somehow related to his central work. He may teach, lecture, write journalism, accept special writing assignments, carry on research. In societies more advanced in communications facilities he may write for the movies, radio, and television (and even in some cases for advertising); he may serve as an editor, a publisher, or a reader in publishing houses. What is essential is that he consider the total round of his life to be consistent with his self-image as a writer. In each society the total round of the writer's life is somewhat different from what it is in other societies.

Most writers in the transitional societies must make their living from something other than their writing. The most important of these supplementary sources is journalism. Since journalism makes use of the writer's skills, enabling him to exercise them even when he is not doing his "true" work, he may feel it entirely consistent with his vocation and his self-image as a writer. Some writers therefore are driven to journalism by economic need or by their desire for a publishing outlet. How well the press meets these depends upon its economic condition, its degree of specialization, and its traditions with respect to literature. "Nobody in this country can seem to live by his writing," complains Filipino novelist N. V. M. Gonzalez—who himself depends upon his professorial post at the University of the Philippines: "Why? There are many reasons. . . . To begin with, he is poorly paid for his fiction and verse. His immediate market is the limited one offered by weeklies. As the history of literature will show, in other countries the newspapers—as dailies instead of weeklies—have been also his marketplace. I have asked some editors about this and their reply has been: they have not got enough paper supply. Or there's the American syndicated column which can be had for thirty pesos a week. Why pay a Philippine writer one hundred and fifty pesos? My guess is that unless we can do something on a day to day basis for our writers, our literature will stay where it is."[44]

In spite of Mr. Gonzalez' generous beliefs, however, the American daily press today provides practically no outlet for serious creative writing. But many of the transitional societies are more influenced by European models, where there is a closer relation between journalism and letters. In Japan, for example, journalism remains a firm part of the round of Japanese literary life.[45] In spite of the scale of professionalism, which is much the same as in any Western country, the journals take vast quantities of work from non-professionals, that is, from free-lance writers. They are enormous consumers of literary production; and if we add to this radio, television, and the movies, we find that they provide perhaps the main source of writers' incomes. Beyond the daily press, Japan has perhaps a uniquely developed "intellectual journalism," the materials for which are almost entirely provided by free-lance writers. Not only are the journals of opinion, comment, criticism, political analysis, entertainment, and literature numerous; they reach very considerable audiences and provide the main continuous outlets for writers. Writers are called upon not only for work that corresponds to their true vocation but also for more narrowly journalistic tasks—to report, comment, express political views, analyze political and social problems, and so on. The conception of the writer as an undifferentiated expert on any and all public issues remains a very strong tradition in Japan—with, one might add, both beneficial and harmful aspects. Even apart from economic need, therefore, writers in the transitional societies often consider it part of their vocation to bring their ideas to the wider audiences provided by journalism. This is especially the case among the politically committed.

But there are other things that bring journalists and writers together. As users of the word they are both deeply involved in the development of a language sufficiently differentiated to be capable of expressing modern ideas, sentiments, and sensibilities. The writer plays a key role by domesticating the new ideas and neologisms,

[44] N. V. M. Gonzalez, "The Status of Contemporary Philippine Literature," *Diliman Review*, October 1953, p. 350.

[45] For a discussion of the Japanese writer, see Herbert Passin, "A Nation of Readers," *Encounter*, March 1957; and Donald Keene, "Literary Currents in Postwar Japan," in Hugh Borton et al., *Japan Between East and West*, New York, Harpers, 1957.

standardizing them so that they can enter the normal vocabulary of modern life. But the journalist is equally involved in this work. Modern newspapers, no matter what their ideological commitments, must reach a wide public. Therefore they must be readable, at least for the literate public. The earliest literate public may be one that is reached in the traditional, classical language, but as literacy spreads among wider layers of the population—and in the extreme case of Japan right down to the "masses"—the newspapers must continuously accommodate themselves to the new audiences. In such a development there is a continual interplay between the work of the journalist and the writer, insofar as they can be separated out. The writer, to some extent, sets standards; but since journalism must be more continuously responsive to changes in the audience, it often forces the pace. In some respects the writer tends to be conservative, partly because of his greater respect for form, his dislike of neologisms, the offense to his taste of incongruous foreign-sounding words, and his search for order. But he may also be open to much bolder innovations far in advance of the average audience of the newspaper. While the journalist may approach things more crudely, his role is essential in stabilizing new words and concepts and in giving them currency among the public at large.

Both equally need a large literate audience. Some languages have so few literate speakers that they cannot provide a sufficient audience for the resonance a writer needs. He may be able to write in his own language, but there may be too few readers at the required level. This is a very acute problem in India, the Philippines, and Africa, where the vernacular languages provide much too small a literate audience. In India, except for Bengali, the vernacular writer can count on few readers. Marathi is a language spoken by some forty million people, and yet a Marathi writer is lucky to have a sale as large as 1,000. Newspapers too are held down by high illiteracy to a low level of quality and of commercial viability. "Why has the short story in Tagalog faltered in its development?" asks the Filipina critic, Florlinda F. Soto. "One reason is the problem of language. Tagalog is not yet as widespread in the Archipelago as might be expected of a national language. English alone enjoys the privilege of being both the medium of instruction and communication throughout the Philippines. Hence the short story in English bridges tribal distinctions and reaches more people."[46] And as for English, Manuel

[46] Florlinda F. Soto, *op.cit.*, p. 379.

Viray tells us that although "English seems to be fairly understood in almost all parts of the Philippines . . . the understanding does not rise above the lingo of the streets, the parlance of commerce, the slang of the teenagers, and the broken English of the schools."[47]

POLITICAL COMMITMENT VERSUS OBJECTIVITY
IN THE NEW JOURNALISM

The result of the professionalization of journalism, which seems to follow an even moderate measure of economic growth, is the sundering of that close union of literature, politics, and journalism that was so striking in the earlier and intenser phases of the nationalist movements. Even though the writer has not gained the economic base for an independent literary life, he is often cut off from the growing mass audiences and from his former sense of vital connection with the problems of the country. In Japan, where journalism and literature remain in such close connection, this is not the case. The Japanese writer has to struggle to maintain his detachment from politics. But in the Philippines we hear growing murmurs about the "alienation" of the writers, and their "indifference" to national problems:

"Although all of them [writes Jose Ortega] would assert a desire to achieve progress for their country, few, if any, would conceive of their writing as an instrument to help bring it about. . . . Most . . . seem to prefer [the notion of literature as] a slender vase, with flowers, preferably imported. They prefer not to use literature as a pot in which to boil and cook together the ingredients of the society around them. . . . [Therefore] . . . the dominant tendency . . . of most of the serious fiction of today . . . is one of introspection. . . . Sterility of theme and substitution of experimentation for something to say are the consequences of such subjectivity. . . . [Even in the regional literature, which is essentially nationalist in outlook] what emerges . . . is not the sensation of a Filipino speaking strongly of his country and of his people, but a quaintness. The portraits of provincial types and characters that appear frequently are aimed at revealing the peculiar and amusing, the quaint."[48]

I can also recall a distinguished Nigerian educator and politician charging, with much less justification, that "our *literati* live in an

---

[47] Manuel A. Viray, "A New Perspective for Philippine Writing," *Diliman Review,* October 1953, pp. 360-361.

[48] Jose Y. Ortega, "For a Significant Filipino Literature," *Literary Apprentice,* 1949-1950, pp. 48-50.

ivory tower and refuse to take part in the struggles of the people."
The tension between the writer's vocation of personal detachment and
public commitment is most easily resolved when the institutional
structure and the prevalent ideology permit him to exercise both.
The earlier stages of modernization, the first period of contact with
the Western challenge, usually permit this exhilarating fusion, but
the first advances in modernization may separate them out. It is
here that the institutional structure of opportunity and the ideological
outlook are decisive. This, I would suggest, may have much to do
with the appeal of Communism to writers in the underdeveloped
countries.

The problem of attachment and commitment is therefore a very
complex one. It depends upon how writers and journalists view the
politico-historical situation as well as upon their "objective" position
within it. The ideal of the writer as detached observer, or of the
journalist as objective reporter of the facts, does exist. But how
fragile this posture is can be seen whenever crises arise. The great
political crises of modern China, exemplified in the May 4th Movement, for example, directly involved writers as writers. The "literary
movement" was as much a part of the May 4th Movement as the
anti-foreign, student, and anti-warlord "movements." But the Chinese
writer was paradoxically fighting for both detachment and commitment at the same time. We might even say that he was attached to
detachment. However, it was detachment from the old that he was
talking about. He wished to be free of the dead hand of the ancient
language, of restrictive canons of literature and poetry, of didactic
obligations. He was in revolt against the old Confucian concept that
literature is for "chastising evil and rewarding good." What he
wanted was to be free to express the new attitudes and ideas without
regard for the canonical—and political—obligation to turn them
to the support of the traditional morality or of authority.

But once this victory against the old was achieved, new forms of
attachment appeared: attachment to the new ideals as well as to
specific political goals. The united literary front against the Confucian tradition included two elements—those who believed in "art
for art's sake" and those who believed in literature as a weapon in the
service of a new polity, the revolutionary writers. After the breakthrough, then, this unity collapsed, and the anti-Confucian Chinese
literary world divided in the struggle over "art for art's sake" and the

formation of the Revolutionary Writers' Association,[49] which was completely committed to a "progressive" solution of China's problems. What is clear is that the ideal of detachment expressed in the May 4th Movement was conditional and, for many, tactical. In the totalist conception, characteristic of modern revolutions—already present, as Tocqueville has shown us, in the French Revolution[50]—the writers (and the intellectuals) opposed the old, which was the embodiment of evil, in the name of a new perfection. Therefore "objectivity" in relation to the old is fine, but not in relation to the new. The perfect state they envisage requires a new commitment, and hence a struggle against detachment, objectivity, subjectivism, etc. The same process may be seen in the great debates on the "obligations of the intellectuals" that took place in Japan in the mid-Meiji period.

The relativity of detachment or commitment as an ideal may also be seen in the relation of the intellectual to the "establishment." He can favor a detached position when he is a private citizen outside of, and often antagonistic to, the establishment. But when he enters it, as government worker, advisor, professor, or editor of "responsible" publications, he often develops a new commitment. This applies not only to the establishment in power but to revolutionary movements and governments as well. The Chinese writers who took positions in the Yenan regime during the 1930's accepted a responsibility as writers for advancing the new morality, in fact a full *partinost*. We would not be far wrong, I suspect, to relate this inclination towards commitment to the Confucian tradition. The *literati*—the mandarins, or the scholar-gentry—were members of the ruling apparatus of Imperial China. Literary attainments were essential to achieving public position, and the *literati* were in fact civil servants, bureaucrats, imbued with a strong civic responsibility. There-

[49] In 1930. Its purpose was "promoting and engaging in the production of proletarian art."

[50] His description of the men who made the Revolution has a completely modern ring: "Firmly convinced of the perfectability of man, they . . . set no bounds to their devotion to his cause. They had that arrogant self-confidence which often points the way to disaster yet, lacking which, a nation can but relapse into a servile state. In short, they had a fanatical faith in their vocation—that of transforming the social system, root and branch, and regenerating the whole human race. Of this passionate idealism was born what was in fact a new religion, giving rise to some of those vast changes in human conduct that religion has produced in other ages. It weaned them away from self-regarding emotions, stimulated them to heroic deeds and altruistic sacrifices, and often made them indifferent to all those petty amenities of life which mean so much to us today." (*The Old Regime and the French Revolution*. Garden City, N.Y., Doubleday and Co., 1955, p. 156.)

fore even when the traditional scholar-gentry disappeared, following the fall of the Manchu dynasty, and they were no longer in the establishment, their sense of public vocation and responsibility remained.

In Japan too the importance of intellectuals and writers in public life can undoubtedly be related to a strong samurai element. As in China—and indeed to a large extent based upon the Chinese example—letters were considered an important pursuit of the administrative classes. Literary attainments were an essential attribute, or at least adornment, of the cultivated person, whatever his usual functions. As early as 1615 Shogun Ieyasu, the founder of the Tokugawa dynasty, had laid down the instruction that samurai were to devote themselves equally to arms and to letters.[51] Periodically over the next two hundred years various shoguns repeated these injunctions in one form or another. For the first few decades after the Meiji Restoration the modern educated classes were largely of samurai origin, or strongly infused with the samurai ethic of public responsibility.[52] In India, by contrast, writers in the narrow sense were entertainers and servants rather than members of the ruling class. However, in the strongly Buddhist countries, such as Burma, Ceylon, and Tibet, the monks, although not *literati*—and certainly not secular *literati*—were the guardians of the intellectual and literary traditions, and they appear to have had a similar kind of public vocation. In Burma a very considerable pre-modern education, even if it reached only the rudiments of literacy and piety, was carried on in the temple schools; and in Tibet the governmental offices were staffed mainly by monk-officials. It would be worth exploring, I think, the connection between this tradition of public responsibility and the vigorous political activity of monks in those countries.[53]

[51] *Buke Sho-Hatto* (Law of the Military Houses), 1615.

[52] I realize that this point can be argued in detail, but I feel that it would take too much space here. There is undoubtedly a strong merchant (*chōnin*) element in the modern Japanese elite, and its influence in literature, particularly since the Genroku period, is incontestable. However, characteristically, when the "lower orders" rose to respectability, they tended to accept a samurai morality and style. We know that in the early decades of Meiji, samurai were very active in the fields of journalism, literature, and translation; Sansom lists these fields as among their most important outlets in the new society (*op.cit.*, p. 477). Even among contemporary leaders of Japan, James Abegglen and Hiroshi Mannari found that 34 per cent of their category of "intellectual leaders" listed father's father as samurai (as against 11 per cent of "political leaders" and 15 per cent of "business leaders"). (See their "Leaders of Modern Japan: Social Origins and Mobility," *Economic Development and Cultural Change*, Vol. IX, No. 1, Part II, October 1960.)

[53] This is quite clear in Tibet, where monks constituted the main elements of the administrative cadres, and perhaps in Ceylon too, where the Buddhist pressure

For the journalist also objectivity is contingent and relative. The prevailing outlook in each country depends both upon traditional elements and on the specific historical experiences leading to modernity. As we have seen, most of the journals of the early stages of modernization were committed to modernization and reform and against the government (even if it was not a colonial government). In some cases, where the traditional culture explicitly enjoined "responsibility" and "obligation" on the intellectuals—as in the Confucian societies—"objectivity" itself became a battle cry: the journalists were committed to non-commitment. But with the development of a commercial (or a mass) professionalized press and of a firmer modern sector and government, new pressures arise. Japanese journalism tended to remain oppositional because of its long history of conflict with autocratic governments. During periods of censorship journalists either avoided controversial issues or gave the appearance of objectivity; but the oppositional tendency remained just below the surface, ready to break forth at any opportunity. Today the ideal of journalistic objectivity remains in Japan, but it is a highly qualified one. Journalists share the same political passions that stir the intellectual classes in general, and the highly polarized politics reflects itself in a very political journalism.

Japanese journalism has by now developed its own tradition, and this has much to do with the question of whether or not there is a trend towards more responsible reporting. As a result of their experiences, both in the Meiji period and in the oppressive atmosphere of the 1930's and 1940's, newspapers have come to acquire a fundamentally oppositional posture towards government. This carries over even when by any reasonable definition the government is not oppressive. Somehow it seems more progressive, modern, and liberal—in short, more *chic*—to oppose the government than to support it. Moreover, editors and owners have far less control over their subordinates than in the United States or Europe because Japan has a strongly entrenched tradition of departmental autonomy. Bending over backwards to avoid charges of political bias, the newspapers are open to all political points of view, almost to the point of schizophrenia. The cultural department may put forth a leftist line, while the editorial of the day is rightist or moderate; the foreign news and

---

for the establishment of Singhalese and of Buddhism has played an important part in recent politics. But in Burma also, as close observers know, the voice of the Buddhist clergy is very important indeed, entirely apart from U Nu's personal inclinations.

the music commentary may reflect completely contrary political views. Within the same department the political slant may change from day to day, depending upon the writer. We therefore have the extraordinary spectacle of an organism, each of whose parts may be moving in entirely different directions, with an apparent absence of central control. An extreme case was the *Chuo Koron* magazine, one of the leading journals of comment, which for many years carried on a policy completely contrary to the wishes of its proprietor, who was also its nominal editor-in-chief. Given this tradition of departmental autonomy, the dominance of left-wing views among journalists virtually entrenches a leftist bias in much of Japanese journalism. Trade unions in the journalistic world are largely under leftist control, and Communist journalists are extremely well organized in "fractions" in leading journals and departments. Their influence is exerted not only for the protection of journalists and of their cherished departmental autonomy but also on behalf of specific political goals.

There are signs of change, but it would be over-optimistic to look for immediate results. What can be expected is a gradual permeation of journalism by the long-range political and social development now in process: the beginnings of some de-politicization because of the continued high level of economic growth, the expansion of the middle elements, the greater outlets and opportunities, and the marked recovery in national self confidence. But from these tendencies alone we cannot predict the exact outcome. We can only expect that they are likely to influence larger numbers of journalists towards a more objective position—and also towards a new definition of objectivity—and perhaps to restore a somewhat better balance between management authority and trade-union pressures. In this respect Japan is to be compared more to some European country with a strong Communist vote, say Italy or France, than to the underdeveloped countries. The political atmosphere, the structure of journalism, and the outlook of the journalists (as members of the intellectual class) are no longer those of an underdeveloped country but rather those of an advanced industrial society in a period of political instability.

In the less-advanced transitional societies as well the commitments of journalists depend upon the particular tradition within which they are working as well as the particular political situation they are confronting at particular stages of their country's development. Where the political temperature is high, the journalist usually considers "objectivity" and "commitment" to be the same thing, because both are identified with "the truth"; what is "true" is naturally "objective," and what he believes is naturally "true." This linkage holds whether the journalist is in opposition, say to a colonial government, or in support of a movement or a government in power. When the political temperature is low, and national politics divided, "objectivity" tends to become more important. In the Communist states as well as in the dynamic guided democracies neutrality is derided or even forbidden. But in the states where opposition is more normal the ideals of journalistic detachment are given more play. Except in the authoritarian states lip service is usually paid to the ideal of the neutral reporter standing outside and above politics. But in reality most serious journalists are deeply *engagé*. It would be a mistake, however, to assume that these attitudes are an automatic imitation of Western attitudes. Journalists in transitional societies are equally familiar with the Western models of the non-partisan, objective reporter and of the passionately committed intellectual; their preference for commitment is not an accidental choice among equally available merchandise but the result of particular internal developments that lead them to a similar conclusion. Western ideas may be quoted to lend authority or justification, but the specific form of the issue of detachment versus commitment is an indigenous response to the course of political development in transitional societies.

CHAPTER 7

COMMUNICATIONS AND CIVIC TRAINING
IN TRANSITIONAL SOCIETIES

WE HAVE been concerned with writers and journalists because they are the important teachers in the process of political development. They are the communicators in a favored position to disseminate to others their visions of the realities and the potentialities of politics. As we have observed, they clearly occupy a vanguard role in urging people to widen their horizons and to absorb the spirit of the modern world. The diffusion of such new ideas and the stirring of new emotions all have their eventual consequences for politics.

In transitional societies there are usually a variety of diverging and contending notions and sentiments about the nature and the purpose of politics. There are invariably many people of both high and low station in such societies who tend to cling to traditional views and to conceive of politics as primarily designed to provide opportunities for expressing differences in status. Other people may have gained their comprehension of politics during a colonial era, and hence they may continue to expect that government should be a distant, impersonal system of public administration. Still others may have been the children of revolutionary and nationalist movements and have the permanent expectations that politics should be a pure expression of emotion and idealism. Others of the same era may have arrived at a cynical and essentially opportunistic outlook as they have learned to cope with radically changing times. In all transitional societies there are those with mature sentiments and rational outlooks on the functions of government.

The writers and journalists have a unique role in helping the people with all of these different orientations to arrive at working agreements on fundamentals. The building of consensus does not call for a single, common orientation of all toward the state and toward the political realm. On the contrary, pluralism is the very essence of modern society. But pluralism requires that there be a minimum shared fund of understanding; and it is indeed the unique technological character of the mass media which makes them a preeminent agent for establishing that fund of understanding. By the very act of reaching out to a broad audience with a common message, the mass media can instill in people the feeling that they in turn belong to a definable community in which it may not be either necessary or likely for everyone to be in general agreement on all matters. It would seem that the mass media in the new states can be either an instrument of collective indoctrination seeking to replace confusion with one point of view or they can become vehicles for community building through which people with different points of view can learn to associate with each other.

The position of the mass media in the new states is more complex than that of being an agent of political socialization, for these modernized components of the communications process are really involved in political re-socialization. That is to say, in seeking to train people to an understanding of the new institutions of the state the mass media must communicate with people who have already reached what they feel to be a mature understanding of politics but is in fact an understanding relevant to a traditional or a colonial world which no longer exists. Hence the mass media are not simply a part of a continuous and coherent training process, as the major socializing agents can be in a stable society, but rather they must be a part of a process of discontinuous change. Thus it is that the mass media, in providing a new basis for understanding politics and for interpreting the realm of government, become involved in the most complex and psychologically intense problems of transitional societies. We shall have to deal in depth with the more intensely human problems of value changes and of psychic motivations. First, however, we must examine the potentialities of the mass media to influence the cognitive dimensions of people's understanding of politics.

Much of recent research on the influences of the mass media on American audiences might bring into question the extent to which the mass media can be reasonably expected to contribute to a quickening understanding of responsible politics among transitional peoples. This research suggests that underlying a population's response to the mass media is a principle of selectivity according to which individuals are likely to expose themselves only to communications which they find to be meaningful and which confirm their predispositions. People are therefore inclined to be responsive only to the familiar and that which matches their interests and *their standards of taste. It is this principle of selectivity which apparently limits the educational potentialities of the mass media and therefore casts in doubt the possibility that in the new states the process of consensus building can be rapidly realized by the conscious employment of the media.*

There are, however, grounds for questioning whether the principle of selectivity applies, at least to the same degree, in transitional societies as it does in industrial ones. In the West the individual finds himself in an environment which is nearly saturated by the mass media, and he must develop mechanisms for warding off the massive and omnipresent pressures of all the different competing forms of communications. Clearly it is impossible in such societies for a person to expose himself to the overpowering bulk of the communications being disseminated, and therefore, as a means of self-defense, he must develop the capacity to ignore much and to become selective in his responses.

In most of the new states the atmosphere is not saturated with communications; the mass media are novel and can still provoke curiosity. In many Asian and African countries there is only one local radio station or at best two stations that compete for attention; and the volume of newspapers and magazines is so limited that competent readers are usually constantly hungry for more reading matter. Under these conditions of relative sparcity of media it appears that people do not develop the same attitudes of selectivity, and therefore in transitional societies the media can in fact play a far more potent role in political education than in the saturated societies.

In suggesting that a more positive view should be taken of the political socializing capabilities of the mass media in the new states we do not want to minimize the difficulties that still exist. In many of these societies people may be willing and even eager to expose themselves to the media, and they may be fully able to comprehend the messages, but the results still may not be more effective political participation. There is in many transitional societies a need for people to develop a new appreciation of the possible functions of political information and in particular to learn that knowledge can appropriately lead to action. In many traditional systems the mass of the people might be quite well informed about high politics; they might be eager followers of court politics and even appreciate many of the fine points of elite intrigue and maneuver. But it would never occur to the subjects in such societies that their information and knowledge about politics should in any way guide their behavior. They have always been observers, and even if they became connoisseurs they would remain observers. At present there are still in many of the transitional societies large segments of people who should be changing their status from observing subject to participating citizen but who, in spite of being adequately knowledgeable about public affairs, remain immobilized.

Indeed it may often be that too direct an approach toward citizen education can be unproductive since people reacting according to a variation of the selectivity principle feel it necessary to resist that which is either too novel and unfamiliar or too manifestly designed to be manipulative. Even the most docile and tradition-attached population can sense the humor and the wisdom in frustrating those with authority and who are their intellectual betters whenever they become too intent upon changing the ways of others.

Our conclusion may thus be that even though the mass media have great potential for citizenship training in the new states this potential can be realized only through a subtle and understanding approach. For example, new messages and new ideas may be more readily accepted if they are related to old symbols and concepts. Indeed, it generally seems to be the case in most transitional societies that the material which surrounds the explicitly political communications and is in a sense a part of the context of a general learning process is likely to be more significant in influencing attitudes than the directly political material.

It is for these reasons that when we now turn to a detailed analysis of the role of the mass media in political socialization we must devote particular attention to the "packaging" which surrounds political messages. We can expect that this "wrapping," which consists of advertisements, the basic format of the newspapers and radio programs, and the presumably "non-political" communications that fill the mass media, may be peculiarly important in inducting people in transitional societies into the realities of the modern world. And, of course, the way they first learn about this modern world is certain to be critical in coloring their understanding of the problems of political development and modernization.

CHAPTER 8

Mass Media and Political Socialization: The Role of Patterns of Communication

HERBERT HYMAN

MAN AND WOMAN, LOVING YOU, ROCK BABY ROCK, NIGHT HEAVEN, BEAUTIFUL BUT BAD, EXPRESSO BONGO, THE YOUNG LIONS, DRACULA, SHE DEMONS, THE DEFIANT ONES, AND GOD CREATED WOMAN, STEEL JUNGLE, JAILHOUSE ROCK, IMITATION OF LIFE, BLACKBOARD JUNGLE, OBJECTIVE BURMA, ABDULLAH THE GREAT, SON OF ROBIN HOOD

THESE were among the memorable Western films reported by a sample of Burmese movie-goers as having created for them some impression of life in the West. Before shuddering at the prospect, pause to consider another finding: the impression was predominantly favorable.

Such a finding, fragmentary and seemingly trivial, reminds us of an aspect of the totality of communication content which we might otherwise neglect in a discussion of mass media and political socialization. It will introduce the first point in my treatment of patterns of communication. When we study the mass media as instruments of political socialization, our attention is immediately directed, perhaps exclusively directed, to that part of the total content which has manifest functions for political socialization. But the news of the wider world, items about the local and national scene, political commentary, or editorial matter are lessons in politics which are imbedded in a larger media package containing assorted religious, artistic, scientific, commercial, and entertaining content all surrounded by flashy wrappings.

In the spirit of a latter-day saint of Gestalt psychology, Lucian Pye has asked whether political communication has different outcomes for political socialization depending on the package within which it is contained. The simple general answer must be "yes." Ever since the Gestalt psychologists revolutionized the study of perception it cannot be doubted that the whole is more than the sum of its parts and that a part is dependent on the context within which it is imbedded; but the details of the answer that will follow from applying such a principle or law of perception to the analysis of mass media and political socialization must wait upon further inquiry. I shall review what meager evidence I can find and present some speculations and suggestions in the hope that this fruitful problem will be explored.

I

In pondering the significance of patterns or packages of communication content for political socialization, the relations between core political content and non-political wrappings, one soon realizes that the wrapping alone may make some contribution by itself. Not only have we neglected the study of the relations of the parts; we have neglected some parts by exclusive attention to others. There are implicit political lessons within the most innocent subject matter. Long ago, in what is a now neglected work in social psychology, Ellis Freeman made the point vividly by a re-examination of a well-known arithmetic primer.[1] He found "no fewer than 643 problems which not only deal with but also accept and stress the concepts of capitalism and of our familiar commercial practices. These 643 consist only of those which, in one obvious way or another, place stress on commercial transactions in which monetary gain was ever the motive. There is selling, buying and reselling, rent, working for wages, employing others for wages, and interest on loans. These concepts are presented as the most important situations to which the child is supposed to learn to apply the arithmetical apparatus." He illustrated an alternative vehicle by the hypothetical problem appropriate to that Depression era: "If a family needs $15 a week for food but receives $5 on the dole, what is the percentage of undernourishment."

Even that part of the media package designed merely to entertain the audience, or to sell a product and make money for a producer, may well serve the latent function of political socialization. It is a wonder we are not politically socialized and re-socialized more quickly, but, as we shall see, it is not for lack of an extensive curriculum in the mass media; the trouble lies elsewhere—some of it with the learners, some of it with the conditions intervening between the learners and the media.

[1] E. Freeman, *Social Psychology*, New York, Holt, 1936, pp. 264-265.

That the popular culture purveyed by mass media may socialize the audience is in itself an old idea. The critics of popular culture have long talked of such consequences, but they have always seen them as dysfunctional, as producing undesirable patterns of conduct. To be sure, their claims are exaggerated, since widespread undesirable effects for the most part remain to be proved, but practically no one has argued the reverse: that the outcomes may be desirable.[2] This part of my argument is novel and, until specified, somewhat outrageous. The place and the stage must be considered. The critics of popular culture are looking at societies and masses already modernized and would prefer that refined and cultivated media content be available and chosen by these audiences. But this is a choice between alternatives all equally modern. In such a situation the modern product of higher quality is understandably to be preferred. By contrast, for the population of a traditional society in process of modernization the popular culture of the mass media may be vulgar, but it is at least modern and may be an opening wedge in the political re-socialization process. The refinement of popular taste through improved media content is a question perhaps better postponed to a later societal stage; modernization is something to be welcomed even at the price of vulgarization.

On this score, since the Burmese finding is only suggestive, let me cite a more elaborate case, a cartoon movie titled in pidgin English *Put Una Money For There*, produced in 1956 for Barclays Bank, D.C.O., by the Film Producers Guild, Ltd., for showings throughout West Africa. Here all the apparatus and talent of a modern mass medium was put at the disposal of a commercial client interested in persuading more West Africans to open savings accounts in Barclays Bank. Even the appurtenances of modern market research were employed, and the theme and drawings were pre-tested on Nigerian students in residence in London. The three-minute product is a delight to the eye with its sophisticated, colorful drawings; a pleasure to hear with its "high-life" sound track created by Mr. Samuel Akpabot, a young Nigerian composer. It amused me; and it so edified film critics that it won a First Prize at the Venice Film Festival. More important, it was eminently successful in bringing in new depositors among the West African peoples. To prove the effect of a communication is very difficult and properly requires elaborate research techniques, but my

[2] For two recent reviews of the empirical literature on the effects of mass media, see Joseph Klapper, *The Effects of Mass Communication*, Glencoe, Ill., The Free Press, 1960; Raymond A. Bauer and Alice H. Bauer, "America, Mass Society and Mass Media," *Journal of Social Issues*, 16, No. 3, 1960, pp. 3-66.

own skepticism on this score was satisfied after interviewing the Barclays personnel. Three such films have been produced for Barclays for West African showings and a fourth for showings in East Africa. The details of the production process, the kinds of decisions which made film content compatible with and viable in different cultural and linguistic settings, are deserving of study by communication researchers but will be omitted here. Rather, I would return to my basic first point. Nothing could be more modern in nature than the institutions of banking and money, and savings and investment and interest. And nothing is more distinctively modern in character structure than the deferment of gratification, "putting una money for there," instead of spending it. Barclays Bank profited from this venture in mass communication engineering; but, manipulation and commercialism aside, many individuals modified their patterns of economic activity and, insofar as political modernization has an economic aspect, were indirectly politically socialized.

Considered in isolation, the non-political content within which political communication is imbedded may thus make its own independent contribution to political socialization and modernization. Certainly the Soviet Union must have a keen awareness of this possibility, for how else shall we understand the periodic violent opposition to Western popular music and popular culture unless it be regarded as an irrational and obsessive reaction against all things Western, no matter how innocuous? The Russians may well have felt, to steal a phrase from Frederick Wertham, that the music accomplished a seduction of their innocent youth, delivering them, through one means or another, into the clutches of the West—either because non-political communication has a latent political function all its own or because it is the attractive wrapper which captures the audience for the political messages which are imbedded within the patterns of content of the Western media.

II

This last point may serve to move our discussion from the independent effects of non-political communication to the way it mediates the effects of political communication on socialization. The wrapping on the package may be of indirect significance without in any way modifying the perception and experience of political communication. Consider the amusing fact reported to me by an official involved in international broadcasting. The radio audiences of the Middle East are a target group of much importance, whether one sees them as strategic to win over to a particular political position or as populations in process of transition to modernity. A good deal of news and political communication is broadcast, but a good deal of the time there is just no news happening, and there are large empty spaces in the extensive program time which must be filled. There is no mystique to the endless Arabic music that is broadcast. It is simply filler in the empty slots but essential to keep the audience ready and in hand for the moment when there will be more political communication to be broadcast.

The non-political content mediates and modifies the response to political communication by acting not merely as filler but also as buffer between the audience and the political world, insulating them from the undesirable effects of an overdose of politics. Once upon a time politics may have been fun to watch, a good spectator sport, but now so much of it is unrelieved crisis that the audience can't take it. Certainly political communication serves the function of bringing home reality, of inducting the citizen into his proper responsibilities and concerns; but it may also make him flee when his anxiety mounts too high.[3] The buffer provided by the non-political content may thus produce a responsive audience for political news, and one that reacts in less extreme fashion.

The alternative view entertained by many critics of the mass media is that apathy, passivity, flight from reality, escapism are all encouraged, perhaps even created, by the preponderant non-serious content. Perhaps there is some truth in that formulation when it is given careful qualification and considerable specification, but most of the empirical evidence does not give support to the idea.[4] One escapes into something when one is escaping from something else. Political news of overwhelming complexity creates the sense of futility and in turn apathy; news that is too threatening creates the need to escape. Of course the design of the media package must be just right; if there is too much buffer, the reality is not perceived at all. And the design must be suited to the audience. Individuals and groups no doubt differ in their tolerance level for crisis, in how much unrelieved frustration and anxiety they can stand, and should be pushed as far towards their thresholds as possible.

[3] For a review of the various functional and dysfunctional consequences of mass media, see Charles R. Wright, "Functional Analysis and Mass Communication," *Public Opinion Quarterly*, 24, 1960, pp. 605-621. See also the Bauers' treatment, *op.cit.*, especially p. 53.

[4] Klapper, *op.cit.*; Bauers, *op.cit.*

Indirect support for the "buffer" formulation and refined evidence on the relations between effectiveness of a communication and magnitude of threat are provided by the well-known experiment of Janis and Feshback in which three messages varying in magnitude of threat were employed to persuade subjects to conform to proper dental hygiene.[5] The message containing the maximum threat was found to be less effective than the moderately threatening message, and the subjects exposed to it did not differ from a control group. The buffer may not only allay anxiety but also work in still another fashion to reduce one of the major obstacles to the effectiveness of the media. Selective exposure, attention and memory, by which individuals defend themselves against hostile information, is less operative when the first part of a medium or communication to which they are exposed is pleasurable or congenial. Hovland and his associates have demonstrated this by other experiments in their research program.[6]

In the laboratory situation Janis and Feshback varied magnitude of threat by manufacturing three different messages. The mass media can also manipulate level of threat implicit in real news by editorial handling of political news, but an alternative approach is through a proper mixture of buffer material. It would be interesting to repeat the Yale experiment, using as the independent variable variations in the pattern of content within which a message of constant level of threat is imbedded.

An exotic experiment of long ago also bears on the argument. Razran had two groups of subjects indicate their responses to various socio-political slogans which had been presented to the accompaniment of, respectively, a free lunch and an unpleasant odor. At earlier stages there had been obtained base-line measures of response to the slogans when presented independently of the accompaniments. The "free lunch" group showed favorable changes in response and the "odor" group unfavorable changes.[7] Razran's model of the process is in terms of conditioned response theory in contrast to the psychodynamic model

[5] I. Janis and S. Feshback, "Effects of Fear Arousing Communications," *Journal of Abnormal and Social Psychology*, 48, 1953, pp. 78-92.

[6] C. Hovland, et al., *The Order of Presentation in Persuasion*, New Haven, Yale University Press, 1957. Geiger has demonstrated a similar phenomenon under natural conditions. By wrapping an unpopular radio program in a palatable label, exposure can be increased and, what is even more crucial, the audience can then be held. See T. Geiger, "A Radio Test of Musical Taste," *Public Opinion Quarterly*, 14, 1950, pp. 453-460.

[7] G. H. Razran, *Psychological Bulletin*, 37, 1940, p. 418.

employed by Janis, but both experiments, by analogy, argue the value of pleasant packaging.

These are admittedly only laboratory analogies to the real-life situation in which an audience is responding to the varied contents of the mass media package. There is available from natural settings evidence on whether non-political content encourages complete escapism or works in desirable fashion as a buffer increasing attention to serious content. As already noted, when the independent, separate effects of exposure to non-serious content are examined, the findings do not support the argument of escapism. The problem may also be examined empirically by analyzing the way in which different discrete types of media behavior cluster together. If exposure to non-serious content were an escape from serious content, then high exposure to the one should accompany low exposure to the other.

Patterns of audience behavior, the kinds of overlapping exposure to various media and classes and types of content, have been a subject of considerable study in media research in the United States, and the many findings do not lend themselves to easy summary.[8] Some of the relations observed seem to favor the model of opposition; some subgroups concentrate on one type of exposure to the detriment of other types of exposure, easy pleasurable content being far more popular than serious content; but there is much evidence to suggest a simple typology of those who show a diffuse and general interest versus those who are not interested in anything at all in the media. When we come to the findings just now beginning to emerge from media research in the newer countries, the conclusions seem to be even less ambiguous. Given the difficulties of research pioneering, the techniques of inquiry are still rudimentary. Field work, sampling designs, and instruments must be greatly improved. The clustering, intercorrelations, of preferences and exposures must be analyzed for individuals and sub-groups in order to arrive at unambiguous interpretations; but the over-all findings lend themselves to a fairly confident conclusion. For example, in East Africa those individuals who have come into the orbit of the mass media seem to have a diffuse interest in most of the output. Popular music is one of their very strong interests, but so too is news.[9] In a more sophisticated inquiry among urban popu-

[8] See for example P. F. Lazarsfeld and P. Kendall, *Radio Listening in America*, New York, Prentice-Hall, 1948, pp. 4-9.

[9] See for example "Focus on Kenya Broadcasting Service; Listener Research Survey, Tanganyika, 1960" and "The Public and the Kenya Broadcasting Service" (Market

lations in West Africa, again, both news and music form a constellation in which the audience is highly interested. Overlapping exposure to several different media seems also to occur. Radio listening and cinema attendance go with reading the press.[10]

Highly elaborate and sophisticated surveys of audience behavior in transitional societies have been analyzed intensively and reported on by Lerner in his recent work on the Middle East, and his conclusions seem in accord with the formulation presented.[11] The transitional and modern groups within the populations have the kind of character structure which makes them responsive to new experience, empathic, and participant; and they have high exposure to the media. It is the traditional groups, who do not exhibit exposure to the mass media, who are passive and non-political. Certainly Lerner's model of the process of modernization is far more complex than I have phrased it, and certainly a variety of social and technological factors are regarded as prerequisite to media exposure and to modernization; but the contribution of the media as such to the on-going socialization process is acknowledged, and the diffuse exposure to the media package is demonstrated among the more modern groups.

A vivid example of the way in which the individual from a traditional society is caught up by the mass media, intrigued by the total package, is provided by Mahmut Makal in his autobiographical work. Makal, a boy from a Turkish village, was educated to be a village teacher, and in the process exposed to the mass media. He describes his experience:

"You may wonder where I get this passion for newspapers. When I left the primary school, and until I passed into the school to which I went afterwards, I had no notion even that anything was published other than school-books. I mean newspapers, novels, periodicals, and so on. . . . Then . . . I suddenly got a taste for papers and periodicals. And how fond I got of them! Before long my passion was such that I got into the habit in my studies of not touching a lesson-book, so many periodicals did I read. It was as though whole worlds of fairy tales were disclosed to me in the pages of every newspaper, magazine, and

Research Company of East Africa, Nairobi). See also Derrick Sington, "Broadcasting in East Africa," *The Listener*, August 3, 1961, pp. 167-169.

[10] Quota samples of 1,000 cases were queried in each of four cities, Accra, Lagos, Abidjan, and Dakar; the work was conducted through the cooperation of the French Institute of Public Opinion in 1960.

[11] Daniel Lerner, *The Passing of Traditional Society: Modernizing the Middle East*, Glencoe, Ill., The Free Press, 1958.

book; and that terribly narrow world of mine became wider and wider. . . . It was just then that I got hold of the address of one or two periodicals and became a subscriber. I used to wait excitedly for the first of the month. Watching for the post became more and more of an obsession with me. . . . What dreams I had for the future! I imagined that I was sent to a busy place. The post would come every day with books, newspapers, periodicals for me. Oh! I would be so happy!"[12]

To reconcile the various comparative findings on patterns of exposure to the diverse contents of the media may call for a kind of developmental model. As a society and population experience their first exposure to the mass media, diffuse and general interest is created, and perhaps the simple and palatable contents—the fancy wrappings of the media package—help initiate and, as buffer, then maintain the high interest. Later on, interests may become differentiated and canalized into more exclusive types of exposure.

The model may also have to take into account certain gross differences in the size of the media package available to the audiences of transitional versus modern affluent societies. Consider the brute problem of reading the entire Sunday edition of *The New York Times* in one day, and this is only the beginning of the problem. Add the round-the-clock domestic television and radio programming, the productions of Hollywood, the endless supply of other print media. Selective exposure—missing something from the total media package—is essential to survival. Even in our leisured society, where members of the average American home can find time to watch TV for five hours a day and listen to radio for another few hours, get in a movie during the week, read a daily paper, a couple of magazines, and perhaps once or twice a year a book, a great deal of the media supply cannot be absorbed. Contrast the size of the TV package in America with, for example, the TV program log for Salisbury, Rhodesia, one of the very few TV stations in Africa, where one channel broadcasts for perhaps four hours a day. Perhaps the best documented finding in all of Western media research is the phenomenon of self-selection; individuals select content that is congenial to their prior ideology. For the most part the finding has been explained in dynamic terms as the individual's method of defending and maintaining his ideological position against hostile information, but certainly the prime condition for such a phenomenon is that he

[12] M. Makal, *A Village in Anatolia*, London, Vallentine, Mitchell, 1954, p. 99.

cannot possibly expose himself to everything available and perforce must select something. In the society with the less lavish media package, selective exposure may not be necessary at all, and the individual's need for stimulation from the media may be nowhere near satiation.

Non-serious content in the media package mediates the exposure of the audience to serious content by keeping them captive; and it mediates the response by preventing too much anxiety from accompanying exposure to what would be otherwise unmitigatedly threatening. There are many other subtle ways in which the context within which a communication is imbedded affects the perception, meaning, and response an audience gives; and here we come to the heart of the problem Pye posed for us. Thus far I have analyzed the media package in terms of a very simple classification of serious political versus non-serious or popular non-political content. Obviously the variety of content is much more complex. On first analysis Western packaging of communication seems global and all-inclusive. Our mass media, with huge and heterogeneous audiences and ever seeking larger audiences, appear omnibus in their packaging, trying to cater to every type of individual and all human needs. Politics, fashion, the weather, the stock market, health, domestic and physical science, consumption, gossip, diplomacy, religion, and the higher man as well as baser pleasures all seem to be provided for by the same vehicle. And yet a little reflection shows that the mixture is not that disorderly. Some things are never mixed together in the same package or at least are kept in separate compartments. A beer company does not sponsor a religious program or interrupt the sermon with a commercial. And this is not only because they think their message will fall in vain on the ears of religious teetotalers. The mixture of the two dimensions of content—the sacred and the profane—seems improper or at the very least incongruous to most Westerners, even drinkers, and the response might be quite different from exposure to the same pure religious message uncontaminated by the beer packaging.

Some combinations of communication content are congruent; they make, to lift a phrase, a good gestalt. Other combinations, while experienced as incongruous, are perhaps inconsequential in their effect. They may simply be amusing juxtapositions, perhaps even slightly grotesque but regarded by the perceiver merely as instances of poor taste and bad judgment on the part of the producer. Some may verge on the nightmarish, and others may, by the slight shock they create, have a heightened impact on the audience. Some incongruous combinations, however, are serious mistakes in packaging which may undermine the effects of the component parts by producing in the audience confusions in meaning, changes in evaluation and response, and doubts as to the validity of a communication. The principles that predict the good gestalt, that guide us toward the best packaging of communication to produce the greatest gains in socialization from exposure, will have to be developed empirically from comparative work in different cultures. Societies must vary in what kinds of communications can be packaged together, in what kinds are segregated from one another, in which media vehicles can carry what combined loads, in what kinds of wrappings are appropriate to particular classes of content.

These suggestions are stimulated by a paper by Eisenstadt which goes right to the heart of the problem of patterns of communication as determinants of socialization.[13] Within the boundaries of Israel, Eisenstadt was able to find various sub-societies contrasted culturally and located at points along the continuum of modernization ranging from the most traditional (a Yemenite group) to the transitional (a North African group) to the most urban and modern (a group of European immigrants). For each group he mapped out the characteristic patterning of communication, the way different classes of communication content are mixed and the vehicles by which they are carried. Such an inquiry might have remained purely descriptive or ethnographic, but Eisenstadt begins to explore the way in which the effectiveness of external communications from the state of Israel intended to instruct and socialize the immigrants is dependent on whether the new packaging matches the culturally prescribed patterning of communication. Eisenstadt's method of conceptualizing classes of communication, a necessary prelude to describing patterns of communication, is also most appropriate to our discussion of socialization. Three main classes of communication content are distinguished: technical content, which provides instruction and information; general cognitive content, which covers news ranging from gossip to politics; and normative content, which defines what is proper behavior and is oriented to the transmission and maintenance of social norms. This third class of content, which is central to the problem of the assimilation of immigrants into Israeli society and to our discussion of political socialization or re-socialization, is further subdivided into

---

[13] S. N. Eisenstadt, "Communication Systems and Social Structure: An Exploratory Comparative Study," *Public Opinion Quarterly*, 19, 1955, pp. 153-167.

more refined categories depending on the particular types of norms being communicated.

Eisenstadt observes something fundamental to our discussion. While all the different kinds of communication content were found in the three groups studied, "there are . . . important differences in what may be called the pattern of communication, in the interrelation between various types of communications, in the extent to which they go together or are segregated in their transmission and reception."[14] Eisenstadt devotes most of his treatment to the analysis of the various patterns. Thus, for example, the Yemenite group does not combine what he terms "hierarchical normative" content with other normative communications. But the consequence of this institutionalized pattern is noted, for the Yemenites "have quite often proved a despair to the various instructors who have been sent to guide them, and who usually cannot understand the almost complete apathy of the people to communications in which this separation does not exist."[15]

The paper contains many other suggestive findings on patterns of content and their effects on the audience, although it is not always easy to follow Eisenstadt's analysis or the interpretation of or allusion to certain cultural patterns of communication. Thus there is the suggestion that the sub-cultures differ in whether local versus society-wide communications can be blended in one package. There is another suggestion that the tone or style surrounding a communication must be the appropriate one for its meaning to be accepted. For the Yemenite subjects, messages boomeranged because "the agricultural instructor speaks every day as if it were Yom Kippur [The Day of Atonement] and wants to be taken seriously."[16] One is reminded of the findings of the Keesings for elite communication in Samoa.[17] There the clash of cultures manifests itself in the different oratorical wrappings which Western and Samoan parliamentarians customarily employ for political discourse. Each group is offended by the other's packaging although they understand perfectly well the inner core of the other's communication.

More anthropological descriptions of the wide variety of patterns of communications plus studies of the effect of exposure to patterns that are congruent or incongruous in light of the cultural background of the audience would be desirable. Other methods besides ethno-

[14] *Ibid.*, p. 155.   [15] *Ibid.*, p. 156.   [16] *Ibid.*, p. 157.

[17] F. M. and M. M. Keesing, *Elite Communication in Samoa*, Stanford, Stanford University Press, 1956.

graphic description could also be adapted to determine patterns of communication content that characterize particular cultures, and the existing findings from some of these approaches could be reinterpreted. One thinks of the classic work of F. C. Bartlett, who developed the method of "serial reproduction" to observe the changes that were wrought in an originally presented stimulus as it was transmitted through a chain of subjects. Bartlett, the social psychologist, and later Nadel, the anthropologist, used this method with subjects from different cultures; and still later Allport and Postman used it to examine rumor transmission among subjects with certain cultural biases. The method and the findings have been used to demonstrate social factors in perception and memory, but it is just as correct to use the method and past findings to reveal, by what is left out and what is added to an original communication, the patterning of communication that is congenial to a given culture. One recalls for example the finding that Westerners dropped out non-essential aspects of a complex communication. The message became reduced; simplification was the principle that guided the patterning as the stimulus moved down the line. The subjects who were Indian, by contrast, added aesthetic frills to the message. Embellishment was their principle. The original message did not have enough wrapping to suit them.[18]

Responses to a communication are governed in part by whether or not the package within which it is contained is experienced as incongruous. This experience in turn seems dependent upon cultural factors which define appropriate patterns for communications. Responses to a communication are also mediated by the packaging through effects on judgmental and cognitive processes. Here we turn from the tradition of anthropology to experimental psychology, which provides well-established principles readily applicable to our problem.

Ponder the suggestion advanced by Pye. "Can the world really be very badly off if we read about it in a context which is surrounded by the women's page, the sports page and the comics, and an accent of a few violent accidents? This sort of thing puts politics in a definite perspective. It must mean quite a different world when you learn your politics in a much starker context."[19] The media contents within which a communication is framed provide a frame of reference and somehow

[18] F. C. Bartlett, *Remembering*, Cambridge, England, Cambridge University Press, 1932; S. F. Nadel, "A Field Experiment in Racial Psychology," *British Journal of Psychology*, 28, 1937, pp. 195-211; G. W. Allport and L. Postman, *The Psychology of Rumor*, New York, Holt, 1947.

[19] Personal communication.

modify the meaning we give something, the weight we assign it, the judgment we make of it. Intuitively, Pye's suggestion is most appealing, and the concept of frame of reference has become a fundamental principle, universally accepted and supported by massive experimental proof. But predicting the influence of packaging of communication from the application of such principles is anything but simple. No doubt the edge of political news can be blunted, the impact softened, by the predominantly pleasant tone of the mass media for reasons apart from the buffering process already described. Prior exposure to a particular train of media experiences has a directive influence in organizing the way we perceive and define and interpret some ambiguous item of information. There is much experimental support for such a formulation, perhaps the most classic study being that by Asch, in which word descriptions and adjectives take on altered meaning depending on the particular series of adjectives which precede them. Other experimental evidence comes readily to hand to support the formulation.[20]

Yet there is another tradition in experimental psychology equally well supported by evidence which would argue the very opposite prediction. A mildly unpleasant odor is terribly offensive to someone who has been accustomed to smelling sweet things. A moderate weight is heavy as lead to someone who has been lifting light things. Our scales of judgment are anchored in our past experience, and new stimuli are located along particular dimensions of judgment by comparison processes. Therefore, is it not equally tenable that the audience fed on mild news is bowled over by the slightest shock? The stark event becomes catastrophic by contrast with what they have grown accustomed to. Whichever prediction is sound, it should be emphasized that the consequence of too extreme and uniform media packaging is undesirable. Either it creates a false glow in the face of bad news or a disruptive reaction. But which prediction is sound? Both are equally plausible and equally well founded in past evidence.[21]

[20] For a summary see S. Asch, *Social Psychology*, New York, Prentice-Hall, 1952, Chapters 8, 15. See also C. Hovland, et al., *The Order of Presentation in Persuasion*, especially the chapters by Luchins, which show the influence of initial material in creating a set which influences response to subsequent communication.

[21] The work of Osgood and his associates is also relevant. Formulated in terms of a "principle of congruity," in which there is a stress upon the individual toward resolving experiences which are cognitively inconsistent, various experiments have been conducted in which discrete items differing in meaning are juxtaposed, and the resultant process of judgment or evaluation examined. In the experiments most relevant to the mass media, one finds that an ambiguous item is assimilated to the

The final answer must wait upon new empirical evidence, and the research should not be hard to design since the paradigm is available in the experimental literature I have mentioned. Both formulations may well be applicable to the mass media, for what distinguishes their sphere of application is the character of the discrete item that is imbedded in particular contexts. Where it is simple and unitary in nature, a stimulus located on some unitary dimension of judgment, something that can be only heavy or light, the concepts of anchoring and comparative judgments account for the outcome. Where the discrete item is itself complex in character, ambiguous and subject to alternative definitions, locatable on multiple dimensions, it is redefined for the person in the direction suggested by the prior context. The packaging of communication may influence response via both processes.

III

In my exploration of the special problem of the pattern of communication within the mass media I have begged the more general question of how much the mass media, however they may package communication, can contribute to political socialization. In the face of the challenge of rapidly modernizing many traditional societies around the world they are a major hope. As instruments of socialization, they are efficient and their sweep is vast enough to cover the huge populations requiring modernization. Their standardization, a point of attack for many critics, is the very thing suited to producing widespread national uniformities in patterns of behavior; and their spirit is modern, no matter what else is wrong with it. By contrast, while the conventional agencies of socialization in a society—parents, teachers, peers, neighbors, and the like—can be more flexible in suiting the lesson to the capacities and needs of the particular learner and more potent an influence, the outcomes cannot be as uniform, and their efforts are often directed against modernization. The time and the stage must be considered in weighing properties of the different agencies of socialization. For our society perhaps more flexibility, less uniformity and conformity, even a little less modernity, would be

meaning that is suggested by the context. But there are contradictions in the findings from some of the studies where discrete items varying in meaning are juxtaposed. Sometimes one type of process eventuates; other times a different process occurs. The findings are thus suggestive of the paradox we have posed. For a summary of this work, see C. E. Osgood, "Cognitive Dynamics in Human Affairs," *Public Opinion Quarterly*, 24, 1960, pp. 341-365, especially pp. 343, 363-364.

fine. For the transitional society the properties of the media as socializers may be the more appropriate.[22] They are a hope, but just how much hope can we rest in them?

There are obvious barriers to their effectiveness. Most fundamental is the limitation in the supply of the mass media in the poor countries of the world, only now beginning their process of economic development. A recent UNESCO report vividly conveys the problem. Per 100 inhabitants, the standard of ten copies of newspapers, five radios, two cinema seats, and two television receivers is used to classify countries as to the adequacy of their media facilities. Any yardstick has elements of arbitrariness, but that this is a most conservative standard for diagnosing adequacy cannot be questioned. For example, both radio and television receivers are present in almost 100 per cent of all households in the United States in contrast to the 2-5 per cent standard employed by UNESCO. "As many as 100 states and territories in Africa, Asia, and Latin America fall below this very low 'minimum' level in all four of the mass media. These countries have a combined population of 1,910 millions or 66 per cent of the world total."[23]

The effective supply of mass communication in many of the developing countries may even be overstated by gross national statistics on facilities, for these are only the vehicles which might carry a supply of content from its source to the recipients. In many of the newer countries the political power of the state has been employed to suspend publication of newspapers and jail editors and journalists. As if the sheer physical scarcity of facilities were not severe enough, the state thereby further reduces the effective supply. In addition, for print media, very high rates of illiteracy cut down on the effective supply; for electronic media, the power and character of the transmitters must be considered; for movies, the concentration of conventional facilities in the urban areas and the rarity of mobile projectors for the rural areas should be noted; and for all types of media vehicles, the multilingual nature of the audience in many of the countries increases the cost and difficulty of effective communication. A recent article on "Broadcasting in East Africa" describes such barriers:

". . . Kenya radio provides transmissions in no fewer than twenty different languages. The tribes of Nyanza Province in the north-west

[22] For discussions of media vs. other agencies of socialization, see C. R. Wright, *Mass Communication*, New York, Random House, 1959; David Riesman, *The Lonely Crowd*, New Haven, Yale University Press, 1950, Chapter IV.

[23] *Mass Media in the Developing Countries*, UNESCO, Reports and Papers on Mass Communication, No. 33, 1961, p. 16.

are served by a regional station at Kisumu which broadcasts in Swahili, Kalenjin, Kisii, Luo, and Luhya. The Mombasa regional station which serves the Arabized coastal strip puts out programmes in Arabic, Kimvita, and Swahili. The National Service from Nairobi broadcasts for Indian listeners in Hindustani, Gujerati, Punjabi, and Konkani (for Kenya's small Goan minority); and also relays the B.B.C.'s programmes in Hindi and Urdu; European listeners are provided for in English (including much relaying of the B.B.C.); and African listeners get a Swahili programme. The Kikuyu, Masai, and Kamba tribes—as well as the Somali minority—are specially catered for by a Nairobi Regional Service. Yet even this complex machine is far from sufficient. There are still no broadcasts in many important tribal languages. Medium-wave transmitters powerful enough to carry the national programmes all over Kenya are too expensive for the country to afford and are confined to the densely populated parts. They have to be supplemented by short-wave systems for wider coverage, and by medium-wave transmitters specially fed by very high frequency links. Tanganyika, a poorer country than Kenya, has not been able to afford any regional broadcasting, and some areas in Tanganyika get only a weak signal. Financial limitations are severe. Expenditure on broadcasting in Kenya, at £18 per hour, is only about a thirtieth of what is spent hourly on B.B.C. programmes."[24]

To be sure, other factors which mitigate the situation must be considered. Trend statistics on the mass media show a rapid rate of growth in recent years, and the forecasts of future growth are optimistic. Patterns of group listening mean that one radio can serve many individuals. The large numbers who are barred by language, poverty, or illiteracy from direct contact with the medium can be brought into the audience via the gatekeeper or interpersonal communicator who himself is literate, perhaps bi-lingual, and wealthy enough to have access to the media, and who can relay the original messages. Nevertheless, our optimism must be tempered. The delight social scientists have in finding out some subtlety, and the enthusiasm with which they have greeted the phenomena of group listening and the two-step flow of influence as it reinstated the human factor in what at first appeared to be too impersonal and mechanical a process of communication, have perhaps led them to neglect some of the implications of these phenomena. In studies of rumor, classic examples

[24] Sington, op.cit., p. 168.

of interpersonal chains of communication, the prime finding is that the interpersonal link distorts the original message. One recalls Cantril and Gaudet's *Invasion from Mars*, their study of the panic that followed listening to Orson Welles' Broadcast of H. G. Wells' *War of the Worlds*, where those members of the audience who turned for interpretation of the facts to other individuals were often led by misinformation to panic, whereas those who turned to other mass media for clarification learned the truth.[25] The amusing story reported by Yasa for the Turkish village of Hasanoglan comes to mind. Almost all the villagers were illiterate, but Halime Hoca, an influential and interpersonal communication link since she was literate, came to their rescue. But what did this old lady do when asked to read letters addressed to the villagers? "She used to recite things without any reference to the letter."[26] Research into the quality as well as the quantity of communication which the interpersonal communicator passes along is needed for a balanced conclusion.

Where the role of communication as socializer, as agent of modernization, is being examined, one should ask as well what the ideology of the interpersonal communicator is. In contrast with the conventional human agents of socialization in the traditional societies, I have emphasized that the spirit of the mass media is modern. The interpersonal link inserted into this process could very well be the agent of tradition, reintroducing the very thing we wish to avoid and creating new opportunities for social control since any subversive modern impulse in the masses is under his scrutiny. At least the mass media cannot inform on their audience! Fortunately it appears to be the fact that interpersonal communicators in the transitional societies are also innovators, more modern in temper than the mass; but again a balanced appraisal of their influence will require comprehensive evidence on the ideological slant they add to or detract from the original message.[27] So too the phenomenon of group listening requires careful appraisal. While it expands the coverage of the mass media, it also creates heightened opportunities for social control. We are inclined to interpret it as a natural carry-over of a cultural pattern from the folk society, in the image of the storyteller surrounded by his audience. Yet it is in the Soviet Union, rather than Africa or Asia, where

[25] H. Cantril, *The Invasion from Mars*, Princeton, Princeton University Press, 1952, pp. 117-118.
[26] Ibrahim Yasa, *Hasanoglan*, Ankara, 1957.
[27] See, for example, Eisenstadt's remarks about gatekeepers and influentials in the Yemenite community, *op.cit.*, p. 158.

this pattern of radio listening has seen much expansion, for the Russians were aware that the group setting permits greater scrutiny, manipulation, and control over the audience than does solo listening.[28] Until all these factors have been examined we should view the supply problem with, at best, cautious optimism.

The interpersonal link may not always be an advantage. And the apparent disadvantage of the mass medium when not combined with such links, that it is too impersonal for cultures accustomed to an oral tradition in communication, may simply be an illusion fostered by our own analytical distinctions. Why prejudge the way a mass medium is perceived in such cultures? It may well take on human features. Perhaps this is what was implied to me by one official involved in international broadcasting who remarked that the successful radio stations in the new countries were ones which had a radio personality. Even Westerners may see the movies as the vital embodiment of Sophia Loren, the impersonal newspaper as the voice of Walter Lippmann or James Reston. Before we prejudge the perception of the medium, some research into the phenomenology of the experience is called for.

There are also psychological barriers to the effectiveness of the mass media stemming from the audience. The mass media are instruments of socialization, but one must have some prior socialization before the media can work their effects. One has to be prepared to understand the media, to accept the technical conventions that govern each particular form of communication. The cultural prerequisites for use of a modern medium are well conveyed in another case reported by Makal, who had let a Turkish villager listen to his radio.[29] This was at mid-century, but it conjures up the behavior of Americans perhaps thirty-forty years ago. The villager's reaction was:

" 'Efendi, how can it be possible—that the call to prayer should be cried in Egypt and heard over here? And think how many voices there are in the world, from morning till evening, all the world over! How is it that the radio doesn't get them all?'

"We try to explain the working of the radio to him, but he's very obstinate. 'No. There's somebody hidden under that set where the talk is coming from. *He* does all the talking and tries to fool the public

[28] For a brief account, see C. R. Wright, *Mass Communication*, p. 26.
[29] *Op.cit.*, p. 102. This last section of the present paper is taken almost in entirety from my "The Role of the Mass Media in the Formation of Public Opinion," in *The Role of the Mass Media in a Democratic Society*, D. C. Reddick, ed. Austin, University of Texas Press, 1961, pp. 17-21.

into thinking otherwise.' Then the teacher commented, 'He is not the only one who thinks like this.' "

As the mass media become part of the fabric of a society, and individuals obtain some experience with them, they come to accept the media as genuine and incorporate them into their lives. This stage, I might suggest, without too much evidence, is quite different from the one at which Western publics have arrived. Since the novelty has not yet worn off, the experience may have great vitality with powerful consequences for opinion change. Yet it may still be recognized for what it really is, something stylized, conventionalized—not real life, but life seen or distorted through an artificial, technical medium. Perhaps the excitement and the critical awareness blend in just the right measure. The earlier autobiographical remarks of Makal may exemplify this stage.

It is a long way from our Turkish school teacher to the stage Western publics are now at in their use of media. For practically all of us, the media are a regular part of our daily lives. For most of us, the social and cultural conditions that are prerequisite are long since met. But the media have become so commonplace that perhaps some of their vitality is lost on us; some of their dynamic for changing our opinions is perhaps reduced. The familiarity of the experience may also reduce the critical awareness I mentioned. The media are so much a part of our lives that the pictures they present are accepted as reality, rather than a representation or an artificial rendering of something through a medium. The blend is now perhaps just the one that would account for two facts: the Western public doesn't suddenly change many of its topical opinions as a result of particular exposure but, at the same time, the media do mold the rather odd ways some see the political world and relate to it.

Both the cultural stage of Western publics in their experience of mass media and the overabundant supply of mass communication with the possible satiation effects mentioned earlier should qualify the current generalization that the mass media are relatively ineffective in producing massive and desirable changes in opinions but at the same time may have subtle and undesirable effects in molding our political behavior. The generalization may hold for Western societies but be inappropriate to the contrasted conditions of the societies just recently introduced to mass media. That brief period when the brute problems of supply are solved and before the next stage sets in may provide the ideal opportunity to capitalize on; and the effects on political socialization and modernization may be large. Whether this developmental model that I have postulated is correct remains to be proved by comparative research. The findings of such research will then serve the cause of social change and lead to a truly general theory of mass communication.

CHAPTER 9

COMMUNICATIONS AND MOTIVATIONS FOR MODERNIZATION

~~~~~~

WE HAVE examined the numerous ways in which the communications process can facilitate citizenship education and influence the process of political socialization in transitional societies. Our analysis suggested that possibly in societies not saturated by the mass media these forms of communication may have a greater influence on people's conscious, cognitive learning about politics than they appear to have in the advanced countries. We also noted, however, that in transitional societies the experience of learning about politics also entails the deeper problem of coming to understand all the complex dimensions of modern life. For this reason it seems that the context of the learning experience and thus the "packaging" surrounding the more explicitly political information may be peculiarly important in shaping the feelings and sentiments of transitional people toward politics.

In moving from the more cognitive aspects of learning about politics to the subtler and emotionally deeper feelings about participating in the modern world we are brought to a wide range of very difficult questions about the motivations of people who are caught up in profound social changes.

Part of the process of modernization involves the learning of new skills and the acceptance of new ideas about the nature of the world and of human relations. Another part of the process entails the acceptance of new values and the changing of preferences. A still deeper dimension of the process calls for a fundamental change in motivations and in the direction in which it is felt that human energies can be properly directed. The problems which impede easy political development are clearly less related to uncertainty over rational choices than to deeper confusions and ambivalences over motivations and desires. In recent years we have been greatly expanding our knowledge about how the experience of breaking from the bonds of a traditional order can produce complex ambivalences which in turn may affect the motivations and the productive capabilities of the individuals involved.

It is no longer possible to assume that people in traditional societies will readily experience a "revolution of rising expectations" simply by being exposed to the prospect of new standards of material life. Communications about the modern world do not always stimulate ambitions and uncompromised desires to take on new ways and to shed familiar conventions. Indeed, historically in most transitional societies the modern world has been communicated as a foreign threat which should properly be resisted and distrusted. Confronted with such a menacing challenge, people may respond by wanting the material benefits of modern technology without, however, being capable of making the necessary commitment of effort. It is because of deeper problems of motivation that many transitional people seem so often to be superficial in their commitments and opportunistic in their calculations.

Instead of having to cope with an agitated population carried away with exaggerated expectations, most governments in transitional societies are confronted with the problem of a disturbingly apathetic public which is inured to all appeals for action on the part of the small band of impatient activists within the government. Apparent political apathy in transitional societies is not always associated with lingering traditional attitudes; frequently it hides deep resentments and frustrations over how the modern world has been communicated. Apathy can be a psychic device for covering humiliations and hostilities toward those who have damaged one's self-esteem by trying to push aside one's own world and replace it with a world that is foreign. Indeed, apathy can be only a short step removed from violent, aimless, and apparently spontaneous outbursts. In all too many transitional countries apathy and outbursts make up the fundamental anomic movements which constantly surround, and in a sense lay siege to, the political process.

If modernization is to be facilitated at greatly reduced human costs, it will be essential to discover more about how the general communications process can operate to reduce psychic damage and to build up the crucial sets of motivations which a people must have if they are to perform as members of the modern world. Unquestionably the problems of motivations and attitudes have their genesis in the basic socialization process. The psychological foundations are laid within the family, and hence there is little that public policy can do to effect radical changes in many aspects of the socialization process. At the same time, early schooling and first experiences with the written word can also be a crucial factor shaping the outlook of people and making them more or less capable of grappling with the modern world. At this sensitive point in the socialization process, public policy in relation to communications can make itself felt. Thus the problem of motivation can be brought within the scope of the communications process and be influenced by rational decisions about the allocation of communications resources.

We cannot in this study attempt to examine all the many facets of the psychological reactions to the process of modernization, but it is appropriate to examine in considerable depth the ways in which personality formation in two different transitional cultures has kept people with different capacities from effectively carrying on the tasks of modernization. For assistance in understanding how basic values may be transmitted and how the general communications process can condition the motivations of a people we turn next to a summation of the research and theories of a social psychologist who has studied extensively the human basis of the modernization process.

CHAPTER 10

NATIONAL CHARACTER AND ECONOMIC GROWTH
IN TURKEY AND IRAN[1]

DAVID C. MCCLELLAND

NATIONAL character is not taken very seriously in discussing economic and political developments today. To be sure, everyone pays lip service to the anthropological credo that cultures are different and that therefore nationality differences should be studied and taken into account in describing and planning for social and economic development. Often travelers, technical advisers, or "old-hands" from a given country return with tales of how disorganized, dishonest, or untrustworthy the people are; but once the tales have been told, everyone settles down to a theoretical description of, or plan for, the economy of that country which does not take into account in any formal way the psychological characteristics of the people just described. Experts are informally convinced that people differ and that these differences should be taken into account somehow, but they have as yet discovered no way to include such variables in their formal models of economic and social development.

The difficulty lies in the nature of the data which supposedly define different national characters. When anthropologists describe the cultural norms for a small tribe or village, they seem to be on firm ground; but when they or others apply similar techniques to discovering consensus in a complex modern nation-state, doubts quite naturally arise as to whether they can succeed. The problem of the representativeness of the people they interview becomes much more acute. Obviously a given anthropologist or student of national character can interview or observe only a small number of people in a given nation, and normally these people are not chosen in a random or even systematic way. Thus the impressions he forms, no matter how careful he is in documenting them, may not be typical of the nation as a whole. Furthermore, since the impressions are usually

[1] I am indebted to Norman M. Bradburn, Richard D. Robinson, Max Thornburg, Joseph M. Upton, and others attending the Harvard Faculty Seminar on Social and Cultural Aspects of Development in 1960-1961 for what little I know about Turkey and Iran, though, of course, none of these men should be held responsible for errors either of fact or interpretation in this chapter.

stated in qualitative terms—e.g., the Iranians are pretty "dishonest" by Western standards[2]—it is often impossible to make a meaningful comparison between two countries. Are the Iranians measurably more dishonest than the Turks, for example? Or, for that matter, how could we prove that they are more dishonest than, say, Americans under similar circumstances? Only quantitative measures can provide meaningful answers to such questions. It is for these reasons that social psychologists interested in national character have been fairly pessimistic about the usefulness of the concept in recent years. Both Klineberg and Inkeles and Levinson have rather discouragingly concluded that the concept of national character has not been of much value to date and that it is not likely to prove of value until there exist in various countries national survey organizations which can select and interview or test representative samples of individuals in the country.[3]

However, another method of measuring variations in national character exists which yields results that are in some respects even more interesting than those that would be obtained from interviewing national representative samples of individuals. It involves content analysis of organized verbal or artistic "symbol systems" from a culture. For example, folk tales or vase designs can be coded for the frequency with which certain types of symbolic forms appear in various cultures and the resulting indices used to predict certain other cultural phenomena, such as the form of religious organization, the type of games played, or the rate of economic development.[4] In this method, representativeness is attained by choosing "symbol systems" that are widely diffused throughout the culture, not by selecting a random sample of individuals to be studied. That is, very few individuals, and certainly not representative ones, ordinarily produce designs for vases;

[2] R. D. Gastil, "Middle Class Impediments to Iranian Modernization," *Public Opinion Quarterly*, 22, 1958, pp. 325-329.

[3] O. Klineberg, *Tensions Affecting International Understanding*, New York, Social Science Research Council, 1950; see also A. Inkeles and D. J. Levinson, "National Character: The Study of Modal and Sociocultural Systems," in *Handbook of Social Psychology*, ed. by G. Lindzey, Cambridge, Mass., Addison-Wesley, 1954, Vol. 2, pp. 977-1,020.

[4] See D. C. McClelland and G. A. Friedman, "A Cross-Cultural Study of the Relationship Between Child-Training Practices and Achievement Motivation Appearing in Folk-Tales," in *Readings in Social Psychology*, ed. by E. G. Hartley, New York, Holt, 1953, pp. 243-248; G. O. Wright, "Projection and Displacement: A Cross-Cultural Study of Folktale Agression," *Journal of Abnormal and Social Psychology*, 49, 1954, pp. 523-528; and D. C. McClelland, *The Achieving Society*, Princeton, Van Nostrand, 1961; and H. Barry, "Relationships Between Child Training and the Pictorial Arts," *Journal of Abnormal and Social Psychology*, 54, 1957, pp. 380-383.

but so long as those artists are successful in the sense of producing what people in general in the culture want, they apparently reflect the norms of the culture well enough for measures based on their productions to be meaningful.

A specific instance of this general approach is provided by the research that makes a quantitative comparison of the national characteristics of Turkey and Iran possible. It is summarized in *The Achieving Society*,[5] where I have taken considerable pains to test the hypothesis that a high concern for Achievement in a nation is associated with its more rapid economic growth. The hypothesis was originally formed from studying the behavior of individuals whose thought patterns as reflected in the imaginative stories they wrote showed a frequent concern for achievement, i.e., for doing a good job of work, for getting ahead in the world, for discovering some new and better way of solving a problem. Such individuals are assigned high *n* Achievement scores because of the frequency with which they spontaneously think about achievement under relaxed conditions. Furthermore they behave in many ways which seem symptomatic of their concern for achievement. They work harder when working hard is likely to lead to a result which can be interpreted as a personal accomplishment. They prefer to work on a problem with technical advisers that are really expert rather than just good friends; they prefer working in situations that are neither safe and traditional nor extremely risky but, rather, involve a moderate challenge, so that a successful outcome is both likely and interpretable as a personal accomplishment. They prefer tasks in which there is concrete feedback as to how well they are doing. In short, they behave as if they have the entrepreneurial spirit which should lead to success in the world of business where moderate risk-taking, concrete knowledge of results, and hard work when it counts are all key parts of the executive role. Further studies showed that in fact individuals with high *n* Achievement do turn out to be more successful as business managers or executives.

But then the question arose as to whether one could diagnose the concern of a whole culture for achievement in much the same way as we had diagnosed it for individuals. So we sought brief, imaginative stories like those scored for individuals but which would be as representative of the culture as possible, coded them in the standard way for *n* Achievement, and correlated the resulting scores with measures of rate of economic development, since the work with individuals

---

[5] D. C. McClelland, *The Achieving Society*, Princeton, Van Nostrand, 1961.

had demonstrated that high *n* Achievement was peculiarly suited for success in business. Various types of imaginative "stories" were sampled in different studies. For example, Bradburn and Berlew used street ballads, accounts of sea voyages, and dramas to assess *n* Achievement levels at half-century intervals in England from 1400-1800.[6] The sampling was done randomly within the categories of material which were chosen to be representative of what people in England were thinking about at the time. They found that waves of concern with achievement in such popular literature preceded waves of economic growth in the English economy by about fifty years on two separate occasions, one centering around 1600 and the other late in the 18th century, at the time of the beginning of the Industrial Revolution. In short, here was a clear case in which assessment of a national psychological characteristic from a cultural symbol system in the form of popular literature was useful in predicting other modal behavior of the country.

For more recent times the measure of national *n* Achievement levels was obtained from coding stories used in the public schools to teach children to read in the second, third, and fourth grades. Twenty-one such stories were chosen at random from the textbooks of twenty-three countries published in the 1920's and from the textbooks of forty countries published around 1950. When the stories had all been coded for *n* Achievement, it turned out that the countries with higher scores in the 1925 period showed more rapid economic growth subsequently than those with lower scores in the same period. The same result was obtained for the larger sample of countries studied around 1950. A high national *n* Achievement score at that time signified a more rapid rate of economic growth in the 1950's.[7] What is particularly interesting theoretically about such findings is that neither set of measures is taken from individuals. Both the national *n* Achievement levels and the national rates of economic growth are group products representing the actions, decisions, and demands of many individuals. In a sense, one could almost say that one aspect of national character—the concern for Achievement—is related to another aspect of national character—the eagerness and success with which economic goals are pursued.

Having established that such a relationship holds on the average

[6] N. M. Bradburn and D. E. Berlew, "Need for Achievement and English Economic Growth," *Economic Development and Cultural Change*, 1961, 10, pp. 8-20.
[7] McClelland, *op.cit.*, Chapter 3.

for most countries, one can then attempt to apply it to individual cases. The problem of application is particularly important because economists, political scientists, historians, and planners are often interested in particular countries, not in broad generalizations across countries that hold on the average but not in every case. What is the usefulness of such general knowledge as *The Achieving Society* provides in understanding particular countries and their varying rates of economic development? The purpose of the present paper is to answer this question and to show, with a concrete illustration, how quantitative measures of national psychological characteristics can be useful in understanding rates of economic development and even in planning for their future acceleration.

Turkey and Iran were chosen for a comparative case study for a very simple reason. They are essentially similar in background characteristics, yet they have recently had very different rates of economic development. The problem they pose is why Turkey has developed so much more rapidly than Iran when the two countries started at more or less the same level as recently as the 1920's. As Table 1 shows, they are both large Middle Eastern countries, not very densely populated, both solidly within the religious tradition of Islam, both with relatively stable governments for the past forty years, both with roughly equivalent natural resources in land and energy potential. Both are, of course, seriously underdeveloped economically and socially as contrasted with a typical West European country like France. Yet they have clearly had different rates of economic growth since the 1920's. It is difficult to get accurate figures as to their comparative economic levels at the earlier period, but the one figure shown in Table 1 (for electric power production per capita in 1929) confirms the general opinion among experts that although Turkey may have been slightly ahead in the 1920's, her economic advantage was nowhere near as great as it is today. Certainly by almost any economic measure—electric power production, gross national product, consumption of steel, or road density—in the 1950's Turkey was several times as developed as Iran.

The difference in their rates of growth in the 1950's is also marked and measurable. In *The Achieving Society* it is argued that electric power production figures provide the best estimates of comparative rates of modern economic growth because they are readily available from all countries, they do not have to be converted into comparable units as national income figures do, and they do not have to be cor-

TABLE 1: GEOGRAPHIC, DEMOGRAPHIC, ECONOMIC, AND SOCIAL
CHARACTERISTICS OF TURKEY, IRAN, AND FOR COMPARISON, FRANCE

	Turkey	Iran	France
Area Km²	776,980	1,630,000	551,208
Population (1959) millions	27	20	45
Density (1956) per Km²	32	12	79
Population growth rates %	2.8	3.4	.8
Energy-potential, millions of			
Kwh per capita*	1.30	1.90	2.50
Cultivated land (1956)			
hectares per capita	.93	.79	.49
Electrical production in			
Kwh per capita (1929)	7	8	378
(1950)	38	11	790
Gross national product per capita			
in U.S. dollars (1956)	276	100	1,046
Consumption of steel (1956)			
Metric tons per 1,000 population	19.0	14.7	235.0
Road density (1955) Km per			
Km² of territory	6.0	1.2	133.0
Adults literate (1956) %	30-35	10-15	96-97
Proportion of children 5-14			
in primary schools	33	15	78
Physicians and dentists (1956)			
per 100,000 population	33.3	13.1	121.5
Religious tradition	Islam (Sunni)	Islam (Shi'i)	Catholic Christianity
Government	Relatively stable, parliamentary democracy	Relatively stable constitutional monarchy with parliament	Stable, parliamentary democracy

* An index computed in N. Ginsberg, *Atlas of Economic Development* (University of
Chicago Press, 1961), showing combined resources of inanimate energy (e.g., coal, oil, water-
power, timber, etc.).

Data from United Nations Statistical Yearbooks; McClelland, *The Achieving Society*;
Ginsberg, *Atlas of Economic Development*.

rected for variations due to over- and under-production. Finally, of
course, they represent the chief source of energy on which all modern
societies depend in both the industrial and household sectors. Turkey's
gain in electric power production between 1952 and 1958 was well
above average in comparison with the forty other countries studied,
even after the effect of the negative correlation between size of gain
and initial level had been removed by a regression analysis.[8] The
figures were not available for the whole period for Iran, but those for
1955 and subsequent years indicate that its rate of gain was well
below average. Increases in electric power production in a given

[8] *Ibid.*

country year by year nearly always show a positively accelerating growth function which assumes a remarkably linear form when plotted on semi-logarithmic paper. When this is done for both countries as in Figure 1, it becomes crystal clear that Turkey outgained Iran to a very marked degree in the 1950's. Figures have also been

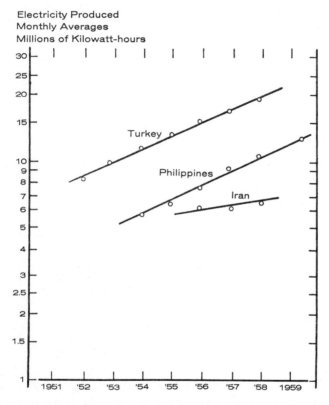

included for one other country, the Philippines, to demonstrate that the slower rate of gain in Iran is not necessarily due to the fact that it started at a lower level. The Philippines has been developing as rapidly as Turkey by this measure despite a level of production initially very close to Iran's.

Two other sets of figures indicate both the greater strenuousness of Turkey's economic effort and the means by which it accomplished the gains illustrated in Figure 1. Inflation was considerably higher in Turkey than in Iran. The cost of living index (1953 equals 100) had gone up in 1959 to 208 in Turkey and to 160 in Iran. In a sense, inflation represents a mobilization of capital resources which can be (and in Turkey were) put to use by the government. Increase in the cost of living in a sense mobilizes savings in the private sector and requires that they be spent in productive ways if the person is to maintain his normal standard of living. National budget figures for the two countries are also of interest. In 1958, eight per cent of the budget in Turkey, as contrasted with one-half of one per cent in Iran, was set aside for interest on debt. In other words, Turkey was living much more beyond its means in the sense of borrowing money to finance its expensive public works programs. Over all, the Turks appear to have been trying harder. They borrowed more, but it cost them more in standard of living to achieve the more rapid rate of economic growth shown in Figure 1.

How can one account for the difference in the rates of growth of the two countries? Several reasonable explanations come to mind.

Perhaps Turkey has planned more for modernization, as the higher rate of borrowing suggests; yet Thornburg writes that the Iranian government has three times in the "past 35 years given evidence of its desire for national advancement by launching vast programs of 'modernization,' the third of which is now (1960) in its fifth year.[9] In addition to internal resources, these programs have had the benefit of foreign aid in the form of finance, technical consultants of many kinds, competent foreign contractors, participation of private foreign entrepreneurs, and access to world markets for buying and selling." He goes on to argue that it was not lack of plans but lack of coordination that made them relatively ineffective in Iran. But can one demonstrate that they were less coordinated than those in Turkey? Perhaps Iran's relative lack of progress was due (as Mossadegh and his supporters contended) to the exploitative attitude of the British, who controlled the all-important petroleum industry in Iran. But if so, why is it that the rate of development did not accelerate as soon as the British were thrown out?

Perhaps the Iranians are not unified enough as a nation, or too corrupt, or the Shah is too interested in preserving traditional institutions to support his constitutional monarchy. Evidence for any of these explanations could be found, but it is difficult to know how

[9] M. Thornburg, *Notes on Iran as an Illustrative Case*, seminar paper on Social and Cultural Aspects of Development, Center for International Affairs, Harvard University, Cambridge, Mass., 1961.

crucial or correct they really are. In the first place, no one has shown that any of them is regularly associated with slower economic growth. Secondly, it cannot readily be shown that these factors are stronger in Iran than in Turkey, or that they outweigh equally negative factors in Turkey. The Turks too have been accused of dishonesty and corruption, have had a prime minister (Menderes) who tried to consolidate his personal power, and are widely known for their fatalistic attitude toward life and progress in general.

The reasoning in such comparisons tends nearly always to be circular. We know that Iran has done less well economically than Turkey. We think of an explanation—such as disunity or lack or coordination among planning authorities—and since we have no way of measuring the relative strength of the factor in the two countries, we conclude that it must have been stronger in Iran than in Turkey since Iran has accomplished less than Turkey. No matter how reasonable such explanations sound, we are not on very firm methodological ground in believing that we have added anything to what we already know—namely, that Iran has done less well than Turkey. Our attempt at an explanation turns out to be untestable and possibly very little more than a restatement of what it is supposed to explain.

But if we turn to n Achievement levels as an explanation of the differential rates of growth, we are on much firmer methodological ground. We know that in general higher n Achievement levels as assessed from children's stories are associated with more rapid rates of economic growth, and we have the stories for Turkey and Iran; so we can see whether the concern for achievement is quantitatively greater in Turkey than in Iran. Table 2 shows the results of this analysis. The Turkish children's stories score very high in the concern

TABLE 2: STANDARD SCORES* FOR N ACHIEVEMENT,
N AFFILIATION, AND N POWER IN
TURKISH AND IRANIAN STORIES FOR CHILDREN IN 1950

	n Achievement	n Affiliation	n Power
Turkey	+2.16	−1.60	−.88
Iran	−1.08	−2.43	+.23

* Standard scores (z-scores) are computed from the usual formula, e.g., $\dfrac{X - M_z}{SD_z}$, in which X is the mean number of instances of the imagery in question (e.g., n Achievement) for that country out of 21 stories, M_z is the mean of the country scores for that imagery for the 40 countries in the sample, and SD_z is the standard deviation of the distribution of country scores. Thus +2.16 is a very high score, well above the average for other countries; −2.43 is a very low score—so low that one would expect less than 2 in 100 countries to score lower in a normal distribution.

for achievement, in fact highest of the forty countries studied in 1950, whereas the Iranian children's stories score very low in *n* Achievement, in fact in the bottom quarter of the distribution of country scores.

The Turkish score is probably an overestimate of the national *n* Achievement level for two reasons. In the first place, several of the Turkish stories deal with bravery in battle, a type of imagery which is often on the borderline between *n* Achievement and *n* Power (concern to control or master another person). For example, in one story the heroic son of a captain hides in the ammunition hold of a ship after the enemy has captured it and killed his father and the rest of the crew. The next day, when all the enemy "high brass" is on board celebrating the victory, he blows the ship, and himself, up—an heroic *achievement* with strong overtones of exercising *power* over one's enemies. For technical reasons, such stories tended to get scored more often under *n* Achievement than under *n* Power, thus elevating the former score possibly somewhat artificially. Interestingly enough, however, these stories accurately reflect the most potent concern of the very group that was crucial in modernizing Turkey—namely, the young army officers under Ataturk who spearheaded the modernization movement in the late 1920's. Certainly they had a strong concern for achievement for their country, which frequently expressed itself in terms of power imagery since they were after all military men. In the second place, the Turkish *n* Achievement score may be somewhat higher than normal for the country as a whole because, as Bradburn has shown, Turkish educators tend individually to have higher *n* Achievement scores than comparable groups in other occupations, particularly business.[10] Thus they may have injected more concern for achievement into the stories than would be typical for other high-level occupational groups in the country.

Nevertheless, even with these cautions in mind, the fact remains that the difference in *n* Achievement score between Turkey and Iran is so great that even allowing for some overestimation in Turkey would not change the basic conclusion. The concern for achievement is measurably higher in Turkey than in Iran, a fact which may account at least in part for their differing rates of economic growth since high *n* Achievement normally promotes faster economic growth.[11]

[10] N. M. Bradburn, "The Managerial Role in Turkey: A Psychological Study," unpublished doctoral dissertation, Harvard University, 1960.
[11] McClelland, Chapter 3.

Table 2 also presents the scores on two other motivational variables for which all the national samples of stories were scored in *The Achieving Society*. The need for Affiliation score reflects the frequency with which the stories mentioned concern for establishing, maintaining, or repairing friendly relations among individuals. In even simpler terms, it reflects an interest in people and a concern to be on friendly relations with them. In the countries studied the *n* Affiliation score turned out to have an interesting though slightly complicated relationship to the birth rate.[12] Since rate of population growth is normally considered by economists and sociologists to be related to rate of economic growth, it is important to see how *n* Affiliation enters the picture.

To oversimplify a little, a high *n* Affiliation score is associated with a low birth rate when infant mortality is high, and with a high birth rate when infant mortality is low. The explanation seems simple: in both instances people with high *n* Affiliation like babies or big families, but presumably they do not like to see babies die. Thus, when the risk to an infant's life is fairly high, parents with high *n* Affiliation will observe that babies do die often and will consequently have fewer babies and take better care of them. On the other hand, after modern public health measures have been introduced and the risk of death to children is greatly reduced, they will tend to indulge their natural liking for children and will have as many as they want, unchecked by the fear of not being able to care for them very well. What this has meant in the past generation is that the birth rate declines less in countries high in *n* Affiliation as they move into a period of greatly improved public health. On the other hand, countries low in *n* Affiliation, which are more careless in the production of children, show a sharper drop in the birth rate as public health improves. That is, when public health standards are low, they over-produce children in the expectation that a certain proportion of them will die, but once this expectation is removed, they do not have sufficient interest in children as such to go on producing large numbers of them.

Both Turkey and Iran, but particularly Iran, are low in the need for Affiliation. So birth rates are high in both countries in what might be called the "careless over-production" pattern. Medical care is still quite poor by Western standards, as the figures in Table 1 show, but it has improved enough to cut the death rate, which means that the net reproduction rate for the moment in both countries is quite high (Table 1). That is, both countries are in a transitional period where

[12] *Ibid.*, Chapter 5.

people have not yet learned that they do not need to over-produce babies in order to have a sufficient number of survivors. Such an interpretation is the normal one among demographers, but the *n* Affiliation scores add something new. They predict that, as far as these countries are concerned, continued improvement in public health will lead to a sharp drop in the birth rate, much sharper than if they had high *n* Affiliation scores, because their people are simply not that interested in people or in babies. By way of contrast, Israel, which has a high *n* Affiliation score, a high birth rate, and low death rate, should go on having a high net reproduction rate much longer than either Turkey or Iran if public health continues to improve greatly in the latter two countries. In short, the motivational analysis suggests that the population problem is not likely to become extremely serious in economic terms for either country over the long run, especially since neither country is densely populated at the present time.

Table 2 also gives the scores for *n* Power, the concern to control another person's behavior or tell him what to do. Among the countries examined in *The Achieving Society* those whose stories were both high in *n* Power and low in *n* Affiliation were governed almost without exception by dictatorial or totalitarian regimes. Countries showing this pattern included Russia, both in 1925 and 1950, Germany in 1925 (shortly before Hitler), Japan before Tojo, Argentina at the time of Peron, and Spain both in the earlier and later periods under Franco. Since almost none of over forty countries with democratic or non-totalitarian regimes showed this pattern, its presence in stories from a country is almost a sure sign of totalitarian trends in the country. What the finding apparently means is that certain elites in the country, in particular the governing elites, want to have their own way (high *n* Power) and do not care enough about other people (low *n* Affiliation) to avoid treating them ruthlessly if need be.

A country can be high in *n* Power, as the United States is at the present time, but so long as it is high in *n* Affiliation, as the United States is, it apparently avoids enforcing its desires for control in a way that tramples on the rights and wishes of individuals. Contrariwise, a country may be low in *n* Affiliation and consequently not care very much what it does to individuals, but it may not have a sufficiently high power drive to crush and kill off the opposition. Such is the case with Turkey. Its readers show both a low *n* Affiliation and a low *n* Power, and it has behaved toward the deposed members of the Menderes regime as these facts would have predicted. They have not been treated in a particularly careful fashion so far as the rights of the individual are concerned (nor for that matter, were they respectful of the rights of the individual when they were in power); but they have not been ruthlessly exterminated or sent to concentration camps as they doubtless would have been in either Russia or Germany. The case is quite different in Iran, whose stories show the totalitarian pattern—low n Affiliation and moderately high n Power. On the basis of findings with other countries, one would have to predict a bloody future for Iran. The mood is an authoritarian one. Either the Shah will succeed in suppressing opposition by force, or he will be "suppressed" by a revolutionary force. (Interestingly enough, the same totalitarian pattern appeared in the children's stories from neighboring Iraq—except that the n Power score was much more elevated, and Iraq, of course, has just had one of the bloodiest revolutions in recent history.)

What this motivational combination apparently reflects is a mood in Iran, or at least among significant elites in the country, which supports violence as a solution to difficulties. It does not predict what kind of totalitarianism will prevail—whether of the right or the left, for example—or whether the Shah will continue in power or whether he will be overthrown. It only suggests that whoever rules will do so ruthlessly, or be overthrown by a stronger counterforce. The mood of the people at present supports totalitarian rather than democratic methods of dealing with political problems. So far as economic development is concerned, the motivational analysis suggests that, while there is not the generally high n Achievement needed to promote it, a few people at the top might develop an overriding concern for it that they could enforce ruthlessly. At least, something like this apparently happened in Russia in the 1920's, when its children's readers showed a pattern almost identical to that of Iran today. The ruling Russian elite at the time had a strong concern for economic development growing out of Communist ideology, and, by a variety of dictatorial measures from forced industrialization to forced liquidation of peasant holdings, they succeeded in accelerating the pace of Russia's economic growth despite the generally low level of n Achievement in Russia. The difficulty is, of course, that the Iranian ruling elite has not shown anything like the zealous dedication to economic goals that has normally characterized Communist party elites.

One other finding in *The Achieving Society* is relevant to our comparative case analysis. Not only were stories from more rapidly developing economies higher in *n* Achievement; they also mentioned more often a type of relationship to others which is fairly adequately summarized by the term "other-directedness."[13] The issue here is not how much initiative or achievement drive an individual in the story shows, but how he is described as conforming to the demands of society. Three coding categories define this variable, as shown in Table 3.

TABLE 3: PERCENTAGES OF 21 TURKISH AND 21 IRANIAN
CHILDREN'S STORIES (1950) SHOWING CHARACTERISTICS
RELATED TO "OTHER-DIRECTEDNESS" AND THEIR
RELATIVE RANK AMONG SAMPLES
FROM 40 COUNTRIES

Stories Showing	TURKEY	Rank	IRAN	Rank
A. Pressure from tradition	12.5%	24.5	33.3%	10
B. Conformity pressure from peers	56.3	13.5	55.8	15
C. Social demand effective for getting conformity	47.6	9	42.9	15
Total "other-directedness" rank (B + C − A)		8		21

A person can conform or do what he is supposed to largely for traditional reasons. In such cases the story often does not even make it very explicit why a child (for example) is good, obedient, loyal, or cooperative. He just *is*, presumably because that is the way children should be. Similarly, people act not so much in an individual as in an institutional capacity—as a judge, a saint, a butcher, a baker, or a candlestick maker. In sociological terminology they simply act out their institutional roles. As Table 3 makes clear, more of the Iranian than Turkish stories show individuals interacting in a traditional or institutional manner. The alternative method of describing interaction is to show it as a specific response to pressure from a particular other individual. Scoring categories B and C in Table 3 represent two aspects of this process. On the one hand, the pressure can come from a peer, as opposed to a superior or a subordinate (category B), and on the other hand, it can be described as effective in the form of a simple demand or request (category C), as opposed either to being ineffective or as requiring some additional reward or punishment to be

[13] See D. Riesman, with N. Glazer and R. Denny, *The Lonely Crowd*, New Haven, Yale University Press, 1950.

effective. Categories B and C combined represent *effective public opinion* or a kind of "other-directedness" in which the individual does what his peers either ask or insist that he do. Stories from countries developing more rapidly economically mentioned traditional types of interaction less often and peer-directed conformity more often,[14] just as the Turkish stories do in contrast to those from Iran. So we have discovered another reason why Turkey may be developing more rapidly than Iran: the Turks place greater stress on "other-directedness," which is typical of societies that develop more rapidly.

Since the other-directedness rank is quite unrelated to the *n* Achievement score of a country, the reason for its relationship to economic development must be sought elsewhere. An explanation is not hard to find. A country that wants to modernize rapidly is faced by two key problems: on the one hand, it must discover a source of energy or devoted commitment to realizing economic goals; and on the other hand, it must break with traditional ways of doing things and promote new social norms. If *n* Achievement solves the first problem, then "other-directedness" can be viewed as the means of solving the second. For modernization implies change, breaking with traditional religious or social institutions. Specifically, in Turkey it has meant such things as abolition of the fez, more nearly equal rights for women, the disestablishment of Islam, and a new type of government.

However, breaking with old ways of doing things is not enough: it may simply leave people confused as to how they should behave. What takes the place of tradition in countries that have modernized rapidly is public opinion as organized and presented by various means of mass communication—radios, newspapers, or public address systems. People can be told by these means what the new social norms are, and they can be encouraged constantly to follow them—e.g., to give women more nearly equal rights, to encourage bright boys and girls to continue in school, to shift one's loyalty from the immediate kin group to the nation, to separate religious from civil authority. The extent to which public opinion has become an effective force for spreading new social norms is apparently reflected in the children's readers by the frequency with which the stories describe people who conform because of pressures from others like themselves (i.e., peers). The way the stories are written reflects the importance of public opinion in the country. In Turkey the stories stress this type of other-directed reliance on public opinion more than in Iran; and, as would be expected from this fact, its mass media are better organized and more in a position to influence people. That is, in Turkey more people are literate and can read the newspapers; a larger proportion is becoming literate in the primary schools; newspaper circulation is five times as great as in Iran; and there are nearly ten times as many radios. (See Table I and the current *United Nations Statistical Yearbook*.) Both aspects of public opinion are important for economic development—namely, the psychological willingness to pay attention to it, or "other-directedness," and the physical means of making sure that the people get exposed to it—the mass media. To put it in a nutshell, what Iran, and to a lesser extent Turkey, needs to promote rapid modernization is a good five-cent battery-operated radio and a government willing to broadcast programs that present the social norms of a modern society.

Hopefully even such a cursory analysis has been enough to illustrate how quantitative measures of national psychological characteristics can be useful in understanding and predicting political, social, or economic trends for a country. However, a certain air of mystery surrounds the procedure that should be dispelled so far as possible. After all, it seems strange or even absurd that one should be able to get significant clues from the content of third-grade readers as to future political or economic developments in a country. Some social scientists, to say nothing of policy experts, will undoubtedly find it difficult to take children's stories as seriously as they take national budget accounts, military adventures, or political victories, no matter how many statistical tests are conjured up to demonstrate the usefulness of data based on such stories. A perfectly natural assumption would be that the character of children's literature is trivial and unrelated to important matters of national life. So we must do the best we can to explain why figures based on children's stories should be taken seriously.

The most obvious reason, of course, is that the figures work; that is, they do in fact predict general trends among groups of nations, and in particular cases like Turkey and Iran they do give a rational account of differences in national rates of economic growth. In fact, the faith in the stories increases in almost direct proportion to the amount of time one has spent studying the scores based on them and relating them to particular trends in the countries concerned. Over and over again, one is impressed by how accurately the stories reflect important trends in the country. Several examples have already been given; e.g., the salience of the "bravery in battle" theme in the Turkish stories as diagnostic of the importance of the military junta in the modernization of Turkey. Many others could be cited.

Nevertheless, empirical demonstrations are not by themselves wholly convincing. How is it that the stories turn out to be so useful? An answer would seem to require two basic assumptions. The first is that what is on people's minds in a country, what they spend their time thinking about and planning, ultimately determines what they spend their time doing. If they spend their time thinking about and planning for achievement, they will put themselves in situations where they can get achievement satisfaction. For theoretical reasons too complex to review here, they get such satisfaction most readily through expansion of business which involves moderate risk, concrete knowledge of results, personal accountability, and other factors making a sense of personal achievement more likely. If they spend their time thinking about establishing good relations with other people, they will act in ways that respect other people, and so on. The second assumption is that children's readers tell us what is on the minds of some significant elites in a country.

The first assumption probably does not need much defense among social scientists or the man in the street, although it might among psychologists. Most people accept as fairly good common sense that, in broad general terms, what people spend their time thinking about determines what they do. But the second assumption requires some justification. Why should people who write stories for children inject into them what "significant elites" in that particular country are concerned with? Why aren't educators more concerned with children's needs and interests, for example?

One might naively assume from looking at collections of children's stories from all over the world published in the United States that stories for children are child-centered and pretty much the same the world over. As a matter of fact, such collections are carefully screened so as to include only those stories considered appropriate for an American audience. Certain popular stories from Grimm's fairy-tales are normally rewritten in the United States to remove much of the cruelty and physical aggression present in the originals. Even greater care is exercised by a culture in selecting stories for use in a public school. Educational authorities everywhere seem concerned to make sure that children read what is considered normal, right, and proper. Although many different kinds of stories may be written in a country (or read in educated families), only those are chosen for public school textbooks that are considered representative of the way people usually think in that country. The point can be documented in many ways. For example, only one of twenty-one Turkish stories and one of twenty-one Iranian stories has a girl as the central character. On a worldwide basis, boys are more often the heroes in stories than girls, but usually by a ratio of three or four to one, not twenty to one.[15] Since it is well documented that males are overwhelmingly dominant in Moslem culture, the stories accurately reflect the cultural norm as to the relative importance of the two sexes in these two countries. In both countries the single story about a girl is the same one. It tells how a simple little girl comes to ask a wise old man for an ember to carry to her mother to start their fire. He is surprised because she has nothing to carry it in but her bare hands. She demonstrates how it can be done by putting ashes under the ember in her hands. The moral seems to be that women, like dogs, sometimes surprise you by how clever they are.

Similarly, the importance of charity as one of the "pillars" of Islam is well known, and stories from both countries stress charity as a key virtue. In an Iranian story some wounded soldiers are suffering from thirst, lying in the desert after a battle. A little water becomes available, but each of them refuses it, saying that it should be given to a wounded comrade. In the end they all die, but the nobility of their charitable behavior is obviously the moral to be drawn from the tale. In a Turkish story a little boy who is poorly clothed in winter suffers so much from the cold that his feet become frozen. A poor old woman who is no relation of his and has very little herself nevertheless finds a pair of shoes to give him. Later he grows up to be a famous man (in a Turkish version of the Horatio Alger theme), seeks out the old woman, and rewards her with gold. It is difficult to imagine that the people who write such stories for children, or the educational authorities who select them for inclusion in children's textbooks, are consciously motivated by a desire to pick what is typical or representative of their cultural norms. Nevertheless, they do so more or less unconsciously probably because they are, after all, members of the culture and think as other members of the culture do, and also because they are charged with the responsibility of bringing up

[15] See I. L. Child, E. H. Potter, and E. M. Levine, "Children's Textbooks and Personality Development: An Exploration in the Social Psychology of Education," *Psychological Monograph*, 60, No. 3, 1946.

children to think and behave "normally"—that is, in the way that other adults in the culture approve.

The fact that educators know more or less unconsciously what is proper in a story for children can be illustrated by their reactions to stories used to teach children to read in another culture. For example, most American educators, primary schoolteachers, and even parents of young children regard themselves as quite broadminded about what kind of stories they consider appropriate for their children. Furthermore, stories from other lands are viewed favorably in the United States. Nevertheless, when Americans read stories that every school child, say, in certain North African countries like Algeria and Tunisia reads, they are shocked. They are disturbed by the inclusion of a number of themes which they consider inappropriate for young children—to take just one example, death openly and explicitly described. In one such story a camel driver is walking across the desert with his old and faithful camel who has been his constant companion for many years. The camel suddenly collapses of old age, and the driver realizes that he will have to leave him there in the desert to die. There is a touching scene in which the man looks into the big eyes of his faithful friend and then, regretfully, with tears in his eyes, goes off and leaves him. But then the reader stays with the camel as he goes through the successive stages of his death agonies. It is a beautifully told story, but American educational authorities and parents regard it as quite unacceptable for public school use, though of course it might appear in a collection of stories to be bought in a bookstore. It is simply too "abnormal" or bizarre for Americans to accept. The example is by no means atypical. Educational authorities in one country commonly regard stories used in the public schools in other countries as inappropriate for their schools because different social norms are being presented. Even Aesop's fables, which are widely diffused throughout children's textbooks from many lands, are rewritten so that they express somewhat different values in different countries. The ultimate proof is, of course, the fact that countries vary quantitatively in the stress they place on achievement, affiliation, power, and other matters.[16]

Nevertheless, while stories in children's textbooks may on the average reflect characteristic thinking in a country more or less unconsciously, they need not always do so. It is for this reason that we spoke above of what was on the minds of some significant elites in a

[16] McClelland, Chapter 3.

country. Large, complex modern nations are not like simple, unified cultures. They are usually a congeries of sub-cultures among which values may differ in important particulars. So it might happen that one or the other of the sub-cultures runs the educational system while still another runs the economy or the army.

To consider only the most obvious examples, what happens when the educational system of a nation is dominated by a foreign power, as in the case of a colony, or by a militant internal minority, as in the case of countries run by Communist parties? In such instances stories in the children's readers might very well be unrepresentative for a country as a whole. In fact, it is surprising that such anomalies did not arise often enough to destroy the general relationship found between indices based on the children's stories and rates of national economic growth for such countries. If they had arisen very often, the significant correlations reported in *The Achieving Society* between the two types of measures could not have been obtained. The explanation probably lies in the fact that in countries in which the school systems were dominated by unrepresentative minorities, those same minorities also controlled the government and the economy. In this sense, since they were the significant elite, what was on their minds as they told stories to children was diagnostic also of the way they would guide the economic and political life of the country. A significant elite can be either democratic, as in the United States, where cultural norms are widely shared by educational, government, and business elites, or dictatorial, as in Russia in the 1920's, when the Communist party elite promoted values in the children's textbooks which may have been very unrepresentative for the country as a whole but which, nevertheless, were diagnostic of the direction in which the country was going to move because the same Communist elite controlled other sectors of the national life.

Reader data may not be representative in cases between these two extremes, however. Turkey provides a good illustration. As we mentioned earlier, testing of individuals by Bradburn strongly suggests that *n* Achievement levels may be higher among educators than among businessmen in Turkey for peculiar internal reasons to be discussed below. Even more significant, younger Turkish businessmen have lower *n* Achievement than older Turkish businessmen who may have been more under the influence of the revolutionary ideals of Ataturk's day. Thus they apparently do not have the same spirit of enterprise as the older men do, and consequently the rapid rate of growth of the

Turkish economy in the 1950's may slow down significantly ten years from now, when the younger men get into positions of business leadership. Yet if the estimate of national n Achievement level based on children's stories was taken at its face value and used blindly without such further knowledge to predict the future of the Turkish economy, quite a different conclusion would be reached—namely, that since Turkey has the highest level of n Achievement of any of the forty countries, it should have the most rapid rate of economic growth over the next decade. Obviously, generalizations based on average relationships over a number of countries cannot be applied so simple-mindedly to an individual case without further detailed study. Further study may show, as in the case of Turkey, that the reader data are unrepresentative. In fact, it may very well be the type of case—neither an extreme dictatorship nor a democracy based on a literate majority—in which reader data are most likely to be unrepresentative because different sub-cultural groups may get control over different segments of the society: the educational system, the economy, or the government.

Social scientists may be reassured to learn that a few psychological statistics are no substitute for the kind of detailed knowledge they have specialized in acquiring for particular countries. Quite the contrary. The psychological information should be simply added to the general fund of information that an expert has on a country and used by him as he uses other facts in forming his over-all judgment or policy recommendations. Psychological findings do not replace other knowledge. In fact, they must be evaluated in terms of that other knowledge, just as that other knowledge must be evaluated in terms of them. In the social science of the future, economic development of a country must be understood not only in terms of such economic variables as rate of capital formation but also in terms of n Achievement levels (which apparently affect incremental capital-output ratios). Neither economic nor psychological variables by themselves are sufficient. Political developments will likewise have to be understood not only in terms of power relationships between various subsections of the society but also in terms of the motivational characteristics of those sub-groups and the presence or absence of the dictatorial motivational pattern described above. Such an approach blurs lines somewhat among various social science disciplines, but certainly at no cost to our understanding of such phenomena, which has been hindered by over-specialization.

The importance of more detailed information is nowhere more obvious than when one is trying to draw policy implications from social science analyses. Consider an obvious possible outcome of the above case study. Suppose some key members of the Iranian government read it and are sufficiently impressed to respond: "Well, suppose you are right. It looks as if Iran is developing less rapidly than Turkey, and let us assume for the sake of the argument that it has something to do with this psychological variable you call n Achievement. We would like to increase our rate of economic development. We have asked and received advice from all sorts of experts—economists, engineers, technical assistance advisors, and so on. It doesn't seem to have been particularly effective. What does the psychologist recommend?" The psychologist might be flattered at being asked such a question, but he should be extremely cautious about answering it, most particularly because he has so little knowledge of the economic and political institutions of the two countries. Yet despite my own lack of knowledge, I feel under some compulsion to show how the question might be answered, because what is most important at this stage is to demonstrate how psychological knowledge of the sort presented above can be useful in making policy recommendations if added to other kinds of information. The illustration will have to be lacking in depth and detail because of my lack of experience in the two countries, but perhaps it will serve its general didactic purpose.

Let us start with the question of why n Achievement level is so low in Iran. Here we are fortunately on pretty firm ground empirically. Several research studies have shown that authoritarian fathers usually tend to produce sons with low n Achievement.[17] Families in Middle Eastern cultures, according to Islamic tradition, are strongly dominated by the father.[18] Some Turks reported to Bradburn that they escaped paternal control only when their fathers died. The reason why such dominance regularly leads to low n Achievement is that the son does not learn to set his own achievement goals and to learn to find his own ways of achieving them. He is told what to do and learns to be obedient and responsible. Since fathers are no less authoritarian in Iran than elsewhere in Islamic Middle Eastern cultures, this traditional way of organizing family life is, in all probability, responsible for the low level of n Achievement in Iran. The

[17] *Ibid.*, Chapter 9.
[18] See for example E. T. Prothro and L. Melikian, "The California Public Opinion Scale in an Authoritarian Culture," *Public Opinion Quarterly*, 17, 1953, pp. 353-362.

interesting question then is: How did the Turks escape the effects of this type of family, since they too are a Middle Eastern country solidly within Islamic tradition? The answer should provide some policy guidelines to Iran if that country wants to raise its general level of n Achievement and accelerate its rate of economic development. Since in many respects, as we pointed out earlier, Turkey was very similar to Iran thirty or forty years ago, the changes Turkey introduced may be those which are more feasible in the general Middle Eastern type of Moslem culture.

What happened in Turkey to undermine the power of authoritarian fathers and promote national achievement aspirations may be conveniently discussed under two headings—institutional changes and ideological changes. On the institutional side, many of Ataturk's reforms had the indirect effect of diminishing the males' authority. He abolished the fez, traditional symbol of male dignity. He separated church and state so that, at least symbolically, marriage was governed by civil rather than Islamic law. He gave more rights to women than they had ever had. To be sure, these changes were effective, if at all, only in the cities. Even today they are not much honored in rural areas. Nevertheless, it became generally known all over the country that new norms were being promoted in the cities, and young people, if they were discontent, could always leave home and go to the city and learn the new ways.

Furthermore, emancipation of boys was promoted by at least two important social institutions—the army and the village institutes (now converted into teacher training colleges). The army helped a son to get out from under an autocratic father in two ways. If either a father or his son goes into the army, the son escapes his father's absolute control. In fact, one of the curious side effects of a prolonged war in which many authoritarian fathers are called into the army is that a generation of sons may grow up with less than normal paternal control because the fathers are away so much or are killed in battle. At any rate, there are a number of suggestive instances, mentioned in *The Achieving Society*, in which the n Achievement level of a country characterized by strong father dominance, like Germany, goes up after a prolonged war. Even in peacetime, if the army is a strong, prestigeful institution which drafts every able-bodied male into service for considerable periods of time, opportunities for sons to escape their fathers' control are considerably increased. Such has certainly been the case in Turkey to a greater extent than in Iran. The Turkish army spearheaded the modernization movement and has remained a large and important social institution which drafts all ablebodied young men even to this day. In fact, one reason for rapid urbanization in Turkey today is said to be the unwillingness of young Turks to return after their army service to the villages where they will be under strict paternal control.

The village institutes were another means by which young boys in the villages could escape their fathers. Bright young boys from various villages were selected at the age of fourteen and sent way to these institutes to be trained at government expense to become future teachers. This very probably explains the higher *n* Achievement level among teachers recorded by Bradburn. He found in three different samples in Turkey that men who had left home by the age of fourteen, or whose fathers had died or left home, tended on the average to have higher *n* Achievement than men who had continued to live at home in the normal social pattern. In other words, Turkish boys who escaped their authoritarian fathers had higher average levels of *n* Achievement, and at least two Turkish social institutions—the army and the village institutes—to say nothing of the lures of modern city life, made it distinctly easier for them to make their escape. If Iran wants to increase its *n* Achievement level, it could take a leaf from Turkey's book and find ways of putting boys in their middle teens into a youth corps that would remove them from traditional home influences and create in them a sense of national purpose.

The ideological changes that took place in Turkey can best be traced by comparing the children's stories from the two countries. A traditional value in Middle Eastern culture is an almost fanatical loyalty to one's master. In Iran, for example, textbooks include a story which describes the extreme faithfulness of a dog. One day a villager goes to a city and sells his goods. He ties his money in a bag on the back of his horse and starts off for home with his dog following faithfully behind. Suddenly the dog runs in front of the horse, barking and carrying on so wildly that the man cannot proceed. He tries to calm or control the dog, is completely unsuccessful, decides the dog must be mad, and finally cuts his throat with much regret. The dog keeps barking, but 'more and more feebly, and the man rides on and leaves him. Finally he looks back and sees that the dog is dead, but also that his bag of money is missing. It had fallen off; the loyal dog had kept trying to call it to his attention even though it meant in the end that he was killed for his act of devotion. The master is very sad and touched by such extreme loyalty, as presumably is the child who reads the story.

In Turkey the same theme appears more often in stories, but with a significantly different emphasis. For example, a boy of thirteen who is carrying shells on board ship during a furious battle with the enemy suddenly feels dizzy and weak and lets one drop overboard. His father, who is the captain of the ship, whips him in a fury of rage, raising huge welts on his bare back. (Parenthetically, one can imagine the reaction of American educational authorities or parents to the inclusion of such an episode in a public-school textbook!) The boy does not say a word. "He did not even stumble. He stood erect. He looked at his protector, at his father, with his innocent eyes. A sweet smile spread over his handsome face, 'Father, was the whip necessary to remind me of my duty?' said he." Then, to the consternation of all on board, he throws himself into the sea; but he manages to find the shell which he had dropped and is pulled by three sailors back onto the deck, to the tremendous relief of his father and everyone else who witnesses the episode. Like the faithful dog, he is willing to sacrifice his life for his master, but the context is different: the father's anger and the boy's sacrificial loyalty occur in time of war, when the whole nation is involved. In other words, in Turkey loyalty and bravery are treated in a patriotic context. It is as if the Turks had capitalized on the traditional Middle Eastern value placed on loyalty, but switched its object from the individual master to the nation. The story nicely illustrates how the Turks manage to change or extend the object of one's loyalty; the boy's act of devotion is simultaneously for his father's and his country's sake.

The virtue of this ideological shift is that it tends to undermine somewhat the father's absolute authority by supplanting it with a larger, institutional loyalty and that it creates a sense of nationhood completely missing in the stories from Iran. Both changes promote the development of n Achievement in boys—the former by decreasing father dominance ideologically, and the latter by setting a high level of achievement aspiration for the country as a whole. Furthermore, patriotism tends to promote a concern for the country as a whole, or loyalty to the "generalized other," which favors the development of "other-directedness," which is the other psychological variable associated with more rapid economic development. So, again to judge by Turkey's example, Iran should stress ideologically patriotism and a high sense of national purpose if it wants to develop more rapidly in the economic sphere.

Another important theme in Middle Eastern culture centers in the value placed on cleverness, trickery, or outwitting another person. To Westerners it often seems to involve downright dishonesty or lying, but as the stories from Iran make very clear, it is viewed as a positive virtue in the Middle East.[19] In over two-thirds of the stories from Iran trickery is the main theme. Typical is the tale of the cruel governor who one day goes on a walk in the countryside. He comes across a peasant and asks him if he knows his governor. The peasant replies that he certainly does, that the governor is oppressive, bloodthirsty, wicked, and tyrannical. "Aha," says the governor, "then you don't recognize me? I am your ruler." Quick as a wink, the peasant replies, "Aha, then you don't recognize me? I am one of those people who go crazy three days a year, and this is one of those days for me." The governor is so amused that he forgives him and leaves him alone. The moral is clear: use your wits to get out of trouble. In another story a man has a very bad temper and keeps blowing up all the time. A friend sends him some medicine and suggests that he take it every time he feels like blowing up. He does, and cures his bad temper. Finally he asks his friends what was in the medicine. The friend replies that it was nothing but pure water, that taking the time to take the medicine was sufficient to calm him down and cure him of his bad temper. Finally, in still another story, a man has a horse with bad habits that he cannot control, so he sells it. The buyer quite naturally comes back in a short while, complaining that whenever he wants to ride, the horse goes backwards. The seller says, "There is an easy solution to that: put the tail of the horse in the direction you want to go."

From these examples it is easy to see how the theme can have a very positive, humorous connotation in the Middle East and yet be regarded by Westerners as promoting dishonesty and intrigue. For honor goes to the man who can outwit his opponent by fair means or foul. In Turkey the traditional theme of trickery is still present, but it is modified in the direction of positive achievement. For example, in one story a young man gets a job with a business firm by saying that he wants wages of only one cent the first day, two cents the second, four cents the third, doubling the amount every day from then on until the end of the month. The firm thinks that it has made

---

[19] See also Gastil, *op.cit.*

a very good deal and hires him on this basis. At the end of the month he presents the bill for his wages, which comes to over $10 million, to everyone's shock and dismay. However, all ends well because the young man explains that he only wanted to demonstrate how smart he is with figures and how qualified he is for a good position in the firm. He outwits them—not to take advantage of them or to get out of trouble, but to pursue a realistic achievement goal for himself.

So the Turks have changed the significance of trickery so that it can contribute to long-range personal achievement. The Iranians might do likewise if they are interested in increasing their national n Achievement level. Furthermore, emphasis on outwitting other people has implications for social relations as well as for personal achievement. Looked at from the viewpoint of the person being outwitted, it strongly implies that people are not to be trusted, that everyone is out to "get" you. There is certainly no support here for the valuing of the opinion of others that we found regularly associated with more rapid economic development. Quite the contrary. You must never trust the opinions of others for the simple reason that they are out to "get" you, to trick and deceive you, or injure you in some way. It is hard to see how the Iranians can learn to trust public opinion so long as they view the motives of other people with such suspicion.

Again, it is instructive to note how the Turks have modified the traditional Middle Eastern view of authority, or the way society or government affects the lives of individuals. The traditional view is nicely illustrated by an Iranian story in which two boys fall to arguing over who should get a walnut they find. They finally call on a passer-by to serve as a judge in the classic Moslem tradition. He gives one half of the shell to one boy, the other half to the other boy, and eats the kernel himself as his wages for deciding the dispute. The moral must be clear, even to third-grade children: authority is bad; government is bad; society in the abstract is bad; it only exploits the individual and steals from him. In no sense can the "generalized other," the government, or public opinion serve as an important source of morality, of guidance in learning what to do. The best strategy is to stay out of its way altogether.

In Turkey the theme is still present but modified in a socially useful direction. Other people are still out to "get" you, but not to exploit you. Rather, they will act for your own good, to correct your bad or foolish behavior. For example, a lazy child is sitting down, supposedly reading his lessons for school, but with the book upside down; he falls asleep, and his head droops down to form a wonderful target for a passing goat, which promptly butts him. Society, in the form of the goat, will "get" you if you don't watch out; it may even hurt you a little, but it will be for your own good. You shouldn't be lazy or foolish, but should stay awake and study your lessons. Thus cleverness is used not so much to exploit someone but to teach him how to behave properly. In another story a fox observes a bear eating a horse he had killed; the fox creeps up and tries to steal some meat for himself. The bear catches him but instead of killing him, decides to teach him a lesson by asking him whether he would like to catch a horse for himself. The fox is delighted to get off so easily and to learn such a trick. So the bear tells him that the next time he sees a horse lying down, he should creep up behind the horse, tie his tail to the horse's tail, and then bite him hard. The fox tries it, gets kicked hard by the horse and dragged through the woods, bumping from side to side to the great amusement of a passing rabbit.

This story points a very important moral. If you try something dishonest, the authorities will trick and shame you into good behavior. The story concludes that the fox never went near a horse again. There is no such moral tone in the Iranian stories. The boys squabbling over the walnut do not learn that they should not squabble over walnuts or that authority will step in to teach them a lesson. Instead they learn that if they get involved with authority it will step in and steal from both of them. The distinction is important so far as learning other-directedness is concerned. From the Turkish story one can learn that outsiders, or authorities, can act to influence one for his own good. The "other" becomes a source of morality rather than of exploitation. Public opinion should therefore be listened to with respect. It is for this reason that other-directedness is greater in Turkey than in Iran (see Table 3). What we learn from such stories is that the Turks took the traditional Middle Eastern delight in trickery and cleverness and modified it in a socially useful direction by making sure that it contributes to conformity and public morality. Again, it should not be difficult for the Iranians to make a similar reinterpretation of their traditional pleasure in trickery if they want to promote economic development.

Thus the psychologist's knowledge might prove useful in formulating recommendations for national policy. He can suggest to the Turks that they find some way of increasing the n Achievement level of their younger businessmen. He can suggest to the Iranians that perhaps they should establish a youth corps to get young men away from their fathers and to promote nationalistic goals of high achievement; that they should spend more money on the mass media to develop the power of public opinion; and that the messages they send via the media—including the school books—should modify the traditional theme of loyalty to one's master into loyalty to one's country, and the theme of tricking and exploiting others into tricking them in the interest of honest personal achievement and public morality. To be sure, many more questions need to be considered. Who will carry out these policies? Is it correct to picture authority in the mass media as a source of public morality if, in fact, government officials are venal and corrupt? And so on. The only point I am trying to make here is that the psychologist's advice, like the economist's or the political scientist's, can be useful if taken in conjunction with other knowledge.

The approach sketched in this paper has research as well as policy implications. If the generalizations across countries made in *The Achieving Society* are useful as applied here, behavioral scientists should get to work and discover more such generalizations. Studying national characteristics by public opinion surveys, while useful when possible, has proved difficult because of the lack of survey organizations and of its great expense.[20] Content analysis of representative "symbol systems" from a culture is much less expensive and can be carried out at a distance for a large number of countries at once. It could certainly be used to discover what national psychological characteristics have been associated with such important variables as speed of urbanization, political stability, spread of medical care, development of technical science, military aggressiveness, etc. There is no reason at all why these problems could not be attacked by the method used in *The Achieving Society*, and if the results obtained in that book are typical, one can anticipate a rich yield of research findings from applying the method further.

Another type of investigation centers not in establishing generalizations across the countries but in carrying out more detailed psychological investigations within a given country, much as Bradburn did in Turkey. Here such questions as the following would arise: What is the relationship between levels of motivation as assessed in children's textbooks and in other types of verbal or written material, like folk tales, letters to the editor, or public speeches? What is the relationship between indices obtained from public documents and from sam-

[20] See H. H. Hyman, A. Payaslioğlu, and F. W. Frey, "The Values of Turkish College Youth," *Public Opinion Quarterly*, 22, 1958, pp. 275-291.

ples of individuals tested to represent different occupational groups—farmers, soldiers, businessmen, or government officials? Are there age or sex differences in levels of motivation? How do the indices obtained from content analysis of various types of verbal material change from year to year? If one were interested keenly in a particular country like Communist China, one could monitor the textbooks for children year by year to discover what changes, if any, were taking place in various motivational or other indices. The possibilities for assessing intra-national variations in values or motives by such methods are almost endless.

Finally, the true behavioral scientist cannot help wanting to try an experiment even at the national level. The ultimate test of a hypothesis is always an experiment. Nowadays many nations as a matter of public policy, and both national and international organizations, are trying to help underdeveloped countries to achieve either rapid economic development or political stability. Why would it not be possible to persuade one of these organizations to choose two countries that are matched in every way possible and to try, for example, to raise the n Achievement level in one, while the other is treated in more traditional ways, to see which of the two countries develops more rapidly economically? If a high level of n Achievement facilitates economic development, policies focused directly on increasing n Achievement should accelerate the rate of economic growth more than aid policies not specifically focused on this objective. With so many countries in the world currently seeking rapid modernization, and with so many different agencies trying to help them, it should not be impossible to find a way to carry out such an experiment over a five- or ten-year period. The psychologist would like to see what the effect would be of this kind of investment in human motivational capital as contrasted with more traditional investments in material capital—or even in technical skills. Whatever the outcome of such an experiment, it would contribute to our knowledge of how group psychological characteristics are related to the behavior of complex social organizations like nation-states. No behavioral science territory has been less explored empirically, and no knowledge is more greatly needed today. Research inquiry into national character is in its infancy, but, after having been rejected as nearly impossible, it may now have taken one or two steps toward being reinstated as both feasible on a large scale and worthwhile.

CHAPTER 11

NATION BUILDING AS A MANY-SIDED PROCESS

IN THE COURSE of this study we have examined different levels of the communications process and different dimensions of the modernization process. In moving from the formal structure of the mass media to the general and informal process of cultural diffusion and communications, and in treating both the conscious rational and the unconscious emotional ways in which transitional people learn about the modern world, we have sought to illuminate the many sides of the problem of political modernization and national development. We have sought to show how both the communications and the modernization processes can be broken down analytically and studied in considerable depth.

At each level of our analysis we have noted both problems and opportunities. Up to a certain point it is possible to conceive of the nation-building process as calling for strategies to grapple with these problems and to exploit these opportunities as they appear in their separate sectors. Much of policy planning must proceed from such intense but limited views of the total range of problems inherent in nation building. Indeed, in order to appreciate the full complexity of the nation-building process it is essential to bring together again all the separate parts of our analysis and see how they relate to each other. This can best be done within the context of a case study of a particular country.

Once the problem of communications and political development is approached on a country basis it soon becomes apparent that the various aspects of communications and social change can easily get out of pace and rhythm with each other and thus set in motion new waves of tensions which may create new dislocations. In the chapters which follow we shall examine ways in which such vicious circles can be prevented and more positive multiplier effects in the opposite direction may be realized.

It will be helpful to begin this aspect of our analysis by first turning directly to a case study in which all the communications patterns in a transitional society are brought out into the open. For our purpose there are great advantages in selecting a country which is not confronted with extreme problems and in which the impact of the modern world has not caused revolutionary or pathological reactions. On these and other grounds the choice of Thailand is readily justified.

CHAPTER 12

COMMUNICATION PATTERNS AND POLITICAL SOCIALIZATION IN TRANSITIONAL THAILAND

JAMES N. MOSEL

~-~

IN TRANSITIONAL societies the mass media system is the great secondary political socializer. In such societies a discontinuity arises between the political culture into which the child is inducted through socialization and the role demands of a modern political state. The strategies of action and the "calculus of power" learned through en-culturation tend to be incompatible with, or at least non-supportive to, the skills and attitudes required for political development. Under these conditions the learning of modern political roles must in part come from later adult experiences with the mass media system since this is a major purveyor of modern influences.

As an agent of political socialization the mass media system teaches its political lessons not only through the information it disseminates but also through the *way* in which people participate in the system. In enculturation the child learns his culture not only from the content of what is taught but also from his experiences with the method whereby it is taught. And so it is with communication systems. This indirect learning which comes as a by-product of the *way* in which one learns has been called "deutero learning" by Bateson.[1] Thus attitudes toward the communicator and habits for using and relating to information—as taught by the style of media participation—may sometimes have greater significance for political behavior than the content of the information itself. It would seem that deutero learning in mass media systems is controlled not by the media system alone but to some extent by the general culture in which the media system is imbedded.

The nature of the dependency of political socialization upon the mass media system varies according to the society. In countries where few if any traditional political roles have been available in socialization the society must start from scratch, and the communication system may provide the only mass training in modern political behavior.

---

[1] Gregory Bateson, "Social Planning and the Concept of Deutero-Learning," in T. M. Newcomb and E. L. Hartley, eds., *Readings in Social Psychology*, New York, 1957, pp. 121-128.

In such cases there has been a cultural break due to the imposition and withdrawal of colonialism; hence in studying the role of mass media as an agent of political socialization it is profitable to focus on the consequences of that break.

In Thailand, however, with its absence of colonial experience, a traditional political culture has long existed and continues to be reinforced through the socialization process. Thailand has suffered no traumatic break with its cultural past, no wholesale jettisoning of earlier behavioral forms, no forceful injection into its culture of discordant alien institutions. Instead there has been cultural continuity and persistence. Thus there is a genuine process of political socialization, but it is not supportive to effective political modernization. Rather, it continues to prepare citizens to behave effectively in a benign but absolute monarchy, and it does this with amazing success. While there is no discontinuity between political socialization and what the political community *is*, there is considerable inconsistency between political socialization and what the political community avowedly is striving to *become*. Consequently the modern mass media system of the Thai runs the risk of playing into the hands of the traditional political culture; instead of revising old roles it may actually help to perpetuate them.

I. Continuity and Cultural Change in Thailand

Thai cultural continuity can be largely attributed to three factors: a very loose role structure which has given Thai social organization considerable flexibility in accommodating to innovations from abroad, acculturation mechanisms which have been able to modify the traditional and reinterpret the new so that compatibility becomes possible, and an historical context of non-colonialism and enlightened leadership which has encouraged self-change without undue external interference. The result is that Thailand has been able to undertake modernization without incurring disruptive internal tensions arising from the disarticulation of the traditional and the modern. And while the society has thrived on change, it has also been able to preserve a curious kind of stability.

HISTORICAL CONTEXT

Thanks to its non-colonial status and the wisdom of its monarchs, Thailand has developed a "tradition of change" with the following characteristics:

(a) Change has been largely initiated from within the culture, not inserted from without by alien pressure. This has permitted a considerable degree of choice and control in the adaptation and re-interpretation of concepts, social roles, and techniques borrowed from abroad. While some changes have been initiated by foreigners, these have tended to be implemented through existing patterns of culture.[2]

(b) Change has been initiated and executed by the society's own *political* leadership; it was for the most part consciously planned and under their control.

(c) Change was made in response to leaders' own perceptions of the country's needs for the future, not in response to popular pressures and discontentments in the mass society.

(d) Planned change has been under way in Thailand for approximately one hundred years. This has created considerable ease in accommodating to change and promoted a balanced set of attitudes toward innovation. Expectations toward modernization are therefore more seasoned and modest, more inured against disenchantment.

(e) The fact that social change was not imposed from without via colonialism has greatly simplified Thai attitudes toward the Western content of modernism. Like other developing peoples, the Thai have adopted the West as a reference group for the new social roles required by a modernizing society, but there is very little of the emotional ambivalence and reaction-formation which so frequently characterizes ex-colonial peoples who have internalized the values of their colonial parent-surrogate and then experienced considerable guilt and uncertainty after the parent has been rebelled against and parental ties severed. Nor has there been any occasion for the Thai to confound their attitudes toward modernization and the West with their sentiments toward nationalism and political independence.

(f) Finally, the above factors have also simplified Thai attitudes toward the psychological self. The Thai do not suffer much from the ambiguous or double psychological identity which, as Pye[3] has observed, plagues identity-formation in the ex-colonial transitional man. The Thai do experience conflicts between traditional and modern modes of acting, but they tend to keep such conflicts at psychological

[2] Lucien M. Hanks, Jr., "Five Generalizations on the Structure of Foreign Contact—a Comparison of Two Periods in Thai History," in V. F. Ray, ed., *Cultural Stability and Cultural Change*, Proceedings of the Annual Spring Meeting of the American Ethnological Society, Seattle, Wash., 1957, pp. 72-75.

[3] Lucian W. Pye, *Politics, Personality and Nation Building*, New Haven, Yale University Press, 1962, pp. 42-56 and *passim*.

arms-length by relegating them to the level of role enactment, not the level of self-identity. Clinical studies conducted by the writer over a period of 18 months on 15 members of the Thai administrative elite reveal considerable ability in distinguishing between self and "modern" roles. By incorporating change into roles instead of self, many Thai are able to preserve self-identity while undergoing modernization.

SOCIOCULTURAL FACTORS: LOOSELY STRUCTURED ROLES

The most salient feature of the Thai culture is the extremely vague and undemanding character of its social roles. By social roles we mean society's expectations concerning the behavior to be displayed by the incumbent of a social status. Among the Thai such expectations are broad, ambiguous, and permit exceptional leeway for individuality and idiosyncrasy. The result is a lack of sharp role differentiation and a proliferation of role overlap. It is this lack of role clarity which is behind Embree's characterization of Thailand as a "loosely structured social system."[4]

Prediction of behavior under such circumstances is naturally difficult and fraught with uncertainty about the actions of others, factors which have placed a premium on wariness and concern for the motives of others. But the insecurities of such a system are effectively reduced by a set of Buddhist values which places high cultural emphasis on benevolence and respect toward all human beings, great tolerance for the autonomy of others, and strict control over aggressive behavior. The diffuseness and overlap in social roles have given the Thai great ease in role shifting and considerable skill in role empathy. Typically the Thai shows a relaxed flexibility in slipping from one role to another—as long as the roles are of the same status level.

While the Thai social system is loosely structured, it is not of course devoid of structure. The structural prerequisites to social order are provided mainly by a hierarchical status system in which it is possible to distinguish for almost any two persons a superior-subordinate relationship. Social organization occurs when subordinates can "lean" on superiors for benefits and resources which are reciprocated in terms of services and followership. The relationship is impermanent and fragile, and it is expected that it will shift opportunistically.

[4] John F. Embree, "Thailand—a Loosely Structured Social System," *American Anthropologist*, LII, 2, April-June 1950, pp. 181-193.

Whatever role clarity that exists is largely due to the respect and dependency prescriptions of such relationships. The limits of role behavior are so closely linked to status that one is tempted to say that there are only two well-defined roles: superior and subordinate. Skill in these two roles is the prime prerequisite for successful participation in the world of politics, government, religion, or rice farming. The socialization process provides considerable role continuity in that the child is effectively prepared to play these roles.

The status hierarchy itself has its origins in the 15th century, at which time it was a formal reality with technical embodiment in a code of laws.[5] As an aspect of cultural continuity it has persisted into modern times as an informal system based on cultural consensus; but it is just as real. Contrary to the usual expectations concerning traditional societies, recruitment to the statuses of the Thai hierarchy has always given generous recognition to universalistic or achievement criteria—a situation which has generated an appreciable amount of social movement up and down the status scale. This mobility has given the Thai a great ease in shifting "role personalities" which in turn has strengthened the ability to separate social role from self. Because social organization is defined vertically in terms of status, rather than laterally in terms of role differentiation, innovation and change have occurred most readily when change involved a lateral, not vertical, revision of role content.

ACCULTURATION MECHANISMS

The diffuse structure of Thai social roles has greatly facilitated the transitional process by offering no highly crystallized, rigid social organization which would resist change and innovation. Since there is so very little highly defined social structure to be threatened by change, we do not find the defensiveness of the traditional order which Lerner[6] observed in countries of the Middle East.

The same circumstances have also made it possible for the transitional process to preserve cultural continuity. When existing roles are loose and permissively defined, new functions and behavioral elements can be incorporated without violating the essential identity of the role. Thus very little social organization had to be "broken" to ac-

[5] James N. Mosel, "Thai Administrative Behavior," in W. J. Siffin, ed., *Toward the Comparative Study of Public Administration*, Bloomington, Indiana University Press, 1957, pp. 278-331.
[6] Daniel Lerner, *The Passing of Traditional Society*, Glencoe, Ill., The Free Press, 1958, p. 141.

commodate modernization; it had only to assimilate, something it could do with relative ease. As long as there is no compromise of the status hierarchy, roles can be extended, enlarged, and revised with little resistance and conflict; and in general this is what has happened historically. The grafting of modern functions onto traditional roles is not only an empirically descriptive generalization; it would also seem to be a rule for policy and planning.

Lastly, we must note that the motivation to accept change has not come from any of the dysphoria or unhappiness which Lerner[7] reports for the Middle East. On the contrary, the Thai seem to be characterized by euphoria rather than dysphoria. Acceptance derives from a very utilitarian concern for finding new ways of implementing old values, and from compliance with the prescriptions of the status hierarchy. Historically planned change has been conceived at the political top of the hierarchy and communicated downward through an all-encompassing bureaucracy, with acceptance becoming a matter of accedence of rank.

We can now understand why planned change in Thailand has been most conducive to modernization in such sectors as education and public health but rather inept in creating basic change in political behavior. The traditional political culture is the very instrumentality whereby planned change in other sectors has been wrought. For the political culture to change itself would be to destroy the habitual mechanisms for producing change.

II. Mass Communications and the Mediation of Change

Exposure to mass media contributes to cultural change not as an isolated single variable but through interactive conjunction with a larger pattern or system of variables. The structure of this patterning in the acceptance of innovations by Thai villagers has been neatly demonstrated in the research of Goldsen and Ralis.[8] These investigators set out to discover what social, cultural, economic, communications, and attitudinal attributes were associated with the acceptance of five agricultural and medical innovations among the farmers of Bang Chan. The matrix of Table 1, which has been constructed from their data, shows which attributes were found to be linked with the adoption of the gasoline engine, fertilizer, the cultivation of mush-

[7] *Ibid.*, pp. 101-103.
[8] Rose K. Goldsen and Max Ralis, *Factors Relating to Acceptance of Innovations in Bang Chan, Thailand*, Data Paper No. 24, Southeast Asia Program, Cornell University, Ithaca, N.Y., 1957, *passim.*

rooms and tilapia fish, and the use of medical clinics. Of course the existence of such linkages does not mean that the associated personal attributes are a direct cause of acceptance. According to the notion of systemic patterning, such associated variables are best viewed as the context in which acceptance takes place.

TABLE 1: PERSONAL ATTRIBUTES ASSOCIATED WITH ACCEPTANCE OF INNOVATIONS AMONG THAI VILLAGES IN BANG CHAN

	PERSONAL ATTRIBUTES						
Innovation	Use Credit	Mass Media	Literacy	Urban Ways	Eco- nomic Level	Social Con- tacts	Attitude
Motor	X	X	X	X	X	X	X
Clinic		X	X	X			
Mushrooms			X	X	X		
Tilapia					X	X	X
Fertilizer							X

The mark X indicates a statistically significant association.
Source: Constructed from the data of Goldsen and Ralis, *op.cit., passim.*

We see that exposure to radio and motion-pictures is associated with the adoption of only two innovations: the gasoline engine and medical clinics, and that in both cases other attributes are patterned with these mass media. Especially interesting is the gasoline engine, which involves the most complex patterning, while fertilizer is linked only to favorableness of attitude toward the innovation per se.

Other aspects of these data show that villagers who are exposed to mass media also tend to be modernized in other respects. For instance, those who have adopted the fork and spoon in eating are more likely to participate in radio listening and motion-picture attendance, make visits to nearby urban centers, use fertilizer and gasoline engines, and raise tilapia fish.

It is also noteworthy that the arrays of Table 1 comprise an indecomposable matrix, that is, by permuting the columns and rows the matrix can be arranged in the form of a parallelogram. Thus the matrix meets one of the criteria set forth by Coombs for a unidimensional domain; this indicates that the rank order of both innovations and personal characteristics represents positions along a single underlying attribute.[9] Only the gasoline engine violates the scale pattern because of the complexity of its determinants.

[9] Clyde H. Coombs, "Theory and Methods of Social Measurement," in L. Festinger and D. Katz, eds., *Research Methods in the Behavioral Sciences*, New York, Holt, 1953, p. 513.

These considerations suggest that at the national level too the process of modernization involves a conjunctive and patterned development in a number of spheres—the economic, demographic, educational, and social. The maintenance of a proper balance among these would seem to be a serious problem for transitional societies; thus the growth of mass communications can be evaluated only in the context of this balance.

When we examine various indices of modernization in Thailand, as displayed in Table 2, we note two major types of imbalance. The first relates to the very visible discrepancy between a relatively high literacy and educational output on one hand and a very low level of urbanization and industrialization on the other. Although Thai literacy was 67 per cent in 1956, only 9 per cent of the population could be considered as urban, and only 6 per cent of those economically active were engaged in commerce and industry. According to the

TABLE 2: INDICES OF MODERNIZATION FOR THAILAND

Population: 25.5 million (1960)

Population Density: 128.6 per square mile (1960)

Urbanization
    7% of population in cities over 50,000 (1956)
    9% of population in municipalities of 1,000 or more households (1956)

Population Mobility, 1948-1954
    25% of population migrant
    11% of all migrants moved to urban areas
    9.5% of all migrants moved to Bangkok-Thonburi

Literacy: 67% of population over 15 years of age (1956)

Education: 17% of population in schools (1958)

Electoral Participation
    44% of qualified voters (21% of pop.) voted in last general election (1957)
    Average of 38% of qualified voters voted in eleven elections held since 1932

Mass Media Consumption (per 1,000)
    Daily newspaper circulation: 13.7 (1960)
    Radio ownership: 7.5 (1956)
    TV set ownership: 1.6 (1960)

Industrialization, 1954
    12% of those economically active are in non-agricultural activities
    6% of those economically active are in business and industry
    2% of those economically active are in manufacturing
    2% of industrial establishments have more than 50 employees (1957)
    Average wage earned in business and industry: $480

Sources: Thai Central Statistical Office, *Final Report of the Demographic and Economic Survey of 1954, Vol. 1,* Bangkok, 1959; Thai Department of Interior, *Elections in Thailand,* Bangkok, 1959; Bunchana Atthakor, *Thailand's Economic Development,* 1950-1960 (publication of Thai Technical and Economic Cooperation, National Development Board), Bangkok, 1961; Adul Wichiencharoen, "Movements of Population within Thailand," *Ratthaprasatsanasat,* Vol. 1, No. 2, October 1960, pp. 29-35.

calculations of Lerner,[10] for its literacy a country like Thailand should have an urbanization in excess of 25 per cent to ensure an even growth. The imbalance is further compounded by low media accessibility, which means that literacy skills have restricted opportunities for employment.

The above inequities reflect the fact that for historical reasons the major pressure for social change has been in education. Indeed, the Ministry of Education can be considered the traditional headquarters for planned social change in Thailand. It has always attracted large budgets and the most competent personnel.

At the same time, as Table 2 indicates, the imbalance is perpetuated by Thai migration patterns. The Thai are a very mobile people, with 25 per cent of the population being migrant in the six years between 1948-1954.[11] But contrary to the usual theories about the transitional process, the greatest amount of migration is not to urban centers but from one rural area to another. Only 11 per cent of all migrants are rural dwellers moving to urban centers, and of these 85 per cent were moving to Bangkok. Urbanization in Thailand is almost entirely a matter of Bangkok growth. In this six-year period the city's population grew at a rate of 7.7 per cent of the base year—more than twice the rate of the nation as a whole.

Lerner has shown, however, that a discrepancy between urbanization and literacy is likely to occur in countries having a low population density.[12] Thus Thailand's low density probably mitigates to some extent the imbalance. The main unfortunate result is one of waste: failure to convert the literacy advantage into improved economic and political participation.

DISTRIBUTION AND ACCESSIBILITY OF MASS MEDIA

The second major imbalance relates to the accessibility of mass media, a more detailed audit of which is given in Table 3. It is apparent that media availability lags behind literacy and education for the country as a whole, and that Thailand must be included among the 60 per cent of the world's population adjudged by UNESCO as underdeveloped in informational media.[13]

[10] Lerner, op.cit., pp. 59-64.
[11] Adul Wichiencharoen, "Movements of Population within Thailand," *Ratthaprasatsanasat* (Public Administration), 1, 2, October 1960, pp. 29-35. (A publication of the Institute of Public Administration, Thammasart University, Bangkok.)
[12] Lerner, op.cit., pp. 66-67.
[13] UNESCO, *World Communications*, Paris, 1956, pp. 30-51.

TABLE 3: AVAILABILITY OF MASS MEDIA[a]

Daily Newspapers in Bangkok[b]
    Number in Thai: 14; 22 (1955); 16 (1959)
    Number in Chinese: 4; 5 (1956); 6 (1958)
    Number in English: 2 (plus two weeklies)
    Combined total circulation of Thai dailies: 220,000

Weekly, Fortnightly, and Monthly Publications
    In Bangkok: varies between 30 to 60
    In Chiengmai: 5 weekly newspapers

Radio
    Number of licensed sets: 150,000 (1956)
    Number of stations: 17 (including experimental stations)

Television[c]
    Number of licensed sets (in Bangkok): 38-40,000
    Number of channels: 2

Motion Picture Theatres
    Number of theatres: 195 (1958)
    Number of seats: 99,300 (1958)

Books and Pamphlets
    Number produced: 1,081 (1959)

---

[a] All figures are for 1960 unless otherwise indicated.
[b] The number of newspapers was reduced through closings in 1958 as consequence of the *coup d'état* in October of that year.
[c] Television began experimental telecasts in 1952 and has been available since 1955; reception only in Bangkok.
Source: UNESCO, *Basic Facts and Figures*, Paris, 1960; and official government sources in Bangkok.

A more interesting aspect of this lag, however, is a demographic one. While the Bangkok-Thonburi municipality contains only 7 per cent of the Kingdom's population, it is the origination and irradiation center for virtually all of the country's mass media. Consequently the concentration of accessibility is extremely high for this small urban group but rather low for the great majority in the rural areas. Thus for the 1.2 million of people in the Bangkok-Thonburi metropolitan area there were in 1960 a total of 20 newspapers, 17 radio stations, 2 TV channels, about 12 luxury motion-picture theatres (excluding a great many Chinese theatres), and from 30 to 60 weekly and monthly publications. All daily newspapers are published in Bangkok; all TV sets and the majority of radios are located there. One reason for the centralization of media sources in Bangkok is the structure of media ownership and control: virtually all radio and TV stations are government-operated, and about one-third of all newspapers are controlled by individual officials in the central government.

The result is that urban residents, especially those in the middle and upper classes, are a bit "over-communicated" in comparison with the rest of the country. Actually, accessibility of media to rural villagers is better than one would think, but it is the relative difference that counts, and this has tended to preserve, if not widen, the traditional gap between the urban and rural worlds, even though both are moving into modern times.

For the rural population, as one might expect, radio is the most important medium because it transcends the barriers of illiteracy and transportation. In almost every village of the north, northeast, and central valley there will be at least one radio; but this is not true of the south. The availability of radios in four villages is shown in Table 4. Availability appears to be increasing sharply, as is suggested by the addition of 33 radios in six years in Bang Chan. In none of these villages, except Phong Saen Thong, do newspapers arrive regularly. When the writer visited Phong Saen Thong in 1954 there were two families who subscribed to a local newspaper which was delivered by bicycle once a week from nearby Lampang. Kingshill found two copies of a newspaper (in addition to his own) during his residence in Ku Daeng.[14]

TABLE 4: DISTRIBUTION OF RADIO SETS IN FOUR THAI VILLAGES

	Bang Chan[a]	Bang Khuad[b]	Ku Daeng[c]	Phong Saen Thong[d]
Year	1955	1953	1954	1954
Location	Central valley 32 km. from Bangkok	Central valley 25 km. from Bangkok	North 10 km. from Chiengmai	North 6 km. from Lampang
Population	1,600	744	842	1,000
Households	333	147	168	190
Radios	47 (14 in 1949)	8	1	26

Sources: [a]Goldsen and Ralis, *op.cit.*, *passim.* [b]H. K. Kaufman, *Bang Khuad—a Community Study in Thailand* (Monograph of the Association of Asian Studies), Locust Valley, N.Y., 1960, *passim.* [c]Konrad Kingshill, *Ku Daeng—The Red Tomb*, *A Village Study in Northern Thailand*, Bangkok, 1960, *passim.* [d]Unpublished data of the writer.

III. Participation in the Mass Media System

It is the ability to read that prepares people to receive the political lessons of the printed word. Thai literacy is perhaps the highest in Southeast Asia—67 per cent for the Kingdom as a whole and 81

[14] Konrad Kingshill, *Ku Daeng—The Red Tomb, a Village Study in Northern Thailand*, Bangkok, 1960, pp. 223-224.

per cent in the urban population.[15] But even in rural villages there is an ample number of literates to ensure a core who can respond to printed mass media. In the village of Bang Chan, for instance, Goldsen and Ralis[16] found in 1955 that 67 per cent of all household heads could read. Madge[17] in 1955 reports that in the northeastern village of Pa-ao all men under forty years and all but two in the age group from forty to forty-nine had received primary education (four years), and of the 21 men over fifty only four were illiterate.

MASS MEDIA EXPOSURE

Literacy has enabled newspaper readership to maintain a workable balance with radio listening. Table 5 gives an overview of exposure to radio, newspapers, magazines, books, and motion-pictures of over 2,500 urban "middle" and "upper" class Thai, based on a probability sampling of Bangkok and six provincial towns in 1955 (henceforth referred to as the "National Urban Survey").[18] In this table towns are grouped according to the geographic regions of Thailand. (It should be remembered that in Thailand there is really only one "city"—Bangkok; all provincial towns are very small communities by Western standards.) These data may be considered as conservative estimates since more recent checks by the writer indicate increases in exposure to all media. To this table may be added the fact that in a survey of 1,825 Bangkok elite which the writer helped conduct in 1959, 67 per cent were found to possess TV sets.[19]

[15] Thai Central Statistical Office, *Final Report of the Demographic and Economic Survey of 1954*, Vol. 1, report of the National Economic Development Board, Bangkok, 1959, *passim.*

[16] Goldsen and Ralis, *op.cit.*, p. 47.

[17] Charles Madge, *Survey Before Development in Thai Villages*, United Nations Series on Community Organization and Development, Paris, 1957, p. 34 (mimeographed).

[18] This study was conducted under contract between The George Washington University and the U.S. Information Agency. The following towns were surveyed: Bangkok (central valley), Lampang (north), Udorn, Khon Kaen, Ubol (northeast), Songkhla and Nakhorn Sri Thammarat (south). Seventy-nine per cent of the respondents were male. While the usual notions of social class do not hold for Thailand, the sample can be described for purposes of convenience as "middle" and "lower-upper" class. Composition of the sample is suggested by the educational distribution: 14 per cent had less than 10 years of education, 26 per cent had 10 years, 25 per cent had 12 years, while 35 per cent had some or completed university.

[19] Business Research Ltd., "Communications Evaluation Study," Bangkok, June 1959 (mimeographed). This study was conducted jointly by the writer and Frederic Ayer. The sample was drawn from a list of 3,937 names culled from 14 organizational sources, both governmental and private.

TABLE 5: MEDIA EXPOSURE OF MIDDLE AND UPPER CLASS
URBAN THAI IN FOUR GEOGRAPHIC REGIONS

	Total	Bangkok	North	Northeast	South
Radio					
Listen occasionally	95%	99%	87%	95%	89%
Listen every day	75	84	71	65	65
Own radio	77	96	75	54	60
Newspapers					
Read in last two weeks	98	99	98	97	97
Read almost every day	77	85	75	74	34
Motion Pictures					
Saw movie in last 6 months	92	94	91	90	68
See movie at least twice a month	74	76	70	73	69
Have never seen movie	1	0	1	3	1
Books					
Read at least once a month	87	79	94	96	95
Read once a week	42	22	54	63	57
Magazines					
Read occasionally	92	96	86	86	94
Read at least once a week	46	30	40	60	65
Receipt of Mail					
Received in last month	72	68	80	75	74
Number of respondents	(2,546)	(1,209)	(174)	(720)	(443)

Source: Unpublished data from writer's National Urban Survey, 1955. See footnote 18.

It will be seen that media exposure is high indeed, and compares not unfavorably with media habits in many Western countries. Specifically we note that: 75 per cent of the total sample are "heavy" radio listeners (i.e., listen at least once a day). Newspapers are read frequently, daily readership being 77 per cent. Motion-picture attendance is equally high, 74 per cent going twice a month or more. Only 8 per cent are not movie goers (i.e., have not seen a movie in six months), while only 1 per cent have never been to a motion-picture. Exposure to magazines is comparatively lower, with 46 per cent reading at least once a week. Book reading is even less, with 42 per cent reading once a week.

While there are absolute differences among geographic areas, the pattern of media participation is quite similar for all areas. Radio listening in each case exceeds radio ownership, especially in the northeast (Thailand's depressed area), where radio listening is the highest and ownership is the lowest of any provincial region (a possible reflection of the greater frequency of group listening). The northeast also shows a slightly higher frequency of book reading, while magazine reading is highest in the south.

Exposure to all media is greater in Bangkok than the provinces with the exception of book and magazine reading and the receipt of mail, which are invariably higher in the provinces. This finding is significant in view of the popular assumption that in underdeveloped societies participation in printed media increases with urbanization. In the present case the data probably mean that book and magazine reading in Bangkok suffers from competition with other more attractive media which are denied to provincial residents.

VILLAGE MEDIA EXPOSURE

Participation in radio listening and motion-picture attendance at the village level may be seen in Table 6, which is based on 1955 data from the central-valley rice village of Bang Chan. Located 32 kilometers from Bangkok, Bang Chan is within the radius of modernizing influences from the capital city. Fourteen per cent of the 333 householders in the village owned radio sets, although 78 per cent reported doing some listening. Motion pictures can be seen in the nearest provincial capital since virtually every rural town of 3,000 or more has one motion-picture theater of some kind. In the last fifteen years it has become popular in the more proximal villages to rent newsreels, old cowboy movies, and various informational films from the U.S. Information Service for outdoor showing at *wat* (Buddhist temple) fairs and the many festivals and religious celebrations that punctuate the yearly cycle. In Bang Chan only 10 per cent had never seen a motion picture, a smaller number than those who had never listened to the radio.

TABLE 6: MASS MEDIA PARTICIPATION OF 333 HOUSEHOLDERS
IN THE VILLAGE OF BANG CHAN

Radio Listening	Per Cent	Motion Picture Attendance	Per Cent
Daily	14	10 times or more in life	48
Occasionally	20	4 to 9 times in life	18
Seldom	44	1 to 3 times in life	23
Never	18	Never	10
Not Ascertained	4	Not Ascertained	1
Total	100	Total	100

Source: Goldsen and Ralis, *op.cit.*, pp. 52, 65.

SOME SOCIAL CORRELATES OF URBAN MEDIA EXPOSURE

Analysis of the urban audience characteristics that correlate with the amount of media exposure reveals that radio listening and newspaper readership have similar patterns. In both cases exposure varies positively with education but scarcely at all with age. Occupational groups are rather evenly exposed to both media. There are sex differences: very slight for radio but favoring women; larger for newspapers, favoring men.

For motion pictures, magazines, and books, frequency of exposure shows a negative correlation with age, but the variations with occupation are negligible. Motion picture attendance and book reading are positively related to amount of education but display negligible variations with sex. Magazine reading, however, is more frequent among women than men.

Very significant is the discovery that police-military groups are the most highly participant of all in heavy radio listening and daily newspaper reading. In contrast are the students, whom we might expect to be very communications-oriented; actually they are the lowest of all groups in heavy radio listening. On the other hand they are the highest in magazine readership. As will be seen later, these findings are also consistent with exposure to foreign media. From this and other evidence it can be concluded that police-military groups are among the most acculturated and outwardly oriented of all social categories.

The difference between the interest orientations of middle- and upper-class men and women is well illustrated in their preferences for radio programs. The average rank order of interest for programs is as follows:

Women	*Men*
Modern Thai music	Traditional Thai music
News	Educational features
Traditional Thai music	Western music
Discussions of world events	Short plays
Educational features	Religious programs
Western music	News
Short plays	Serial stories
Religious programs	Modern Thai music
Serial stories	Discussions of world events

There is a hint here that women are more oriented toward the wider world than men. This is consistent with other evidence to the effect that women, despite their traditionally high status in Thai society, are more actively concerned with modernizing their social roles.[20]

READERSHIP, PREFERENCE, AND PERCEIVED RELIABILITY
OF NEWSPAPERS

Thai expectations concerning the accuracy of their newspapers are notoriously and uniformly pessimistic, and consequently the credibility of newspaper content is low.[21] Almost all respondents believe that radio news is more reliable. Within such expectations there is considerable variation in the reliability ascribed to various newspapers. In 1959 the writer collaborated in a study of 1,825 Bangkok elite (henceforth called the "Bangkok Elite Study") which, among other things, obtained data concerning which newspapers respondents read, those they thought most interesting, and those they considered most reliable.[22] The results for the leading newspapers are displayed in Table 7, together with similar data on readership and perceived reliability from the 1955 National Urban Survey, and newspaper preference data from a 1958 study of 394 university students conducted by Schuler and Thamavit.[23]

The 1959 figures for Bangkok elite show that in terms of absolute percentages the agreement between readership and interest is substantially greater than the agreement between readership and perceived reliability. However, the rank order of newspapers is the same on all three variables. The rank order of readership, but not reliability, is the same for both 1955 and 1959; thus readership appears to be more stable than perceived reliability. Especially noteworthy is the fact that for both 1955 and 1959 readership almost always exceeds (or at least is equal to) perceived reliability; that is, the number of individuals who read a paper tends to be greater than or equal to the number who choose it as most reliable. The two exceptions to this trend are the paper with the highest perceived reliability and

[20] Henry M. Graham, *Some Changes in Thai Family Life*, a report of the Institute of Public Administration, Thammasart University, Bangkok, 1958, *passim* (mimeographed).

[21] Albert G. Pickerell, "The Press in Thailand: Conditions and Trends," *Journalism Quarterly*, XXXVI, 1, Winter 1960, pp. 83-96.

[22] Business Research, Ltd., *op.cit.*, *passim*.

[23] Edgar Schuler and Vibul Thamavit, *Public Opinion among Thai Students*, report of the Faculty of Social Administration, Thammasart University, Bangkok, 1958, pp. 81-82 (mimeographed).

TABLE 7: READERSHIP, PREFERENCE, AND PERCEIVED RELIABILITY OF
LEADING THAI NEWSPAPERS IN THREE SEPARATE STUDIES

	1955[a]		1959[b]			1958[c]
Newspaper	Perceived Reliability	Reader-ship	Perceived Reliability	Reader-ship	Pref-erence	Pref-erence
Siam Rath	43%	60%	63%	52%	50%	47%
Sarn Seri	*	*	9	12	11	28
Phim Thai	10	49	6	12	11	10
Siam Nikorn	79	41	5	5	6	10
Chao Thai	10	21	3	3	3	1
Thai Rawan	*	*	1	1	2	28
Kiattisak	6	2	†	†	†	†
Prachathipatai	5	16	†	†	†	†
Daily Mail	4	32	†	†	†	†
Thai Mail	1	4	†	†	†	†

[a] Per cents based on multiple-responses of 2,546 respondents of writer's unpublished National Urban Survey. See footnote 18.

[b] Per cents based on single-responses of 1,825 respondents of Bangkok Elite Study. See footnote 19.

[c] Per cents based on multiple-responses of 394 university students in Bangkok studied by Schule and Thamavit, *op.cit.*, pp. 81-82.

* Not published in 1955.

† Per cent is less than one.

the paper with the lowest readership. In both cases and in both years perceived reliability exceeds readership.

PUBLIC OPINION AND EDITORIAL LINE

A very careful analysis of data from the National Urban Survey was made to determine whether the opinions of a newspaper's audience were related to its editorial position. The opinions of persons who usually read one of five newspapers with reasonably clear editorial lines were studied with respect to some fifty statements. The distribution of opinion responses was extremely similar for all five papers. The amount of cross-paper similarity, however, depended somewhat on the extent to which opinion was structured (as indexed by the proportion claiming no opinion). Similarity was greater for well-structured opinions than for the less structured. In the case of unstructured opinions, however, the cross-paper differences did not correspond to differences in editorial line.

Thus it seems clear that readers show virtually no tendency to be self-selective in their exposure to newspapers. Nor does editorial position have any immediate effect upon readers' opinions. The situation is especially noteworthy in the case of pro- and anti-Communist readers. While pro-Communist attitudes in Thailand are rare and mild,[24] it was possible to identify 535 readers who on the basis of open-ended questions revealed favorable attitudes toward Communism. Table 8 compares the newspapers read by this group with a larger group who were identified as anti-Communist. Differences in readership are small and show no trend toward correspondence with editorial line.

TABLE 8: NEWSPAPERS REGULARLY READ BY GROUPS WITH
FAVORABLE AND UNFAVORABLE ATTITUDES
TOWARD COMMUNISM

		Per Cent Who Read	
Newspaper	Editorial Position[a]	Anti-Communist	Pro-Communist
Daily Mail	Leftist, anti-government	36	34
Kiattisak	Anti-government	20	23
Siam Rath	Independent, slightly rightist	61	68
Phim Thai	Strongly leftist	52	51
Siam Nikorn	Slightly leftist, anti-government	38	45
Number of respondents		(1,421)	(535)

[a] As of time of survey.
Source: Unpublished data from writer's National Urban Survey, 1955.

IV. Informal Oral Communication

While the urban Thai is exposed to a considerable degree to formal mass media, he also participates even more in a continuing pattern of informal social communication.[25] The social sources from which urban middle- and upper-class Thai obtain news are shown in Table 9, based on data from the National Urban Survey. The relative rank of frequency of mention for each source is noticeably consistent from one geographic area to another, with letter-writers in first place, followed by government representatives, shopkeepers, people met in eating and drinking places, and Buddhist priests, in that order.

Buddhist priests are frequently consulted for astrological counsel, and it is generally recognized that the timing of most political and

[24] For the reasons underlying this situation, see David A. Wilson, "Thailand and Marxism," in F. N. Trager, *Marxism in Southeast Asia*, Stanford, Stanford University Press, 1959, pp. 58-101.

[25] The persuasive effectiveness of Thai oral communication is suggested by a study in which 14 presumably qualified observers, both Western and Thai, rated the persuasiveness of 9 media on a 5-point scale. Oral communication received the highest rating—4.8, in comparison with radio at 3.9 and newspapers at 2.9. See Imogene Okes, "Effective Communication by Americans with Thai," M.A. thesis, American University, 1960, p. 114.

TABLE 9: EXPOSURE TO INFORMAL SOCIAL SOURCES OF NEWS
FOR MIDDLE AND UPPER-CLASS URBAN THAI

Social Source	Total	Bangkok	North	Northeast	South
Shopkeepers	43%	43%	41%	38%	50%
Postmen	14	13	12	14	18
Letter writers	58	64	43	51	56
Government repre-sentatives	43	45	44	41	42
People at *wat*	17	15	16	15	25
People in eating-drinking places	30	35	29	24	30
Travellers	14	18	15	8	13
Priests	25	21	26	25	38
Novices	5	4	6	6	6
Peddlers	13	13	9	11	17
Attended *wat* fair in last 6 months	43	40	56	38	63
Number of respondents	(2,546)	(1,209)	(174)	(720)	(443)

Source: Unpublished data from the writer's National Urban Survey, 1955.

administrative events is based upon astrological calculations, made usually by the counselee's favorite Buddhist priest. According to the 1954 census, there were 165,000 priests in 20,000 *wats*—which is about 8 priests per 1,000 population, more' than the official number of radio sets.

Contacts with government representatives take place within the territorial administration system, a vast bureaucratic hierarchy which has points of contact with almost every citizen and through which official information is passed downward.

Four sources are mentioned with greater frequency in Bangkok than in any provincial town: travellers, letter-writers, government representatives, and people in eating and drinking places. People met at the *wat* or Buddhist temple, Buddhist novices, and postmen tend to be mentioned more frequently as sources in provincial towns than in Bangkok. Attendance at *wat* festivals, a traditional occasion for social contacts and entertainment, is unexpectedly high in Bangkok, where 40 per cent report such attendance within the last six or seven months. Among provincial towns those in the south show the greatest amount of overall contact with social sources of news. The south has the highest percentages of mention in 6 of the 11 social sources.

INFORMAL TRANSMISSION AMONG THE URBAN UPPER
AND MIDDLE CLASSES

Based on intensive participant observation in the Thai language over a period of eighteen months of the informal network among fifteen Bangkok Thai, the writer would make the following tentative conclusions:

Social transmission of information is rarely persuasive, almost never argumentative. It is simply a relay with elaboration. One of the reasons behind this appears to be the character of the communicator's motivation to communicate. His incentive derives not so much from an intrinsic interest in the topic or information or from a desire to convince others of his own views; rather, it comes from his desire to pursue a personal relationship or to conform to the demands of a social situation. Any persuasion that occurs is largely incidental and occurs as a consequence of the listener's response to the communicator's status. For this reason the informal transmitters of news are better described as "mediators" rather than "opinion leaders." Opinion leadership in the more narrow sense emerges as an accidental consequence of the speaker's status rather than from his attempts to convince.

The informal relaying of information serves to supplement the content of mass media more than to reinforce and reiterate its content. Government control of all radio, the low credibility of newspapers, and the fact that the government public relations office is the sole source of official news on domestic affairs means that there is always a need to know the "inside story." It is this additional information (or more correctly, "speculation") which the informal system supplies.

RURAL INFORMAL TRANSMISSION

In rural areas the informal transmission of news is enhanced by patterns of short-term geographic mobility found in all but the most remote villages. Generally speaking, the frequency and distance of this mobility reaches its peak after the harvest season and is at its ebb during the rainy season. Also, the longer the distance the more likely it is that the transient is a man.

Travel has long been a favorite recreation of the Thai, and a considerable amount of mobility has been traditional, especially in the central valley region, where an abundant network of waterways and *khlong* (canals) makes movement easy. In the northeast it has been customary until 1960 for young men to journey to Bangkok, where they work as *samlor* (tricycle ricksha) drivers for a year or two, then return with some small savings to resume the life of a farmer.[26] Textor[27] estimates that of the approximately 12,000 samlor drivers in Bangkok about 57 per cent were born in the northeast. Virtually all were literate. A recent analysis of population movements by Wichiencharoen, cited in Table 2, showed that between 1948 and 1954 25 per cent of the total population was migrant, with 89 per cent of the migration being from one rural area to another. The propensity for travel has served to give the Thai a feeling of membership in a community larger than his immediate village; he does not think of himself as a member of an isolated self-sufficient little world. He has a sense of identity with some larger consensus and group which is to be enjoyed through travel and visiting.

The significance of mobility for modernization is especially great for those who are illiterate. There is evidence to suggest that physical contacts with urban centers and other areas beyond the immediate community can act as a substitute for literacy in making the villager more sophisticated about improving his standard of living and level of production. Goldsen and Ralis[28] found that among illiterate farmers those who made frequent visits to urban centers, agricultural fairs, and the nearby airport were more likely to adopt the gasoline engine than those who were less mobile. Among literate farmers, however, this relationship did not hold. If the farmer could read and write, he was just as apt to adopt the motor irrespective of whether he had been in contact with urban culture. Mobility also brings new information. For instance, villagers who visited the medical clinic in nearby towns were found to possess more information about Thailand's public figures.

Table 10 shows the mobility patterns in two Thai villages, Bang Chan in the central valley near Bangkok and Pa-Ao in the northeast near Ubol. We note that in Bang Chan over three-fourths of the householders had visited Bangkok, a distance of 32 kilometers, at

---

[26] *Samlors* in Bangkok were abolished by governmental decree in January 1960.

[27] Robert B. Textor, "The Northeastern Samlor Driver in Bangkok," in *The Social Implications of Industrialization and Urbanization*, publication of the UNESCO Research Centre in the Social Implications of Industrialization in Southern Asia, Calcutta, 1956.

[28] Goldsen and Ralis, *op.cit.*, pp. 25-26.

least once within the last year, and that 4 per cent had travelled beyond the boundaries of Thailand. In Pa-Ao we note that 61 per cent of the men in the 20-29 age group had driven *samlor* in Bangkok, and that the older a man is, the more likely it is that he has never left his village. This latter observation suggests that travelling has increased over the years.

TABLE 10: MOBILITY OF VILLAGERS IN TWO THAI VILLAGES

	BANG CHAN[a]	
Mobility Experience		*Per Cent*
To Bangkok (32 km.) at least once in last year		78
To Don Muang (13 km.) at least once in life		55
To Minburi (4 km.) at least twice in last month		79
To clinic in Bangkok or Minburi at least once in life		64
Lived or worked in Bangkok		34
Beyond boundaries of Thailand at least once in life		4
Number of respondents		(333)

	PA-AO[b]			
		Age Groups		
Mobility Experience	*20-29*	*30-39*	*40-49*	*50-*
Never left village	24%	14%	20%	41%
Traded in Ubol province	9	40	36	18
Traded farther afield	6	14	40	41
Served in army	0	18	0	0
Drove *samlor* in Bangkok	61	14	4	0
Total	100%	100%	100%	100%
Number of respondents	(33)	(22)	(25)	(22)

Sources: [a] Goldsen and Ralis, *op.cit.*, pp. 57-58; [b] Madge, *op.cit.*, p. 44.

The most active mediators of outside news in the village are those whose social roles give them an opportunity for mobility, such as the village headman who must attend monthly meetings in the district (*amphur*) seat, the housewife and daughter who make frequent visits to the nearby market town for trading purposes, and the young man who is conscripted into military service.

Within the provincial town the market or *talat* serves as a link-pin to unite town and village, and one village with another, into a single informal communication network. Early in the morning village women arrive from outlying districts to sell their produce, socialize, and return home bearing the news. Recognizing this common communications center, the government has equipped the markets of all provincial capitals with a large public address system whose loudspeakers blare out music, market prices, and local news items.

News is also brought into the village by outsiders, the most recurrent carriers being itinerant peddlers, medicine venders, travelling Buddhist priests, local government officials, and entertainment troupes imported for festivals. The medicine vender has unusual propaganda potential but is more limited in mobility than the itinerant peddler. The medicine vender may arrive with a small sideshow, an ancient cowboy movie, and sometimes a *like* (folk play) or *tua talok* (comedian). The itinerant peddler, while not so glamorous and persuasive, is not hobbled by a cartload of impedimenta that defies transportation to the less accessible villages.

There have been instances in the northeast where Communist propagandists have used the medicine vender to considerable advantage. In one northeastern area, villages were visited by medicine venders who offered their medicines and penicillin injections (which are in great demand by the Thai) at amazingly low prices while subjecting their clients to subtly presented Communist propaganda. In another area free medicines were given away after mobile entertainment troupes had deftly worked a propaganda theme into their songs and patter.[29]

V. Some Thai Innovations in Communications Media

In Thailand there are several indigenous institutions which have been adapted to extending and supplementing the impact of formal communications media. We shall examine five of these: group oral newspaper reading, pass-along readership chains, the verse editorial, *like*, and the *mo lam*. The first two are social innovations which serve to extend tremendously the range of audience exposure to newspapers; the third increases the attractiveness and informal circulation of newspaper editorial content; while the last two represent traditional folk entertainments which mediate oral transmission of the news and which in the last ten years have come to provide a new communications "package" for political information and ideas.[30]

Group Oral Readership. In villages there are occasional instances of newspapers being read aloud by one person to others; however,

[29] Lewis Pate, "Some Important Informal Means of Communication in Rural Thailand," unpublished report to the U.S. Information Agency, Bangkok, 1958.
[30] For a discussion of "packaging" or context factors in communication, see Chapter 8.

such occasions appear to be rarer in Thailand than in the Middle East, and their occurrence is irregular, casual, and spur-of-the-moment.

Pass-Along Readership. In provincial towns the writer has uncovered numerous instances of multiple readership wherein a newspaper is passed from one person to another along a fairly regular circuit. The membership is not rigid, but it does tend to be stable. In Chiengmai the writer found one such "chain" that contained twenty people. Thai newspapers, especially the weeklies and fortnightlies, contain a liberal amount of non-temporal news; thus interest can survive the delay of pass-along.

The extent of pass-along readership can be judged from Table 11, which shows the extent to which the copy of a person's newspaper is read by other people. We see that only two per cent of the total sample report no multiple readership for the paper they read. Pass-along readership is slightly greater in provincial towns than in Bangkok, and this is what we would expect. Readership by other family members is greater in Bangkok than in any provincial town, being the least in the northeast. Readership by non-family persons is more frequent in the provinces than in Bangkok, with the northeast showing the greatest amount of all.

TABLE 11: PASS-ALONG READERSHIP OF NEWSPAPERS AMONG
MIDDLE AND UPPER-CLASS URBAN THAI

	Total	Bangkok	North	Northeast	South
Read by family members	46%	55%	49%	33%	38%
Read by non-family	66	57	66	76	73
Not read by others	2	3	1	2	2
Number of respondents	(2,546)	(1,209)	(174)	(720)	(443)

Source: Unpublished data from writer's National Urban Survey, 1955.

Table 12 shows the usual age of the newspaper when read. Eighty-one per cent of the total sample report that it is less than four days old, while only 8 per cent say "four days to a week." The paper is over a week old for only 1 per cent. The percentage for "less than four days" is greatest in Bangkok, least in the south. These figures indicate that even in the provincial towns the transportation and pass-along of newspapers is sufficiently rapid to handle even temporal news.

Verse Editorial. This is a commentary written in verse, appearing

TABLE 12: AGE OF NEWSPAPER WHEN READ BY MIDDLE
AND UPPER-CLASS URBAN THAI

Age of Newspaper	Total	Bangkok	North	Northeast	South
Less than four days	81%	87%	75%	80%	70%
Four days to a week	8	2	10	12	17
More than one week	1	1	3	1	*
Number of respondents	(2,546)	(1,209)	(174)	(720)	(443)

* Per cent less than one.
Source: Unpublished data from writer's National Urban Survey, 1955.

on the editorial page, and usually accompanied by a montage cartoon.[31]
The purpose is not to prescribe opinion but rather to raise doubts,
suggest issues, and introduce sentimental and moral aspects of a problem which would be awkward in prose. The language employed is
invariably clever and witty, full of *double-entendre*, innuendoes, and
word plays. The verse form is *klon*, the simplest and most popular
of the five classical verse forms; it originated in ancient times as an
unwritten folk verse but became written in the mid-17th century.

Interestingly enough, the verse editorial is not a traditional device
which is dying out under the impact of modernism. It is a recent
innovation (beginning around 1950) with strong traditional roots
which has been precipitated and strengthened by such modern forces
as governmental censorship and the economic pressures on newspapers
to capture readership. Its significance lies in the fact that it is an extremely effective form of communication. Because of its popular
appeal and easy rhythmical remembrance, editorial material can readily capture public attention and acquire considerable oral transmission.
It is not uncommon for certain verses to become the sayings of the
day and to be recalled years after their initial appearance. By moving
editorial material from the printed page into the oral system the
verse editorial can greatly magnify public impact.

Like (also *yike*). This is a vulgar form of the classical dance-drama
which has been in existence for about one hundred years.[32] Among
villagers and urban lower classes it has attained tremendous popular-

[31] For a report on this technique with examples in translation, see James N. Mosel,
"The Verse Editorial in Thai Journalism," *Journalism Quarterly*, XXXIX, 1, Winter
1962, pp. 70-74.
[32] For descriptions, see Faubian Bowers, *Theatre in the East*, New York, Evergreen,
1956, pp. 156-162, and H. K. Kaufman, *Bangkuad—a Community Study in Thailand*, Monograph of the Association for Asian Studies, Locust Valley, 1960, pp.
170-171.

ity; no festival or religious celebration would be complete without it. In Bangkok there are no less than twenty *like* theater houses. *Like* has also been adapted to radio and television, but among the urban middle classes its appeal is primarily to the older generation. The National Urban Survey found that among the middle and upper classes in the northeast and south *like* was the favorite radio program of over 20 per cent, whereas in Bangkok it received very little favor.

A *like* troupe consists of about seven performers who are usually professionals. Formerly all actors were men, but today girls also appear. A performance may last from three to four hours, and many are serialized over several days. Action is accompanied by speeches and songs but there is no script; the words are improvised on the spur of the moment with ingenious attempts at risque *double-entendre*, bawdy humor, word plays, and witty repartee—all in accordance with strict poetic rules for rhyme and metre. The themes and plots are almost always historical and until 1955 usually dealt with medieval wars with the Burmese.[33]

In recent years the government has encouraged *like* troupes to put on anti-Communist plays. *Like* lends itself admirably to this; its themes are always heroic ones, involving banditry, conspiracy, and uprisings against a local prince or king. By simple adjustment these have been made to refer to the Communists. According to the current practice, the villain must wear red, attempt to overthrow the ruling power, set out to destroy the Buddhist religion, and owe allegiance to some foreign power.[34]

Mo Lam. This traditional entertainment is peculiar to northeastern Thailand and Laos. The words *mo lam* mean "doctor of sung verses."[35] The performance consists of a declamation sung to the accompaniment of the *khaen*, the indigenous panpipes. Typically there are two singers, a man and a girl, and the *khaen* player, but at times there may be more singers and percussion instruments as well. The declamations are improvised from a store of traditional melodies in a simple Lao verse form, replete with wit, double meanings, and risque insinuation, so that almost any kind of message can be conveyed with great effect. Performances last around four hours and themes range widely: political events in Bangkok, local gossip, the beauties of

[33] Bowers, *op.cit.*, p. 160.
[34] For an example of an anti-Communist dramatic plot, see *ibid.*, pp. 161-162.
[35] Sometimes mistaken as *mo ram* ("doctor of dances") by Westerners and central-valley Thai who are unfamiliar with the northeastern dialect. For a brief account of a performance, see Madge, *op.cit.*, pp. 65-70.

nature, commentaries on courtship, the assassination of the late King, progress, airplanes, New York City, the Buddha's renunciation, the Thai Constitution of 1932. A favorite song having many versions is *Long Khong* ("Descending the Mekhong River").

The *mo lam* enjoys great popularity in the northeast. Audiences have been known to remain the entire night to hear a performance. Most northeast villages have their own *mo lam*, but there are also professional teams who tour the festival circuit and earn comparatively high fees. Phonograph records of *mo lam* are available in the towns of the northeast, and occasionally performances are presented on radio.

In other parts of Thailand other entertainments serve as similar function: the *so* of the north; the *lam tat*, originally from the northeast but now popular in the central valley; and the Malayan-inspired *nang thalung* or shadow play in the south. All of these have considerable potential for the communication of political ideas in rural areas, a potential which has sometimes been activated, but usually not from design or intentional exploitation.

VI. Orientations Abroad

Political information reaches the Thai not only through indigenous mass media but also from the world abroad through direct exposure to foreign media and personal contacts. Such exposure is facilitated by the prevalence of English-language skills. Table 13 shows the distribution of foreign language skills for the respondents of the National Urban Survey. All such skills are decidedly more common in Bangkok than in any provincial town. It is remarkable that 94 per cent in Bangkok can read some language other than Thai. English greatly outweighs any other Western language; in Bangkok 92 per cent are able to read it, with French in second place with only 10 per cent. Schuler and Thamavit in their survey of university students found that five per cent had an opportunity to use English at home.[36]

DIRECT EXPOSURE TO FOREIGN MEDIA

The participation of middle- and upper-class urban Thai in foreign radio listening, English-language newspaper and magazine reading, and American movie viewing is summarized in Table 14.

[36] Schuler and Thamavit, *op.cit.*, p. 78.

TABLE 13: FOREIGN LANGUAGE SKILLS OF MIDDLE AND
UPPER-CLASS URBAN THAI

Foreign Language Skill	Total	Bangkok	North	Northeast	South
Read language other than Thai	85%	94%	78%	74%	79%
Speak language other than Thai	76	87	65	71	62
Read English	82	92	75	70	78
Speak English	68	83	60	52	53
Read French	6	10	4	3	2
Speak French	5	9	1	2	1
Number of respondents	(2,546)	(1,209)	(174)	(720)	(443)

Source: Unpublished data from writer's National Urban Survey, 1955.

TABLE 14: FOREIGN MEDIA EXPOSURE OF MIDDLE AND
UPPER-CLASS URBAN THAI

Media Exposure	Total	Bangkok	North	Northeast	South
Radio Listening					
Listen to English-language broadcasts	48%	55%	49%	32%	57%
Listen to Voice of America	45	44	53	31	53
Listen to BBC	41	45	53	33	44
Listen to Radio Peiping	9	9	16	9	9
Listen to foreign broadcasts	58	59	61	54	61
Heard someone discuss U.S. broadcasts	65	66	80	59	69
Reading					
Read newspapers in English	43	59	35	25	43
Read U.S. magazines	21	26	20	10	17
Motion Picture Attendance					
Have seen U.S. movie	96	97	97	99	97
Believe U.S. movies give fairly true picture of American life	44	38	52	18	57
Number of respondents	(2,545)	(1,209)	(174)	(720)	(443)

Source: Unpublished data from writer's National Urban Survey, 1955.

It will be seen that in all parts of the country greater numbers are exposed to American motion pictures and foreign radio broadcasts than English-language newspapers.

Foreign Radio Listening. Slightly over half of the entire sample listen to foreign broadcasts, while slightly less than half listen to

English-language broadcasts. The percentage who listen to the Voice of America is very slightly greater than that for the BBC. In all categories of foreign radio listening there is always one provincial area, usually the north or south, that exceeds Bangkok.

"Heavy listening" (once a day or more) is much less frequent than the occasional listening shown in Table 14—only 24 per cent of the total sample fall into the heavy listener category. Among listeners to U.S. programs, the proportion of heavy listeners is greatest in Bangkok (84 per cent) although regional differences are not great. Listening to U.S., BBC, and Peiping broadcasts is also slightly higher among men than women; and while there is no significant correlation with age, there is a positive correlation with education. (It will be noted that these findings are consistent with the trends for domestic radio listening.)

Students and police-military groups are atypical radio listeners in several respects. Students show the greatest proportion of non-listeners to American broadcasts of any group, although they were unusually high in listening to the BBC. They also showed the least interest in programs having an ideological commitment. Police-military groups, in accordance with their previously noted strong outward orientation, were above average in listening to the VOA, BBC, and Radio Peiping.

Throughout Thailand the most favored U.S. programs were news, political commentary, and music. In general more importance was attached to U.S. news broadcasts in the provinces than in Bangkok.

U.S. broadcasts appear to have received considerable informal oral relay at the face-to-face level. Respondents were asked if they had heard anyone recently mention or discuss U.S. programs. As Table 14 shows, well over half in each region reported such experiences, the frequency being greater (as in direct listening) in the north and south.

English-Language Newspapers and Magazines. Over one-third of the total sample report reading English-language newspapers, the frequency being much greater in Bangkok than in provincial towns. (The newspapers read are all published in Bangkok; see Table 3.) Slightly over one-fifth of the total sample read English-language magazines, and in contrast to domestic magazine readership, this tendency is greatest in Bangkok. In a later study of university students 20 per cent were found to read American magazines at one

JAMES N. MOSEL

time or another; 9 per cent mentioned *Life* and 3 per cent mentioned *Time*.[37]

U.S. Motion Pictures. Almost all respondents (96 per cent) had seen an American movie; there is very little regional variation in such exposure. On the other hand, there is considerable regional variation in the extent to which respondents believe that American movies give a true picture of American life. Slightly more than two-fifths of the total sample believe that movies present at least a fairly true picture, the greater credibility being in the north and south, where over half accept American movies as true representations. In contrast, credibility is extremely low (about one-fifth) in the northeast, with Bangkok somewhat higher. Oddly enough, further analysis shows that women are less credulous than men. In general the older and better educated the individual, the less likely he is to believe that American films truly reflect life in the United States.

PERSONAL CONTACT WITH WESTERNERS

For urban Thai, especially those in Bangkok, direct personal contact with Westerners provides a very important source of information about the West and new role models. The frequency of such contacts within Thailand, particularly with Americans, is rather high for middle- and upper-class urban Thai, as shown by results from the National Urban Survey in Table 15. Well over half of the entire sample reported contact with Americans during the last year, while about two-fifths reported contacts with British. Contacts with other Westerners were reported by only ten per cent.

TABLE 15: PERSONAL CONTACT WITH WESTERNERS IN
PRECEDING YEAR OF MIDDLE- AND UPPER-CLASS URBAN THAI

Type of Contact	Total	Bangkok	North	Northeast	South
American	63%	76%	55%	42%	66%
British	41	55	41	13	52
Other Westerners	10	15	5	3	10
Number of respondents	(2,546)	(1,209)	(174)	(720)	(443)

Source: Unpublished data from writer's National Urban Survey, 1955.

All foreign contacts are greater in Bangkok than in the provinces, and in the provinces the greatest frequency is in the north and south

[37] *Ibid.*, pp. 83-84.

for all categories of Westerners. The difference in frequency of American and British contacts is much less in the north and south; this reflects the greater presence of British in these areas due to teak interests in the north and rubber and tin in the south.

The Bangkok elite have also had considerable personal contact with Westerners as a part of travel or residence abroad. The extent of this is shown in Table 16, where data from the 1959 Bangkok Elite Study indicate that 48 per cent had been abroad, 18 per cent having been to the United States. Manheimer in a study based on depth interviews with Thai student exchanges has documented very well the political socialization effects of such experiences.[38] Within Bangkok the same elite group displays a relatively high rate of contact with Americans, as shown in Table 17. We note that about one-fourth have contact with Americans at least once a week and that about two-fifths have contacts at least once a month.

TABLE 16: FOREIGN EXPERIENCE OF BANGKOK ELITE

Country of Visit or Residence	Per Cent
United States	18
Britain	9
France	2
Australia	1
Other countries	18
Never abroad	50
Not ascertained	2
Total	100
Number of respondents	(1,825)

Source: Bangkok Elite Study, 1959.

TABLE 17: FREQUENCY OF EXPOSURE OF BANGKOK ELITE
TO AMERICANS

Frequency of Contact	Per Cent
Almost every day	14
At least once a week	11
About once a month	14
Two or three times a year	15
Hardly ever	23
Never	21
Not ascertained	2
Total	100
Number of respondents	(1,825)

Source: Bangkok Elite Study, 1959.

[38] Dean Manheimer, "Thai Student Exchanges—a Research Report," unpublished report of International Research Associates, New York, 1955, passim.

SOURCES AND CREDIBILITY OF INFORMATION ABOUT
THE UNITED STATES

The concentration of mass media and foreign contacts in Bangkok has given the Bangkok elite unusual exposure to certain kinds of information about the United States. Table 18 from the Bangkok Elite Study shows the proportions exposed to eight categories of such information. Also shown is source of the information and respondents' evaluation of the truthfulness of the information.

TABLE 18: SOURCES AND CREDIBILITY OF INFORMATION ABOUT
THE UNITED STATES AMONG BANGKOK ELITE

Topic	Per Cent Exposed	Personal Experience	SOURCE Mass Media Newspaper	SOURCE Mass Media Radio	Persons Thai	Persons Americans	All or Fairly True
y of life	80%	30%	33%	22%	9%	16%	76%
story and overnment	77	7	33	22	2	5	74
s, lit., music	56	8	14	34	1	3	49
entific	96	7	75	60	3	0	91
eign policy	73	5	59	41	4	3	67
cognition of reedom	84	4	63	47	2	3	73
gional greements	73	2	56	42	2	2	62
ncern for velfare of Thai	92	18	72	55	6	4	81

Note: Total number of respondents is 1,825.

Source: Bangkok Elite Study, 1959.

There is a fairly high exposure to all topics, the greatest (over 80 per cent) being to information about American scientific activities, American concern for the welfare of Thailand, and America's recognition of the freedom of every country. The topics about which respondents had received least information were American art, literature, and music. Topics with the greatest exposure are also the topics where mass media are cited most frequently as the source of information. Striking is the fact that information about the American way of life shows a higher association with personal experience as a source than does any other topic.

Truthfulness is rated highest for information about American scientific achievements and American concern for Thai welfare, while it is lowest for American foreign policy and the arts. If topics are ranked in order of frequency of exposure and also for informational credibility, the resulting rank-order correlation (*rho*) is 0.78, indicating that the more widespread a topic's informational exposure, the higher its adjudged truthfulness.

COGNITIVE NEEDS REGARDING FOREIGN COUNTRIES

While foreign media exposure gives a picture of the informational environment, it does not reveal what kinds of information the Thai seek. The informational needs of respondents in the National Urban Survey were studied by asking what they wanted to know about six countries. The results are shown in Table 19.

TABLE 19: INFORMATION NEEDS REGARDING FOREIGN COUNTRIES OF MIDDLE AND UPPER-CLASS URBAN THAI

Topic about Which Information Is Desired	Russia	Red China	Nation-alist China	United States	Great Britain	Indo-China
Form of government and political situation	20%	18%	19%	13%	14%	23%
Individual civil rights, freedom	10	8	3	3	2	2
Military strength	4	1	8	3	2	2
Economic situation	15	19	13	21	18	11
Technology	3	2	1	14	7	1
Education, students' life	5	5	4	13	10	4
Life of people, customs	25	29	20	28	26	20
"Everything"	2	2	1	2	2	2
No information desired	25	25	31	15	24	34

Note: Total number of respondents is 2,546.

Source: Unpublished data from writer's National Urban Survey, 1955.

It is remarkable that the relative distribution of interests is rather similar for all six countries. For all countries the greatest interest is shown for information about the country's life and customs, followed by economic situation and government and political situation. Matters such as individual civil rights, military strength, technology, and education are on the whole rather low in frequency of mention.

The United States is somewhat different in that technology and education receive a relatively higher mention, while Russia and Red China are unique in receiving a comparatively higher interest in individual civil rights and freedom. There is somewhat stronger interest in military strength for Nationalist China than for any other country, while interest in government and political situation is greater for Indo-China than for other countries.

If we use the response "no information desired" as an index of disinterest in gaining information, we get the impression of rather widespread informational apathy. One-fourth or more of the respondents are apathetic concerning each country, with the exception of the United States, where only 15 per cent display disinterest in learning more. It is significant that informational·apathy is greatest for Thailand's immediate neighbor, Indo-China.

VI. Thai Personality in Communications and Opinion Formation

We have seen that the upper- and middle-class Thai are rather well involved in a fairly extensive communications system which also has numerous linkages with the world abroad. We know, however, that the modernization process must be accompanied by changes in personality and self-concept that are supportive to the new economic, political, social, and communications roles required by a participant society. Thus the adequacy of a nation's communications system cannot be assessed solely in terms of its size, accessibility, and range; it must be judged relative to the psychological capacities of its citizens in handling information and in relating attitudes of action.

VALUES OF THE TRANSITIONAL THAI

A good point of departure is the value pattern of the "modern" man in transitional Thailand. In transitional societies it is possible to identify the "transitional man" as one who is midway between the values of tradition and those modern values that are available in his society. But we must also recognize that in Thailand at least the "modern man," as identified by sociological criteria, is also psychologically a "transitional man" in that he is midway between the modernism available in his own society and that more ulterior modernism of the "world culture."

This mixed, transitional character of persons who have presumably "crossed over" into the modern world is revealed by 1958 data on the values of the 394 Thai university students referred to earlier.[39] These students (a random sample of 5 Bangkok universities and colleges) were asked to choose from a group of 15 values those 3 that were most important in their lives. The 15 values presented were

[39] Schuler and Thamavit, op.cit., pp. 96-97.

equally divided among traditional, modern, and mixed, on the basis of a consensus of Thai and American researchers. The meaning of "Thai modernism" is clearly suggested by the fact that the 3 most frequently chosen values were: "education" (82 per cent), a modern value; "fame" (43 per cent), a mixed value; and "Buddhist morality" (41 per cent), a traditional value. It is extremely significant that "Westernization" as a value was chosen by less than 1 per cent—significant indeed in view of the easy assumption that tomorrow's leaders would be the most open to Western influences.

The mixture of traditionalism and modernism that characterizes the "modern" Thai is also revealed when students were asked about their post-educational aspirations. The two most frequent categories of aspiration were "successful in chosen occupation" (69 per cent), a modern aspiration, and "be of service to others" (33 per cent), a very traditional value in Thailand. The distribution of students along the continuum of traditional versus modern was metricized by scoring each student according to the values he chose. Traditional values were given a weight of zero, modern values a weight of two, and mixed values a weight of one. The distribution of these scores is shown in Table 20.

TABLE 20: DISTRIBUTION OF TRADITIONALISM-MODERNISM
VALUE SCORES OF UNIVERSITY STUDENTS IN BANGKOK

Score	Per Cent
0 (Traditionalism)	1
1	1
2	7
3	38
4	26
5	24
6 (Modernism)	3
Total	100
Number of students	(394)

Source: Schuler and Thamavit, op.cit., pp. 96-97.

We note a decided skewing toward the modern pole. Ninety-six per cent of the students are mixed, however, and the midpoint of the scale, which represents the equal balance of traditional and modern values, is the most frequent score. We may conclude that these students are typified by a mixture of values, and that, while they favor modern values, their preference is neither blind acceptance of modernism or the West nor a rejection of the traditional. Although these data are somewhat superficial, the balance of values they suggest is supported repeatedly by many other observations made throughout the whole of Thai culture. Perhaps we have here a hint as to why the Thai can span two worlds with relative psychological ease. Exactly the same conclusions have been drawn by Manheimer in his study of the adjustment of Thai students in the United States.[40] Manheimer was impressed with the relaxed, unstrained moderation that deterred the Thai from strong identifications with either extreme. The 18-month clinical study of 15 modern Thai, referred to earlier, focused among other things upon the psychological mechanisms used to avoid and mitigate endopsychic conflicts arising out of the modernizing process. While these findings are properly the subject of another paper, it should be pointed out here that much reliance is placed on pragmatic value selectivity, avoidance of ego-involvements in either the traditional or modern extreme, and the undemanding nature of Thai role expectations—a reliance which apparently the Thai have traditionally used in dealing with conflicts.

While the modern Thai's orientation with respect to traditional and modern values contributes to the maintenance of psychic integrity in the midst of transition, the interesting question is whether these benefits encourage the media responses which are essential to the development of a participant society. There is evidence to suggest that these benefits are achieved by means which inhibit the emergence of the processes whereby communicated information is converted into effective opinion and action. In tracing out these consequences, in what is admittedly a somewhat tenuous way, we shall examine four aspects of Thai personality: self-concept, self-potency, cognitive role, and psychological mechanisms for relating to mass media.

CONCEPTION OF SELF AND PERCEIVED NEEDS FOR SELF-CHANGE

The appropriate question here is whether the Thai self-image is compatible with the demands of media response imposed by a participant society, and whether the perceived needs for self-change would strengthen development in the required direction.

To begin with, let us consider the model of the valued personality which is held out and reinforced by the Thai socialization process. While there are a number of components in this ideal self, we shall focus upon four qualities which comprise the foundations of the ethical component. These four qualities have received some degree of formal

[40] Manheimer, op.cit., passim.

embodiment as the Buddhist *Brahma Vihara* (the Four Faces of the Temple of Brahma). The traits, known by their Pali names, are: *karuna* (compassion), *metta* (loving kindness), *mudita* (empathic joy), and *uppekha* (equanimity achieved through impersonal serenity and noninvolvement). (The English equivalents are only approximate and suggestive.) These four qualities are cultivated in the home, in school, and in the adult world. For instance, in a study the writer made of government officials' concept of a good supervisor the *Brahma Vihara* was mentioned by almost everyone. It is also expected that the higher a person's status, the more completely he should display these qualities.

In general the Thai perceive themselves as an ethnic group possessing these valued attributes. This has been confirmed in a study by the writer using Stephenson's Q-sort technique[41] and in large-scale surveys. Many of the major implications of these studies are conveniently illustrated in the responses of university students when asked to characterize the Thai people. These Thai perceptions of the Thai people are shown in Table 21.

TABLE 21: STUDENTS' PERCEPTIONS OF THAI PRESENT SELF
AND DESIRED SELF

Categories of Ascribed Traits	Present Self	Desired Self[a]
Carefree	50%	0%
Generous	39	11
Gentle	37	6
Religious	11	4
Comfort-loving	9	4 (less)
Progressive	8	15
Conservative	6	7
Considerate	1	1
Ambitious	0	59
Self-confident	0	21
Nationally-minded	0	19
Number of respondents	(394)	(394)

[a] For "Desired Self" the percentages indicate the proportion of respondents believing that the Thai people should possess *more* of the trait listed, with the exception of "comfort-loving" where *less* of the trait should be possessed.

Source: Constructed from the data of Schuler and Thamavit, *op.cit.*, pp. 99-100.

The three most frequent response categories are "carefree," "generous," and "gentle"—traits which clearly reflect the *Brahma Vihara*

[41] For a basic presentation on Q-methodology, see William Stephenson, *The Study of Behavior*, Chicago, University of Chicago Press, 1953.

and which actually are salient in the Thai traditional personality. (Thai literature, for instance, is full of instances where these traits are cited in characterizations of heroes and heroines.) This rather high congruence between perceived self and desired self is further evidenced by the second column in Table 21, which shows opinions on what qualities the Thai *ought* to have. These responses give us a picture of the discrepancy between what the Thai self *is* and what it should *become*, and thus of the felt needs for self-change.

In examining the qualities of the desired self we can make some very interesting observations. The traits mentioned as *already possessed* are also mentioned as those which *should be possessed more.* Furthermore, the more frequently a trait is mentioned as possessed, the more frequently it is felt that it should be strengthened. This seems to mean that *personality development for these Thai is to an appreciable degree a matter of becoming more of what they already are.* The one exception is the trait "carefreeness," which, while the most frequent characterization of the present self, is not mentioned at all as a quality that should be possessed by the desired self. It is also significant that the "should be" traits mentioned most frequently of all, namely, "ambitious," "self-confident," and "nationally-minded," are not perceived at all as part of the present Thai self; they are new and must be added.

These observations suggest the following interpretation: there is considerable acceptance of the present organization of the self, and there is very little self to reject. Perceived needs for self-change are not a matter of rejecting parts of the existing self; rather, they are a matter of becoming more of what the self already is, and especially becoming some new things which have no precedents in the existing self. These widespread attitudes of self-acceptance seem to be due in part to the introjection of cultural attitudes. Since other people are so undemanding and accepting of one's self, these same attitudes are introjected in childhood and are applied to one's own evaluations of self.

Turning now to content of the trait categories, we can make three observations: (1) All of the traits comprising the present self (with the possible exception of "progressive") stress ethical and social character and are typical of Thai traditionalism. (2) All of the self-changes lacking precedents in the present self (i.e., the "new" traits) are distinctly modern and are of the kind needed to encourage achievement, success, and civic responsibility. (3) The categories used to perceive both present and desired self are exclusively of the personality and social variety; there is a total absence of traits referring to abilities, cognitive capacities, or anything having implications for information-handling skills. Thus, while there are felt needs for self-change in the direction of the "modern" personality, the new self which is sought would contribute mainly to increased motivation for exposure to information, but it is largely irrelevant to the cognitive skills required for responsible information-handling. As we shall see, such skills are one of the most "underdeveloped" aspects of Thai personality.

SELF-POTENCY

Effective political socialization involves the development of a sense of "self-potency," by which we mean the extent to which an individual perceives himself as having some degree of control over his world, the extent to which he believes his opinions and actions can affect the solution of his problems.[42] Without self-potency the socializing effects of mass media would be greatly curtailed. It seems obvious that a certain amount of self-potency is required for opinion to be translated into action, and for an individual to be vigilant of information about new roles and modes of political action. Unless an individual feels that his ideas and actions can make a difference, he is not likely to make the effort; nor will he be sensitive to information about such fruitless efforts. Lerner has suggested that self-potency for larger goals is a vital part of the movement of the "constricted personality" of traditional society to the "expanded personality" of participant society.[43]

In Thailand cultural expectations about the manipulatability of man and nature, especially man, have been traditionally rather optimistic. The world of people and events is seen as essentially an open, on-going affair, offering reasonable promise that one's efforts to influence it will succeed—providing one is so moved.

In the National Urban Survey respondents were asked what they thought were the most serious problems facing the nation. The multiple responses were about equally divided between "economic" and "political" categories. We then asked what they thought they themselves could do to solve these problems. Only 2 per cent indicated a total lack of self-potency by the reply "can't do anything," while 11

---

[42] For a brief review of some notions concerning self-potency, see David McClelland, *Personality*, New York, Holt, 1951, pp. 538-542.

[43] Lerner, *op.cit.*, pp. 73-74, 147-152.

per cent were unable to answer, which suggests an inability to appraise one's self-potency. The positive responses were classified as to whether they denoted a "self" action (those which an individual personally could carry out) or a "non-self" action (those which could be carried out only by someone else). The proportional split of self and non-self actions provides us with a measure of self-potency for the associated problems. The distribution of these classified responses is shown in Table 22.

TABLE 22: SELF-POTENCY FOR ECONOMIC, POLITICAL, AND
EDUCATIONAL PROBLEMS OF MIDDLE- AND
UPPER-CLASS URBAN THAI

| Problem Type | PER CENT MENTIONING PROBLEM WHO PROPOSE SELF-ACTION | | | | |
	Total	Bangkok	North	Northeast	South
Economic	73	75	74	65	76
Political	75	90	76	72	73
Educational	51	35	40	63	58

Source: Unpublished data from writer's National Urban Survey, 1955.

Self-potency is clearly quite high both for economic and political problems; in both cases over 70 per cent of the proposed solutions are self-actions. Very similar results were obtained in a recheck study done on a much smaller sample in 1959.

Focusing upon political problems, we note that the self-potency percentage is much higher (90 per cent) in Bangkok than in provincial towns. One might expect, then, that political participation would follow a similar pattern. But this is definitely not the case. The explanation of this paradox will help illuminate the nature of the relationship between self-potency and many forms of Thai public action.

Political Participation and Self-Potency. Political participation in the form of voting is higher than for the Middle East countries studied by Lerner and compares not unfavorably with many Western countries. The percentage of qualified voters who actually voted in the eleven elections since the establishment of the Constitutional Monarchy in 1932 has never been below 25 per cent, and in the election of February 1957 it was 58 per cent. The average for all eleven elections is 38 per cent.[44] During the same period the rate in the United States varied between 54 and 64 per cent.[45]

[44] Thai Department of Interior, *Elections in Thailand*, Bangkok, 1959, p. 20.
[45] Robert E. Lane, *Political Life*, Glencoe, Ill., The Free Press, 1959, pp. 19-21.

Strangely enough, and quite contrary to the usual assumptions about developing countries, the voting density in urban areas is decidedly below that in rural areas. Bangkok, for instance, has one of the lowest of all voting densities. In every election it has lagged considerably behind the national average; the lowest rate was 17 per cent (1949), the highest 54 per cent (February 1957), and the average for all eleven elections 28 per cent.

Furthermore, among urban areas the voting rate exhibits a rather close *inverse* relationship with the amount of urbanization (i.e., size of municipal population). Among the seven towns studied in the National Urban Survey we find the following: the most urbanized towns have the highest political self-potency but the lowest voting rate, while the least urbanized towns have the lowest political self-potency but the highest voting rate. Urbanization thus seems to be positively related to political self-potency but negatively related to voting. Also, a measure of political interest, indexed from questions about political affairs and opinions, reveals a uniformly low level of interest in political events.

The explanation of this paradox appears to be that while interest in politics is apathetic in both rural and urban areas, in villages and less urbanized areas there are face-to-face influences and status demands that take the place of direct political interest and thus encourage voting. For instance, at election time it is one of the duties of the village headman to instruct the villagers in voting procedures. Sometimes the district officer or other officials will supplement his efforts. In this way villagers tend to acquire the notion that failure to vote would be committing a crime, or at least a violation of obligations due within the status hierarchy. Furthermore, the election itself often becomes a festive occasion. These and other primary community influences, which have been interestingly documented by Phillips,[46] serve to involve the villager in voting for social and respect reasons, but not from political interest per se.

In urban areas, however, there is an absence of such administrative pressures and social inducements, and there is no strong political interest per se to take their place. Thus in Bangkok political self-potency is very high, but there is no motivation to precipitate action. In villages it apparently does not matter whether political self-potency and interest are high or low, since political participation has

[46] Herbert Phillips, "The Election Ritual in a Thai Village," *Journal of Social Issues*, XIV, 4, 1958, pp. 36-50.

a non-political meaning. It seems, therefore, that for political behavior at least, self-potency is somewhat irrelevant to action, since action arises out of traditional non-political motivations. Considerations such as these should be borne in mind by those who would use voting density figures as a measure of "political participation."

Self-Potency and Communist Attitudes. Attitudes of approval or disapproval toward Communism were not found to relate to political self-potency in any direct way. Both the pro- and anti-Communist groups mentioned earlier contained almost identical proportions of self-actions for political problems. Nor did readers of the leftist press differ significantly from readers of the rightist press.

On the other hand, those who embraced consistent attitudes were higher in self-potency than those whose attitudes were inconsistent. Among the pro-Communist group those who gave responses in agreement with the Communist position on a battery of opinion questions had a higher score on political self-potency than those who were in disagreement. Similarly, among the anti-Communist group those who responded in agreement with the anti-Communist position were higher in self-potency than those in disagreement. It seems, then, that attitude consistency and self-potency are interactively linked.

PSYCHOLOGICAL MECHANISMS FOR RELATING TO MASS MEDIA

The modes for relating to the content of mass media provide one way for examining the "deutero" learning that occurs through participation in the mass media system. Only the most general conclusions will be given here; the supporting data come from the previously mentioned clinical study of the Thai administrative elite and from the depth probes used in the National Urban Survey.

Thai orientations toward media content can be summed up in the notion of "spectator role," wherein the individual permits himself only to view impersonally the content of communications, without much sense of involvement and without any impulsion to act. This spectator orientation is an extension to mass media of a very pervasive cultural mode for relating to the world in general, supported in turn by the Buddhist value of *uppekha,* one of the four virtues of the *Brahma Vihara. Uppekha* means internal equanimity achieved through non-attachment, or, in more psychological language, the withholding of ego-involvement and cathexis. Thus while it is undeniable that mass communications have given the Thai an enlarged field of awareness and new moral standards for evaluating their political scene, all of this has taken place within the basic role of the spectator. The principal effect has been to increase competence in spectatorship and to expand the arc of spectacle. This suggests that deutero learning in the mass media system has reinforced the general cultural habits of spectatorship and focused these habits on specific spheres of experience such as politics, thereby impeding political socialization. In spectatorship empathy is employed primarily to obtain vicarious gratification and catharsis for feelings of hostility, passion, and aggression which have few approved outlets in Thai culture. This is especially true for newspapers and motion pictures, where even the most casual observation confirms that the Thai love to witness the mediated display of violence, passion, and malevolence toward others.

The net result is that much satisfaction is gained from media participation alone; since it is enough to view, to believe, action is not psychologically necessary. This tendency to substitute media participation for overt action produces a curious kind of "narcotizing dysfunction,"[47] something which also occurs in the mass society of the West but for different reasons. And since gratification comes directly from the witnessing of information, there is little pressure to consolidate it into an opinion that would form an adequate basis of action. Lerner has pointed out that empathy is a psychological prerequisite to modernization.[48] We note here, however, that we must also consider how empathy is *used* by transitionals. While the spectator role may help preserve the integrity of the Thai self-concept by providing an outlet for unwanted and otherwise unexpressible feelings, it does not encourage the activities of a participant society. Psychological development of the Thai does not require further growth in empathy; what is needed is that satisfaction be derived not from the empathy process itself but from the enactment of the new roles acquirable through empathy.

COGNITIVE ROLE

By cognitive role we mean the information-handling processes acquired by playing a social role. This new concept is needed to account for the fact that in Thailand cognition and social relationships are closely connected. While there are several cognitive processes which could be mentioned here, we shall confine ourselves to one which appears most salient, namely, the "social pragmatism" which fre-

[47] Paul Lazarsfeld and Robert Merton, "Mass Communication, Popular Taste and Organized Social Action," in L. Bryson, ed., *The Communication of Ideas*, New York, 1948, pp. 95-118.
[48] Lerner, *op.cit.*, pp. 47-52.

quently governs the organizing of communicated information.[49]

At the most general level this may be described as a tendency to evaluate and organize information not in terms of empirical antecedents but in terms of social consequences. The Thai do not have any implicit theory of truth which places strong reliance upon documentation in empirical reality or upon the operations employed to obtain information. They seem to view information and knowledge as an economic commodity possessing a certain social utility, and its quality, i.e., validity, is dependent upon the craftsman who made it, or more specifically, the social status of the information's source. Nowhere is this attitude seen more clearly than in the traditional attitude toward education and learning, as has been well described by Hanks.[50]

This means that the assimilation and reorganization of incoming information is to a large degree governed by the anticipation of social purposes and the individual's intended social strategies. Two broad social utilities are discernible: the manipulation of the behavior of others, and the maintenance of status relationships. In either case the organization process is guided by prescriptions of the "looking-glass self"; that is, information is organized in anticipation of how the communicator will look to his audience and the effect that the relayed information will have upon his audience's perception of him. For instance, in intensive interviews respondents retraced their reactions to the newspaper they had read earlier that day. Virtually all respondents showed frequent indications of having mentally rehearsed, at the time of reading, the anticipated occasions for using the information vis-à-vis some person or persons in the immediate future.

Opinions which emerge from the assimilation of information in this way are socially anchored more than data anchored. And since a person is continually involved in playing two generalized roles, i.e., a superior and subordinate, it is not inaccurate to say that he tends to have two opinions.

VII. Some Conclusions on Political Socialization

All considered, one gets the impression that as an agent of political socialization the Thai communications system has in many respects

[49] Much of the interpretation that follows was originally developed in Bangkok with Douglas Ellson of the Department of Psychology, Indiana University.

[50] Lucien M. Hanks, Jr., "Indifference to Modern Education in a Thai Farming Community," *Human Organization*, XVII, 2, Summer 1958, pp. 9-14.

both strengthened and accommodated to the process of cultural continuity and persistence. While mass media give the Thai "modern" information, they do not cause him to relate to information in the manner required by a modern political state. Media behavior is largely a continuation of general cultural behavior. Traditional cognitive habits and opinion-action relationships become practiced rather than unlearned; consequently, participation in the mass communication system tends to encourage the traditional political culture by providing new ways for playing old roles. While this contributes to social stability and political conservatism, it delays the learning of new political behavior.

In those few instances where more modern political behavior has emerged it has been the content of communications, not the "deutero" learning which accompanies exposure, that is the contributive factor. Content does this by creating a consensual awareness of new standards of political elite behavior and by advertising the transgressions of the elite from these standards. The so-called "dirty" elections of 1947 are a case in point. As Pickerell and Moore have shown, we have for the first time the emergence of true popular involvement and distinguishable campaign platforms.[51] But the benign paternalism of Thai autocracy has made such instances few indeed.

On the whole the "latent" political lesson that is learned from mass communications is that traditional Thai expectations of political behavior continue to be valid, and that, after all, the most realistic and pragmatic posture must be basically and typically Thai. The flavor of some of these latent learnings (or relearnings) is succinctly suggested by a few of the Thai aphorisms which abound in political contexts:

"All is impermanent; only Karmic merit and demerit remain."

"A tame elephant, a cobra that masquerades as a fish, an old family retainer, and a loving wife—put not your trust in these things."

"He whose head stands out gets his head cut off."

"Don't spit at the sky."

"It's best to be like a bamboo reed—it bends but doesn't break."

"Push but don't pierce."

"If you run from the tiger, you encounter the crocodile."

[51] Albert G. Pickerell and Daniel F. Moore, "Elections in Thailand," *Far Eastern Survey*, XXVI, 6, 1957, pp. 92-96.

CHAPTER 13

COMMUNICATIONS POLICIES IN DEVELOPMENT
PROGRAMS

~·~

OUR ANALYSIS to this point has been directed primarily toward gaining insights into the nature of the communications process in transitional societies and an appreciation of the problems inherent in political modernization. We have reached a stage when it is appropriate to turn our attention more directly toward questions of policy and the issues which may confront governments seeking to develop their societies. In our introduction we suggested that the task of nation building in the new states is of such an urgent priority for free men that we are anxious to combine scholarly analysis with a concern for programs and policy. It was our hope that the communications approach to the problems of political development might be especially rewarding in producing guides for action.

Given our current state of knowledge it is impossible to design an effective general doctrine for the role of communications in political development. We do not have fully formulated and tested dynamic theories to provide the necessary intellectual support for such a doctrine of communications. Indeed, it would be quite unrealistic to hold out the hope that within the foreseeable future the social sciences will be able to produce a complete dynamic theory adequate for guiding nation building in all societies.

Social developments can never be expected to be ruled by such simple blueprints. In the underdeveloped regions there are great differences among the individual countries; each is at a different stage of development and therefore each will need somewhat different policies. Some countries are at the stage of very early transition, and all the instruments of communications must be directed to giving support to the legitimacy of the government and to the administrative structures of states which will in time be necessary for guiding further social changes. In those countries with a small modernized elite the weight of communications policies should be on the side of protecting the freedom of these leaders and strengthening their influences throughout the society. At later stages of development the elite may have expanded and the prime problem of communications becomes that of mobilizing increasingly larger segments of the mass of the people. At this phase the communications media must be used to reinforce an essentially tutelage process; the time is ripe for broad appeals and for the repetition of theses basic to civic education. At still later stages in the transitional process the problems of communications tend to center more on facilitating adjustments among different emerging interests and on the need for providing the population with effective channels for communicating its views to the elite.

Clearly the communications policies appropriate at one stage of development may be either irrelevant or, more likely, directly damaging if applied at other stages. The problem of policy, however, is even more complicated than merely distinguishing different stages, for the process of national transformation manifestly does not follow a linear course of development. The impact of the modern world has struck different traditional societies in different ways and with quite different results. The great differences in the tensions and stresses basic to all the various transitional societies makes it impossible to think of them as simply at different relative stages of development. Some countries may never experience some of the profound problems which have been fundamental to the histories of others. Similarly, some of the transitional societies have long histories of civilization and must adjust to the modern world on the basis of a sophisticated heritage, while other countries are now being catapulted into the modern world without a prior experience with the higher phases of human life.

The possibility of demonstrating the theoretical limitations to the designing of general policy plans for political development does not, however, require that we go to the other extreme of settling for a mere list of ad hoc propositions and random practical suggestions. There would of course be considerable value in such forms of wisdom but this is the kind of task which can best be done by operators and policy implementors. Between the two extremes of the overall blueprint and the collection of items of practical advice there is the domain of the general strategic approach or that of the basic orientation toward policy where the scholar should be able to make useful contributions and find a common meeting ground with those responsible for public affairs.

In short, in our effort to be of assistance in the nation-building process we should probably at this time focus primarily on trying to outline a general philosophy toward the role of communications in political development. The objective is to combine the advancement of theory with forms of analysis which will alert those responsible for action to the various possible implications of particular policies. The planning and implementation of nation-building policies call for an appreciation of not only the many facets of development but also the interrelationships among them. The intellectual preparation for policy making thus calls for a sense of perspective and a basic orientation which will highlight the possible levers which may move the process of development along constructive lines.

More specifically, the policy orientation should be one of searching for all the ways in which purposeful communications can facilitate every aspect of development with the least damaging consequences. It is necessary to stress the last qualifying phrase for, as our study has shown, many changes have been brought about in the underdeveloped areas but at a cost that has been so high as to prove eventually quite counter-productive. Colonialism, for example, was often highly effective in initiating a process of modernization, but it did so in such psychologically damaging ways that in the post-colonial period many of the formerly subjugated are still reacting to these experiences and are unable to advance in creative ways to the handling of contemporary problems of development. Only in part should a communications policy for development focus on the dissemination of new ideas, new techniques, and new images. In larger measure a successful communications policy must also provide reassurance for a people that they do have a common history, that they are in the process of experiencing a common challenge, and that in the future they will still have their common identity as a people and as a nation. In short, the successful communications policy must capture at any particular moment the appropriate balance between a people's search for innovation and their need for continuity. Sometimes this may mean putting new wine in old bottles, while at other times incremental changes may have to be dramatized as great events.

Governments in transitional societies generally do not have complete strategies for the role of communications in political development. Nor do they generally have a sensitive understanding of the full potentialities of communications in building coherent polities. Many governments have had an exaggerated expectation about the *influences that the mass media in isolation can have in changing the ways of tradition-bound peoples. Other governments have assumed that the mass media can be readily used to indoctrinate an entire citizenry with a common outlook and thus presumably resolve all problems of consensus. Still other governments have sought to rule by propaganda and thus institutionalize demagogy. None of these approaches embraces any sense of the proper place of communications in furthering national development.*

The experiences of international communications and psychological warfare have encouraged the view that no form of communications can be a substitute for policy, and that all efforts at manipulative communications must be governed and strictly limited by the bounds of political policy. These experiences have strengthened the belief that communications policy should always be treated as a stepchild of "substantive policies." This conclusion about the relative importance of communications or information policies is applicable to the problem of political development only to the extent that in treating with the mass of their people the ruling elites of some transitional societies are in a position essentially analogous to that of persons employing psychological warfare across national boundaries. To a limited degree governments, in seeking to encourage their more tradition-bound people to adopt new ways, need to be reminded that information programs cannot substitute for substantive administrative policies and that words can neither replace nor completely disregard actions.

The analogy with international communications and psychological warfare does not apply to the broader dimensions of the role of communications in the process of political development. The dichotomy between policy and communications does not exist with respect to the building of a polity; as we have repeatedly observed, the very process of communications is coterminous with the political process. The development of the structure of communications, the creation of more coherent modes of communication, and the strengthening of all forms of reciprocal communications are also inherent in the development of a more integrated and a more responsive polity.

Thus the role of communications in political development is considerably more than merely supporting and facilitating the acceptance of the specific policies of government. The very act of communication and the experience of sharing and responding to communications represent in themselves the essence of political involvement in a polity. This means that fundamental to any strategy of communications for political development must be the objective of transforming what we have characterized as transitional communications into our model of a modern system. The highest priority must thus be given to building up the necessary systematic and orderly relationships between the mass media and the patterns of face-to-face and more personalized modes of communication.

Whether the objective is that of employing communications to facilitate the realization of administrative policies or of directly strengthening the flow of communications as an immediate measure in building the polity, the critical problem in most transitional societies will be that of relating what we initially described as the two prime levels of the communications system. Government programs can expect to be popularly received only when they are mutually supported by both the mass media and the more informal social processes of communications. A people cannot be aroused and mobilized by the mass media alone, and hence the need for political parties and popular movements to bring into play also the other level of communications in support of the national objective. Similarly, the continuing strength and adaptability of a polity can be guaranteed only when the social processes of communications and the mass media systems are coherently related to each other.

Thus in seeking an orientation for policy we must begin with an examination of precisely this relationship between the mass media and the more personalized systems of communications.

CHAPTER 14

THE MASS MEDIA AND POLITICS IN THE MODERNIZATION PROCESS

ITHIEL DE SOLA POOL

I. Introduction

THERE are four policy issues about the development of mass media which most emerging nations must resolve. As countries pass from the conditions of traditional society to modernity, sometimes they are resolved by deliberation, sometimes by happenstance.

First, and most important, developing nations must decide how much of their scarce resources to invest in mass media. Second, they must decide what roles to assign the public and private sectors respectively. Third, they must decide how much freedom to allow or how much control to impose; how much uniformity to require and how much diversity to permit. Fourth, they must decide at how high a cultural level to pitch the media output.

The Communist and non-Communist countries make very different decisions on these matters. The practice in non-Communist countries is for development plans to provide large amounts for the education of children and for the eradication of illiteracy but relatively small amounts for other communications investment. The practice in the Communist countries also is to spend heavily for literacy and education but in addition to support expensive programs of exhortation addressed to adults. They invest much in the press, movies, loud speaker systems, etc.

The neglect of mass media development in most of the new non-Communist nations may be documented best by reference to that medium which is most often operated by the government itself, radio. Since in most developing countries it is the medium most effectively available to the planners themselves, what they do with it is a good index of the importance they really attribute to media development. Egypt has made of radio a major instrument of foreign policy. Most developing countries have done something by way of developing village-oriented radio programs and educational programs, but their efforts are small.

The practice in India is typical of the priorities. There are two radios per 1,000 persons in India. The First Five Year Plan allocated two-tenths of one per cent of outlays to developing of broadcasting. It allocated 14 times as much as that to posts and telegraph. It allocated about 60 times as much to education. But that was only the Plan. Across the board, actual outlays for the five years slipped 15 per cent below the Plan, but outlays for broadcasting were allowed to fall short by 45 per cent, leaving actual outlays at somewhat over one-tenth of one per cent of the total. In the Second Five Year Plan development of broadcasting was given no greater role, being again allowed two-tenths of one per cent of outlays. In the Third Plan it is cut down to one-tenth of one per cent.

The willingness of countries faced by foreign exchange shortages to ration newsprint or impose severe excise taxes, tariffs, and quotas on radios and TV sets, and even to exclude TV entirely for fiscal reasons, attests to the fact that few non-Communist countries have assigned to the development of the mass media the same significance they have to steel mills, roads, railroads, and dams.

The situation in the Communist underdeveloped countries is, of course, quite different. Castro's use of TV, the Communist avidity for the Ministry of Information in a coalition regime, the blare of the Chinese omnipresent loud speaker system, and many other examples testify to the great importance attached to the exhortation of adults. The circulation of newspapers in the Soviet Union grew from 2.7 millions in 1913 to 9.4 millions in 1928, to 38.0 millions in 1939, to 44.0 millions in 1954.[1] Frederick Yu gives us comparable figures from China.[2] Capital investment in the production of words is not stinted in Communist countries.

It might be argued, though erroneously, that the reason for low public investment in mass media in non-Communist developing countries is that the media are thought to belong properly to the private sphere. It is indeed true that media in the private sphere have developed more rapidly than those in the public sphere. The few commercial radio stations in Asia (e.g., in Goa and the Philippines) have built far larger audiences than the publicly owned stations with which they sometimes compete beyond their borders.

[1] 1913-1939 figures from Alex Inkeles, *Public Opinion in Soviet Russia*, Cambridge, Mass., Harvard University Press, 1951, p. 144; 1954 figures from UNESCO, *Basic Facts and Figures*, Paris, 1956.
[2] See Chapter 16 of this volume.

TV on any scale exists in underdeveloped countries only where it has been commercial. Publicly owned TV has been stillborn. TV exists in 16 underdeveloped countries in the Eastern hemisphere, with commercial stations in only 5 of them. No one of these 16 countries had more than 20,000 sets in 1958, but the two countries with most sets were ones with commercial stations. In Latin America TV has evolved much faster and further; among the 14 countries there with TV only one bars commercial broadcasting.

Newspapers, which in virtually all non-Communist countries are private, can now be found everywhere, and movies have become a major industry in a number of underdeveloped countries.

But non-Communist developing countries do not limit their governmental efforts in media development in order to gain the efficiencies of private enterprise. They do so rather because they accept the clichés of European socialism about the evils of commercial media; they see government radio and TV as the only proper kind. One might expect governments which hold that view to take up media development seriously, but they seldom do.

A favorable governmental policy is important even for the development of private media. Policy on import of newsprint, development of newsprint sources, placing of legal advertising, telegraph rates, and many other policies may either facilitate or inhibit growth of private media. Thus it can hardly be argued that government need pay little attention to media development because the media are private. There must be other reasons for the policy decision that is usually made to play down investment in mass media. One reason, which we shall shortly consider, is disillusionment with their usefulness. Whatever the reasons, the practice is unmistakable.

Characteristic of non-Communist developing countries is a policy which attaches great importance to literacy and the education of children but little importance to the mass media, and which looks down with some disdain on those more popular mass media which do develop at low cultural levels in the private sphere. Characteristic of Communist developing countries, on the other hand, is a policy which attaches enormous importance to hortatory communications through the mass media, and which uses these not only for political control but also as a major stimulus to the carrying through of development plans.

Behind these divergent investment policies lie two different theories of communication as well as two different theories of economic organization. Our objective in this paper is to examine these implicit theories of communication and test them against social science knowledge.

II. Disillusionment with the Mass Media

The implicit view about the operation of the mass media which we have been describing as widely held by elites in non-Communist nations may be labeled that of disillusionment. The media are conceded a potential function of educating people to support urgent national tasks for development, but they fail at it. The media, so it seems, are ineffective agents of action on behalf of the planners. Agricultural advice broadcast on radio seldom gets followed in practice. Exhortations in the press to change established family or social patterns seem to have no results. People may learn that caste discrimination, or a low protein diet, or spitting, or dowries are disapproved in the modern world, but they do not change as the planners exhort them to.

But while the Westernizing leaders become disillusioned about the power of the media in their own hands to engender desired actions, they simultaneously believe in the vast powers of the hidden persuaders for evil. It seems that while the media are not effective instruments of constructive action, they have a considerable power to disorient and engender confusion in a society. They produce, for example, a demonstration effect. They engender the revolution of rising expectations. They engender desires for new things about which their readers and viewers learn, but they do not thereby create a willingness to take the actions called for to obtain these good things.

Now what we have just described may seem to be a caricature of a jaundiced view of the role of the mass media in development, but it is more than that. It is indeed a view with a firm foundation in social science research. It is perfectly true that the mass media alone, unlinked to word-of-mouth communication, fail in generating action but do not fail in creating information and desires. We shall document this point later. Here let us simply note that the lukewarm attitude of the governments of most developing countries toward the mass media is a natural concomitant of the weakness of political organization underpinning their regimes. Without an effective political organization at the grass roots to provide word-of-mouth support for the messages in the mass media, the latter do not produce desired action results.

From a broader point of view than that of a particular government, other effects of the mass media, such as demonstration effects or raising the level of information, may be either good or bad in the long run. But a regime resting on weak political organization can hardly be expected to look with pleasure on forces which introduce shocks to the social fabric while not facilitating control of the short-run action consequences. A regime based on a strong organization of face-to-face leadership can use mass media with great effectiveness as an associated instrument of action. A regime without such organization cannot substitute mass media propaganda for organization. The media do not produce the same results.

Thus the theory of communication that underlies the media investment pattern in most non-Communist developing countries is one which says, first, that the media do not seem to produce major changes in action. (That is true if one considers the media alone.) Secondly, other changes in the short run, such as changes in beliefs and values unaccompanied by appropriate changes in practices, tend to be disruptive. Third, despite the impracticality or dangers of trying to produce changes in the minds of men, it is recognized that such changes are needed for modernization. That is why a seemingly safe investment is made in the very slow-acting medium of education. From the perspective of history we know how disruptive to the old ways education may also be, but the quick-acting media (press, radio, film) act in periods coincident with the span considered in political decision making while education in general does not. For the short run, then, this theory says the mass media are not of great importance; and that is correct if one focuses on the objective of producing action and assumes the media to operate without concomitant political organization.

III. The Communist Theory of Media Use

The Communist theory of mass communication differs at many points from that which we have just outlined. In the first place, and most obviously, it is even more emphatic on the possible negative effects of some messages; oppositional messages are simply banned. Terror assures that only the approved ideas are in the flow to the public, without tolerance of even slight deviations. While this is the most important single difference between Communist and free world communication, we do not dwell upon it here since our subject concerns other matters.

The Communist theory of mass communication, in the second place, while much concerned with the immediate action consequences of propaganda, is not quite so exclusively focused on them. Although the Communist propaganda rulebook requires that the agitator always exhort to specific actions rather than simply advocate attitudes, at the same time Communist doctrine recognizes propaganda objectives other than those which action-advocating propaganda may serve. Much more than their opponents, the Communists think of using the mass media to produce characterological change. Also they are aware of the possibility of using the mass media as organizational devices, for in Communist theory the media are just an adjunct to political organization, not an independent base for political power.

That part of Communist theory with which we are here concerned is developed in two pamphlets by Lenin, *What Is to Be Done*, and *Left Wing Communism, An Infantile Disorder*.[3] It has been codified in a number of books by students of Soviet affairs.[4] In *What Is to Be Done* Lenin polemicized in favor of the revolutionists establishing a nationwide legal newspaper inside of Czarist Russia. He conceded the point of his opponents that such a paper under Czarist censorship could not tell the truth as the Marxists saw it, could not agitate effectively, could not, in short, be a spokesman for the views its publishers held. Why then did he want it established, and why did he regard it as of utmost importance? His main reason was that he recognized something which American racketeers have also recognized: that a newspaper distribution system is an excellent nucleus for a political machine. Actually his view was a little bit broader; the whole newspaper apparatus would provide both a function for and a cover for the revolutionary organization on a nationwide basis. There would be reporters who would have to travel around, inform themselves, get themselves in contact with sources of news on legitimate grounds. There would be jobs in distribution for less literate party members. For all of them the existence of something to do in the otherwise stifling environment of a dictatorship, and something which brought them into face-to-face contact with each other in a legal way, would be

---

[3] "What Is to Be Done," 1902, in V. I. Lenin, *Collected Works*, New York, International Publishers, IV, 1929, pp. 89-258; *Left Wing Communism, An Infantile Disorder*, New York, International Publishers, 1940.

[4] See, especially, Philip Selznick, *The Organizational Weapon*, New York, Mc-Graw Hill, 1952, for a discussion of the relation of the media to organization; Raymond A. Bauer, *The New Man in Soviet Society*, Cambridge, Mass., Harvard University Press, 1952, for Soviet views on the possibilities of producing characterological changes; and Nathan Leites, *A Study of Bolshevism*, Glencoe, Ill., The Free Press, 1953, for a general codification of Communist doctrines of political tactics.

a major boon to morale. These are the reasons why he wished the newspaper established.

While this approach to the media may in part be explained away as a response to the special situation of maintaining a subversive organization against an inefficient authoritarian regime,[5] it has nevertheless been canonized into general doctrine. The model of media use set in the first decade of this century remains in generalized form the model in Communist countries today.

Let us try to codify the operational doctrine briefly.

One: the important thing about a medium is not what it says per se but the social function (a) of its existence as an institution and (b) of the statements in it.

Two: discipline in making the "correct" statement in the media is indeed important—not primarily because of any direct impact of the statements made, but rather as a means to inducing characterological changes in the speakers in the direction of discipline and conformity.

Three: media provide an important activity around which to build organizations. Worker correspondents, discussion groups around key articles, local wall newspapers, etc. involve people deeply in the media.

Four: the media provide an instrument for central direction of organizations dispersed to all-corners of a country.[6] The media give the orders of the day to be carried out in face-to-face organization.

Five: words in the media alone do not effectively change people. It takes a combination of the media and direct personal contact to move people to action. It is only through participation in action that deeply held attitudes are changed. By action, however, these can be changed, even down to changing the basic personality of man.

The last point, and to some extent point one, may be clarified by reference to *Left Wing Communism*. In that work Lenin was replying to a group of Marxists who took the view that Communists had no business advocating such short-run goals as higher wages, racial equality, and social security. In the first place, the Leftists argued, such goals were unachievable under capitalism, so it was misleading to propagandize for them. Secondly, insofar as the goals were partly achieved, such progress might satisfy the masses; from the Communist

[5] Lenin's approach to media use may also be regarded as a generalization of the materialist conception of history, which minimizes the importance of the ideas expressed and exaggerates the importance of institutions.

[6] Note that the most important magazine in Russia is probably *The Agitators Notebook*, a journal which gives the two million oral agitators their guidelines for the next few weeks of meetings.

point of view the worse things got, the better. Lenin rejected both these theses. He conceded that immediate demands were unrealistic, a critic might say demagogic. He too regarded them as unachievable under capitalism. But in that fact he found their tactical merit, for the struggle was everything, the goal nothing. Lenin argued that the Communists had to put themselves on the side of what people wanted. There was no danger that success would undercut their revolutionary program, for with unachievable goals disappointment was sure. Finally, and most important, it was in the process of struggle for immediate demands that the masses would be transformed.

That was the old Marxist answer to the challenge: how could socialism turn over factories to obviously lazy, irresponsible, often dissolute people such as one found in fact among many of the workers? The Marxist answer was that capitalism made the workers that way. The experience of expressing autonomy through strikes and revolution would transform their personalities, making new men out of them. In line with that image of the learning experience in the modernization process, Lenin regarded the stimulation of action for immediate objectives as an essential part of all agitational efforts.

Thus it is not some abstract truth-value by which the media are to be judged in Communist eyes, but their contribution to action by organized groups of people. The media thus conceived acquire enormous importance to Communist regimes. They are an effective organizational device, and, when linked to face-to-face organization, they can be powerful influences on individual action.

IV. Traditional Modes of Communication

In the developing nations Westernized deracinated action-oriented elites without well-organized mass following tend to adopt the first view of the media outlined above, that which we called disillusionment. Certain other elites obviously find the Communist approach to mass communication genial. Ever since Sun Yat Sen a surprising number of leaders of developing countries have found the practical political methods of democratic centralism appealing even though they have cared but little about the economics of Communism. Indeed it is its approach to propaganda and politics which has been the most effective part of Bolshevik doctrine in the underdeveloped countries. That is not surprising, for in a few important respects the Communist doctrine is closer than is the Western approach to the theory of communication which characterizes traditional societies. It is closer in that it values the social function of a communication above its truth-value. It is closer also in its recognition of the primacy of word of mouth over mass media. It is closer in conceiving of communication as embedded in a process of elaborately organized particularistic relations among persons rather than as a uniform output from the media to a faceless mass.

The similarities that we have just noted between Communist and traditional conceptions of communication are not explained by any glib assertions of influence of one on the other, nor by a comforting assertion that the Communist approach to communication is backward or primitive. The fact that two of the three theories we have been describing are alike on a number of points is better explained by some peculiar and unique features of the third, or Western theory of communication which set it apart from most human behavior through all time the world over.

To evaluate assertions primarily by a criterion of objective truth is not a natural human way of doing things; it is one of the peculiar features of the Graeco-Roman-Western tradition. This one cultural heritage among the many in human experience has tended to make truth-value the main test of the validity of statements. And truth-value is a rather curious criterion. It is ruthlessly two-valued and dominated by the law of the excluded middle, something which classical Indian logic, for example, never accepted; statements in the latter system could be simultaneously both true and false. The Western criterion of truth-value also assumes that a statement has a validity or lack of it inherent in itself and quite independent of who says it and why. That too is something Brahminical philosophy did not accept; a statement true for a man in one Varna might be false for one in another. The Western criterion of truth assumes further that validity can be tested independently of who does the testing provided certain rituals of procedure are followed. Most cultural traditions do not make these assumptions. For one thing, only in a society with an unusually high degree of mutual trust in interpersonal relationships would people accept statements regardless of source. In most societies facts must be validated by an in-group authority before they can be considered credible. Word of mouth is therefore more trustworthy than written sources. Distrust of those who are not in one's own family, tribe, or caste dominates any objective test of truth in most economically non-expansive societies.[7]

[7] F. and M. Keesing, *op.cit.*; cf. also Thomas Blair, "Social Structure and Information Exposure in Rural Brazil," *Rural Sociology*, xxv, March 1960, pp. 65-75.

Furthermore, most of mankind does not regard the truth-value of statements as terribly important. For most of the men who have inhabited the earth the consequences of a statement—e.g., whether it will bring the wrath of God upon you, whether it will help you earn a living, whether it will win a loved one—are considerably more important than whether it matches certain abstract rules of transformability into other statements. The Western tradition is unique in the value it has attached to the latter consideration.

So when we say that traditional societies are more concerned with the social function of communication than with its truth-value, we are only saying they are human. Yet their concern with the social function of communications is an important fact.

A statement is valid in a traditional society if it comes from the right oracle. It is not necessarily everyone's right to judge its validity. There are statements within one's own sphere of propriety, and there are those which are outside one's proper role. Daniel Lerner has introduced all of us to the peasant whose reply to the question, what would he do if he were someone else—a foreigner, a radio station manager, a politician, is in effect, "My God! How can you ask me a question like that? I could never be him."[8] The peasant's statement, even in role playing, is considered of no validity. Felix and Marie Keesing document the same point even more extensively in their study of communication behavior in Samoa.[9] There are certain words and certain topics of discussion reference to which is proper only by certain individuals. In Samoa references to those domains in which power is demonstrated by chiefs and talking chiefs is improper for their subordinates. It is not, as in Western dictatorship, that the inferior is obliged to say approved things. It is rather that it is shocking for him to say anything at all in what is not his proper sphere.

The frequent application of social rather than truth-value criteria in traditional societies is further documented by studies of political movements in them. Lucian Pye has shown how to the Malayan Communists the primary criterion applied to Communist ideology was the power of the leaders. If the Communists seemed likely to win, then what the Communist leaders said was valid; if they seemed likely to lose, then it was not. It was personal leadership and power which determined the validity of what might be in the mass media.[10]

---

[8] *The Passing of Traditional Society*, Glencoe, Ill., The Free Press, 1958.

[9] Felix and Marie Keesing, *Elite Communications in Samoa*, Stanford, Stanford University Press, 1956.

[10] Cf. Lucian Pye, *Guerrilla Communism in Malaya*, Princeton, Princeton University Press, 1956; Edward W. Gude, *Buddhism and the Political Process in Cambodia*, manuscript, 1961, p. 15.

A study of Cambodia tells us that "information itself is considered sterile by the individual villager until someone of status has interpreted it. The individual does not see it as his role to judge the news."[11]

One might cite examples indefinitely. We could talk about honorifics and the problem of communication in Japan, where it may become hard to express what one has to say until one has gotten around to finding the words appropriate to the person to whom one is talking.

Our concern here, however, is to consider the significance of these matters to the mass media. The mass media represent a peculiar mode of communication in which one does not know to whom one is talking. Broadcasting or writing for the press is like dropping a note in a bottle over the side of a boat. The man who receives it may be king or pauper, relative or stranger, friend or foe.

This is less of a problem in a traditional society, although it is not a problem which is altogether new. All traditional societies have their equivalents of mass media. There is a literature of sagas or folk songs sung to all and sundry. There are assemblages at temples, festivals, or markets where the hawker or priest or actor addresses himself to a motley crowd of persons of all stations. There are proclamations to the multitude. There are ways of calling out to a stranger in the dark. But for all of these there are established conventions. The rules of etiquette prescribe the form of language in which a folk song is sung. The modern media create a host of new situations for which new conventions must be established. How does one answer the phone or talk on radio or write for the newspapers? New conventions will be established, but new conventions are always by definition crude, coarse, and vulgar.

So the mass media in a stratified society inevitably have the problem of vulgarity in a particularly acute way. They can avoid vulgarity by pretending they are addressing their most cultured superiors. This results in media which use only the highest form of the language and which are not understood by the bulk of the population. This happens extensively in Arab countries. It happens often where the media are in the hands of well-educated civil servants aspiring to be intellectuals. The All India Radio, for example, says that its small village audience is its top priority audience, but it also often refuses to use the low Hindi forms which the villagers can understand.

Alternatively, the media may seek out their natural mass audience

[11] Edward W. Gude, *op.cit.*, p. 14.

and alienate themselves from their national elite and its goals. They can do this by turning radical or by turning commercial and sensational or both, for these alternatives are not exclusive. Tawdry apolitical yellow publications or movies may well be produced by a largely leftist press corps. (Private entrepreneurs of sensation may be building part of the political machine Lenin prescribed.) Or it may be that the radical publications themselves provide low-level popular culture, some sort of so-called people's art. It takes either a callous unconcern with the values of one's culture or else an ideology which justifies alternative values to permit intellectuals, bred among the elite or elite aspirants of any society, to produce the kind of more or less debased materials which can communicate to the masses who share only a watered-down version of the culture.

In a traditional face-to-face communication system this problem is not too serious, for there is a high degree of differentiation of communication according to the interpersonal situation involved. The village singers or traveling troupes, though they tell ancient tales, are usually quite skilled at adapting themselves to their audience, often indeed introducing local matters or topical events into the classical frame of their stories. These bards or their equivalents are a kind of bridge between their unsophisticated audience and their own teachers or urban colleagues from whom they learn. Such traditional communicators at the lowest level have at least one foot deeply in their pre-industrial society, and they have at best very modest intellectual or cultural attainments. But in the great non-Western cultures they are in turn in contact with a more elevated group of traditional teachers and sages. At each level communication is appropriate to its environment both in literary form and content. Any kind of interpersonal organization, traditional or modern, has such a graded structure of face-to-face communication. Its absence is a problem for a pure mass media communication system.

Granted it is not an insuperable problem. The mass media are also graded, and they divide up a national audience among them by taste and cultural level. But a problem does exist. Some media do have to serve the total society. Where there is but a single local newspaper or radio or TV station, dissatisfaction with it is bound to arise in any differentiated society, and especially so in a dual society such as any developing society is. Even more important is the fact that highly educated or Westernized elites produce the modern media and guide them; such men are often unable or unwilling to address their masses, or they are in conflict when addressing them.

Educating the masses to become like their elite is normally offered as the answer. But that is obviously an illusory solution. Village schools or even new colleges may produce literacy. They do not thereby reduce the circulation of lowbrow highly popularized media; they increase it.

A recent study in Israel documents an obvious point. It compares the achievement in school of children whose fathers come from culturally advanced countries with children whose fathers come from underdeveloped countries. Although in the same grade-school classes in a heterogeneous community, by the end of the second grade 80 per cent of the former could read sentences but less than one third of the latter. Similar results appeared in arithmetic and other tests.[12] The supporting family environment largely determines how much the school communicates. So too with any medium, be it education or a mass medium. What it can accomplish is severely limited, depending upon the functionality of the medium as perceived in the interpersonal environment.

What this signifies is, first, that mass education may be expected to create an audience for only the most popularized and simplified media. Second, media of that kind are the only ones which can serve to induct into modern ways precisely those persons whose familial environment does not push them in the same direction. Education may modernize a child or young man from a household which instills motivation for that goal. It will not effectively modernize the masses. The media, plus associated personal influence on adults, must take over the job at the very low level which schools will achieve.

Media at that low level of popular culture include movies, comics and picture books, and potentially radio and TV. Also particularly effective at this level are the traditional media to which we referred before, and which can be used effectively on behalf of birth control, agricultural conservation, or nationalism. The Communists have done a good deal of this, putting out material through traditional storytellers, priests, or players. Some non-Communist movements have done the same. Conservative religious traditional parties, such as provincial movements in India or that of Prince Sihanouk in Cambodia or of the Muslim Teachers in Indonesia, of course rely particularly heavily

[12] Sarah Smilansky, "Evaluation of Early Education," in M. Smilansky and L. Adar, eds., *Evaluating Educational Achievements*, Educational Studies and Documents, No. 42, UNESCO, Paris, 1961, p. 9.

on a machine built up of bards, or bronzes, or Maulanas. But experiments have been conducted, and quite successfully, in using such channels for modernizing messages too.[13]

These traditional media are particularly effective because they involve an organized machine for word-of-mouth communication. We know that in many traditional societies word-of-mouth is more trusted than the written word, that word-of-mouth everywhere is an essential stimulus to action, that it is more adaptable to the variations in style and manner which are so particularly important in a dual and transitional society; and we might add here that at the early stages of transition, mouths may be more common than newspapers or radios. (Cambodia, for example, has roughly one full-fledged priest for every 80 inhabitants, against one weekly paper in circulation for each 120 inhabitants, one daily in circulation for each 500, and a similar number of radios.[14])

But it would be a mistake to minimize the equal and often greater importance of the new mass media which contain the new-style popular culture, vapid and lacking in identity as it often may be. There is something universal in the appeal of the film song or soap opera.[15] And there is something significant in their contribution to modernization. In order to understand just what their significance may be, we need to digress here to consider what social science research has shown about the effects of communications on individuals.

V. The Social Science View of Media Effects

In conjunction with development programs there have been many studies of how to get farmers (and occasionally others) to adopt modern practices. The general finding has been that what occurs when a new practice is adopted is what Katz and Lazarsfeld call the two-step flow of communication.[16] That is to say, the mass media do not lead to

---

[13] Cf. Y. B. Damle, "A Note on Harikatha," *Bulletin of the Deccan College*, XVII, Poona, for a discussion of the role of such traditional sources in dissemination of ideas about caste. For descriptions of this kind of communication, see Milton Singer, *Traditional India: Structure and Change*, Philadelphia, The American Folklore Society, 1959.

[14] Edward W. Gude, *op.cit.*

[15] For a description of comics, popular songs, radio, soap operas, movies, and magazine stories in a non-Western culture, see Hidetoshi Kato, ed., *Japanese Popular Culture*, Tokyo, Charles E. Tuttle Co., 1959.

[16] Elihu Katz and Paul F. Lazarsfeld, *Personal Influence*, Glencoe, Ill., The Free Press, 1955. For a review of the literature see E. Katz, "The Two Step Flow of Communication," *Public Opinion Quarterly*, 21, 1957, pp. 61-78.

adoption directly. They create an awareness of the existence of the new practice, and they provide guidance to innovating leaders. However, actual adoption of a new practice requires either personal persuasion or personal example by a respected opinion leader. Thus the spread of an innovation can be traced from an initiating center, by direct personal contact, out to the periphery.[17] It can also be traced from younger, well-educated, somewhat alienated and relatively cosmopolitan individuals in a community to older, highly entrenched, above average educated individuals with whom the former are in touch, and then finally to other people in the community who follow the leaders.[18] The adoption of an innovation advocated in the mass media has been shown to depend on interpersonal discussion of it.

The last point has been most dramatically demonstrated in a series of UNESCO sponsored studies of radio listening and TV viewing groups. J. C. Mathur and Paul Neurath, for example, conducted a study of village radio broadcasts in India. In the control situations where these broadcasts were listened to by individuals in usual fashion the radio programs had virtually no effect. Where, however, listening groups were organized and discussions of the programs took place immediately after, the suggestions were often followed.[19] The same thing was found with TV viewing groups in France, and in other places too.[20] Similar results on the role of word-of-mouth communication in clinching media advice have been obtained in marketing studies.[21]

All of these studies add up to the conclusion foreshadowed above: that to stimulate action, mass media exhortations need to be coupled

[17] Cf. Torsten Hägerstrand, *On Monte Carlo Simulation of Diffusion*, mimeographed.

[18] Cf. James Coleman, Elihu Katz, and Herbert Menzel, *Doctors and New Drugs*, Glencoe, Ill., The Free Press, forthcoming. Foundation for Research on Human Behavior, *The Adoption of New Products*, Ann Arbor, 1959. Everett M. Rogers, "Categorizing the Adopters of Agricultural Practices," *Rural Sociology*, 8, 1943, pp. 15-24. E. M. Rogers and G. M. Beal, "The Importance of Personal Influence in the Adoption of Technological Changes," *Social Forces*, Vol. 36, No. 4, 1958. Bryce Ryan and N. C. Gross, *The Acceptance and Diffusion of Hybrid Seed Corn in Two Iowa Communities*, Iowa Agricultural Experiment Station, Ames, Ia., Research Bulletin No. 372, 1950. E. A. Wilkening, "Informal Leaders and Innovators in Farm Practices," *Rural Sociology*, Vol. 17, No. 3, 1952, pp. 272-275. H. F. Lionberger, "Community Prestige in the Choice of Sources of Farm Information," *Public Opinion Quarterly*, 23, 1959, pp. 110-118.

[19] J. C. Mathur and Paul Neurath, *An Indian Experiment in Farm Radio Forums*, Paris, UNESCO, 1959.

[20] Henry Cassirer, *Television Teaching Today*, Paris, UNESCO, 1960. Cf. also UNESCO series on Press, Film, and Radio in the World Today, J. Nicol, A. Shea, and G. J. P. Simmins, Canada's Farm Radio Forum, 1954; J. Dumazedier, *Television and Rural Adult Education*, 1956; Anon, *Rural Television in Japan*, 1960.

[21] Katz and Lazarsfeld, *op.cit.*

with the organization of face-to-face leadership. Here, however, we must raise the question of whether exhortation to action is indeed the most important use of mass media in the modernizing process. While many studies have examined how to persuade the citizenry to take specific actions, only a few studies have looked at the role of the media in producing transformations in values and personality. Such changes in values and attitudes, it can be argued, are far more important to modernization than are mere changes in actions.

That is perhaps an unusual view, for it is common to assume that changes in men's actions are the really important objective and that changes in attitudes are but a means toward the desired actions. We would argue, however, that it is the other way around. It is, for example, relatively easy to get peasants to plant a particular kind of seed a foot apart instead of six inches apart. This action can be induced by money payments, by terror, by authority, by persuasion, by proving it to be the will of the gods, and by many other means. But the improvement of one such practice does not mean that the peasant has been in any way modernized. A far more significant change would be the development of a scientific attitude toward the adoption of new practices. It is only that kind of internal change in the latent structure of his attitudes that would produce self-sustaining movement toward modernization. Yet the effects of communications in the process of transition has been much studied in relation to specific actions, but only little studied in relation to the much more important matters of values and attitudes.

In this area the most notable contributions have been by Daniel Lerner and David McClelland. They have both put forward the daring thesis that the mass media can have profound characterological effects. Lerner convincingly argues that the media provide their consumers with a capacity to conceive of situations and ways of life quite different from those directly experienced.[22] To have such a capacity for empathy is necessary if a person is to function in a great society. A great society is characteristically one where every business firm must anticipate the wants of unknown clients, every politician those of unknown voters; where planning takes place for a vastly changed future; where the actions of people in quite different cultures may affect one daily. If, as Lerner argues, the media provide the means for empathically entering the roles that affect a man in a great society, then the characterological contribution of the media to modernization is indeed significant.

[22] Lerner, op.cit.

McClelland's thesis has less face plausibility but is documented persuasively. It is that certain types of media content may help to raise achievement motivation and help to develop a consensus supporting it, and that such high achievement motivation is in turn a major necessary condition for development.[23] If McClelland's results, based in part on studies of children's literature, are even partly confirmed, they too are vitally important to any theory of development.

Now the interest of the Lerner and McClelland theses for our present paper is that neither of these depends upon a two-step flow of communication. Neither of them is predicated upon opinion leaders or political organizations paralleling the media. They are concerned with effects which the media have directly.

This suggests that the conclusion that the effectiveness of the media in the process of modernization depends upon their being linked to a well-developed organization of face-to-face influence is too simple. It is not wrong, but it is partial. It is true for certain of the potential effects of the mass media but not for others. And so we stop here to set up a typology of what the effects of the mass media are.

These effects are of two main kinds: effects upon the individuals exposed to them, and institutional effects arising from the very existence of a mass media system.

Among the direct and immediate effects which exposure to the media may have upon the individuals are changes in: 1. Attention. 2. Saliency. 3. Information. 4. Skills. 5. Tastes. 6. Images. 7. Attitudes. 8. Actions. Changes in any one of these may in turn change each of the others: changes in one's actions may change one's attitudes just as changes in one's attitudes may change one's actions; changes in the information one has may change one's distribution of attention, or changes in what one attends to may change one's information. Yet it is possible analytically to distinguish these changes and to consider the differences in the conditions for each kind of change.

Various experimental and survey results suggest that the mass media operate very directly upon attention, information, tastes, and images. Election studies, for example, show that the campaign in the mass media does little to change attitudes in the short run, but does a great deal to focus attention on one topic or another.[24] It also affects the saliency of different issues. Television studies have shown that TV

[23] David McClelland, *The Achieving Society*, Princeton, Van Nostrand, 1961.
[24] Paul F. Lazarsfeld, Bernard Berelson, and Hazel Gaudet, *The People's Choice*, New York, Columbia University Press, 1948. Bernard Berelson, Paul F. Lazarsfeld, and William McPhee, *Voting*, Chicago, University of Chicago Press, 1954.

has relatively little direct effect on major attitudes, but it does develop tastes (good or bad) and provides much image material to stock the mind of the viewer.[25] Harold Isaacs' studies of image formation also support the notion that these scratches on the mind can be picked up casually from the most diverse sources, including literature, movies, etc.[26] The effect which media have on images is also the effect on which Lerner built his theory; empathic capacity is the ability to imagine a situation. And such effects are indeed ones which the media have directly.

Changes in skills and attitudes are less apt to be brought about by the mass media operating alone. Here the best we can say is that sometimes they are but often they are not. Often face-to-face relations with a human being toward whom the learner has considerable cathexis is essential for producing changes in those variables. We can, for example, classify attitudes as being of greater or lesser rigidity and saiiency. Lightly held attitudes may readily be molded by mass media alone, but not deeply entrenched ones. The experimental literature on the framing of survey research questions is probably as good evidence on this point as any. Responses to low-saliency questions are shifted readily by question wording, new information, or almost anything. Other attitudes stand up under any media barrage. Psychotherapy shows that to change deeply rooted attitudes requires the development of an intense relationship with a reference person. So too the literature on teaching, i.e., the imparting of skills, demonstrates that while many skills can be learned from reading, or TV, or movies, the learning of difficult matter requires a level of motivation that is engendered only in a relationship with an important reference person who demands the effort.

Finally, we return to actions, changes in which, as we have already noted, are almost always checked with reference persons before an individual embarks upon them.

Changes of all of these variables are important in the process of development. But they enter the process in different ways. For example, a conclusion stated much earlier in this paper holds, we now see, for some of these kinds of change only. Changes in actions and in some skills and attitudes will not be effectively produced by mass media alone; rather, the effectiveness of the mass media in influencing

[25] Hilda Himmelweit, A. Oppenheim, P. Vince, et, et al., *Television and the Child*, London, Oxford University Press, 1958. Wilbur Schramm, Jack Lyle, Edwin Parker, *Television in the Lives of Our Children*, Stanford, Stanford University Press, 1961.
[26] Harold R. Isaacs, *Scratches on Our Minds*, New York, John Day, 1958.

them will be a direct function of the effectiveness of political organization to which the mass media are an adjunct.

On the other hand, certain of these changes toward modernization will occur as the mass media develop, whether or not strong political organization exists. Note what these changes are. They are changes in attention, tastes, information, images. That is exactly the revolution of rising expectations! General findings of social psychology based largely upon American experiments and surveys have led us to exactly the same results as area students have formulated from experience with the politics of development: a happy but rare conjunction of observation with theory in the social sciences.

VI. The Media as Institutions

What functions can the mass media perform in the process of political development? We have just noted that there are certain kinds of impact on their audiences which they easily produce, and certain others which they can produce only in conjunction with political organization. We remarked above that in addition there is another class of effects which mass media have (a class of effects well noted by Lenin): namely, effects by virtue of the existence of the media as institutions in the society.

For example, the existence of media gives politicians a vastly increased opportunity for leadership. As happened also in the West, the growth of plebiscitarian politics goes hand in hand with the growth of the press. The press enables the politician to act on a national scale. It puts into the headlines all over the country topics which are otherwise no part of the experience of the citizens in each separate locality. It transforms these topics into issues. It enables the political leader to give the word of the day simultaneously to the whole country on something which the press has made salient for all of it. It makes national parties possible because some issues are the same throughout the country. And a modern media system with wire services does this better than a set of struggling local print shops putting out papers.

The press also gives the politicians a recognized national code of procedures by which to confirm status. A highly segmented society is apt to suffer from lack of consensus not only on matters of substance but even on the facts of what has been decided. Anything which establishes a public record of policy decisions, of assignments of prestige (by column inches or anything else), and of responsibilities can be useful. Of course a party press in which the different papers give very different pictures of the world does not achieve this purpose. But under many circumstances a press consensus enables everyone (including the party leader himself) to know, for example, who is the party leader.

A mass media system permits the unification of a nation in many non-political ways similar to those we have just been describing. The existence of daily price quotations facilitates the establishment of a national market. Media encourage a national art and literature by holding up products against each other. The media broaden the relevant reference groups in discussions. The same kinds of processes of national organization through the media take place in social life, in cultural life, in economic life, and in party politics.

The media also serve as educators for and employers of a new kind of politician, one who is issue oriented and ideologically oriented rather than oriented to personal identifications. The media provide some of the few jobs in mobile professions in many underdeveloped countries. Those are miserably paid and grossly exploited professions, but they are ones not tied rigidly to either traditional statuses or castes nor to a Western style educational system. The media thus provide a niche where political men of a new kind can ensconce themselves. They provide a base from which such men can operate in attacking the old elites. The media often provide a livelihood for such politicians while they wait for the opportunities of politics or while they engage in the day-to-day work of political organization. The media create some of the few chances for men who are not notables to become politicians by vocation in poverty-stricken countries.

VII. Conclusions

Neither these points about how the media can give rise to a political class and to political activity nor the earlier points about how the media generate rising expectations make rapid mass media development seem a happy prospect to leaders attempting to hold together a fragile balance in barely viable states about to explode. But in this field as in others the processes of change are not going to be stopped. The media can be a far more potent instrument of development than has yet been recognized in almost any non-Communist developing nation or by American development planners. But for their potential to be effectively used, their development must also be linked to effective grass-roots political organization.

CHAPTER 15

ALTERNATIVE PATTERNS OF DEVELOPMENT

~·~

*IN FIRST DISCUSSING questions of policy we put aside any hope
of uncovering fixed formulas for the use of communications in nation building. Instead we stressed the need for each transitional
society to search creatively for the most appropriate way of accelerating modernization in the light of its own circumstances. Certain gross distinctions in national approaches, however, can be
made, particularly between the ways of the Communists and those
of all others. The realities of the divided world of today call for
a special awareness of Communist techniques and for hard-headed
appraisals of their advantages and disadvantages.*

*Historically the Communists have been unique in the degree to
which they have consciously sought to exploit every potential of
communications in the service of propaganda. Basic to the history
of Communism has been a peculiar faith in the potency of the
political word. In the struggle first for existence and then for
power, Communist parties have tended always to believe that the
secret of politics is locked in the power of agitation and propaganda.
As small bands of people seeking to upset entire societies or as elite
cadres striving to control mass movements, they have steadfastly
valued the two extremes of secrecy and of endless propaganda and
communications.*

*The Communist movements in the underdeveloped areas have
displayed this same compulsive concern with exploiting every possible dimension of communications. One of the first activities of
the struggling Chinese Communist party was the publication and
dissemination of barely legible leaflets and pamphlets, and
throughout the years of the Long March and of sustained guerrilla warfare duplicating machines became a basic piece of equipment of Communist military units. In the Malayan jungles the
Communists in their decade of unsuccessful struggle made every
sacrifice to produce leaflets and printed sheets which they always
dignified with the title of a newspaper or journal. Similarly,
throughout the rest of Asia a fundamental difference between the
Communist parties and all others has been the constant stress upon*

the production of literature and propaganda, upon utilizing the advantages of printing.

The Communists' concept of communications has not, however, been limited to the printed word or to the mass media. In their view, agitation and propaganda are equally face-to-face activities. The direct confrontation, the utilization of personal channels of acquaintanceship, the management of "informal" discussions and of even casual conversations are all explicitly recognized as vital elements in the propaganda process. The limitations of illiteracy are not to be taken as obstacles to the passing on of the message of revolution.

Out of these experiences of political conflict the Communists, wherever they have gained total power, are propelled into a massive utilization of communications for national development. Once in command of a country they have a more sensitive understanding than most ruling groups of all the different facets of communications which governments can control and manipulate. In their view the realization of power requires absolute monopoly over all the possible channels of communications in a society. Until this goal is achieved the struggle must continue and an "enemy" continues to threaten the success of the revolution.

This restless, compulsive concern with control over all forms of communications is the first distinctive characteristic of the Communist approach to political development. The second unique element in their approach is the manner in which they seek to eliminate the gap between the mass media and the social and informal processes of communications which we have observed to be the fundamental work of the communications process in all transitional societies. In striving to control and manipulate all the available channels of communications in a society the Communists seek to transform the relatively casual and unreliable processes of informal and personal communications into uniform and highly predictable forms of communications; and thus in a sense they seek to transform all forms of communications into "mass media." That is to say, they strive to make all face-to-face means of communications take on the essential characteristics of the mass media; and in making the two levels of communications indistinguishable from each other in the standardization of messages and the control of content they hope to realize a completely unified system of communications and control.

In Communist China, as in Russia, the party has emphasized the role of the primary communicator, the man who can directly confront his audience in bringing to it the messages of the party. Well-trained party members, or cadres as the Chinese call them, are expected to utilize all the old and even quite traditional forms of communications, as well as such new ones as loudspeakers, in striving to project themselves into the communications processes of every sub-community within the society. Instead of seeking to eliminate the fragmented and essentially atomized communications pattern of transitional China by investing in higher levels of communications technology, the Communists have engaged in a massive effort of exploiting the primitive forms which have long been available within Chinese society. In this effort they have been able, as we shall see in the next chapter, to organize these older means of communications so as to give them the essential attributes of the modern mass media.

It should be noted that this Communist strategy of transforming face-to-face means of communications into a form of mass media may appear to eliminate the gap between what we have called the two levels of communications in transitional societies, but it does not produce what we have called a modern system of communications. The result is not a coherent society in which there is mutual exchange and mutual influencing between the mass media and the informal means of communications. In the short run it may appear as though the Communists' approach can alleviate some of the difficulties inherent in transitional societies, but eventually what we have described as the test of modernization must be met.

This brings us to the basic question of the degree to which the Communist techniques of massively indoctrinating an entire population can succeed in changing their ways of thought and provide continuing and autonomous support to the regime. It has become increasingly apparent in recent years that the Communists may be paying a heavy price for over-propagandizing their populations. Endless exhortations can result in boredom, apathy, and exhaustion. Indiscriminate demands for great sacrifices for small goals can wear away the potential for great sacrifices for great goals. There are limits in all cultures to the extent to which a community will allow its social life to become politicized, for the civic ideal of every society reflects the knowledge that man cannot live by community values alone. Similarly, the individual does not need at every turn guidance from a total ideology for the demands of daily life do not require constant reference to "a large map of the universe."

It is evident then that there are stages or conditions of affairs in transitional societies when the Communist approach of mastering and monopolizing all channels of communications can apparently facilitate the progress of modernization and nation building. But there are limits to the Communist techniques, and in other stages or conditions their approaches become counter-productive and disruptive to the creation of modern nationhood. This is dramatically apparent in the history of Communist China, which is now entering a phase of crisis after early years of apparently rapid advances. In Chapter 17 we shall be examining many of the Communist practices which first gave China the appearance of unity but which have not solved that country's basic problems of development. Although the Communists may be able to reduce greatly the gap between the mass media and the personal level of communications, their approach seems to create a new gap between the manifest level of social communications and a people's private and intensely subjective reactions. Their skill in communications cannot in itself support for the long duration a sense of collective identity and national unity when their actions tend to heighten each individual's sense of isolation and powerlessness.

Effective development in any transitional society can occur only as individuals find a secure basis for relating themselves to both the mass media and the more informal social processes of communications within their immediate communities. Sound policy must seek therefore to balance the development of both levels of communication, respecting the peculiar role which each must play in providing change and continuity, innovation and a persisting sense of collective identity. Thus in all transitional societies, whether Communist-ruled or not, there is no escaping the need to achieve certain prerequisites for the establishment of a coherent society. The universalistic qualities of the mass media must be balanced with the human loyalties of the social processes of communications; modern standards must be fused with parochial sentiments; the need to be a part of the cosmopolitan world must be related to the equal need to have a distinctive, historically based identity. In short, nation building rests upon nationalism, but a nationalism that provides assurance and competence in international relations.

It is appropriate that after examining in detail communications in Communist China we should turn directly to a nationalist example and examine the place of communications in the relatively successful evolution of modern Turkey.

CHAPTER 16

COMMUNICATIONS AND POLITICS IN COMMUNIST CHINA[1]

FREDERICK T. C. YU

PERSUASIVE communications play a conspicuous part in the total policy of the Chinese Communist regime. The rulers in Peking do not govern China solely by naked force. They have always depended upon hypnotic indoctrination and stirring propaganda to mobilize the minds and effort of the population, to carry out tasks of the party leadership, and to facilitate control of the nation.

To be sure, persuasive communications are indispensable political tools in all Communist or totalitarian societies. For in a Communist state solidarity and achievement depend upon ideological unanimity,[2] and communications provide the model with which to conform. But the extensive and vigorous manipulation of communications in Communist China is a startlingly new phenomenon—new both to China and to world Communism. Although the idea of controlling the thinking and action of the populace is not totally strange in China, no precedent can be found in Chinese history for mass ideological conversion of the sort now being attempted by the Communists. Although many of Peking's principles of propaganda and techniques of persuasion are obviously borrowed from or inspired by the Soviet Union, the Bolshevik attempt to remould the thinking of the Russian population (not just party members and government cadres) in the post-1917 era does not warrant comparison with the Chinese Communist performance in intensity, scope, and skill.

[1] A major part of the research was done while the writer was a postdoctoral fellow at Harvard University and the Massachusetts Institute of Technology recently under a Ford Foundation grant, which he wishes gratefully to acknowledge. All observations and conclusions are, of course, strictly his own and do not in any way reflect those of the administration or personnel of the Ford Foundation.

[2] Friedrich and Brzezinski refer to this as "passion for unanimity" which, they observe, "make the totalitarians insist on the complete agreement of the entire population under their control to the measures the regime is launching." They add that "the totalitarian regimes insist that enthusiastic unanimity characterize the political behavior of the captive population." See Carl J. Friedrich and Zbigniew K. Brzezinski, *Totalitarian Dictatorship and Autocracy*, Cambridge, Mass., Harvard University Press, 1956, p. 132.

To understand the incredibly important role of persuasive communication in Communist China it is important to keep in mind the Communist belief that "thought determines action." The *Jen Min Jih Pao* put it this way: "Work is done by man, and man's action is governed by his thinking. A man without the correct political thinking is a man without a soul. If politics does not take command—i.e., if the proletarian ideology does not take command—there can be no direction. In every work we undertake, we must always insist that politics take command and let political and ideological work come before anything else. Only when we are both thorough and penetrating with our political and ideological work can we guarantee the accomplishment of our task."[3]

In other words, if people can be made to think "correctly," according to the Communist reasoning, they can naturally act "correctly." The Chinese Communists seem to be singleminded about this, and their press is flooded with stories of how various tasks are accomplished under almost impossible conditions mainly because "the correct political and ideological work takes command." It may be the task of killing 1,700,000 catties of flies in one day in Peking;[4] it may be the task of making Chinese intellectuals "turn over their hearts to the Party."[5] How much truth there is in such stories is not the point; what is significant is the Communists' nearly fanatic faith in their "correct political and ideological work."

The Communist "political and ideological work" is more often known as propaganda (*hsien chuan*) or persuasion (*shuō fu*). In the lexicon of the Chinese Communists this is also called "ideological warfare" or "political warfare," which is supposed to be "vigorously, gallantly, and ceaselessly fought" on every conceivable front. It is, as some Communists put it, "the basic working method of the Party."[6]

The Chinese Communists are not content merely with producing obedient, docile subjects. They have a new gospel to preach and a new world to build; they want converts and believers. They require enthusiastic support of the people, not just silent acceptance. They expect

[3] *Jen Min Jih Pao* (*People's Daily*, Peking), editorial, November 11, 1960.
[4] *Ibid.*, May 26, 1958.
[5] *Ibid.*, April 28, 1958. This refers to the *Chiao Hsin Yun Tung* (Campaign to Give Hearts) which was supposedly initiated by the "democratic parties" in China following the "Hundred Flowers" campaign in 1958 as a pledge of their loyalty to the party.
[6] Yu Kuang-yuan, "To Develop the Ideological Education of Marxism-Leninism from the Discussions on the Story of Wu-Hsun," *Hsueh Hsi* (*Study*, Peking), IV, 6 and 7, June 1, 1951, p. 59.

all people in China to be enthusiastic in accomplishing every task of the party, not from necessity but from conviction. They must therefore capture and reshape the minds of the entire population.

This is a big order. For this means no less than an all-out ideological assault on one-fifth of the human race. Nevertheless, this is exactly the objective of the whole intricate design of propaganda or "political and ideological work" of the party. This is the task which the Communists have set out to do with their penetrating system of persuasive communications—a task on which they have spent more time, effort, and energy than on any other activity in the country.

I. Communist Doctrine and Communication Theory

It has been said that "in the Soviet system, there is not a theory of state and a theory of communication; there is only one theory."[7] Essentially the same thing can be said about communications in Communist China.

This does not mean that the Communists do not theorize about communications. It merely suggests that the Marxist-Leninist dogma which shapes the whole course of development of every Communist society necessarily determines the theory and pattern of every policy and activity of the party. In other words, the best place to start an investigation of the theory and policy of communication in a Communist country is the Communist ideology itself.

Three aspects of the Chinese Communist ideology are especially important in the realm of communication: class consciousness, the mass line, and unity of theory and practice.

CLASS CONSCIOUSNESS

The Chinese Communist revolution is a class struggle, and the entire course of Chinese Communist propaganda and agitation stems from one fundamental concept: class consciousness. The central purpose of propaganda, so a favorite Communist cliché goes, is to "awaken, heighten, and sharpen the class consciousness of the masses," from which the real strength or power of the party is supposed to be generated.

Defining politics as "nothing but a centralized form of class struggle," Ai Ssu-chi, one of China's leading theoreticians, makes this point explicitly clear when he writes: "There are only two kinds of political

[7] Wilbur Schramm, *Responsibility in Mass Communication*, New York, Harper, 1957, p. 81.

tasks: one is the task of propaganda and education, and the other is the task of organization. Both aim at raising the level of political consciousness of the revolutionary class, uniting with the forces of the revolutionary classes and fighting for the ruling power."[8]

Class consciousness is, for Marx, the basis of political consciousness. But Lenin further develops the idea—and this is perhaps his greatest contribution to the propaganda of Marxism—that class consciousness left to itself becomes entirely bound up in the "economic struggle" and will be confined to a mere "trade-unionist" consciousness. Therefore Lenin hammered on the idea that class consciousness must be awakened, educated, and brought into the battle in a larger sphere than the worker-employer relations alone, and that this task should be assigned only to an elite group or professional revolutionaries, "the conscious vanguard of the proletariat."[9]

This Leninist interpretation of class consciousness prevails in Communist China. Liu Shao-chi, Red China's chief of state, has the following to say: "We should lead the masses forward, but there should be no commandism. We should be intimately connected with the masses, but we should reject tailism.[10] We should start from the level already attained by the masses in developing their consciousness and leading them forward.[11] With us, therefore, everything is dependent on and determined by the people's consciousness and self-activity, without which we can accomplish nothing and all our efforts will be in vain. . . . When the masses are not fully conscious, the duties of Communists . . . in carrying out any kind of work is to develop their consciousness by every effective and suitable means. This is the first step in our work which must be done no matter how difficult it is or how much time it will take."[12]

[8] Ai Ssu-chi, *Li Shih Wei Wu Lun She-Hui Fa Chan Shih Chiang I* (*Historical Materialism—Lectures on History of Social Development*), Peking, Workmen's Publishing Co., June 1951, first rev. ed., pp. 83-86.

[9] See Jean-Marie Domanach, "Leninist Propaganda," *Public Opinion Quarterly*, Summer 1951. See also Alex Inkeles "Communist Propaganda and Counter Propaganda," *Proceedings of the 28th Institute of the Norman Wait Harris Memorial Foundation* (1952); stenographic transcription of this lecture is on file in the Social Relations Reading Room, Harvard University.

[10] This follows the Soviet attack on the tendency to drag at the tail of the masses, or *khvostizm*, as it was called by Lenin. See Alex Inkeles, *Public Opinion in Soviet Russia*, Cambridge, Mass., Harvard University Press, 1950, p. 2.

[11] Liu Shao-chi, *On the Party*, Peking, Foreign Language Press, 1950, p. 66.

[12] *Ibid.*, pp. 5, 7, 8.

THE MASS LINE

"The fundamental policy of the party," according to the Communists, "is the policy of the mass line."[13]

Like class consciousness, this "mass line" has acquired a quality of sacredness in China. The Communists talk forever about the "harmonious unity with the masses," "the viewpoint of the masses," "wisdom of the masses," "sanction of the masses," etc. According to them, almost every program or policy of the party is "demanded," "desired," and "initiated" by the masses. For instance, it is almost always the "creative initiative" and "highly elevated political consciousness" of the masses that result in their "volunteering" to go to the Korean front, "demanding" the punishment of rightists in the Hundred-Flower Movement, or "petitioning" for the realization of the commune program.

But how does this mass line operate? And how is it related to class consciousness and communication?

The answer can be found in the Communist formula: "the policy and methods of work of the party must originate from the masses and go back to the masses." A cynical interpretation of this would be that the Communists are trying to make the ideas of the party sound as if they were ideas of the people. It is perhaps more accurate to say that the Communists always attempt to transform the feeling or sentiments of the masses into an idea or notion which seemingly represents what the masses want but actually expresses what the party intends. As early as 1943 Mao preached: "We should go into the midst of the masses, learn from them, sum up their experiences so that these experiences will become well-defined principles and methods, and then explain them to the masses (through agitation work), and call upon the masses to put them into practice in order to solve their problems and lead them to liberation and happiness."[14]

This "mass line" was explained more fully by Mao at another occasion when he wrote: "In all practical work of our party, correct leadership can only be developed on the principle of 'from the masses, to the masses.' This means summing up (i.e., co-ordinating and systematizing after careful study) the views of the masses (i.e., views scattered and unsystematic), then taking the resulting ideas back to the masses,

[13] *Jen Min Jih Pao* (*People's Daily*, Peking), December 11, 1958.
[14] Mao Tse-tung, *Selected Works*, London, Lawrence and Wishart, Ltd., 1956, Vol. 4, p. 153.

explaining and popularizing them until the masses embrace the ideas as their own, stand up for them and translate them into action by way of testing their correctness. Then it is necessary once more to sum up the view of the masses, and once again take the resulting ideas back to the masses so that the masses give them their wholehearted support. . . . And so on, over and over again, so that each time these ideas emerge with greater correctness and become more vital and meaningful."[15]

So much importance is attached by the Chinese Communists to this method of "mass line" that it is formalized as general guide to action in the party constitution: "Whether or not the party leadership is correct depends upon the party's ability to analyze, systematize, summarize, and consolidate the opinions and experiences of the masses, to transform them as the policy of the party and then to return them, through *propaganda, agitation*, and *organization*, to the masses as their own guide to thinking and action."[16]

UNITY OF THEORY AND PRACTICE

"If you want to know the theory and methods of revolution," declared Mao in his often quoted article entitled *On Practice*, "you must participate in the revolution."[17] His explanation: "All truths are obtained through direct experience."

It must be remembered that Chinese Communism as an ideology consists of a variety of components ranging from basic beliefs, such as "labor creates the world," to utopian promises, such as "the elimination of classes." It also prescribes tasks to be accomplished and goals to be achieved.

While outright opposition to the doctrine is obviously forbidden in a Communist society, mere passive compliance with the ideology is equally unacceptable. To the Chinese Communists, apathy is a cardinal sin. Everyone must take part in *tou cheng* (struggle).

Thus, in terms of persuasion, it is not enough for a peasant in a commune to shout that he loves Communism, that he detests feudalism,

---

[15] *Ibid.*, p. 113. This quotation is from a resolution on methods of leadership drafted by Mao on behalf of the Central Committee of the Communist Party. The resolution was passed on July 1, 1943 by the party's Politburo. The Chinese text of the resolution is available in the *Cheng Feng Wen Hsien* (*Documents of the Party's Ideological Remoulding Movement*), Hong Kong, Hsin Min Chu Ch'u Pan She, 1949, pp. 139-144.

[16] *Chung Kuo Kung Chan Tang Chang Cheng* (*Constitution of the Chinese Communist Party*), Peking, Jen Min Chu Pan She, 1956, p. 8.

[17] *Mao Tse-tung Hsien Chi* (*Selected Works of Mao Tse-tung*), Peking, Jen Min Publishing Co., 1953, Vol. 1, p. 276.

and that he adores communes. He has to show by action that he has actually "benefited" from the wisdom of Marxism-Leninism. This means that he has to "accuse," "attack," or "eliminate" the "reactionary elements," participate actively in the tasks assigned by the cadres, "contribute" his labor or production to the government to express his "gratitude" to the Communist party.

The faith must be practiced. Hence the entire process of mass persuasion is forever built around one central task of one kind or another. The tasks vary, but each represents a goal prescribed by the party and creates an opportunity for the people to unite their faith with practice in an approved manner.

One needs only a casual look at the Communist record since 1949 to discover that for twelve years the entire nation has always engaged in one major mass movement along with large-scale campaigns for different sections of the population during a particular time. To name chronologically only a few: Land Reform, *Hsueh Hsi* (study), Resist-America Aid-Korea, Propaganda Networks, Democratic Reforms in Factories, Mines, and Enterprises, Ideological Remoulding, Three-anti and Five-anti, Suppression of Counter-Revolutionaries, Five-Year Plans, Agricultural Coops, "Hundred Flowers," National Reconstruction Through Austerity and Diligence, Reform through Work, "Big Leap Forward," "General Line of Socialist Development," Production of Steel and Iron, and People's Commune.

This is not to say that every Communist movement serves mainly the ideological function of the party. That would be stretching somewhat the role of mass persuasion in Communist China. It merely suggests that the policy of communication is synchronized with every task of the party and that it is through the tasks that some major objectives of propaganda are achieved. Here is the way the Communists have stated their position:

"It is always important to grasp every opportunity which can push our revolution one step further. Always give full support to complete one central task, mobilize the broad masses and attract them to the general slogan at the time. We must know that revolution is a mass movement, and that actions of the masses must concentrate only on one or at most a few definite and clearly-expressed objectives. . . . After one central task is completed, replace it with another central task. Substitute one general slogan for another new slogan. This is the forward-going law of revolution. It is also the law of gradually elevating mass consciousness and organizational ability."[18]

[18] *Hsueh Hsi* (*Study*, Peking), February 10, 1952, p. 44.

II. The Communication System

The Chinese Communists have developed a crude but strangely efficient communication system which reaches almost every segment of the population and which controls virtually all the avenues to the Chinese mind. A French correspondent who visited Red China in 1956 reported: "The head of a good Chinese citizen today functions like a sort of radio receiving set. Somewhere in Peiping buzzes the great transmitting station which broadcasts the right thought and the words to be repeated. Millions of heads faithfully pick them up, and millions of mouths repeat them like loud-speakers."[19]

This must sound hard to believe since Communist China, despite its ambitious program of modernization, continues to be handicapped by a high illiteracy rate and inadequate communication facilities. But one must not think of mass communication in Communist China in terms of the conventional mass media such as newspapers, magazines, radio, television, and motion pictures. Though important, they do not make up the entire communication system in China. The Communists depend upon a variety of communications channels and devices that are rarely considered tools for "mass communication" as the words are understood in the United States. These include blackboard newspapers, *tatzepao* (handwritten posters), street corner plays, folk dances, songs, poetry, plain face-to-face communication used by millions of oral agitators known as "propagandists" (*hsien chuan yan*) in China, and various means of thought reform.

Some features of this communication system are Communist, some are traditionally Chinese, and some are strictly inventions of the Chinese Marxists. Together they suggest something of a revolution in communication. Motivated by the general goals of Chinese Communism and guided by a new communication elite, this revolution has resulted in new images, new symbols, a new language, a new audience, new communication channels, new communication methods and behavior of the masses.

COMMUNICATIONS IN A COMMUNE

To understand some of the peculiarities of this communication system, let us examine a typical Communist communication set-up in Tsao Hsien, a farming town of about 20,000 in Anhwei province.

[19] Robert Guillain, *600 Million Chinese*, New York, Criterion Books, 1957, p. 137.

Like any other Chinese rural area, this town in pre-Communist days probably had a larger number of illiterate peasants who had very little contact with the national government and whose activities were not centrally or vigorously controlled. Education was probably no more than a matter of a few primary schools and private tutors. There might have been a few reading rooms and education centers that were poorly equipped, inefficiently administered, and infrequently utilized. There might have been a mimeographed or poorly printed local paper; a few families in the town might have had access to the provincial or prestige national newspapers. There was no radio station, although radio sets might have been owned by a few well-to-do families. Movies were probably a novelty; the inhabitants depended upon their local talents and small traveling troupes for entertainment.

But let us now turn to this town in 1959 as reported by Ho Pi, the first secretary of the party branch in the area.[20] The town has become a commune known as the Shih Chi Commune of Tsao Hsien. It has 5,253 families, 21,000 people, and a farming area of 64,000 mu.[21]

"Cultural work," according to the party leader, "has already been extended to every corner of the commune." He lists the following:

Newspaper reading groups	267	Kiddie dancing teams	11
Art and literary teams	267	*Huang Chung* dancing teams	8
Production research teams	267	Children dancing teams	34
Cultural association of the communes	1	Weather bulletins	8
Propaganda instrument workshop	1	Radio station (radio diffusion exchange)	1
Production agitation board	80	Local message-relay centers	25
Blackboard newspapers and *tatzepao* (posters)	390	Primary school	20
Movie projection team	1	After-work middle school	7
Libraries	17	"Red" and "expert" schools[22]	1
Cultural centers	8	Young farmers' schools	1
Exhibition centers	4	Art schools	4
Recreation centers	57	Public education schools	1
After-work cultural workers corps	15	Night party school	7
Youth cultural palaces	27	Farmers' after-work grade schools	155
People's fun centers	4	Night youth corps schools	7
Current affairs and political propaganda teams	35	Basket ball teams	56
		Volley ball teams	2
		Playgrounds	2

"Most of these cultural organizations," Ho hastens to point out, "are useful for propaganda activities on a permanent basis and in a variety of ways." Then he explains how these "cultural organizations"

[20] *Wen Hui Pao* (Shanghai), January 1, 1959.
[21] *Mu* is a Chinese measurement of area. One *mu* is about one-sixth of an acre.
[22] This is a popular expression in Communist China, where a person is supposed to be "Red" in his ideology and "expert" in his work.

have "enriched the cultural life of the masses, pushed forward production and central tasks in different periods, and greatly changed the
social atmosphere and cultural outwork of the people."

Ho refers to this as part of a "cultural revolution" now going on in
China and paints the picture in a verse:

> Poetry is all over walls and drawings are everywhere,
> Everyone goes to school, everyone has books to read;
> Like a galloping horse, we break through the cultural gate,
> And now it is on the farms where writers and poets meet.

One must not be misled into believing that the Communists are
interested in this "cultural revolution" for literary or aesthetic reasons.
"Poetry, songs, and wall drawings," Ho says bluntly, "are powerful
weapons to encourage production and to stimulate people to work."
He adds, "the harder the members of the commune are working in
production, the more they write poems and paint." Then he explains:

"All this suggests that cultural work must be integrated with politics
and production. This is the only way to push forward production and
political struggle.

"Poems and songs of the masses are the best forms of self-education.
Ever since the Great Leap Forward Campaign, already 13,000 in the
commune have participated in writing poetry and composing songs and
more than 2,000 have done wall drawings.

"According to incomplete statistics, from March 1958 till now (less
than one year) the people have produced 180,000 folk songs, 87 plays,
170 novels and short stories, 520,000 poems, 190,000 wall drawings.
At the moment members of the commune are busy in writing scripts
for movies and plays for stages as their way to salute the National
Anniversary of 1959. Also appearing in the commune are 18 kinds of
art and literature publications, including the *Shih Chi Art and Literature, Shih Chih Poetry and Paintings,* and *Tung Feng (East Wind).*
Then there are also 17 other kinds of publications such as *Great Leap
Forward Express* and *Tsan Tou Pao (Combat Paper)."*

One must be cautioned about some of the terms used in this dramatic
report. The word "school" here may mean not more than an organized
gathering for the purpose of teaching the peasants how to read and
write; a "youth culture palace" may be just a room where youths
gather for propaganda and recreational activities; a "weather bulletin"
may be just a blackboard with current information about the weather;
a "library" may be just a reading center where a few newspapers and

some propaganda literature are available; a "poem" may be nothing more than a jingle or just some crudely composed rhymed lines.

How much truth there is in this report cannot be easily ascertained. But even if only one-tenth of what is described is true, it illustrates the Communist attempt to utilize various communication channels to achieve political objectives.

THE ORGANIZATIONAL AND OPERATIONAL PATTERN

The switchboard of this whole intricate communication system is the *Hsien Chuan Pu* or Department of Propaganda of the Chinese Communist party. This is directly under the Political Bureau of the party's Central Committee. The long arm of the department reaches all the way from interpreting Marxism-Leninism to answering simple questions from a peasant in a commune; from deciding policies of national newspapers to criticizing some obscure "blackboard newspaper" in a tiny village.

The department operates through three major channels. One is made up of the propaganda departments or committees maintained in every party organization at all levels: central, regional, provincial, and local. The second consists of government agencies, such as the Ministry of Culture, Publications Administration, Ministry of Education, at various levels. The third is formed by numerous mass organizations such as the All-China Federation of Writers and Artists, New Democratic Youth Corps, Sino-Soviet Friendship Association. These are the organizations through which the party maintains its closest and most extensive contact with the population and through which it is able to carry out its program in the name of the people. Everyone in China, it must be remembered, has to belong to some kind of mass organization. Even a retired man who stays at home has to join at least a citizen's group or his neighbourhood group.

Coordination of the three channels is achieved by the party's system of interlocking directorates, in which a few Communist leaders at any level in the Communist organizational structure hold concurrently key positions in the party, the government, and the mass organizations. For instance, the secretary of the party branch (cell) of a commune may be at once chairman of the party's propaganda committee, director of the Department of Culture and Education of the local government, principal of a "Red and Expert School," and member of a number of local mass organizations.

The key link in the entire communication system is the Peking *Jen Min Jih Pao* (*People's Daily*) through which the Department of Propaganda operates and to which all papers in the nation turn for guidance and direction. In recent years the authoritative magazine *Hung Chi* (*Red Flag*), also mouthpiece of the party's Central Committee, has had the same important function.

What is published in the *People's Daily* is reprinted or quoted in the party newspapers at various levels, in special newspapers (such as *Worker's Daily* or the All China Federation of Trade Unions, *Youth Daily* of the Democratic Youth Corps), and in various other newspapers. It is carried by the People's Broadcasting Station in Peking, which transmits its messages downward through broadcasting stations in the provinces and cities, which in turn send the word further down through the line-broadcasting system or "radio-broadcasting network" which makes the message available to the listeners either through collective listening or through blackboard newspapers or wall newspapers. The same message from *Jen Min Jih Pao* will, of course, be noted in various trade, professional, or special-purpose magazines. Eventually it is printed in the form of booklets or pamphlets which are available for *hsueh hsi* (study) groups, cultural affairs study groups, and hundreds of groups or occasions for ideological indoctrination.

It must be noted that the message, unless it has to do with government or party directives or something of similar nature, is not always repeated word for word by various channels. Transmitting a message from Peking, a local newspaper, magazine, or radio station normally integrates the message with local situations. This is not a matter of adding local color. It is partly to relate it to the local situation but mainly to set the stage for agitation purposes.

One naturally wonders at this point whether the message will ever get read or heard. Newspaper readership or radio listenership may be the worry of American publishers and advertisers but not of the Chinese propagandists. To read a newspaper in China today is a political obligation. Any news item that is considered important by Peking is read in newspaper-reading groups, heard at "collective radio listening groups," discussed at various study and indoctrination meetings, and may even become part of the people's "thought conclusions" or "work reports."

If it is news about killing so many sparrows in Town A, one can be sure that the glory of this town will not shine alone. For Town B may be mobilized to kill twice as many sparrows. And if this should be the case, there will be special meetings to discuss the methods and operation of sparrow-killing, poems (jingles) composed, street-corner plays written, slogans coined, and dances planned to popularize the affair. Most certainly there will be criticism and self-criticism meetings, which go on forever in Communist China. It takes no time at all for sparrow-killing to be the central task of Town B, where school children of one class challenge those in another class, where one work brigade tries to outdo the record of another, where one member of the "propaganda network" labors to outdistance all his colleagues. If the model experience of sparrow-killing in Town A has so inspired the action of Town B, what is done in Town B is not to go unnoticed but to be reflected in various communiqués to agitate other towns. The contest goes on. And it stops only when another "central task" emerges.

Tasks vary, but tasks there always are. As noted earlier, one campaign follows another, and one movement is succeeded only by another movement.

In addition to major movements such as land reform or hundred-flowers there are seasonal ones such as the anniversary of the party, the People's Government, the October Revolution, and so on. There are special campaigns inspired by special occasions for special groups. For instance, there is the Teacher's Day for teachers and Journalist's Day for journalists. Then there are forever campaigns of the sparrow-killing kind.

AN ILLUSTRATION

It may be helpful at this point to take the case of one major movement, the communes, to illustrate how various kinds of persuasive communications are mobilized.

There is no doubt that communization was the goal of the Communists even in their early days of revolution. But operating on the cardinal Communist principle that every campaign or movement requires class consciousness at a special level, the Communists then knew that the nation was not "ideologically prepared" for such a drastic move. Thus when the People's Republic was proclaimed in 1949, there was not a whisper about communes. That was the period for the Land Reform Movement. Then came the program of "mutual aid groups." Then came the program of "collective coops." Then came the campaign "to combine small coops into large coops." Then the more ambitious program of "collectivization." Finally, the communes.

The movement of people's communes was officially inaugurated in September 1958. We now turn to the handling of this event by the *Jen Min Jih Pao (People's Daily)*.

In July 1958 occasional stories began to appear in the *People's Daily* to suggest the desirability of having "socialistic families." On July 6, for instance, there appeared in this pace-setting paper a letter written by a housewife telling of the importance and joy of socialistic families and the need to give up the idea of "selfish small families." The following day a long piece appeared on the success of a "public mess hall"[1] of an agricultural coop. This was followed by another piece which advocated "the development of such practices."

On August 11 the paper front-paged Mao Tse-tung's inspection tour in Honan, where he lavishly praised the performance of a "commune" there. "As long as we have a commune like this, there will be more communes," Mao was quoted. Two days later the paper found Mao in Shantung and headlined Mao's statement: "We should do well with communes. The advantage: to unite workers, peasants, merchants, intellectuals, and soldiers. Such a system will facilitate political guidance."

By the middle of August, when the Politburo of the party was reportedly meeting at Pai Tai Ho, stories suddenly mushroomed in the *People's Daily*. There were long articles about a commune in Hsing-yang, Honan (August 18), another in Sinkiang (August 16), another in Chekiang (August 18), and still another one at Tientain (August 19).

There is no doubt that the commune at Hsing-yang in Honan which Mao inspected was one of the Communists' major experiments, for it was heavily popularized. And it is equally evident that what was done there was reported not only to inspire the nation but also to set it as a "model" experience to be followed.

Then on September 1 appeared the front-page story that the Enlarged-Conference of the Party's Political Bureau decided to announce the "great objective of producing 170,700,000 tons of steel and of making the people's commune as the best form to accelerate the transitional period from socialism to communism." But, the story insisted, "The establishment of people's communes must be made on the basis of initiative consciousness of the masses. It must be done through discussions and indoctrination of the masses as done in the Hundred-Flower movement."

Then came the final official notice when the *People's Daily* front-paged on September 10 the "Decisions of the Central Committee of the Chinese Communist Party on the Problem of Establishing People's Communes."

It is significant to note that the action of the Central Committee was taken on August 29, although the official announcement was not made until September 10.

But even weeks before the publication of the official announcement the movement was already carried out in the nation with fanfare. One needs only the beginning paragraph of an editorial of the *People's Daily* (September 3) to realize how vigorously persuasive communications were already at work: "People's communes, which symbolize a new period of our socialist movement in the rural area, are now established very swiftly in various areas. . . . The movement was started as a result of the high level of socialistic consciousness of the masses. After a few early communes obtained their success, many agricultural coops began to study such models and thus started the movement. . . . Peasants in many areas have written huge volumes of *tatzepao* (posters), petitions and letters to express their determination; they requested to establish people's communes. . . ."

To be sure that "all propaganda authorities in the nation were able to carry out their task efficiently," the *People's Daily* released on September 11 the "Propaganda and Education directives of the Central Committee of the Chinese Communist Party." The five-point directive spells out the meaning of the movement, the propaganda content, the methods to be used, the arguments to be advanced, and the steps to be followed. It emphasized: "From the beginning to end, this movement must follow the principles of settling contradiction among people; it should make use of confessions, accusations, debates, discussions, *tatzepao*, demonstration meetings, exhibits, and all kinds of forms to achieve genuine ideological liberation and to make the movement a REAL, BROAD MOVEMENT OF SELF-EDUCATION. . . ."

By this time the movement had already reached its zenith of development. And before the end of the year the *People's Daily* reported on December 31: "Agricultural coops are already a thing of the past in the rural areas of our country. According to our statistics, in November 99.1 per cent of our peasants have already 26,500 big and fair people's communes which include 126,900,000 families. In average, every commune has about 4,756 families."

III. Functioning of the Communication Media

THE PRESS

Lenin's teaching that the press should perform the threefold role as a "collective propagandist, a collective agitator, and a collective organizer"[23] is followed faithfully in Communist China. Apparently inspired by Lenin and possibly trying even to outdo him, Mao Tse-tung has assigned five major functions to the press: "to organize, to stimulate or encourage, to agitate, to criticize, and to propel."[24]

Mao went on to explain:

"1. To organize is to accurately propagate the objectives, policies, and directives of the party; it is to mobilize and organize all people into a powerful force to realize and to struggle for the various great tasks prescribed by the party at different stages in history.

"2. To fully develop the function of agitation and stimulation, editors must wholeheartedly integrate the creativeness of the masses with their emotions and energy to reflect accurately and timely the accomplishments of the various fronts; they should further learn to make use of the experience of the people's success to suggest new demands, to agitate the masses to compete with or challenge those who have gained early successes.

"3. The most important function of criticism of the press is to be able to select issues and to present convincing arguments to attack the various shades of opportunism, conservatism, and destructive capitalism, to assure the establishment of socialism, to conquer pessimism, and to mobilize aggressivism."

Only a few months after the Communists took over the Chinese mainland a National Press Meeting was called in March 1950 and a four-point directive was issued by the government to cover activities of the newspapers, news agencies, broadcasting stations, and other news media.[25]

"1. Newspapers should devote more space and give prominence to reports on the progress of the people's labor and production, publicizing the experiences of success as well as the lessons of error derived

[23] For a detailed discussion of the role of the press in the Soviet Union, see Alex Inkeles, *op.cit.*, pp. 135-222.

[24] This statement was quoted from a letter written by Mao to two party members in Honan. Wu Chi-pu, "Fully Develop the Five Functions of a Provincial Newspaper," *Hsin Hua Pan Yueh Kan* (*New China Fortnightly*, Peking), February 25, 1959, No. 4, p. 160.

[25] *Ta Kung Pao* (Shanghai), April 24, 1950.

from the work of production and financial and economic tasks, and discussing methods of overcoming difficulties in such tasks.

"2. Newspapers should reorganize their functional structure in such a way that direction and management would be centralized in the hands of the editors.

"3. Newspapers should consider the establishment and direction of 'correspondent networks' and 'newspaper-reading' groups as their major political tasks.

"4. Newspapers should assume responsibility for criticism of the weaknesses or mistakes of the governmental agencies, economic organization, and government personnel; but such criticisms should be truthful and constructive. They should pay the greatest attention to the handling of letters to the editor."

The first point of the directive deals with the content of the press. Specifically, this means propaganda of socialism and Communism and agitation for production. Plainly, the political use of the press is a lesson taken from the Soviet experience.

In the earliest days of the Soviet regime Lenin declared that it was a fundamental necessity "to transform the press from an organ which primarily reports the political news of the day into a serious organ for economic education of the mass of the population." Lenin offered the Soviet newspapers the slogan of "less politics and more economics," and he made it clear that when he spoke of economics he did not mean theoretical arguments, learned reviews, and high-brow plans, which he labeled "twaddle." Instead he demanded that more attention be paid to the workaday aspects of factory, village, and military life. The principal task of the press in the period of transition from capitalism to Communism, Lenin asserted, was to train the masses for the tasks of building the new society, and this meant that the newspapers must give first place to labor problems and to their immediate practical resolution.[26]

Even a quick glance at the Communist newspapers in China reveals that news stories and feature articles about the production activities and economic life of the peasants and workers practically flood the columns. This is especially true of the provincial and local newspapers, in which news, as it is understood in the Western world, is kept to a minimum.

This is not to say that the Chinese Communists are not interested in news. It is only to suggest that to Chinese Communists news can be only one thing: the process of developing socialism and eventually

[26] Alex Inkeles, *op.cit.*, pp. 161-162.

Communism. This is their concept of news. This is how news is presented. And this is how the press, as well as other news media, is utilized to aid the political development of the country.

This is why Lu Ting-i, director of the Department of Propaganda of the Chinese Communist party, said: "The press is an instrument of class struggle."[27] This is also why Teng Kuo, editor of the *People's Daily*, said: "The press is the most powerful and effective weapon to mobilize and organize the broad masses for the building of socialism, particularly the fight for agricultural production."[28]

The establishment of "correspondent networks" is similar to the Soviet *Rabsseľkor*, the Worker and Peasant Correspondent Movement. A "correspondent" is any man or woman in factory or field who writes to newspapers about his work, his economic life, his experience in political study movement, and the accomplishments or failures of those around him. Writing ability is a matter of secondary importance. In fact, it is nothing unusual at all to find newspaper stories written by "correspondents" who can barely manage to read and write, poems composed by those who hardly know the fundamentals of the Chinese language.

Less than a year after the Communists took over the Chinese mainland most newspapers already claimed to have a huge army of correspondents. For instance, in 1950 *Ho Pei Jih Pao* (*Hopei Daily*) claimed to have 1,600 correspondents; *Fu Kien Jih Pao* (*Fukien Daily*) 5,000; and *Lao Tun Pao* (*Labor Daily*) as many as 7,000.[29]

How the correspondents help the propaganda function of the party is very explicitly explained in an official report in which the following statement from *Nung Ming Pao* (*Farmer's Daily*) in Shensi is quoted: "It has been verified by our experience that only by depending upon correct propaganda policies can our task of uniting closely with the masses be lively, and that only by tying together the actual life and work of the masses with propaganda can our policies be convincing and effective. We have come to understand that peasants have the following habit in comprehension and understanding: they will not accept a theory or principle if it is not coupled with 'facts'; but they cannot see

[27] Lu Ting-i, "Speech Delivered on the Twentieth Anniversary of the New China News Agency," *Jen Min Shu Tse* (*People's Handbook*), Peking, Ta Kung Pao Company, 1958, p. 144.
[28] Teng Kuo, "Socialist Revolution on the Journalistic Front," *Hsueh Hsi* (*Study*, Peking), April 18, 1958, No. 8, p. 2.
[29] Liu Tseng-chi, "The Press in New China," *Culture and Education in New China*, Peking, Foreign Languages Press, undated, p. 43.

through the 'facts' if no 'reason' or 'theory' is given and therefore cannot raise their level of consciousness. To make newspaper articles appealing and convincing and to strengthen the effect of newspaper propaganda, there must be actual examples together with convincing arguments. Therefore, we will not merely deal with vague facts that are not well organized."[30]

Perhaps even more important than the correspondents' network are the newspaper-reading groups, in which the news is read aloud and discussed.

It is significant to note that even fifth-graders in a Peking elementary school are also organized to read newspapers. "In this particular school," reports a Peking evening paper, "the leadership and the Youth Volunteers are extremely interested in utilizing youth newspapers to engage in political and ideological education among students."[31]

Another major responsibility of the press is the intensive practice of criticism and self-criticism. This is known in Soviet Russia as *kritika* and *samekritika*. In China this public criticism has been formalized and elaborated in a major social institution. Since the practice of criticism is supposed to work from top to bottom and from bottom to top, it is but natural that the press ideally fits the role as a transmission belt between the party and the government on the one hand and the masses of the people on the other.

RADIO

The vast land of China is now blanketed by the round-the-clock din of radio. As Dr. Sripati Chandrasekhar, noted Indian scholar who returned in 1959 from extensive travel behind the Bamboo Curtain, describes it, the radio voice "blares away at you in the bus, in the train, in the trolley, the sleepers, and dining cars, on street corners, in villages, towns, and cities—just about everywhere."[32] He goes on to say:

"Even in a most backward and traditional village I saw a loudspeaker hidden in a treetop. You can escape the sun and the moon but you cannot escape the radio and the loudspeaker. . . .

"This is the most important medium for approved news—news of the nation's progress, industrial output, how to make a smelter, how to defeat the American imperialist, how to be a good Communist, how

---

[30] *Hsin Hua Yueh Pao (New China Monthly,* Peking), II, 4, August 1950, p. 901.
[31] *Peking Wan Pao (Peking Evening News),* February 27, 1959.
[32] Sripati Chandrasekhar, "Red China Today," written for the Associated Press, *Boston Globe,* February 16, 1959.

to be neat, how to denounce the rightists, how to behave in a train, how to kill a rat or a sparrow, how to cook a sweet potato—and a thousand other things, interspersed with traditional Chinese opera with its deafening gongs and cymbals and martial and marching songs.

"A few times in trains I had to feign illness so I could pull out the plug under the loudspeaker to enjoy a few hours of quiet. The citizen does not have a minute of silence in which to rest his mind or reflect on his new life."

Dramatic as this account may sound, it tells only of the pervasiveness of the so-called *yu hsien kuang po* or "line broadcasting" in Communist China. Strictly speaking, this is not a broadcasting system but a system of point-to-point radio communication with dissemination of selected programming at the point of reception by means of wired loudspeakers. This is known as the "radio-diffusion exchange" in the Soviet Union.[33]

The Communist plan to blanket the entire nation with the so-called "radio broadcasting networks" started almost immediately after the regime was proclaimed. Detailed instructions were given by the government in April 1950 when the "Decision Regarding the Establishment of Radio-Receiving Networks" was announced.[34] The latest Chinese claim is that "with the exception of a few remote areas in border regions, radio networks in rural areas all over the country are greatly popular."[35]

The more striking features of radio communications in Communist China must be briefly mentioned. One has to do with what the Communists call "collective listening." Most of the listeners under this system are workers in factories and mines, peasants on farms, and people of low cultural standards in cities. They are organized or mobilized to form radio-listening groups. Trained monitors are

[33] For a detailed discussion on the radio-diffusion exchange in Soviet Russia, read Alex Inkeles, *op.cit.*, pp. 225-286. The same system is developed in other Communist countries. In Communist Poland, for instance, "wired radio" is becoming increasingly important. See Robert C. Sorenson and Leszek L. Meyer, "Local Uses of Wired Radio in Communist-Ruled Poland," *Journalism Quarterly*, Summer 1955, pp. 343-348. For a more detailed discussion on radio communications in Communist China, see Frederick T. C. Yu, "Radio Propaganda in Communist China," *Journalism Review*, I, 1958, pp. 20-26. See also Franklin W. Houn, "Radio Broadcasting and Propaganda in Communist China," *Journalism Quarterly*, Summer 1959, pp. 366-377.

[34] Tse Yung, "Broadcasting in China," *People's China*, 22, 1955, November 16, 1953, p. 29.

[35] Tang Cheng-lin, "To Struggle for Easier Realization of the Directives on National Agricultural Development," in *I Ting Yao Chi Su Yueh Ching (We Must Leap Forward)*, Hong Kong, San Lien Bookstore, 1960, p. 59.

located throughout the country to make certain that the daily messages from Peking find their way to the masses of people. They also see to it that certain messages that require serious attention of the audience are discussed and understood in the political study groups.

Another unusual utilization of radio in Communist China is the program of news dictations. In Chinese this is *chi lu hsin wen*, which literally means "news to be recorded." This program is specially designed for professional propagandists and monitors of radio-receiving networks who engage in a great variety of propaganda activities such as issuing small tabloids, blackboard newspapers, wall newspapers, and pamphlets, or engaging in oral agitation. It generally starts with a preview of the next day's news or features. Sometimes special notes to propagandists and monitors are broadcast. Such notices instruct the monitors and propagandists as to what issue and what angle they should play up in their propaganda publications. Then the announcer gives the topics for dictation as well as the number of Chinese characters of each item. The dictation is very slow, and every sentence is repeated at least three or four times.

POSTERS (TATZEPAO)

That posters are used for propaganda purposes is a common phenomenon; that they should be used as a medium of mass communication is something strikingly new. The fact that they are handwritten normally prohibits any possibility of making them available to a mass audience.

A *tatzepao* means literally "paper of bold characters." It is usually a large sheet of paper posted at any convenient location. Although some Communists choose to trace the beginning of the saga of *tatzepao* to as early as the 17th century,[36] this form of communication was first used on a dramatically large scale during the Communist Rectification Movement in 1957 and is now regarded as the "most effective medium for criticism and self-criticism."[37] In 1960, when the Movement to Increase Production and Practice Austerity was in full swing, *tatzepao* was considered one of the major weapons of indoctrination.[38] Below are four typical cases that illustrate the unique character of this form of mass communication and its use in political development.

[36] Fang Han-chi, "The Saga of Tatzepao," *Jen Min Jih Pao* (*People's Daily*, Peking), June 18, 1958.
[37] *Chinese Literature* (Peking), November-December 1958, No. 6, p. 14.
[38] *Jen Min Jih Pao* (*People's Daily*, Peking), editorial, September 13, 1960.

Chung Min, member of the Shanghai Municipal Committee of the Chinese Communist Party, reported in 1958:

"During this anti-extravagance and anti-conservatism movement, the broad masses and cadres in Shanghai have produced in the period slightly more than 100,000,000 sheets of *tatzepao*. . . . The Shipbuilding Yard posted 538,000 sheets of *tatzepao* in a short period of six or seven days.

"Experience has told us: jointly used with discussion meetings, accusations meetings, and debate sessions, *tatzepao* is the most effective method to bare and solve the problem of internal contradiction among the people. . . .

"*Tatzepao* is a driving force to enable us to accomplish our tasks. It is a form of pressure to those cadres who are at a low level of class consciousness. . . .

"*Tatzepao* is something unique in our country of socialist democracy. It is the best instrument to bring to the open the problem of internal contradiction among the people, to solve the problem and thus to push forward progress. We should follow Comrade Mao's direction to develop and keep this particular instrument and to keep it forever."[39]

In November 1957 a total of 220,000 sheets of *tatzepao* was posted by some 60 units of government offices in Peking, along with 1,400 meetings. "Through these channels the masses contributed some 380,000 items of suggestions."[40]

Wan Ching-liang, the first secretary of the party committee of Putung, a small city near Shanghai, opens his article entitled "Long Live the Commune" with these words: "After the news about the people's communes appeared in newspapers last year, the broad masses of peasants in Putung welcomed the idea enthusiastically and demanded speedy establishment of the commune. When the authorities decided to have the commune established, the masses posted more than 30,000 sheets of *tatzepao* in a few days resolutely asking to join the people's commune."[41]

One New China news agency reporter exults: "There are now so many *tatzepao* in the government agencies that sharply colored 'no smoking' signs have to be put up. Indeed *tatzepao* are plentiful. You see them from one floor to another, on all walls, on windows, at staircases and inside of offices. In corridors, strings or ropes were

[39] *Hsueh Hsi* (*Study*, Peking), June 18, 1958, No. 12, pp. 20-21.
[40] *Jen Min Jih Pao* (*People's Daily*, Peking), November 23, 1957.
[41] *Wen Hui Pao* (Shanghai), January 1, 1959.

stretched from one wall to another to hang the reams and reams of
tatzepao. . . ."[42]

In some quarters the production of *tatzepao* has become a formalized
affair which is run almost like a newspaper complete with "editorial
board, production center, correspondent network, and distribution
center."[43] In others for those who cannot write, special "*tatzepao* writing stations" are established.[44]

There is no set form or style for *tatzepao*; they employ slogans,
satirical prose, comic strips, cartoons, accusation letters, tables, graphs,
etc.

That *tatzepao* should be unusually effective as a means of persuasive
communications is easy to understand. In the first place, it is written
by those and about those whom all readers know. In the second place,
it is not a communication that can be simply ignored or dismissed, for
it may appear on the wall of one's office or at the door of one's house.
In the case of an engineer who was accused of having committed the
unforgivable sin of "individualism"[45] *tatzepao* appeared in his office.
As a matter of self-defense he wrote his own *tatzepao* entitled "My
Difficulties." But his *tatzepao* got nowhere; it only invited more
tatzepao from his accusers. According to the Communist news story,
the engineer, after "repeated education" of the *tatzepao*, was able to
realize his mistakes. He accepted the criticisms in his later *tatzepao* and
wrote many more *tatzepao* to "expose" the various aspects of "extrava-
gance," "waste," and "undesirable behavior" in his plant.

The fact that *tatzepao* is vigorously utilized along with accusation
meetings, study sessions, and almost all campaigns is evidence that
perhaps it serves as a device of control more effectively than the columns of criticism and self-criticism in the newspapers.

FILM

The mission of the film industry, according to Hsia Yen, Vice-
Minister of Culture and China's leading spokesman on the motion
picture, "is to reflect speedily the new era and new society—especially
the new men, new events, new heroes, new ideologies, new emotions,
new morality, and new qualities during this period of socialist revolution and socialist development—and through all this to propagate the
Socialist and Communist ideology."[46]

[42] *Jen Min Jih Pao* (*People's Daily*, Peking), March 28, 1958.
[43] *Jen Min Jih Pao* (*People's Daily*, Peking), August 13, 1958.
[44] *Ibid.*, September 25, 1957.   [45] *Ibid.*, March 28, 1958.
[46] *Ibid.*, September 15, 1960. This is an important address delivered by Hsia Yen

No useful purpose will be served by listing all the accomplishments claimed by Hsia and his colleagues in the film industry, but there is every reason to believe that, as a medium of persuasive communication, motion pictures now reach a much larger audience than before in the country. If the Communists' figures are in any way reliable, the progress is more than impressive. For instance, the figure of movie projection units in the country, according to Hsia, "jumped from about 600 in 1949 to about 14,500 by the end of 1959."[47]

Perhaps it should be noted that until China turned Communist movies were mainly a medium of entertainment and available only to those in urban areas. Although movie teams were tried by the Nationalist government in the 1940's for political and educational purposes, exposure of the Chinese peasants and workers to this medium was never significantly large. This picture has apparently changed drastically under the Communists.

The movie audience in 1949, according to one leading movie producer in China, was estimated at 50,000,000. The figure, he reported, rose to 1,390,000,000 in 1956.[48] In 1954, for instance, the Communists claimed that their "cinema production teams serving mines, factories, villages, and settlements in mountainous and remote frontier districts of the country gave more than 1,100,000 shows to a total audience of 820,000,000 people."[49] Perhaps these figures are not sheer fabrication or exaggeration. For the Communists are quite skillful in mobilizing their movie audience. Consider, for instance, the following case.

In 1951, when the Korean war was in high gear, the Peking Film Studio of the Ministry of Cultural Affairs released the first part of a documentary film called "Resist-America Aid-Korea." The Communists did not go about winning a big audience simply by placing attractive advertisements in newspapers or colorful posters on streets. Instead, a special committee was formed in every major city to see to it that the film was shown to the largest possible number of people. In Canton "The Committee for Showing the Documentary Film Resist-America Aid-Korea" was formed by representatives of the twelve government and mass organizations, and a joint directive was issued to

---

at the Second Session of the Congress of All-China Representatives of the Federation of Chinese Film Workers on July 30, 1960. The full-page newspaper article reviews Communist China's film industry since the beginning of the Communist regime in 1949.

[47] *Loc.cit.* [48] *Jen Min Jih Pao* (*People's Daily*, Peking), February 22, 1957.
[49] *People's China* (Peking), No. 10, May 16, 1955.

all organizations in Canton asking them to mobilize "an audience of 450,000 in Canton."[50] According to the official newspaper in Canton, a few days before the showing of the film, an estimated audience of 525,000 was already reported by many organizations to the committee. And the task of mobilization took only a few days.[51]

ART AND LITERATURE

No discussion on persuasive communication in Communist China can be complete without reference to the various forms of art and literature—drama, opera, songs, novels, propaganda paintings (*hsien chuan hua*) sculpture, comics, cartoons, etc. Mao wrote in 1942: "The literature and art of the proletariat are part of the revolutionary program of the proletariat. As Lenin pointed out, they are a 'screw in the machine.' . . . Although literature and art are subordinate to politics, they in turn exert a tremendous influence upon politics. . . . They are like the afore-mentioned screws."[52]

To understand why various forms of art and literature are, as China's propaganda chief Lu Ting-i puts it, "a major weapon in ideological education and struggle"[53] it is necessary to have some notion of their uniquely important role not only in the tradition of Communist propaganda but also in the political development of the Chinese Communist party.

Perhaps the area where the Communists scored the biggest propaganda victories in the pre-1949 days was the field of art and literature. Marxism-Leninism, it must be noted, grew up in China at a time when China was desperately searching for new helpful ideas for national salvation. It was introduced to the country by intellectuals who discussed it along with the theories of Adam Smith, John Stuart Mill, Tolstoy, Darwin, Rousseau, Montesquieu, Kropotkin, and Thomas Henry Huxley. Among those who either embraced or showed sympathy with the Communistic idea was a small group of artists, writers, and intellectuals in general, although they were perhaps only vaguely familiar with Marxism-Leninism. In the first two or three decades

---

[50] *Liu Ch'ang-sheng, K'ang Mai Yuan Ch'ao Pao Chia Wei Kuo Yun Tung Chung Ti Shanghai Jen Min* (*Shanghai Citizens in the Resist-America Aid-Korea, Protect-Home Defend-Country Movement*), Shanghai, Lao Tung Publishing Co., 1951, pp. 19-27.

[51] *Nan Fang Jih Pao* (*Southern Daily*, Canton), December 26, 1951.

[52] Mao Tse-tung, *Problems of Art and Literature*, New York, International Publishers, 1950, p. 33.

[53] Lu Ting-i, "New China's Education and Culture," *Hsin Hua Yueh Pao* (*New China Monthly*, Peking), II, 1, May 1950, pp. 159-162.

of the twentieth century the whole field of Chinese art and literature was ideologically chaotic. Those seeking inspiration from abroad talked excitedly, often pointlessly, about the aestheticism of Oscar Wilde, the naturalism of Gustav Flaubert, the symbolism of Maurice Maeterlinck, the neo-classicism of Anatole France, the neo-humanism of Goethe and Schiller, or the neo-romanticism of Ibsen. There were other ism's, of which one was Marxism.

Almost from its birth in 1921 the Chinese Communist party has formed a curiously important relationship with artists and writers. It is difficult to decide when the party started to grasp the teaching of Stalin that "literature should belong to the party." It can only be said that the party attempted quite vigorously even in the 1920's to seek alliance with whomever they could win over among the artists and writers. This was especially true of the newly rising self-styled leftists and liberals who, like many others, were frustrated with the problems of China and who, being human, were delighted at getting sympathetic attention from almost any living soul.

In 1930 the "Federation of Leftist Writers" was organized. Communist historians today take pride in pointing out that the group was organized in Shanghai with the leadership of the Communist underground workers. The group had the support and enjoyed the prestige of such great literary figures as Lu Hsun and Mao Tun.

By this time there were already the clashes between so-called "revolutionary literature" as represented by the Federation and the so-called "bourgeois literature." Quickly emerging also was the debate among writers about the problem of the political function or mission of literature. At any rate, it became quite fashionable for a while for writers to promote the cause of the proletariat, although to do so in political circles at this time would be more than frowned at.

It would be wrong to believe that Communist activities in the circles of artists and writers were tolerated by the Nationalists. It is perhaps much closer to the mark to say that the Nationalists were not sufficiently aware of the political usefulness of art and literature to use it or to guard against it. By the time the Nationalists realized what they had overlooked, it was too late.

Shortly after the outbreak of the Sino-Japanese War the Federation of Leftist Writers was dissolved, apparently as a result of pressure from the Kuomintang. But the Kuomintang-Communist coalition only made the activities of the Communists in the field of art and literature easier. As a result the Communists were able to achieve remarkable successes in their manipulation of the channels of art and literature for their persuasive communications.

Today all forms of art and literature are utilized to follow Mao's teaching of "propagandizing only the ideology of workers, peasants, and soldiers."[54] To be sure that this policy is successfully carried out, the Communists now require all artists and writers to "identify themselves with the workers and peasants, labor and write among them and learn from them." This means that artists can no longer simply work in their "ivory tower" even when they agree to sing, paint, or write about the "glorious wisdom" of peasants and workers. They have to be with the peasants and workers. As Minister of Culture Chou Yang decreed: "It is of the utmost importance for a writer to maintain the closest contacts with the life and struggles of the great mass of the people. Only thus can he acquire a feeling for the new and the fresh and develop broad vision."[55] It is therefore no coincidence that thousands of artists and writers often find themselves toiling together with peasants and workers in the countryside and in factories as one of the most important requirements of their work.

As Tien Han, one of China's leading playwrights, puts it: "Ever since the Hundred-Flower Rectification Campaign in 1957 teams of dramatic workers have gone to the mountains, to farms, to factories, to armies, to the front, to be intimately associated with workers, peasants, and soldiers. On the one hand, they participate in the labor of production; on the other, they perform for them."[56]

The Communist single-mindedness of using art and literature solely as a tool of political communication necessarily introduces new characters, new symbols, new images, new expressions, and new forms. We can illustrate a few here.

The *Folk Songs of Great Leap Forward* opens with the following poem profusely praised by Minister of Culture Chou Yang:

We measure songs in bushels now;
The thousand bushels fill a barn;
Don't laugh if we use homely speech—
Out in the fields it turns to grain.

[54] Mao Tse-tung, *Problems of Art and Literature, op.cit.*, p. 23.
[55] Chou Yang, "Building a Socialist Literature," *Chinese Literature* (Peking), 4, 1956, p. 205.
[56] Tien Han, "The Struggle on the Front of Dramatics Since the Establishment of the Nation 11 Years Ago and Future Tasks," *Jen Min Jih Pao* (*People's Daily*, Peking), September 9, 1960.

You need a proper hoe to farm,
You need a proper voice to sing;
Each one of us is a singer now—
We'll sing till the Yangtze flows upstream.[57]

This may very well be a reasonably accurate picture of the mass production of songs and poems. For, as Chou goes on to say, "They have become a mode of political agitation in factories and farms. Weapons in the struggle to increase output, and the creation of the laboring people themselves, they are at the same time works of art the people can appreciate."

"Poetry is now integrated with work, while work has become poetry," say the Communists. Even such work as collecting manure finds its way into poetry. Chou cites "The Little Boat" as an example:

The little boat loaded with dung
Has frightened the moorhens away,
Has shattered the stars in the stream
In smoke that is misty and gray.

The little boat loaded with dung,
Its sculls creaking merrily still,
Is passing the willow-clad shore
To melt into Peach Blossom Hill.[58]

Likewise, new images emerge in love songs that are forever related to labor and production:

He carries earth as swiftly as the wind.
And with her load she follows close behind.
'Though past the fleecy clouds you fly away
I mean to catch you up, cost it may![59]

While plays or shows are far less popular than movies in the United States, the reverse is true in China. Drama is perhaps the only form of mass culture commonly liked in China's rural areas and almost the only point at which ordinary, illiterate peasants participate in the higher form of traditional culture. A great variety of drama exists in China, and every dialectal region has its own operatic, theatrical, or musical form. Almost every Chinese village has a place (sometimes

[57] Chou Yang, "New Folk Songs Blaze a New Trail in Poetry," *Chinese Literature* (Peking), 6, 1958, p. 8.
[58] *Ibid.*, p. 13.
[59] *Loc.cit.*

located in a temple or an ancestral shrine or on the local fair grounds) where performances are given by local talent or by traveling troupes.

The Communists, aware of this unique feature of drama as a means of persuasive communication, have attached special importance to this form of propaganda. For instance, the number of various kinds of dramatic artists or performers in 1949, according to the Communists, was 50,900 in China; it jumped to 260,000 in 1959. The Communists now claim to have 39,000 workers' after-work performing troupes and 244,000 agricultural after-work drama teams and cultural-workers corps.[60]

In addition to revising much of traditional drama in China the Chinese Communists have introduced many new forms of dramatic art for the purpose of political propaganda. Their radio drama, for instance, is now hailed as "the light brigade in propagandizing the party's policies."[61] Then there are street-corner shows which are called "living newspapers." Only one year after the establishment of the Chinese Communist regime the official *People's China* reported:

"Every day during the last few days (late in 1950) in Peking alone more than 5,000 players from schools, institutions, and dramatic clubs have given various street corner shows. Among the most effective 'living newspaper' plays are *Truman Dreams of Hitler* and the Dances of the Devils, the devils being Truman, MacArthur, Chiang Kai-shek, and many others.

"Through the countryside of Hopei province 2,000 locally organized amateur troupes are traveling from village to village to give performances for the peasants in the long winter evenings. Around the theme of 'protect the homeland,' their plays are woven out of the stuff of their own experiences. Their true-life stories impress the audiences profoundly, and often at the end of the shows, the onlookers themselves join the players in shouting slogans. Many enroll immediately as volunteers for Korea on the spot."[62]

In 1958, when the *coup d'état* in Iraq resulted in the overthrowing of King Feisal's regime, the propaganda team of the All-China Playwrights Association lost no time at all in producing a "living newspaper" play, *The Result of a Traitor*, ridiculing the Iraqi premier who failed in his attempt to flee the country in the disguise of a woman.[63]

[60] *Jen Min Jih Pao* (*People's Daily*, Peking), September 9, 1960.
[61] *Loc.cit.*
[62] "Art Fights for Korea," *People's China*, III, 1, January 1, 1951.
[63] *Jen Min Jih Pao* (*People's Daily*, Peking), July 21, 1958.

Such plays are often crude and unsophisticated, but many of them are written by some of the leading writers. The "Ah, Ya, Ya Small American Moon," which ridicules the smallness of American satellites, was written by four leading playwrights, including Chen Pai-cheng.[64]

So important is the manipulation of drama for persuasive purposes that one of the current policies of the Peking regime is "to integrate dramatic arts with teaching in communes" and "to establish fine arts schools" in all basic units of the communes.[65]

PERSON-TO-PERSON COMMUNICATION

One has to stretch very far the meaning of mass communication as it is understood in the West to include person-to-person communication or what is generally known in Communist countries as "oral agitation." But this is definitely a form of mass communication if one takes into account the fact that this is a Communist scheme of communication that involves literally millions of communicators and huge segments of the Chinese population.

Ever since the Central Committee of the Chinese Communist Party issued on January 1, 1951 the order to establish propaganda networks in the nation[66] the system has become an institution in the country. In 1952, for instance, the province of Shantung alone claimed a total of 450,000 "propagandists."[67] These propagandists carry on a variety of activities among the masses, such as interviewing, passing on information, reading newspapers (in newspaper reading groups), monitoring broadcasts, preparing posters, editing wall newspapers or blackboard newspapers, leading discussion meetings, etc. But many of them simply use personal conversation as their form of carrying out their propaganda mission.[68] They are supposed to be constantly at work among people in their homes, quarters, and daily activities and to seize every opportunity to carry on propaganda, even at meal time.

For instance, the following story appears in a book specially compiled for the use of propagandists. It is the "model experience" of a propagandist:

[64] *Ibid.*, February 27, 1958.

[65] *Ibid.*, September 13, 1958.

[66] "Decisions on the Establishment of Propaganda Networks for the Whole Party among the Masses of the People," *Hsin Hua Yueh Pao* (*New China Monthly*), III, 3, January 1951, pp. 507-509.

[67] *Jen Min Jih Pao* (Peking), January 12, 1955; also in *Hsin Hua Yueh Pao* (*New China Monthly*), 2, 1955, p. 193.

[68] Li Chia-lin: "Conversation—the Best Form of Oral Propaganda," *Jen Min Jih Pao* (Peking), May 17, 1955.

Eating Noodles

"On a Saturday we had noodles. . . . At noon time all workmen came to the mess hall. While paying for his meal, one worker said in great delight: 'We have noodles to eat.'

"I (the propagandist) immediately added: 'That's right. Yesterday we had bread, today we have noodles. . . . We are no longer in the days of the Japanese occupation, when we have *hsiang-tze-mien* day in and day out.'[69]

"Because I mentioned this, all the people around me began to remember the days in the past. Who had not suffered? Who wanted to live again the life of those days? Then I (the propagandist) said:

" 'Now there are still people who will not let us eat this (noodles)!'

" 'Who?' people asked, before I had finished my sentence.

" 'Who? The American devils,' I answered, and then continued: 'The American devils started the war of aggression in Korea because they wanted to invade China. Unless we eliminate all the American devils, we shall have no good days in the future. In order to drive away the American devils, we have to speed up production and support the front. . . .' "[70]

Stories such as this are plentiful in the Chinese Communist press. One woman propagandist spends several days aboard the boat of a fisherman's widow in order to bring out the latter's "grievance against landlords, the Kuomintang, and despotism" and thus to prepare her for accusation meetings.[71] Another woman propagandist even moves into the home of a poor peasant woman and successfully "educates" the latter to be an "aggressive element" in *tou cheng* or struggle meetings against landlords.[72] One propagandist in a mine makes a point to carry out his propaganda activities every time he and his co-workers take a break.[73]

Such "model examples" of oral agitation represent one type of propaganda which occupies a uniquely important position in the Communist scheme of mass persuasion. This importance should become immediately apparent when one realizes that to be a propagandist is the natural

[69] *Hsiang-tze-mein* is a kind of food made of chestnut oak which poor people eat during years of famine or war.

[70] Editorial Department of the People's Publishing Co., ed., *Tsen Yang Tso Hsien Ch'uan Yuan (How to Be a Propagandist)*, Peking, Jen Min Ch'u Pan She, 1951, p. 11.

[71] *Nan Fang Jih Pao (Southern Daily, Canton)*, March 3, 1952.

[72] *Ibid.*, February 14, 1952.

[73] *Jen Min Jih Pao* (Peking), May 17, 1955.

duty of every member of the party and the Communist Youth Corps and every "aggressive element" of the numerous mass organizations in the country.

IV. Thought Reform

An adequate grasp of persuasive communications in China cannot be obtained without some understanding of the Communist program of thought reform or ideological remoulding of the nation.[74] This is easily the most ambitious attempt in human history to reshape the minds of men, and one of the most truly important features of Chinese Communism.

But what is thought reform? Many equate it with "brainwashing," and there is already an impressive amount of literature on the subject.[75] The term is not incorrect, but it suggests, figuratively speaking, mainly a process of cleaning one's brain by "washing out" the "poisonous and erroneous ideas." It leaves out the process of filling one's brain with the "universal truth of Marxism-Leninism and Maoism." Moreover, the term is associated mainly with the indoctrination of American prisoners-of-war in China and the re-education of Chinese intellectuals.

[74] Schramm, for instance, observes: "I don't know of any case in which the Communists have put the whole burden of convincing people and gaining members on mass communications alone. They always provide a group structure where a convert can get reinforcement, and meetings to which a potential convert can be drawn. They use mass communication almost as an adjunct to these groups." See Wilbur Schramm, ed., *The Process and Effects of Mass Communication*, Urbana, Ill., University of Illinois Press, 1954, p. 25.

[75] The most recent and thorough study on this problem is Theodore H. E. Chen, *Thought Reform of the Chinese Intellectuals*, Hong Kong University Press, 1960. Other interesting and significant studies: "Brainwashing" (special issue), *Journal of Social Issues*, XIII, 3, 1957 (articles by Robert J. Lifton, Edgar H. Schein, Julius Segal, Raymond A. Bauer, and James G. Miller); L. E. Hinkle and H. G. Wolff, "Communist Interrogation and Indoctrination of the 'Enemies of the State,'" *Archives of Neurology and Psychiatry*, 76, 1957, pp. 115-174; Joost A. M. Merloo, "Brainwashing in Perspective: A Psychiatrist Interprets Peking's 'Thought Reform,'" *New Republic*, 136, May 13, 1957, pp. 21-25; *idem*, "Thought Reform of Western Civilians in Chinese Communist Prisons," *Psychiatry*, XIX, 1956, pp. 173-196; *idem*, "Home by Ship: Reaction Patterns of American Prisoners of War Repatriated from North Korea," *American Journal of Psychiatry*, CX, 1954, pp. 732-739; E. H. Schein, "The Chinese Indoctrination Program for Prisoners of War," *Psychiatry*, XIX, 1956, pp. 149-172; *idem*, "Interpersonal Communication, Group Solidarity and Social Influence," invited address delivered to the International Council for Women Psychologists on August 28, 1958, Washington, D.C. (mimeographed); M. T. Singer and E. H. Schein, "Projective Test Responses of Prisoners of War Following Repatriation," *Psychiatry*, 21, 1958, p. 375; H. A. Segal, "Initial Psychiatric Findings of Recently Repatriated Prisoners of War," *American Journal of Psychiatry*, CXI, 1954, pp. 3,588-3,663; I. E. Farber, H. F. Harlow, and L. J. West, "Brainwashing, Conditioning and DDD (Debility, Dependency, and Dread)," *Sociometry*, XX, 1957, pp. 271-285; Edouard Sanvage, *Dans les Prisons Chinoises*, Provins, Seine-et, Marine, 1957.

To equate thought reform with brainwashing is to overlook the fact that thought reform is a permanent part of the Chinese Communist policy, that it is one form of communication which is designed to reinforce all other forms of persuasion and coercion in China, and that it is conducted not only periodically among the enemies of the state but among all the Chinese people at all times.

Thought reform, says Mao Tse-tung, "is a protracted, gigantic, and complex task." As a method of persuasion and an instrument of control it had been repeatedly tried within the party long before it came to power in 1949. As early as 1929 Mao waged a "thought struggle" against petty bourgeois ideologies in the infant Red Army. It was no longer a new idea in 1937 when Mao said: "We advocate a positive ideological struggle because it is the weapon for attaining the solidarity between the party and other revolutionary organizations. . . . Every Communist party member and every revolutionary must take up this weapon."[76]

Indeed the basic strategy, tactics, and methods of thought reform in China today do not differ greatly from those set down by Mao about two decades ago.

On February 1, 1942, lecturing on the eradication of "muddled" and "dangerous" ideas at the Central Party School of the Chinese Communisty Party at Yenan, Mao Tse-tung concluded with two methodological principles: "Learn from past experience in order to avoid future mistakes," and "treat the illness in order to save the man." He explained:

"We must expose without personal considerations all past errors, analyze and criticize them scientifically so that we will be more careful and do better work in future. This is the meaning of the principle: 'learn from past experience in order to avoid future mistakes.' But in exposing errors and criticizing defects, our whole purpose is the same as the doctor's in treating a case: namely, to cure the patient but not to kill him. A person suffering from appendicitis will recover if his appendix is removed by the surgeon. Any person who has committed errors is welcome to treatment until he is cured and becomes a good comrade, so long as he does not conceal his malady for fear of taking medicine or persist in his errors until he becomes incorrigible but honestly and sincerely wishes to be cured and made better. You cannot

[76] Mao Tse-tung, "Fan-tui tzu-yu-chu-yi" (Opposing Liberalism), in *Cheng-feng Wen-Hsien* (*Ideological Remoulding Documents*), Hong Kong, Hsin Min Publishing Co., 1949, p. 163.

cure him by subjecting him to hearty abuse or giving him a sound thrashing. In treating a case of ideological or political illness, we should never resort to violence, but should adopt the attitude of 'treating the illness in order to save the man,' which alone is the correct and effective method."[77]

Six days later, speaking at a cadres' meeting on certain anti-Marxist ideas and behaviors that are diagnosed as "petty bourgeois ideology," Mao observed that China was a country with a very large petty bourgeoisie and that "a large number of members of this class origin had joined the party without shedding their petty bourgeois tails, long or short." Then he offered this clinical approach: "It is not easy to liquidate these things and sweep them clean. We must do it properly; in other words, we must use persuasive reasoning. If our reasoning is persuasive and to the point, it will be effective. In reasoning we must begin by administering a shock and shouting at the patient, 'You are ill!' so that he is frightened into a sweat, and then we tell him gently that he needs treatment."[78]

The surgery of tail-shedding turned out to be a group therapy, and the actual act of shedding the tail was to be performed by the patients themselves. Mao's surgical method, as popularized later by his disciples, is described thus: "Take off your pants in public and stand the pain of cutting off the tail."[79] In more civilized terms, this means one's application of the method of criticism and self-criticism in group indoctrination to search for, identify, and repudiate his "erroneous" beliefs or ideas.

It is interesting to note that Mao, apparently with no medical training himself, frequently speaks about the problem of thought reform in clinical terms. In 1945, emphasizing once again the importance of the method of criticism and self-criticism, he wrote: "We have said that a room must be regularly cleaned or dust will accumulate in it, and that our faces must be regularly washed or they will be smeared with dirt. The same is true of our comrades' minds and our party's work. The proverb: 'running water does not go stale and door-hinges do not become worm-eaten,' indicates how these things can by ceaseless motion be immune from the harmful effects of microbes or other

[77] "Rectify the Party's Style in Work," *Selected Works of Mao Tse-tung*, London, Lawrence and Wishart, 1956, IV, pp. 44-45.
[78] Chu Min, *Ssu Hsiang Kai Tsou Hsueh Hsi (Thought Reform and Study)*, Shanghai, Ta Hua Publishing Co., 1952, p. 54.
[79] *Loc.cit.*

organisms."[80] Then he went on to discuss methods "to prevent various kinds of political dust and microbes from producing harmful effects on the minds of our comrades and the physique of our party."

Thus in 1949, when the entire Chinese mainland came under the Communist rule, Mao and his followers were not entirely helpless and inexperienced when they had to face literally millions of "patients" who had "petty bourgeois tails," who were "plagued by political maladies of various kinds and degrees," and who were apparently not even cognizant of their "political illness."

Mao's first major measure in thought reform for the entire nation was the gigantic *Hsueh Hsi* (Study) Movement, which has become a permanent institution in China. Then different groups were subjected to different intensified rectification campaigns. Since the Hundred-Flower Campaign in 1957 rectification campaigns have become a regular affair.

Today everyone *hsueh hsi* or studies. Every factory, mine, shop, school, office, army group, or residential unit is divided into study groups. Under party-approved leaders, the groups meet regularly to study party doctrines and government policies, to learn to serve the nation by participating in the endless campaigns and tasks prescribed by the party, and, above all, to strive ceaselessly for "ideological liberation," i.e. "liberation from all ideologies" considered reactionary, hostile, and erroneous by the party.

The main forms of study are reading of assigned documents and discussions and debates. The guiding principles of discussion are to integrate realistic situations with the documents and, if possible, to relate problems of oneself to the documents or question under discussion. Everyone has to talk because all erroneous ideas have to be exposed. This is generally the first step in any study program. Then well-staged struggle meetings, accusation meetings, or complaint meetings are conducted according to the nature of the study program and the tasks involved. Then more discussions, more criticisms, more self-criticisms, and more readings. Then a study conclusion or thought conclusion is expected from each participant who is to expose or confess his "erroneous idea, wrong attitudes, and inadequate outlook" in the light of the newly acquired ideology.

Physical labor also plays an extremely important role in this whole process of ideological conversion. "Reform by labor" is no idle propa-

---

[80] "On Coalition Government," *Selected Works of Mao Tse-tung*, Book IV, pp. 313-314.

ganda phrase in Communist China. It is obviously considered one of the most effective means of persuasive and coercive communication in the hands of Communists, particularly in dealing with intellectuals and those who still fail to see the wisdom and dignity of labor. This is why a major educational policy of the Communists is "Integration of Education with Labor of Production."[81]

The subtlety and skill of the Chinese Communists in thought reform have often made people wonder where, when, and how they acquired the methods and techniques. They have appeared as veterans of what seem to be psychiatric and psychoanalytical practices, and one wonders whether they were reading Freud and Jung along with Marx and Lenin in their early revolutionary days. There is, of course, no evidence that they did so. A reasonably good guess is that the Chinese Communists have acquired their knowledge on thought reform from three major sources.

The first and easily the most important source is their experience throughout the years when they were fighting for the acquisition of power. Their tasks for a generation and more were largely insurrectional. Their political, even military, work was mainly propaganda and agitation. They had a good deal to do with the mobilization, organization, and indoctrination of both the masses and their own party members. Naturally they learned many of their tricks of the trade through a process of trial and error.

The second source is the Soviet Union. It is difficult to determine when the operational, not just ideological or theoretical, principles of the Russian experience of revolution were introduced to and practiced by the Chinese Marxists. The Chinese Communist literature is, of course, flooded with statements testifying to the inspiration and wisdom of the Soviet experience in nearly everything done in China. But such statements can often be expressions of a sentiment rather than fact. It is worth noting, however, that the works of Lenin and Stalin constituted a major part of the required readings of the Chinese Communists in their Yenan days and later, and that certain methods on ideological matters are modified and then applied to Chinese conditions.

The third source can be loosely referred to as the accumulated political and cultural experience of the Chinese. This is very clearly

[81] *Lun Chiao-yu Sheng-tsan Lao-tung hsiang Chieh-ho* (*On the Integration of Education with Labor of Production*), edited and published by Chinese Youth Publishing Co. in Peking, 1958.

and frequently revealed in the writings of Mao Tse-tung, who quotes Chinese proverbs and maxims with both ease and dexterity. Manipulation of persuasion as an instrument of control, one can be sure, is not an invention of the Communists. Mencius probably realized the value of persuasion when he remarked: "When men are subdued by force, they do not submit in their minds, but only because their strength is inadequate." Even an ordinary Chinese illiterate can repeat the old Chinese saying: "Submission by mouth is not nearly as desirable as submission by heart" (*Ko Fu Pu Yu Hsin Fu*).

The complex interplay of psychological and personal factors in this intricate process of thought reform cannot be discussed here, but it is important to recognize this ambitious Communist design of thought reform as a special tool or method of persuasion to bring the thinking of the nation in line with that of the party and to compel the people to internalize, as a social scientist may say, the Communist doctrines and information that are made available to them through various communication channels. This serves another important communication function for the Communists. By constantly making the people expose themselves to intensive and ruthless thought reform the party is in a position to obtain a general picture of the ideological as well as sentimental state of the people. This is of crucial importance to the Communists because, as noted earlier, the party "must never run too far ahead or lag too far behind mass thinking."

V. The Outlook

Just how effective is the Communist system of communication? No single, simple answer is possible, but to adumbrate a final view a few analytical comments may be in order.

There is no doubt that the communication system is both pervasive and penetrating. Employing many crude methods of communication, but placing the greatest emphasis on personal contact between the masses and party cadres, the Communists are able to bring the largest number of people in Chinese history into direct and close contact with the central government. Even if the system is not always successful in producing the particular thoughts and attitudes desired by the party, it appears to be reasonably effective in keeping out information and ideas that may operate to weaken the party's program. Moreover, it provides for the party a continuous flow of information on the sentiment or psychological climate of the people, which obviously gives the Communist rulers an incontestable element of superiority.

This is not to suggest that the impressive and imposing system of communication is truly effective in winning the confidence of the Chinese population or in making complete Marxists out of the Chinese people. The system is far from being a complete success; it is far less effective than the expectation of the Communists. One needs only a casual review of the Chinese Communist press to discover ample evidence of serious problems and difficulties that have profoundly disturbed the rulers in Peking. There are, for instance, frequent and open Communist complaints that many of their comrades still "cannot grasp the usefulness of the work of persuasion"; that too many of them are unimaginative, superficial, impatient, or downright sloppy with their political and ideological tasks; that much of their propaganda work is "outwardly impressive but basically ineffective"; that there is too much formalism or routine-ism in propaganda; and that too many of the party cadres are still themselves "victims of erroneous ideologies and harmful ideas." In fact, in the Hundred-Flower Movement in 1957-1958 alone there were enough such complaints in the Communist press to fill several volumes.

But even successful elimination of these admitted difficulties does not necessarily mean that the Communists will then have an effective system in reshaping the thinking and action of the Chinese people. It must be realized that while persuasive and coercive communications are powerful tools of political development and social control, they are subject to definite limitation.

One inherent limitation is that no matter how shrewdly it is designed and how vigorously it is utilized, "propaganda does not change conditions, but only beliefs about conditions, and it cannot force the people to change their beliefs but can only persuade them to do so."[82] One must therefore ask: Are the actual conditions in Red China today as good as they are claimed to be in the various forms of persuasive communication? As one leading specialist on Chinese Communism points out:

"A major source of trouble besetting the Communists is their double-talk. They talk democracy but practice dictatorship; they stress voluntarism and exercise compulsion; and they preach freedom while they apply rigid control. Theirs is the double-talk of democratic dictatorship, the people's democratic state, and freedom of speech in a

---

[82] Daniel Lerner, "Effective Propaganda—Conditions and Evaluation" in Daniel Lerner, ed., *Propaganda in War and Crisis*, New York, George W. Stewart, Publisher, Inc., 1951, p. 346.

people's democracy. This Communist double-talk inevitably increases the inner contradictions of their regime. It is in the nature of the Communist ideology to try to ride horses racing in two opposite directions, the horse of 'democracy' and the horse of 'democratic dictatorship.' This may well unsaddle them."[83]

One more point should be stressed. Perhaps, ironically, the Chinese Communists are trapped by their own political and economic achievements and particularly by their own success in propaganda. By their incessant use of persuasive communications and other means the Communists have stirred up much of the old, traditional China; they have turned millions of unconcerned, conciliatory, and easy-going peasants and workers into aggressive, agitated, and vicious fighters and revolutionaries; they have introduced a type of political activity and a pattern of socialization that had never existed in the country. The slumber of a sleeping China, to use an outworn cliché, is rudely disturbed. But once awakened, the nation cannot be expected to return immediately to its old inertia. And once a man becomes a converted revolutionary or trained rebel, he is not likely to be submissive again and unresisting. One therefore wonders whether the tremendous power unleashed by the Communists and the new forces now set in motion by the Peking regime may not eventually prove too great for the manipulators to handle.

[83] Theodore H. E. Chen, *Thought Reform of the Chinese Intellectuals*, *op.cit.*, p. 201.

CHAPTER 17

POLITICAL DEVELOPMENT,
POWER, AND COMMUNICATIONS IN TURKEY

BY FREDERICK W. FREY

~~~~~~

I. Communications, Political Development, and Power

IN A CHAPTER exploring some of the relationships between communications and political development in Turkey it is perhaps not inappropriate to begin with a brief glance at these two conceptual foci of our analysis: "communications" and "political development." Their definition will be decisive for the scope and character of what we shall have to say. Of the two, the notion of communication seems to have received far more careful scrutiny as a concept, to have benefited from the development of more elaborate subordinate conceptualization, and to have been more effectively provided with feasible and relevant empirical indicators—though much remains to be done in the second and, especially, the third of these areas. even within the field of communications.

We shall look upon communication as an interpersonal relationship, direct or indirect, involving the transfer of information. As such, it is an analytical aspect of any social system. All such systems can theoretically be analyzed in terms of the amount, patterning, methods, and content of the communications particular to them. Naturally, they can also be analyzed in terms of other types of interpersonal or inter-role relations, such as power, status, friendship, and so on. The search for regularities in pattern and in type between these analytical aspects of social systems would seem to be a most promising avenue for social science research. To speak rather too simply, this research would seek answers to questions like the following: Do certain forms of communications structure tend to be regularly associated with specific types of power configurations? Do friendship patterns and communications contacts vary predictably in the mass, and if so, how? Are there, under specified conditions, regular relationships between distributions of power and status? Such investigations confront a number of serious problems—conceptual and mensurative. Nevertheless, early results as well as inferred possibilities are extremely interesting and promising.

The notion of political development proves to be much more of a submerged reef menacing our Turkish exploration. Initially it seems to be a rather natural extension of the popular idea of economic development, which has been widely and effectively employed. On closer examination, however, marked differences in type between the two ideas emerge. First of all, there seems to be much more intuitive consensus about what constitutes economic development. A real per capita increase in the goods and services produced by a nation is deemed economic development by almost all observers—capitalist or socialist, Western or non-Western. The values brought into play by questions of distribution, which might disrupt this consensus, in fact do not usually seem to be disruptive. Thus if Turkey builds more factories and raises more crops, resulting in an absolute increase in total production per Turk, even if all of this increase goes to the most plutocratic pasha in the society, it seems still to be accepted as economic development. The distributive question is viewed as something apart, solvable later.

On the other hand, any number of views as to what constitutes political development are in vogue; contemporary consensus seems lacking. Some have argued that movement toward the possession of a list of specific political institutions and procedures—a national legislature, an independent judiciary, free elections, political parties, civil rights—is the essence of political development. Others have contended that stability is the vital ingredient, the absence of violence, turmoil, and revolution supposedly reflecting a relatively high degree of popular satisfaction with the existing polity. Yet another view is to consider political development merely as an adjunct to economic development and, hence, to regard it as any change in the political system contributing to the provision of services necessary for that economic development. In this sense primary attention is often given to the development of an increasingly efficient bureaucracy—to politics as administration. Finally, it is quite common to define political development as movement toward "democracy" or toward "Communism," or "totalitarianism," or "monarchy," or whatever one's preferred "ism," "archy," or "ocracy" happens to be. In addition to the obvious teleological traps lurking about the idea of "development" we must also recognize that there is a strong, though not unavoidable, ethical or evaluative content in the term. This content may be somewhat concealed in economic discussions, we submit, because of the apparently simpler and more uniform value patterns involved in the behaviors under analysis. In politics the influential values seem to be more varied and inconsistent, and this situation is reflected in lack of consensus about the meaning of political development.

Not only is there greater intuitive consensus about what constitutes economic development; the ways of measuring this development are far clearer and more accepted than the devices for measuring political development under almost any definition. Such indices as gross national product, per capita national income, available horsepower per individual, and so on seem to bear a close relationship to the idea of economic development and to be relatively easily computed. Input-output analysis is feasible because of the existence of useful standards for measuring units of input and output. Adopting any definition of political development mentioned, we can see that the discovery of similarly effective indices and indicators is a very tricky business and certainly not something that can be regarded as largely accomplished. The result is that comparisons of political development with other variables are forced to be extremely crude and insensitive compared to analogous comparisons involving economic development. A useful query to be addressed to prospective concepts of political development is just this: Are the available and proposed indices so crude as to preclude effective comparative analysis?

A third divergence between the notion of economic development and most conceptions of political development is that they seem to be basically different types of goals. Economic development, defined as a real per capita increase in the goods and services produced by the nation (or produced per unit of labor time), can be crudely labeled an "unlimited value goal." If we plot satisfaction against goods and services produced per man-hour, its graphic form is that of a curve rising to infinity. Essentially, one can never get enough of it; the preponderance of the population in almost all societies wants such goods and services produced per man-hour to rise continuously. On the contrary, many conceptions of political development which have been offered seem to view it as an "optimum value goal," that is, one for which there is a limited range of preferred positions, with undesirable situations at either extreme. Democracy, stability, and the existence of certain institutions and procedures seem to partake more of the idea of balance, of ground to be gained and then essentially held, than of a continuous movement in a given direction. The graphic form of such goals is roughly that of the bell-shaped curve, perhaps with the apex flattened into a plateau. Additional movement in a given direction is sometimes desirable and sometimes not, depending on one's previous location, rather than always desirable or undesirable, as in the case of an "unlimited value goal." The conceptual complexities thus introduced are not inconsiderable.[1]

It is likely that the most common notion of political development in intellectual American circles is that of movement towards democracy. This formulation sounds appealing but obliges one to clarify the meaning of "democracy," since such a term can hardly pass as a logical "primitive" whose meaning is intuitively clear. For us democracy refers to a special sort of power configuration in a social system— a configuration which, relative to others, features wide distribution and great reciprocity of power.[2] It is the opposite of autocracy, which refers to a social system in which, relative to other social systems, power is highly centralized and unilateral. Changes in the direction of greater distribution and reciprocity of power we shall style "political development." As a result, in our Turkish investigation we shall be concerned with relationships between communications and power in Turkish society.

---

[1] For a useful discussion of goal distinctions of this sort see James G. March, "Group Norms and the Active Minority," *American Sociological Review*, 19, December 1954, pp. 733-741. On this point, cf. also William H. Riker, "Voting and the Summation of Preferences," *American Political Science Review*, LV, December 1961, pp. 900-911.

[2] Power is more widely distributed in one social unit than another if, within a given scope, the inequalities in the sizes of the domains of the members of the first unit are less than the inequalities in the sizes of the domains of the members of the second unit. (The terms "scope" and "domain" will be defined shortly.) Theoretically, these inequalities could be expressed by the customary statistical measures of dispersion such as standard deviation. Knowledge of the distribution of power as defined permits no inference to the over-all level of power in the unit, which can be expressed by the ratio of the number of existing power linkages within a given scope to the number of theoretically possible linkages. More is said about these concepts in the following few pages.

Reciprocity refers to a power relationship persisting over time in which if the influencer (R) engages in behavior b_1 then the influencee (E) engages in behavior b_2, but for which it is also true that E can himself behave so as to affect R's doing b_1. For example, when the President of the United States issues an executive order, the behavior of various Americans is (let us trustingly assume) altered. However, on learning that the President is contemplating the issuance of such an order, these concerned individuals can take action to affect the President's action, even though once the order is issued they comply with it. Crudely, the concept of reciprocity refers to such a set of power relationships. Some discussion of this type of power relationship is found in Felix F. Oppenheim, *Dimensions of Freedom*, New York, St. Martin's Press, 1961, pp. 105-106.

Though it is not possible here to discuss the many ramifications of power analysis, just a few words about one or two concepts which will be repeatedly employed seem necessary.[3] Power, very simply, is considered to be an interpersonal relationship in which the behavior of one individual alters the behavior of another. When individuals represent groups in some sense, or act in concert regularly *as* groups, we naturally speak of the power of one group over other groups or individuals, even though in the ultimate analysis we refer to specific individual behaviors. In some senses the concept of power so defined bears a logical resemblance to the concept of force in physics.

Two further concepts from a larger set of subordinate concepts amplifying the basic notion of power seem to be required by our analysis. We shall refer to the "scope" of a power relationship, and by this we shall mean the range of behaviors of the influencee altered by the influencer. We shall also refer to the "domain" of a given individual's power, meaning by this the set of persons whose behavior he alters within a given scope. The concept of scope takes cognizance of the fact that human beings rarely if ever influence every single behavior of another person. Usually, in Harold Lasswell's formulation, X influences Y with regard to Z, where, for us, Z—or the scope of the relationship—refers to certain specific types of behavior.[4] Kemal Ataturk may have had great power over the voting behavior of a typical deputy to the Grand National Assembly of Turkey but none over that same man's bathing practices—unless perhaps they were too odiously deficient. The concept of domain takes cognizance of the fact that within a given scope human beings rarely if ever influence the behavior of all other living human beings. Therefore specification of those influenced and those not influenced becomes crucial.

After defining political development to mean certain changes in the configurations of power in a society we will find it valuable to add a distinction made by Talcott Parsons when reviewing Mills'

[3] A good introduction to the types of thought presently most prominent in this field can be garnered from such writings as Herbert Simon, "Notes on the Observation and Measurement of Political Power," *Journal of Politics*, 15, November 1953, pp. 500-516; James G. March, "An Introduction to the Theory and Measurement of Influence," *American Political Science Review*, XLIX, June 1955, pp. 431-451; Robert A. Dahl, "The Concept of Power," *Behavioral Science*, 2, July 1957, pp. 201-215; Dorwin Cartwright, ed., *Studies in Social Power*, Ann Arbor, Research Center for Group Dynamics, University of Michigan, 1959; Harold D. Lasswell and Abraham Kaplan, *Power and Society*, London, Routledge and Kegan Paul, 1952.
[4] Lasswell and Kaplan, *op.cit.*, p. 75.

The Power Elite a few years ago. Parsons emphasized that power, like wealth, had both distributive and communal aspects, and that we tend to concentrate almost exclusively on the former. This may be particularly unfortunate in studies of the developing areas. Knowledge of the distribution of the power existing within a given social system is of tremendous significance for many purposes. However, it may be a one-sided view. Recognizing that the behavioral coordination permitted by the existence of power relations enables social systems to do things which might otherwise be impossible, one must also attend to what might crudely be called the *over-all level* of power in the society. Thus in developing nations one important trend is usually that of an increase in the amount of power wielded by its citizens over each other regardless of change or continuation in the patterns of relative power distribution. With the greater social coordination produced by this increase in the over-all level of power, formerly impossible activities now become feasible. The conceptual tools which we have suggested, however, seem to be adequate for representing this phenomenon, for it must appear as the establishment of new power linkages—changes in domain—or changes in the scope of existing relationships.[5]

Two very broad points about the relationship between power and communications may guide us in understanding the Turkish situation. First, communications patterns generally seem to act as a limiting factor for power configurations. With minor exceptions, there is no

[5] Cf. Talcott Parsons, "The Distribution of Power in American Society," *World Politics*, X, October 1957, pp. 123-143. The communal aspect of power is also frequently emphasized, for example, in Edward C. Banfield, *Political Influence*, New York, The Free Press of Glencoe, 1961. A rise in the level of over-all power in the society is frequently viewed by crucial sectors of an emerging nation as much more vital than any question of the distribution of power. This emphasis on the development of new power linkages to permit more concerted activity (such as mobilizing and supporting a modern army, developing industry, or establishing a national educational system), and the concomitantly reduced stress given to distributive power considerations, would seem to be integrally associated with the oft-observed tendency of emerging nations to experience various forms of dictatorship or autocracy. The rise in the over-all level of power in the society is achieved, but in its easiest form—by a great increase in the scope and domain of power of a very few groups in the nation. One of the typical, "second stage" problems then confronting the emerging society, at least from our viewpoint, is that of re-adjusting the distribution of power at the new, higher, over-all level, so as to move in a "democratic" direction. It can be seen from this analysis, however, that a non-trivial conflict between economic and social development, on the one side, and progress toward "democracy," on the other, can readily appear. The antagonistic parties can be looked at, in power terms, as those for whom increases in the over-all level of power are of dominant importance versus those who give relatively greater emphasis to distributional matters.

power relationship without some direct or indirect communications linkage. This fact suggests that we could frequently infer the maximum domain of power for a given individual or group from the total communications contacts of that individual or group if we possessed the latter information. With our present primitive techniques for obtaining these data, however, we are commonly restricted merely to getting insights into possibly maximal power domains from rough estimates of communications networks, and this is emphatically true of our Turkish analysis.

Though power relationships in a given social unit are usually no more extensive than that unit's communications network, it is not normally the case that the two are simply coterminous. A power connection without a communications linkage is rare, but the contrary—communication without power—is very common. The ubiquity of laments like, "My words had no effect on him," "You can talk until you are blue in the face and he does what he wants," "I can't reach him," and so on attests to this fact. Learning what sorts of communications influence what sorts of people under what circumstances is vital to the politician, propagandist, publicist, and political scientist, among others.

The old maxim that "Knowledge is power" suggests a second broad point about the relationship between communications and power. Much of man's knowledge is acquired through communication. An individual possessed of appropriate knowledge is better aware than others lacking that information of when, how, and for what to exert influence; he tends, other things equal, to exert that influence more effectively—to be more powerful, in other words. Thus it is that Turkish politicians, for example, work very hard to supply themselves with constant and reliable information about those whom they desire to affect. Looked at the other way around, determining what information another person receives puts one into a choice position to alter his behavior by shaping his values and his perception of situations and phenomena—his cognitions. These are, in fact, two basic *types* of power—duly labeled "motivational" and "informational power"—in a rather useful typology which we shall not explain here.

The consequence of the contributions to power made by access to and control over communications is that positions of communications centrality, in which a person both receives disproportionate information from others and passes on a disproportionate share of information to others, are very likely to give their occupants power not to be anticipated from the other attributes of those individuals. An excellent illustration from Ottoman history is at hand in the "dragoman" (from the Turkish *tercüman*, translator or interpreter) of Western embassies in Istanbul, who formally mediated between the Western nation and the Sublime Porte and exercised considerable power in the process.

Obviously a good deal more can be said in this same general vein about the relationship between power and communications. However, with this brief but essential introduction behind us, if we are ever going to get to modern Turkey we had better pick up our hastily packed methodological valise and begin making the trip. Further insights into the interaction of communication and power relationships will hopefully emerge from analysis of the Turkish experience.

II. Communications and Power in Ottoman Turkey

Toynbee, in his younger days, portrayed the Ottoman Empire as ". . . the strangest congeries of racial and social types that has ever been placed at a single government's mercy."[6] Bernard Lewis, with more restraint, has said that "What existed was not a nation but a domination. . . ."[7] And a team of American investigators not too long ago described the communications structure of this realm in the following terms: "Means of travel and communications were so slender that instead of one Turkey, there were a hundred—or a thousand—little Turkeys."[8] Actually there were probably around 40,001, for the country was essentially bifurcated into a relatively unintegrated set of about 40,000 villages on the one hand and a "ruling elite," distinguished largely by education, occupation, and religion, on the other. While sharp and momentous changes occurred in the power and communications structures within this ruling elite, the broad bifurcation between elite and mass persisted right up until the mid-20th century.

The domain of power of the elite—and this was a situation to which the term "elite" is well applied—seems to have been almost coterminous with its communications net. We find, for example, the "tax revenues per capita and per square kilometer tended to decline

[6] Arnold J. Toynbee, *Turkey: A Past and a Future*, New York, George H. Doran, 1917, p. 5.

[7] Bernard Lewis, *The Emergence of Modern Turkey*, London, Oxford University Press, 1961, p. 228.

[8] Max W. Thornburg, Graham Spry, and George Soule, *Turkey: An Economic Appraisal*, New York, The Twentieth Century Fund, 1949, p. 18.

in direct proportion as the distance from Constantinople increased," even after making necessary allowances for variations in natural resources and development.[9] Laxity in the execution of orders from the capital, banditry, the sway of the local *ağas*, all varied inversely with the excellence of communications contact between elite and mass. As a matter of fact, recognition of this situation on the part of the peasants themselves is evidenced by the pains taken in many instances to locate their villages in extremely isolated and inaccessible spots where the tax-collector, gendarme, and conscription sergeant were less likely to make their presence felt. From government mainly harm was expected; but, under the changed conditions of today, such villages are paying for their evasion with economic and social backwardness largely engendered by communications isolation.

In the absence of studies of Ottoman village social structure we are forced to infer the nature of power and communications in these communities from recent studies of Turkish villages, making the plausible assumption that very little intervening change has occurred.[10] Within the village the relative communications centrality of the powerful is inescapable. In modern Turkish novels of rural life one ubiquitous set of characters is that of the minions of the *Ağa Bey*— the local landlord—who report to him on all that occurs in his villages and their environs.[11] Thus the organization of revolt against him as well as escape from his clutches are both precluded.

Less dramatically, one notes that those persons generally reported as powerful in the traditional Turkish village are characterized by focal positions in village communication; these were the *hoca* (roughly, priest), the *muhtar* (head man), the *Ağa Bey* described above, and a few village elders who were usually affluent compared to other villagers. The communications position of these last, the village elders, is not as plain as that of the others. The elders seem generally to have been the heads of agnatic "lineages" or clans and, as such, privy

[9] William W. Cumberland, "The Public Treasury," in Eliot Grinnell Mears, ed., *Modern Turkey*, New York, Macmillan, 1924, p. 394.

[10] For a general introduction in English to Turkish village life, see Paul Stirling, *The Social Structure of Turkish Peasant Communities*, unpublished doctoral dissertation submitted to Oxford University, 1951, and "Social Ranking in a Turkish Village," *British Journal of Sociology*, 4, March 1953, pp. 31-44; Mahmut Makal, *A Village in Anatolia*, London, Valentine, Mitchell and Co., 1954; Ibrahim Yasa, *Hasanoğlan*, Ankara, Yeni Matbaa, 1957; and Barbara and George Helling, *Rural Turkey, A New Socio-Statistical Appraisal*, Istanbul, Fakülteler Matbaası, 1958.

[11] The most recent example, in English, is Yashar Kemal, *Mehmet, My Hawk*, London, Collins and Harvill, 1961.

to almost all important information garnered by several generations of kinsmen. Also they seem often to have been wealthy enough to have supported a village *oda* (social room) in their houses where male neighbors and relatives regularly congregated in spring, autumn, and especially winter to discuss village happenings for hours at a time. Almost all village contacts with the outside world were mediated by these individuals. Naturally not all were equally powerful in every village, and other factors besides communication position entered into the production of their power. Moreover, power can be, and was, itself used to improve one's communication position. On the whole, though, the association between the two is unmistakable.

In two major respects these patterns of village communication acted to hamper changes in the over-all level, the distribution, and the reciprocity of power in Turkey. First and most obviously, the *isolation of the villages from the ruling intellectual elite* in the society prevented that elite from exerting any decisive influence in most villages, from making any significant alteration in typical village life and power structure, and from spreading to the villages the fundamental psychological changes which were then taking place among the elite—changes which we simplistically call Westernization. Secondly, the *excellence of internal communications in the village*, given the aforementioned power structure and stressing additionally the extremely conservative values of the older, wealthier, and more pious men who headed that power structure, acted to forestall social and economic change. These dominant and interested parties were able to know virtually everything that went on in the village. Almost nothing could escape their attention. Consequently, any deviation attracted notice the moment it began, and the entire force of the community was concentrated on the deviant. With such excellent communications, there was no place to hide, no place for basic change to ferment, no nook free from the glare of the village's vested interests. When seen to be cut off from outside stimulation by a great breach in communications, yet with pervasive internal processes of communication focused around highly conservative interests, the unyielding rigidity of village social structure and values in Turkey right up to our own era becomes quite comprehensible.

Turning to the "ruling elite," as it is customarily called, we see almost the opposite situation. Essentially what we find is that the traditional, conservative authorities lose communications control and ultimately lose power as well. In the Ottoman elite three institutions were politically dominant: the military, the *ulema* (clergy), and the bureaucracy. The Sultan and his court might be considered a fourth, but their power essentially rested on the other three. In a relatively complex society men do not usually obtain power by creating *de novo* great sets of power relationships around themselves. Rather, using a limited number of such personal power relationships, they move into one of the main institutions of the social system—into an established power structure—which multiplies their personal influence many times over. In Ottoman days these institutionalized power structures were the three mentioned. Significantly, they were the three organizations in the country which had the most effective internal communications; and two of them, by the nature of their operations, also had the most frequent contact with other societies. It was in these last two, the military and the bureaucracy, that the massive political and social developments leading to "the emergence of modern Turkey" occurred.

The Ottomans had ". . . from an early stage in their history been in contact with Europe—longer and more closely than any other Islamic state, not excluding North Africa. The Empire included important European territories, in which it absorbed European peoples and institutions. It also maintained contact with the West through trade, diplomacy, war, and—not least—immigration."[12] However, until late in the 18th century these contacts could be treated by nearly all Ottomans as the interaction between their superior civilization and a barbarian West, or at least as the intercourse of cultural equals. A shocking series of unmistakable and bitter defeats in their most prized area of activity—the profession of arms—undermined even the high redoubts of Ottoman self-confidence. Since such defeats could not possibly have been due to any lack of dedication or valor among the Turkish soldiery, they were attributed to certain technical gimmicks developed by the West and giving it an unfortunate advantage. However, it was thought that once the Turk learned the techniques, the advantage would be terminated.

While foreign military instruction had existed in the Ottoman Empire before 1795, intensive modern communication with the West is usually dated from the founding in that year of an artillery school by Sultan Selim III. This school featured instruction in French given by French officers to Turkish cadets who had training in the French language as a compulsory part of their curriculum. It was

[12] Lewis, *op.cit.*, p. 6.

followed in the early 19th century by schools of military engineering, military medicine, and a War College. Largely in this fashion was Pandora's Box opened—the forces of Westernization released. As the author of our previous quotation, Bernard Lewis, has remarked, the main channel for the transmission of Western ideas into the Ottoman Empire was military instruction.[13]

In the latter half of the 19th century the channel was broadened to include vital civil sectors of the society. The School of Political Sciences for the training of top-level bureaucrats was founded in 1859, a law school in 1888, the American-sponsored Robert College in the 1860's, and, perhaps most important of all, the French-influenced Imperial Lycée of Galatasaray in 1868. The differentiating characteristic of the education provided at all these schools was that it was secular and held up Western patterns as a model to be followed. The students who emerged were secular in political orientation and adopted Western governmental practices as their norms. Such attitudes brought them into ineluctable conflict with the members of the third great institution of Ottoman society—the clergy. To quote Bernard Lewis once again, "The history of the reform movements in the nineteenth and early twentieth centuries is largely concerned with the attempt by Western-educated intellectuals to impose a Western pattern of secular political classification and organization on the religious community of Islam."[14]

The reform movement failed several times before the Ataturk Revolution—in the *Tanzimat* (Reforms) era, in the short-lived First Constitutional Period of 1876-1878, in the Second Constitutional Period which commenced in 1908, and under the Young Turk dictatorship. Among the outstanding reasons for those failures was the fact that the inchoate system of secular education had not yet generated enough "new Turks" to ensure the success of such a movement over natural social inertia and the stubborn resistance of the clerics and their various allies.[15] Yet when these strategic schools were sufficiently firmly established so as to be able to provide for their own future instructional needs and to have begun to influence the entire wave of future military and bureaucratic leaders, one might have

[13] *Ibid.*, p. 55.
[14] *Ibid.*
[15] *Cf.* Lewis V. Thomas, "Turkey," in Lewis V. Thomas and Richard N. Frye, *The United States and Turkey and Iran*, Cambridge, Mass., Harvard University Press, 1952, p. 87; Geoffrey Lewis, *Turkey*, London, Ernest Benn, 1955, p. 36; Barbara Ward, *Turkey*, London, Oxford University Press, 1942, p. 31.

said that the point of communications "take-off"—of self-sustaining development—had been reached and that the rough course of future social development had been set.

Sultan Selim III also inaugurated a second program, parallel to the effort to establish Western-type schools in Turkey, and of only slightly less importance as a communications channel for the dissemination of revolutionary modern ideas. In 1793 he established the first regular and permanent Ottoman Embassy in a major European capital. Others followed quickly and were instructed to obtain information about the cultures and institutions of the countries in which they were located. "These missions thus gave an opportunity to a number of young men to reside for a while in a European city, master a European language, and make the acquaintance of some of the revolutionary ideas current among their European contemporaries. Some of them on their return became officials at the Porte, where they formed a Westward-looking minority among the bureaucratic hierarchy similar to that created among the officers by the military and naval reforms." The importance of this contact is reflected in the fact that ". . . almost every one of the reforming leaders and statesmen of the next half-century had served in these embassies. . . . Even the sons of these first diplomats, profiting from the opportunities of a stay in Europe in childhood or youth, filled a disproportionate number of high offices of state in the next generation."[16] Add to these individuals the even larger number of graduates of the new Western and secular schools transmitting Western values within the country, and one obtains nearly the entire reforming cadre of late Ottoman and early Republican Turkey.[17]

While the opening of crucial elements of Ottoman political leadership to Western communications proved fundamental in altering the prevailing power configurations in Turkish society, it was also true that a secondary power conflict provided a contrapuntal theme which must not be overlooked, since it strongly affected communications opportunities in Turkey. Under traditional Ottoman practices there was considerable reciprocity in the power relations between the Sultans and the three great engines of state—the military, the bureaucratic, and the religious. With regard to many types of be-

[16] B. Lewis, *op.cit.*, pp. 61, 89.
[17] The social backgrounds of all deputies to the Grand National Assembly of Turkey, from 1920 to 1957, are analyzed in detail in a forthcoming study by the author.

havior each organ had considerable influence over the other, and it was definitely not the case that the Sultan merely issued a ukase which decided any matter in which he had become interested. By the turn of the 19th century Sultan Selim III and his successor, Mahmud II, as well as a number of other influential persons, had become convinced that this reciprocity of power, this mutuality of influence with regard to specific issues, was a barrier to Ottoman progress in the face of Western pressure. They believed that centralization of power in the hands of the Sultan was a prerequisite to modernization. Selim and Mahmud struck the first blows in a struggle which continued throughout the 19th century to free the ruler from the institutional restraints of the military, the bureaucracy, and the clergy. In the 20th century, and especially in recent times, a major development has been to construct a new reciprocity between new organs of state and elements of Turkish society.

Under Mahmud II the army was temporarily brought to heel by the mass liquidation of the janissaries in the "Auspicious Incident" of 1826. The last feudal fiefs were abolished and, more significantly, the great pious foundations of the clergy were partially subordinated to the Sultan's control, weakening the power of *ulema*. Later Sultans continued the centralization policy with similar, if less bold, measures until the process had its unfortunate but logical culmination in the despotism of Abdulhamit II, the "Red Sultan." For our immediate purposes the most important point is that this drive for centralized power on the part of the Sultans led them to take great interest in certain devices for improving communications within their domain. The first newspaper in the Turkish language, *Takvim-i Vekâyi* (*Calendar of Events*), functioned mainly as an official gazette, informing public officials of the Sultan's aims and policies. The postal system inaugurated in 1834, road improvements, and particularly the telegraph in 1855 and railways in 1856 all served to strengthen the administrative centralization initiated by Selim III and Mahmud II. At the same time they also served to involve thousands of educated Turks more deeply in national life than ever before and to afford dissident elements who were able to get control over one of the communications channels a chance to publicize their views to a wider audience than had ever before been possible. By the end of the century the process had been carried to its unfortunate extreme. The Sultan, Abdulhamit, had gone so far as to erect an elaborate network of spies and informers to alert him to all slightly question-

able activities of his subjects. On the other side, the growing opposition was distributing its newspapers, published in Europe, to enlarged
numbers of disgruntled Turks through the channel of the foreign
post-offices granted to European powers by the Ottomans under the
Capitulations. By this time, however, the great secular schools—the
War College, the medical faculty, the political science school, and
others—had done their work, and the military and bureaucracy were
populated by young officers and officials determined to win respect
from the West for the Turkey which they officially represented by
adopting the methods utilized in the West, even including constitu-
tionalism and representative government. The Sultan was overthrown
by the army in the Revolution of 1908. After a brief period of constitutional government the reforming regime degenerated into a
military dictatorship which collapsed with the defeat of the country
in World War I, into which that regime had sent her.

III. Communications and the Ataturk Revolution

The communications development in the 19th and early 20th centuries which we have described was *relatively* great but *absolutely*
small. The first Turkish language printing press, for instance, had
been introduced in 1727. Its history is a good illustration of the fact
that the mere availability of a Western technique is not sufficient to
produce its utilization—even a technique as revolutionary as printing. The first Turkish newspaper did not appear until over one
hundred years later, in 1831, and it was the official gazette, *Takvim-i
Vekâyi*, described above. The earliest independent newspaper, from
which the Turks date the beginning of journalism in their country,
appeared only in 1860. Significantly, it was followed just five years
later by the first of a series of press laws providing for stern governmental control over the new institution.[18] Moreover, the press was
no longer confined to the capital. The number of dailies increased to
nine in 1911, but fell to six in 1913 under wartime shortages and
restrictions.[19] It is doubtful if at the beginning of the War for Independence in 1919 there were more than two dozen daily newspapers
in Turkey—a sizeable increase compared with several decades before,

---

[18] B. Lewis, *op.cit.*, p. 146.
[19] *Türkiyede Çıkan Gazete ve Mecmualar*, Ankara, Basın-Yayın ve Turizm
Bakanlığı, 1961, pp. 1-4; Ahmet Emin (Yalman), "The Turkish Press," in Mears,
op.cit., pp. 451-467.

but still hardly sufficient to reach great masses of the Turkish population.

The construction of new telegraph and railway lines proceeded somewhat more rapidly, but on the whole a similar comment can be made concerning the development of most other means of communication and transportation. Important relative progress was made, but the over-all result was merely an agitation of the intellectual surface of Turkish society. When Ataturk landed at Samsun on the 19th of May, 1919, to commence the revolution which now bears his name, Turkish social structure was still bifurcated into elite and mass divisions by a great chasm in communications. Even within the elite, which had been significantly affected by the alterations in communications practices previously described, the best that could be said of the position of the Westernized intellectuals in Turkey was that they had established a tenuous beachhead which gave them precarious control over the state apparatus. In the conflict within the elite between the "religious traditionalists" and the "secular modernists" (largely officers and officials) the latter had tipped the balance in their favor, but the issue was far from settled.

It is the essence of the Ataturk Revolution that it *exploited* the communications bifurcation existing in Turkish society rather than lamenting it or immediately attacking it, as a number of other nationalist movements have done. The Kemâlists concentrated on the extension and consolidation of the modernist beachhead within the ruling elite won by the graduates of the great secular schools and those with European training. This effort involved the final expulsion of religion from the temple of politics and the attempt to complete the Westernization of the intellectual elite of the society before plunging ahead to more grandiose ventures with the entire Turkish populace. It also involved the reformers in a drive to make the uncongenial cities and larger towns of Anatolia habitable for the new class of Westernized Turkish intellectuals who were to serve and represent the new state. It was by no means an immediate attempt to remold the society by starting with the peasant masses. Such an attempt was not in keeping with the history of the Turkish revolutionary movement or the psychologies of its leaders. Moreover, the task was simply too immense for such an approach. As in most emergent nations, a smaller handle was necessary—a lever more easily grasped.[20]

[20] This thesis is discussed more fully in the forthcoming work mentioned in footnote 17. *Cf.* also Lewis V. Thomas, *op.cit.*, p. 72.

Put another way, what we are saying is that the communications bifurcation in Turkish society between educated elite and uneducated mass actually provided Mustafa Kemal with a convenient halfway house in the reshaping of the country. He could to a large extent afford to forget about the submerged peasant masses and concentrate his limited resources on solidifying his hold on the dominant intellectual group, to which he could increasingly appeal through such improvements in communications techniques as had been made. Then, once this crucial initial battle was won, once the bulk of the ruling elite had been modernized, he could move on to the greater task of changing the masses. The lack of communications between elite and mass was a vital factor which he used to simplify his task and equate it with his resources.

Both Ataturk's tactics in his combat with the conservative-religious faction and the content of his specific reforms are instructive in this connection. With great shrewdness he would mobilize all his forces on a specific, limited goal, without ever tipping his hand as to his next objective and thus permitting opposition to organize. When the instant goal was achieved, he would then focus upon another target which, once known, usually bore a clear strategic relation to the preceding effort.[21] The Ataturk reforms comprised such things as abolishing the Sultanate and Caliphate, introducing new legal codes from continental Europe, outlawing the dervish orders, proscribing the wearing of the fez, adopting Western time standards, calendar, and weekend, changing the script in which Turkish was written from Arabic to modified Roman, enlarging educational facilities in the country, especially in the cities and at the university level, and so on. The salient point is that most of these reforms were characteristically devoted to increasing the scope and domain of state power over the society, to putting the national house in order so as to command respect in the West, to removing the last possible challenge from the now defeated conservative-religious faction, and to enlarging the size and influence of the dominant body of Westernized intellectuals. The immediate goal was not the fundamental improvement of the peasant's lot or the grant to him of increased political power. Those were for the future.

Ataturk's instinctive sense of the relationship between communi-

[21] For Mustafa Kemal's own statement of his tactics, see his *Büyük Nutuk* (*Great Speech*), available in a mediocre English translation in *A Speech Delivered by Ghazi Mustapha Kemal*, Leipzig, K. F. Koehler, 1929, pp. 16, 18, 19, 598 and *passim*.

cations and power in Turkey's major social institutions is particularly well reflected in his campaign against the clergy. Given the state of Turkish public opinion, a broad frontal assault was impossible. The best he could do in this area was to abolish the Caliphate and the position of the *Şeyh-ül-İslam*, head of the *ulema*, and place the religious establishment formally under the Office of the Prime Ministry. But the more subtle allied measures were quite effective. All possible outward symbols of religious distinction were removed: the Muslim fez was proscribed and replaced by the Western hat (unfortunately that of a Welsh coal miner), and the wearing of religious garb by clerics outside of the precincts of the mosque was prohibited. It became much harder to distinguish the pious from the non-pious and thus to force conformity upon the latter. The contact of organized religion with the mass of the people was curtailed by the abolition of the dervish orders, though this measure, of course, did not effectively stop all dervish activity. Perhaps most important of all, and in accordance with our previous emphasis of the communications role of the educational system in Turkey, was the fact that the educational contact of organized religion with the youth of the country was shrewdly severed. The *medreses*, religious schools, were abandoned, and a national and nationalistic system of popular instruction took over, in which the teaching of Arabic and Persian was dropped, thereby cutting off access to religious literature in the linguistic form held indispensable by the religious authorities themselves. Finally, the schools for the training of professional men of religion, *imams* and *hatips*, were artfully permitted to lapse into desuetude, making it extremely difficult for the clerics to perpetuate their special values even among their own personnel.[22] The result of all these measures was that the ability of the religious institution to communicate with the Turkish populace, elite and mass, and especially youth, declined quite abruptly, and this communications decline was clearly reflected in a loss of power by the institution—the result desired by Mustafa Kemal and his cohorts. Those whom the *Gazi* would destroy he would first isolate.

Several other examples of this same approach are readily available. The first major move of Mustafa Kemal against the group of

[22] On these schools, see Howard Reed, "Turkey's New Imam-Hatip Schools," *Die Welt des Islams*, IV, 1955, pp. 150-163, and the other articles on allied topics by Reed which are given, e.g., in the bibliography to Kemal Karpat, *Turkey's Politics*, Princeton, Princeton University Press, 1959, p. 486.

POLITICAL DEVELOPMENT IN TURKEY

legislator-generals who organized to oppose him in 1924 was to cut off their contact either with the army or with the parliament by insisting that they resign from one or the other post.[23] Indeed, the great script change of 1928, when the Arabic script for Turkish was replaced by Roman, was partly stimulated by a desire to reduce the influence of the Ottoman heritage on the youth of the Turkish Republic—as Lewis says, to erect a "great barrier" against the unwanted voice from the past. (Similarly, to erect barriers against both Islam and the Turks, the Soviets twice changed the script of the Turkic languages in the Soviet Union—from Arabic to Roman, and then when the Turks themselves adopted Roman, from it to Cyrillic.[24])

Major aims of the Ataturk Reform were to increase the over-all level of power in Turkey so as to permit social and economic modernization and to expand the scope and domain of the influence of the state so that it could act as the main agent for that modernization. The top political leadership in Turkey was, after all, overwhelmingly intellectual and official in its social background.[25] At the same time, both from a desire to win respect in the West and from inner conviction, there was a commitment by Ataturk himself and the most prominent Kemâlist leaders to democracy—to expanding popular participation in government, to an increase in the distribution and reciprocity of power in Turkish society as well as to its over-all increase. These two facts together led to another distinctive character-

---

[23] See Frederick W. Frey, "Arms and the Man in Turkish Politics," *Land Reborn*, XI, August 1960, pp. 3-14.

[24] B. Lewis, *op.cit.*, p. 426.

[25] Classifying the deputies to the four Grand National Assemblies of the Ataturk era (1923-1939, Assemblies II through V) according to their formal leadership levels (i.e., offices held) gives the following results for education and occupation:

LEADERSHIP LEVELS[a]	ASSEMBLY			
	II 1923-1927	III 1927-1931	IV 1931-1935	V 1935-1939
Per Cent with University Education				
Top leaders	79%	89%	89%	87%
Middle leaders	75	87	86	90
Backbenchers	68	71	69	70
Per Cent with Official Occupation[b]				
Top leaders	66	61	60	65
Middle leaders	50	65	53	51
Backbenchers	55	53	47	44

[a] Unknowns excluded. For each percentage given, $27 < N < 277$.
[b] Government, military, and educational occupations.

istic of the Ataturk Revolution—the development of an effective political infrastructure to translate high policy into action, to wield power so as to organize large numbers of people into coordinated activity, but at the same time able to serve as a reverse channel to influence the behavior of those in high positions. In short, the new political infrastructure was originally designed to control the elite, but it also provided an opportunity for lower-level members of that elite to influence their superiors and, finally, for spanning the communications and power gap between elite and mass so as to permit reciprocal influence.

Besides the army and the bureaucracy, which of course had been previously well developed, the specific institutions involved were the political party, the press, relatively autonomous universities, an independent judiciary, and a burgeoning public school system. The communications significance of each of these institutions is immediately apparent, most of them reaching vertically farther down into Turkish society than any other organizations. All of these organs had a rudimentary existence prior to the Kemâlist Reform but emerged into real power only in that period. All of them were primarily concerned with symbol manipulation. All of them later on, as we shall see, proved to be the main barriers to the anti-democratic activities of Adnan Menderes and his associates.

By 1938, the year of Ataturk's death, the number of daily newspapers in Turkey had increased to more than fifty, and the total number of newspapers and periodicals had increased roughly tenfold in the eighteen years since 1920, even though extensive coverage outside Istanbul and Ankara was only beginning.[26] In 1938 there were approximately 50,000 radios in Turkey compared to practically none in 1920. Telephone subscribers numbered 20,000, all urban, of course. Nearly 500,000 telegrams were sent within the confines of the country in that year. About 7,000 kilometers of railway lines had been developed which furnished almost 100,000 passenger/kilometers of transportation to Turks. The state airline had just been founded, carrying the grand total of 35 intrepid passengers in that year. Literacy had increased from around 11 per cent in 1927 to approximately 20 per cent in 1938. The number of cities with over 50,000 population had mounted from 5 to 9, and the total urban population resident in these cities had increased from 32 to 40 per cent, though

---

[26] *Türkiyede Çıkan Gazete ve Mecmualar, op.cit.*, p. 2.

the relative total urban population changed only very slightly[27] There was a sharp improvement in education—less on the mass, primary level than on the middle and higher levels which qualified one for membership in the dominant elite. The precise figures and index numbers for selected years are given in Table 1.

TABLE 1: TOTAL NUMBER OF TURKISH STUDENTS
AT EACH EDUCATIONAL LEVEL[28]

SCHOOL TYPE	ACADEMIC YEAR							
	1923-24		1927-28		1936-37		1940-41	
	No.	Index	No.	Index	No.	Index	No.	Index
Primary	341,941	100	461,985	114	714,178	209	955,957	280
Middle	5,905	100	19,858	336	52,386	887	95,332	1613
Lycee	1,241	100	3,819	308	13,622	1098	24,862	2006
Technical and professional	6,547	100	7,354	112	10,358	158	20,264	310
University	2,914	100	4,282	147	8,354	287	12,844	442
	358,548	100	497,298	139	798,898	222	1,109,259	309

Though detailed figures are not available, the judicial system was greatly extended in the cities and towns, and the Republican People's Party of Ataturk and İnönü had covered the entire country, usually down to the *kaza* (*ilçe*) or county level, with political units of varying degrees of organization.

In sum, what had happened was that the Westernization of the intellectual elite had reached an irreversible stage, and that elite had been provided with a rather effective communications network through several important institutions. Moreover, the elite had begun to take quite seriously the values of democracy which had been repeated to it by these institutions. Since the internal religious enemy had largely been vanquished, the elite also commenced to take for granted the necessity and inevitability of modernization and to disagree about means, methods, and subordinate objectives. On the other hand, the basic bifurcation between the elite and the peasant mass largely re-

[27] Data from *Aylik İstatistik Bülteni* (Monthly Bulletin of Statistics), Ankara, T. C. İstatistik Umum Müdürlüğü, 1960, No. 73, pp. 12-14 and *Nüfus Sayimlari 1927-1950* (Population Censuses, 1927-1950), Ankara, T. C. İstatistik Umum Müdürlüğü, 1953.

[28] *L'Instruction Publique en Turquie Républicaine*, Ankara, Matbuat Umum Müdürlüğü, 1936, page and table unnumbered; *İstatistik Yilliği 1951* (Statistical Annual 1951), Ankara, T. C. İstatistik Umum Müdürlüğü, n.d., pp. 186-187, 189-190, 192, 198.

mained to strike the conscience of the idealist and to catch the eye of those elite members who needed an added source of power in their struggle against other elite groups.

IV. Communications and Power in Contemporary Turkey

Turkey can now be said to be in the second stage of the over-all Turkish Revolution. The first stage, that of the modernization of the ruling elite, was essentially completed in the Ataturk Revolution. Broad segments of the intellectual stratum were integrated into an effective communications network and given a larger share of the increasing level of power in the society. They had been inculcated with new, more modern values through training in the major secular schools of Turkey, and they now held the command posts of most of the nation's dominant institutions. As we have suggested, the process had gone sufficiently far so that internal differences within this modernized elite began to be more and more emphasized.

On the other hand, the peasant masses of the society had only just barely begun to be weaned from centuries of isolation and integrated through communications and shared power into the political life of the nation. The second and current phase of the Turkish Revolution consists of the absorption into the Turkish polity of these village communities—the final change from one thousand Turkeys to one. In many ways this present transformation is more difficult and dangerous than the arduous changes which the Kemâlists wrought in Turkey. But it would seem to be a regular phase of the tutelary journey to political development, along which route Turkey has progressed further than perhaps any other emergent nation, and so it warrants especially close scrutiny.

Since the Second World War the momentum of communications change in Turkey has increased tremendously. An almost exponential rise in means of transport and communications has for the first time brought the villager into regular contact with his urban, modern compatriots, with resulting repercussions on the political behavior of all concerned which pose fundamental problems for Turkish stability and development in all fields. Table 2 provides some of the detailed statistics.[29]

[29] *Aylik İstistik Yillïği, op.cit.*; Richard D. Robinson, *Developments Respecting Turkey*, New York, American Universities Field Staff, 1957, Vol. IV, Section III, p. 195 ff.; *Investment in Turkey*, Washington, U.S. Dept. of Commerce, 1956, Table 6, p. 117.

TABLE 2-A

Year	Train Pass. (1,000)	Air Pas- sengers	Tele- phone Subsc. (1,000)	Internal Tele- grams (1,000)	Radios (1,000)	Newspapers and Magazines
1938	1,950	33	20.4	499.3	46.2	364
1946	3,966	3,109	30.6	862.1	184.5	339[a]
1948	4,099	6,022	36.2	651.4	240.5	nd
1950	4,428	7,194	50.9	590.8	362.5	956
1952	5,027	10,375	66.4	660.8	647.0	1,607
1954	5,164	11,554	103.0	855.7	935.8	nd
1956	5,625	18,592	123.7	828.4	1,047.2	1,510
1958	7,707	32,851	161.8	978.8	1,167.1	1,390

[a] 1945.

TABLE 2-B

Year	Roads (km.)	Auto- mobiles	Trucks	Busses	Road Travel (mill. pass./km.)
1938	40,235	4,573	3,882	1,044	nd
1946	42,730	3,406	4,475	988	nd
1948	44,186	5,838	10,596	2,198	1,211
1950	47,080	10,071	13,201	3,185	2,484
1952	49,801	16,427	18,356	4,569	6,023
1954	51,125	27,692	27,549	5,933	8,257
1956	nd	29,970	34,429	6,848	nd
1958	nd	36,800	36,900	8,300	nd

Crude inspection of these figures indicates that the number of rail passengers increased 4 times between 1938 and 1958, the number of telephone subscribers 8 times, the number of domestic telegrams 2 times, the number of radios 23 times, the number of newspapers and magazines published 4 times, the number of autos about 9 times, the number of trucks 10 times, and the number of busses 8 times. Between 1946—the better base—and 1958 the number of air passengers increased 10 times. Generally, in the communications and transportation breakthrough that attends social and economic modernization, improvements in railways, telegraphic connections, and newspapers seem to be the initial developments, just as agricultural and textile movements seem frequently to lead purely economic development. Such a pattern is reflected in the Turkish case. The main growth of telegraph lines preceded the contemporary spurt and was used more for elite modernization and the increase in state power than for mass communications. Thus we see relatively little increased use of this channel since 1946. In the future it will probably proceed at the same rate as general economic improvement rather than pace it as other channels seem to be doing and as it did in the past. A similar comment is true of the railways, though not reflected in the figures, which probably portray a rise in peasant use of train facilities.

The press can be seen to have grown rapidly after 1946, when a multi-party political system was introduced, and then to have declined slightly under the trials of the Menderes period. By 1960 the total number of newspapers and periodicals had increased to 1,658. Of these, 942 were newspapers and 716 other periodicals. Five hundred and six of the newspapers were dailies, of which 41 were in Istanbul and 16 in Ankara. Of the total number of publications, 638 were produced in Istanbul, 295 in Ankara, and 75 in Izmir, making 1,008 of 1,658, or some 61 per cent, which came from these three largest cities. The total circulation of all Turkish daily newspapers in 1960 was 1,411,429, a figure which should be interpreted as minimal since there is probably greater sharing of newspapers than occurs in Western nations. There are locally published newspapers in all but one (Hakkâri) of Turkey's 67 provinces, and 63 of the 67 have daily newspapers. A considerable number of the newspapers are affiliated with varying degrees of closeness to one or another of the nation's four major political parties.[30]

Despite this rather good press coverage and the undeniably great impact of the press on the educated elements of Turkish society, the mere fact that 60 per cent of the total population—and the preponderance of the peasantry—is still illiterate reduces the impact of the press on village life. From this point of view the most momentous communications change of all in recent years may have been that portrayed by Table 2-B concerning improvements in road transportation. Railways, airplanes, the telegraph and telephone, the press, and even radio seem to have been trivial in their force compared to the real revolution created by the motor vehicle. The peasant appears to need tangible evidence of previously unexperienced and strange phenomena introduced to him from outside his environment—to need to see and touch—before he believes. Moreover, the ideas emanating from the newspaper that is read to him or from the radio on the coffee house wall are always very strongly filtered through a cognitive screen manufactured from his own limited experience. A classic example of this is the peasant who thought that most city buildings were made of dung since the words for brick and dung were confused. He under-

<hr>

[30] *Türkiyede Çıkan Gazete ve Mecmualar, op.cit.*, passim.

standably felt that people who lived in dung houses had little to teach someone who merely cooked with it. But such selective interpretation is much less able to mitigate the impression that visiting the town or city and seeing things with his own eyes, feeling it with his own hands, and stumbling over it with his own feet make on him. The development of road transportation in the past decade or so has made this experience possible for untold villagers who formerly remained immured behind mud-brick walls even though only five miles from town. This change in road transport may be the real heart of the communications revolution that has unquestionably struck Turkey in the last few years.

Glancing again at the figures presented suggests also that the change has been less due to road-building, though this is undeniably a factor (our data unfortunately are incomplete for the most recent years), than to a great increase in the number of vehicles available for movement over the existing web of roads. The automobiles have permitted more and more urban Turks to get away from the city and encounter their village brethren, distasteful as it may be to them. But the trucks and autobusses have enabled hordes of villagers to visit nearby towns and cities, so that such travel, even for long distances, is becoming commonplace. The tremendously increased number of inter-city busses are still packed to the luggage racks, and the number of extra passengers hitching rides on trucks mounts daily. Even remote villages are within striking distance of roads along which come two or three trucks per day which will let them clamber aboard. Moreover, most of the 40,000 tractors which have been wisely or unwisely injected into the Turkish economy by American aid are used for regular excursions from villages to towns and cities—though most peasants still refrain from taking their relatives to Germany on the family tractor as one atavistically bold Turk did not long ago.[31] All told, in the eight years between 1946 and 1954 road traffic in Turkey increased eight-fold, and a large share of this increase seems to have been contributed by peasant travel.

The alteration produced in traditional village power structure by this great modification in communication practices could be predicted from our earlier analysis. No longer, in most cases, do the *hoca*, the *Ağa Bey*, and the village elders and *ağas* monopolize all village con-

[31] Kemal Karpat, "Social Effects of Farm Mechanization in Turkish Villages," *Social Research*, 27, Spring 1960, pp. 83-103.

tact with the outside world. No longer can they control what the villager sees and hears and thus what he thinks. No longer are all escape hatches from the village closed. Largely as a result, no longer do these conservative persons dominate the village. Naturally they maintain considerable residual influence, and their power varies greatly from community to community. But it seems to vary inversely with the development of the sorts of extra-mural communication we have been discussing.

An additional extremely important factor altering village power structure by inserting villagers directly into broad and different communication networks is that of political party development in Turkey. The political party leader in the village has come to be a person of import, especially since the multi-party system stimulated widespread grass-roots competition between the parties at the village level. The local party leader may be an *ağa* or elder; this is particularly true in the more backward eastern regions of the country—a fact supporting our general argument.[32] But in the western provinces the party leader quite often serves as an additional pipeline to possibly the most vital sector of the external world, and as such he not occasionally weakens the position of the traditional village leaders. Multi-party competition gives an opportunity to dissident elements within the village to find an acceptable outlet for that dissidence, one which it is too risky to repress in many cases because that party might come to power in the future and even has influential connections in the present.[33]

A final general communications factor—again more of the direct, interpersonal contact type than of the Western mass media sort—is that of the school system. Though Turkish educational development in the past has been biased (not unwisely) toward meeting the needs of the elite, in recent years this task has been sufficiently well accomplished so that the expansion of village education has proceeded more rapidly. Over half of Turkey's villages now offer some sort of primary-level education, and the village schoolteacher, quite

---

[32] See, for example, the description of the 1961 political campaign in the East in *Cumhuriyet*, 25 *Eylul* (September), 1961.

[33] For one illustration, among many, of such changes see Yasa, *op.cit.*, pp. 161-162, 153-175, esp. footnote 1, p. 161, where Yasa observes that "The newspapers and posters of these two parties (People's and Democratic), and information and gossip about them accelerated the life of the country, and contributed to shake (the village of) Hasanoğlan out of its old static order." Unfortunately, *village* party organization is now legally prohibited.

often over the objections of the *hoca* and the elders, has been added to the list of village fixtures. He brings with him another channel to the modern world and another adjustment in village power structure.[34]

It cannot be said that all improvements in communications seem to have pushed the villager in the direction of modernization. One result of his increased mobility is that he has been brought into closer association with the townspeople. However, many of the denizens of small towns in Turkey are among the most conservative, traditional, even reactionary individuals in the country—particularly the *esnaf* class, the small merchants and shopkeepers. Consequently, heightened contact with these persons has worked on numerous occasions to reinforce the waning power of anti-modern groups within the village.[35] Obviously, mere increase of communications has an unpredictable effect on political behavior. The specific content and source of those new communications cannot be overlooked.

The significance of the changes in village communications and power relations for national political development in Turkey is very hard to fathom at this point. There seems to be almost as much cause for alarm as there is for thanksgiving. The peasants have been given the vote, and the parties assiduously woo them to secure the award of that vote to their proffered candidates. The reaction of the villagers to variations in policy are elaborately discussed and estimated by political leaders. The distribution and reciprocity of political power in Turkey have unquestionably been increased and, true to our definition, we must label this political development, largely engendered by communications changes. However, the rub lies in the fact that our third ingredient—the over-all level of power—may have been adversely affected. The peasants newly in receipt of power may utilize that power to reduce the organization and control available to Turkish society, and in the process reduce the chances for economic development.

There is a great temptation presented to all parties to pander to short-run peasant greed and political immaturity by promising tax reductions, fiddling with crop subsidies, incorporating many local

[34] *Cf.* Makal, *op.cit.*, or Kemal Karpat, "Social Themes in Contemporary Turkish Literature, Part II," *Middle East Journal*, 14, Spring 1960, p. 156, among many possible references for this fact.

[35] Bernard Lewis, "Democracy in Turkey," *Middle Eastern Affairs*, x, February 1959, p. 65.

potentates into top-level party and governmental positions, and so on. Fortitude to resist these temptations, even at the price of a reduced chance for power, has not so far been widely displayed. In fact, the key to Menderes' success, despite his anti-democratic tendencies, lay in just such maneuvers. Thus short-run political development can lead to a reverse trend under certain conditions which may prevail in Turkey (and in other developing nations) at the present time.

Within the political party, central control and discipline have been appreciably weakened. Local forces have become so strong as to impair the party's ability even to perform necessary political tasks, such as research into its own organization. The chief contribution to national party planning which local leaders can offer lies in their personal knowledge of conditions in their locality. Consequently they stubbornly resist any attempt by the national headquarters to provide itself with an alternative source of information about local conditions, such as various forms of research or the erection of parallel party organizations. Recalcitrant party leaders who have lost their central posts are now commencing to cater to local interests to regain power despite central opposition.[36]

This tale sounds very much like a description of American politics. The moral may be that the United States is a politically underdeveloped society which, because of development in other areas, can afford such conditions. However, we must not forget another crucial effect of the recent communications explosion of the second stage of the Turkish Revolution. The well-known revolution of rising expectations in the economic sphere has struck. The Turkish villager, newly introduced into the nation's political life, is beginning to voice strong demands for a higher standard of living and indicates a willingness to use his new political power to reject those who do not give him what he wants. Hence, while party control is declining and the ability of the society to integrate the actions of its citizens is decreasing, the emergent peasantry is now demanding that very type of economic development which requires a heightened degree of political discipline and social coordination. The government may be unable to obtain the present sacrifices needed for rapid economic development; and the absence of that development may produce

[36] The activities of Kasîm Gülek, former General Secretary of the People's Party, at the People's Party Congress in the summer of 1961 afford the most egregious example. The same propensities were to be seen in his newspaper, *Tanin*.

dire political instability resulting, at worst, in another but less enlightened military coup some three or four years from now. Certainly top political leaders in Turkey are sincerely worried about such possibilities in these anxious days.[87]

[87] Judgment based on interviews obtained by the author in the summer of 1961 in Turkey. A few top politicians went so far as to say that they felt they had about four years to make unmistakable headway in solving the nation's major economic problems. If such success was lacking, political instability resulting in another, more durable military take-over might well be the result.

CHAPTER 18

Toward a Communication Theory
of Modernization

A Set of Considerations

DANIEL LERNER

In the city of Teheran, in 1954, there were 36 registered "film companies." Only one of these companies had actually produced, distributed, and exhibited any films; the other 35 had yet to complete production of their first film.

How did this odd situation come about? The sequence of events begins at Teheran University, where the old traditions of Iranian learning and the new demands of Iranian modernization are locked in a deadly struggle, from which there issues annually a horde of distorted and disfigured progeny called "graduates." These are the young men who, under the compulsion to maintain or attain an elevated social status, attended or evaded four years of magistral lectures and passed a final examination. They have acquired certain standard adornments—i.e., acquaintance with Persian history and Shariya law, familiarity with the glories of Persian art and poetry, certified by the ability to quote yards of Firdausi and appropriate stanzas of Saadi.

These young men are all dressed up—but they have no place to go. They are much too numerous to be absorbed into the traditional social orders represented by government, army, priesthood. Already the Iranian government periodically discovers itself unable to meet the payroll of its swollen bureaucracy. Nor is Iran developing an adequate supply of new occupations deemed fitting for college graduates. These graduates face only the bleak prospect of unemployment and underemployment. Accordingly they seek to occupy themselves in ways that will be amusing if not rewarding. A half-dozen such graduates organize themselves around a 35 millimeter camera and form a "film company." But their outlook is dismal. Most of them will never produce a film; those who do will never be able to market it. It is unlikely that, even if they wish to show it free of charge, their film will ever be seen beyond their circle of friends. There are few cinemas in Teheran, and they are for commercial hire. Frustration and failure thus await most young Iranians who seek to make a career in the mass media.

The key factor in this unhappy situation is the uncertain and inadequate tempo of Iranian modernization. The supply of new life-opportunities does not keep pace with—is indeed steadily outpaced by—the burgeoning demands of the new literates. In 1958 I summarized the Iranian situation in the following terms, which remain cogent in 1962:

"Incorporation of new men is no easy task in a non-growth economy. Iran develops few of those constantly growing and changing occupational holes which embody young men in the elite structure. The clergy, the military, the bureaucracy—all these are charges on the public treasury, already overburdened and scarcely capable of expansion. The teaching corps is pitifully inadequate, but unlikely to multiply opportunities until Iran develops a modernizing economy in which literacy is an essential skill. Without an expanding business sector, there is little room for the lawyer and accountant, for the specialist in industrial management or labor relations, for the insurance broker or the investment manager, for the account executive or the public relations counsel. Advertising is stillborn and the mass media abortive. Where in Iran is 'the man in the gray flannel suit'? Whatever his unpopularity among Westerners wearied by opinion brokers, in Iran he would be a more useful stimulus to modernization than the agitational intellectual in a hairshirt of vivid hue.

"Given its limited absorptive capacity, Iran suffers from an overproduction of intellectuals. In a society about 90% illiterate, several thousand young persons go through the classical routines of higher education each year. Learning no skills that can be productively employed, these collegians seek outlets in the symbol-manipulating arts toward which their humanistic studies have oriented them. Their effort supplies a poignant instance of usable training rendered useless by its social environment—newspapers without readers that last a week or a month, film companies that never produce a film. The mass media, as distinctive index of the Participant Society, flourish only where the mass has sufficient skill in literacy, sufficient motivation to share 'borrowed experience,' sufficient cash to consume the mediated product. In Iran the mass media are anemic and with them, annually, die a thousand hopes."[1]

[1] Daniel Lerner, *The Passing of Traditional Society*, Glencoe, Ill., The Free Press, 1958, p. 362.

The thousand hopes that die in Iran each year are multiplied into millions throughout the underdeveloped countries around the world that exhibit communication malfunctioning in their efforts to modernize. What is the common mechanism underlying these numerous cases where the communication gears fail to mesh with the motor of modernization? Various formulations have been offered us in the excellent chapters in this book. Each points to essential factors in a comprehensive theoretical understanding of the interaction between communications and political development. No paper achieves such a comprehensive theoretical understanding—a statement of such force as to suffuse us with the beautiful feeling of perfect illumination—as does a Newtonian account of the solar system as a *gravitational* system or a Wienerian account of all systems as *entropic* systems. It may be prudent at this stage of our knowledge about communication systems and social systems to aim at something less than this. The present effort is only a set of considerations drawn from an incomplete theoretical base.

The theoretical base of this paper is the proposition that modernity is an interactive behavioral system. It is a "style of life" whose components are *interactive* in the sense that the efficient functioning of any one of them requires the efficient functioning of all the others. The components are *behavioral* in the sense that they operate only through the activity of individual human beings. They form a *system* in the sense that significant variation in the activity of one component will be associated with significant variation in the activity of all other components.

The terseness of these definitions should not obscure the amplitude of the proposition, which is coterminous with the basic theorem of behavioral science—namely, that the operation of a social system, or sub-system, can be accounted for by the statistical distribution of behavioral components among its members. Thus a society operates its polity as a representative democracy if a large fraction of its members are qualified to vote, and regularly do vote, in elections that actually decide which of several competing candidates shall occupy the offices authorized to make decisions on specified issues of public policy. Thus a society operates its economy under capitalism in the measure that its members are free to decide how they shall use their own savings in order to maximize their own wealth. The statistical distribution of items that form the index—i.e., components of the system—determines how we characterize a society.

There is much that remains to be clarified in the behavioral conception of society. But it does, even in its present condition, authorize systematic efforts to locate linkages between personal and aggregative behavior, to establish reciprocity between individuals and institutions, to associate samples with systems. Operating on this authorization, this paper will seek to clarify how and why it comes about that the mass media function effectively only in modern and rapidly modernizing societies. We know empirically that this is so. Here we wish to develop further the idea that media systems and social systems have "gone together so regularly because, in some historical sense, they *had to* go together."[2]

I. The New Revolution of Rising Frustrations

These considerations arise from reflection on the course of the developing areas over the past decade. It has not been a smooth course nor a consistent one. It has falsified the predictions and belied the assumptions of those who foresaw the coming of the good society to the backward areas. Among its casualties has been the assumption that if some particular input was made—i.e., investment capital, industrial plant, agricultural methods, entrepreneurial training, or any other "key factor" preferred by the analyst—then a modernization process would be generated more or less spontaneously. This is a serious casualty. As the editor of this volume has aptly written in his introduction: "Faith in spontaneity died soon after the first ex-colonial people began to experience frustrations and disappointment at becoming a modern nation."

This bitter experience is new to us and requires careful evaluation—particularly by those among us who want the defeats of the past decade to help prepare the modest victories that may still be hoped for in the next. The decade of the 1950's witnessed the spread of economic development projects around much of the world. This process of reviving cultures, emerging nations, and new states was widely characterized as a "revolution of rising expectations." People throughout the backward and impoverished areas of the world suddenly acquired the sense that a better life was possible for them. Now leaders arose

[2] *Ibid.*, p. 438. See also Daniel Lerner, "Communication Systems and Social Systems," *Behavioral Science*, Vol. 2, No. 4, October 1957; Gabriel A. Almond and James S. Coleman, *The Politics of the Developing Areas*, Princeton, Princeton University Press, 1960, p. 536; Lucian W. Pye, *Politics, Personality, and Nation Building*, New Haven, Yale University Press, 1962, p. 15.

who encouraged their people to believe in the immanence of progress and the fulfillment of their new, often millennial, hopes. A great forward surge of expectancy and aspiration, of desire and demand, was awakened during the past decade among peoples who for centuries had remained hopeless and inert. This forward feeling was shared by those of us whose unchanging task is to understand.

A significantly different mood characterizes our thinking about the decade before us. While rising expectations continue to spread around the underdeveloped world, those of us who retain our interest in comprehending or programming rapid growth have learned that the ways of progress are hard to find, that aspirations are more easily aroused than satisfied. There is a new concern that the 1960's may witness a radical counter-formation: a revolution of rising frustrations. Observers have had to temper hope with prudence, for the limits on rapid growth have become more clearly visible through our recent experience. There is a seasoned concern with maintenance of equilibrium in societies undergoing rapid change. Soberly, responsible persons now tend to look for guidance less to ideology than to theory, less to dogma than to data. A new era of systematic research into the mysteries of modernization has opened.

Any restless area presents social research with an excellent opportunity to meet the need for a theoretically sound, empirically based exposition of the process called modernization. To be sure, there are particularities in each situation. Particularities can be wedded to generalizations, however, if we focus social research in any area upon those aspects of the process which it shares with other regions of the world that are seeking to accompany rapid economic growth with rapid social change. The political function in this process is to maintain stable controls over these rapid changes—i.e., to preside over a dynamic equilibrium.

In these terms there are two main sets of problems that confront the development process everywhere: mobility and stability. By mobility we mean the problems of societal dynamism; by stability we mean the problems of societal equilibrium. Mobility is the agent of social change. Only insofar as individual persons can change their place in the world, their position in society, their own self-image does social change occur. Social change is in this sense the sum of mobilities acquired by individual persons. (In a more precise sense, as we shall see, societal equilibrium can be expressed as a ratio between individual mobility and institutional stability.)

It is fairly well established that a systemic relationship between the major forms of mobility—physical, social, and psychic—is required for a modern participant society. As to sequence and phasing, we have only the Western experience to serve as full-scale model. Historically, in the Western world mobility evolved in successive phases over many centuries. The first phase was *geographic* mobility. Man was unbound from his native soil. The age of exploration opened new worlds, the age of migration peopled them with men transplanted from their native heath. The second phase was *social* mobility. Once liberated from his native soil, man sought liberation from his native status. The transplanted man was no longer obliged to be his father's shadow, routinized in a social role conferred upon him by his birth. Instead, as he had changed his place on the earth, so he sought to change his place in society.

The third phase was *psychic* mobility. The man who had changed his native soil and native status felt obliged, finally, to change his native self. If he was no longer his father's shadow, then he had to work out for himself a personality that fitted his actual life situation. Once he had changed his ancestral home and inherited status, thereby transforming his place and his role, he had to transform himself in ways suitable to his new situation. The acquisition and diffusion of psychic mobility may well be the greatest characterological transformation in modern history, indeed since the rise and spread of the great world religions. It is in any case the most fundamental human factor that must be comprehended by all who plan rapid economic growth by means of rapid social change. For psychic mobility—what we have elsewhere called empathy—is the mechanism by which individual men transform themselves in sufficient breadth and depth to make social change self-sustaining.[3]

This Western experience is what gave us that faith in spontaneity which Professor Pye assures us died a little while ago. We assumed that in any country that was given the right amount of investment or training or whatnot empathy would rise and mobility would be accelerated—and the good society would be attained sooner or later. But the good society can only be attained later in the measure that advances are made to attain it at each stage, for in development terms the long run can only be a sequence of short runs. Hence stability is essential.

[3] Daniel Lerner, *The Passing of Traditional Society*, p. 43. Also K. Gompertz, "The Relation of Empathy to Effective Communication," *Journalism Quarterly*, XXXVII, Autumn 1960, pp. 533-546.

The past decade has taught us that mobility, while indispensable to rapid social change, is not enough. It is a necessary but not sufficient condition of growth. Since mobility is a seeking for something better, it must be balanced by a finding—as, in equilibrium, a demand must be balanced by a supply. It is the continuing failure of many transitional societies to maintain the balance of psychic supply-and-demand that underlies the new revolution of rising frustrations.

II. The Want:Get Ratio

The spread of frustration in areas developing less rapidly than their people wish can be seen as the outcome of a deep imbalance between achievement and aspiration. In simple terms, this situation arises when many people in a society want far more than they can hope to get. This disparity in the want:get ratio has been studied intensively in the social science literature in terms of achievement and aspiration. The relationship we here propose for study can be expressed by the following equation (adapted from an ingenious formula of William James[4]):

$$\text{Satisfaction} = \frac{\text{Achievement}}{\text{Aspiration}}$$

This formula alerts us to the proposition that an individual's level of satisfaction is always, at any moment of his life, a ratio between what he wants and what he gets, i.e., between his aspirations and his achievements. A person with low achievement may be satisfied if his aspirations are equally low. A person with high achievement may still be dissatisfied if his aspirations far exceed his accomplishments. Relative deprivation, as has been shown, is the effective measure of satisfaction among individuals and groups.

It is a serious imbalance in this ratio that characterizes areas beset by rising frustrations. Typically in these situations the denominator increases faster than the numerator—i.e., aspiration outruns achievement so far that many people, even if they are making some progress toward their goal, are dissatisfied because they get so much less than they want. Indeed, in some developing countries aspirations have risen so high as to annul significant achievements in the society as a whole.

How does such an imbalance in the want:get ratio occur? How can it be prevented or cured? What, in short, are the social institutions

4 William James, *Psychology: Briefer Course*, New York, Holt, 1923, p. 187.

that affect the level of aspiration, the level of achievement, and the ratio between them? There are six institutions which function as the principal agencies of social change (or its inhibition): the economy, the police, the family, the community, the school, the media.

About the first five we can be very brief. If the economy can be made to supply all the opportunities needed to maintain reasonable equilibrium between achievements and aspirations—if the want:get ratio can be balanced by simply supplying all that people want—then there is no problem of frustration. Everyone is happy. Similarly, if the frustrations that arise are settled simply by police methods, then also there is no problem—at least, not for social research. Social research has little to contribute in situations of over-achievement or under-aspiration. Where riches outrun wants, where coercion inhibits desires, there social research is not needed. In most transitional societies that concern us, however, neither of these conditions obtains.

A more complex agency of social change is the family. Typically in developing areas the family acts as an instrument of conservatism and the retardation of change. It acts also, however, as an instrument of balance. To the degree that mobility involves the breaking of traditional family ties (and I believe the degree is high), this is a built-in destabilizer of the modernization process. How to replace the stability of traditional family ties by other methods is a deep problem of social equilibrium under conditions of rapid change.

Similarly, the community may act as a powerful force to promote or impede balanced growth. Here the force hinges upon the individuals who function as activators and enthusiasts of modernization. Where these people emerge and prevail, communities tend to become positive agents of the purpose that modernization seeks to accomplish. Otherwise, in the absence of effective activators and enthusiasts, the coalition of adversaries and indifferents that forms within every transitional community will impede growth and disrupt equilibrium.

The schools, under conditions of modernization, are necessarily instruments of social change. They must teach what is new and modern, what is desirable and obtainable, because they have no other curriculum worth supporting. There are of course important variations in the effectiveness with which different schools produce modernizers and their products serve modernization. We shall not discuss schools further here, despite their importance, because their institutional role and behavioral function—in our model of modernization—can be handled as a variant of the mass media in the communication process.

The mass media, finally, are a major instrument of social change. They make indispensable inputs to the psycho-political life of a transitional society via the minds and hearts of its people. Theirs is the critical input to satisfaction in emerging nations and to citizenship in new states. To perceive the communication crux of modernization, we must consider deeply three propositions: (1) that the mass media bring new aspirations to people—and then, since the empathic individual imagination quickly (logarithmically it appears)[5] outruns societal achievement, it brings dissatisfaction conceived as frustration of aspiration; (2) that, despite the now-evident risks of frustration, the mass media continue to spread around the world—inexorably and unilaterally; (3) that modernization—conceived as the maximization of satisfaction—can succeed (achieve more at less cost) if, and only if, a clarifying communication theory and practice are activated.

On the first proposition I have already written so much that I shall simply incorporate in this paper conclusions which any interested reader can pursue further in my (and other) published work.[6] On the second point I have published descriptive studies of the inexorable and unilateral spread of mass media around the world, showing that no society, once it acquires a media system, does go back to an oral system of communication.[7] In the next section of this chapter I want to explore *why* this is so. Then we shall turn to the third—and crucial—proposition about communication theory and practice.

III. How and Why the Mass Media Spread

If the mass media are to have some significant effect on modernization and democratic development—whether to facilitate or impede these desiderata—the first condition is that the mass media must spread. For, if the mass media do not spread, then we have no problem to discuss. We thus consider the question: what conditions determine whether the mass media spread?

One major condition is economic: the level of economic development in a country determines whether the mass media spread. All industrially developed countries produce mass media systems. No pre-industrial country produces mass media systems. Between these extremes lie the range of cases that interest us here, i.e., the developing

---

[5] This refinement of my basic theory I owe to my student Howard Rosenthal. See his "A Statistical Approach to Comparative Politics" (M.I.T. CENIS document number C/62-9, 1962), to be published shortly.

[6] See footnote 2.

[7] See Daniel Lerner, "Communication Systems and Social Systems."

nations. Here the general rule is that mass media spread in a direct and monotonic relationship with a rising level of industrial capacity. Where this rule applies, in general the spread of the mass media facilitates modernization. Where the rule does not apply, one may expect to find that the spreading mass media impede (or, perhaps more accurately, "deviate") modernization. Why does this simple rule have such general force as is here claimed?

The reasoning is clear if we consider information as a commodity. It is produced, distributed, and consumed like all other commodities. This brings information within the rule of the market. Notably, the supply-demand reciprocal comes into operation. This means that, to evaluate the functioning of a communication sub-system within a societal system, it is essential to consider—it may even be wise to begin with—the conditions that determine the efficient functioning of all economic processes: the capacity to produce and the capacity to consume.

We shall consider each of these briefly. Our discussion will draw its substance from the market economy model of the modern Western nations. It is in these countries, where the mass media developed in the private sector, that the mass media spread first historically, and where they remain today the most widespread in quantity of both production and consumption. Any account of this process that wishes to be relevant to happenings in the mass media around the world today must provide some reasonable explanation for the variant economic evolution of the mass media in the Communist countries and the developing countries. The Soviet system provides some especially interesting deviations from the rule of supply and demand, e.g., the political rule of enforced supply and acquiescent demand for a social commodity taken out of the economic market place. Events in the developing countries, such as India and Egypt, do not yet form a "system," but they do alert us to the possibility of new ways of handling information that differ significantly from the historic evolution in the modern West. We shall therefore try to frame our discussion in categories that *must* apply to the operation of mass media whether a country be capitalist, Communist, or neutralist.

CAPACITY TO PRODUCE.

There must be a capacity to produce. No country—whether its ideology be Hamiltonian, Stalinist, or Gandhian—can produce information via mass media until it has an economic capacity to construct and maintain the physical plant of the mass media. I have made a simple checklist of the items needed to produce mass media products. This checklist is neither precise nor comprehensive. It is simply a reminder of what it has taken historically and what it takes today to produce information via the mass media. A glance will indicate how much more complex this list would become if one were considering the most efficient means of producing information according to strict considerations of economic optima. But such considerations lie far outside the present purview of developing countries. For these countries the simple checklist will do.

Capacity to Produce: A Checklist

1. PLANT:
   Buildings
   Utilities (power, light, water)
   Facilities (studios, workshops, offices)

2. EQUIPMENT:
   Books (linotype)
   Newspapers (rotary)
   Magazines (rotogravure)
   Movies (film, camera)
   Radio (amplifier, transmitter)
   Television ("picture tube")
   [Future standard equipment: satellites]

3. PERSONNEL:
   Copy producers (reporters, scripters, features)
   Copy presenters (actors, printers, "layout")
   Managerial corps (editor, publisher, producer, director)

The items required to produce information via the mass media are grouped under the three categories of plant, equipment, personnel. The three categories, as well as the items listed within them, are arranged in ascending order of complexity. They may even be construed as a scale upon which rising levels of economic capacity could be calibrated. Thus, if one thinks of the contemporary United States, it may seem too rudimentary to list the "plant." Yet efforts to spread the mass media in the developing countries have foundered, and continue to founder today, on just the three items listed in this category.

Even the item of buildings is a large hurdle and frequent stumbling-block. For one thing, buildings of adequate shape and size do not exist in most of the villages and towns and small cities of the developing countries. The mass media are perforce restricted to the capital cities for just this reason. But even such a capital city as Teheran, as we have seen, does not have enough buildings of the right shape and size to permit production or consumption of many full-length movies. The buildings in which the mass media operate must be provided with efficient utilities, such as power, light, water. How could a proper newspaper operate in Teheran without efficient telephonic communication, without regular telephone links to the great oil refineries at Abadan, to the summer and winter residences of the Shah, to other capitals of the world—not to mention the electronic equipment needed for receiving the huge volume of daily news files coming from the international press services? Yet which of us does not remember some amusing or frustrating incident connected with his use of the telephone in a rapidly developing country? Which of us has not witnessed the inhibiting, and sometimes paralyzing, restrictions placed upon the mass media in these countries by the inadequacy of their facilities? Of the thirty-six film companies in Teheran, only one had studios. This was the only company that had managed to produce a full-length feature film.

The varieties of equipment required by the mass media are manifold, complicated, and expensive. I have listed the principal media in the historic order of their evolution, which corresponds also to the complexity of the equipment they required at the time their major development occurred. Thus the book publishing industry was able to develop on the basis of the simple linotype machine. A further technological advance made possible the spread of the mass circulation daily newspaper, namely the rotary press. Illustrated magazines were a medium of elite communication because of their cost until the development of rotogravure machines made possible the cheap production of millions of copies of illustrated monthlies and weeklies. Similarly, the rapid development in our century of movies, radio, and television as industries hinged upon the capacity of American industry to produce at acceptable prices the mechanical and electronic equipment which are indispensable to the functioning of these mass media. The communication revolution of our time was technological before it became anything else. It is not implausible that in our century communication satellites will become standard equipment for the efficient functioning of mass media systems in many countries throughout the world.

The economic level of any country hinges also upon the quantity and quality of its skilled personnel. Particularly in the mass communication industries the capacity to produce hinges upon the availability of a corps of communicators, i.e., a substantial body of personnel trained in the array of special skills required for immediate production. Needed first of all are the skills that produce copy—whether it be for the news columns of a daily paper, a feature article in a weekly magazine, the script of a radio program, or the scenario of a movie or television show. Consider in passing the variety of features that fill the pages of every major daily newspaper. What a great variety of tastes, skills, and interests are needed to produce all this copy! Reflect for a moment that the man who has written a novel rarely turns out to be the man best equipped to adapt his own work for production as a movie. The man who does this may well be a person of much less creative talent but with superior specialized skill in "scripting." Consider the further array of skills needed to present copy, after it has been produced, to the consuming public. Actors do this for the spoken word, printers for the written word. But consider the extremely specialized skill required for that essential presentation function performed by the so-called "layout man." To make such large enterprises as a daily newspaper, a radio station, or a film company operate efficiently, a skilled managerial corps is also necessary. These are the editors and publishers, the producers and directors who are the kingpins of the mass communications industries. Without these many and varied persons the mass media have no capacity to produce.

If we simply reflect on the developing countries we know best in these terms, we promptly perceive that these conditions may well determine whether the mass media will spread. In reflecting further on the central question—whether the spread of the mass media will facilitate or impede modernization—we must take account of another condition: the capacity to consume.

CAPACITY TO CONSUME

Three factors determine whether the capacity to consume media products spreads—and how fast—in any country: cash, literacy, motivation. There is a simple side to this matter. A person needs cash to buy a radio, a cinema ticket, a newspaper. If a newspaper costs as much as a loaf of bread, and if his ready cash is in a chronic state of short supply, then there is a diminishing probability that a person will consume newspapers. On the same simple level: only a literate person *can* read a book, paper, or magazine, and only a motivated person *wants* to read. The media flourish therefore in the measure that their society equips the individuals with cash, literacy, and motivation to consume their products.

There is a more complex sociology, however, that underlies each of these factors and their reciprocal interaction. It is no accident that the mass media developed in the monetized sector of every economy. The barter of country newspapers against farmers' produce or artisans' products was a brief and transitory phase—occasionally magnified in the sentimental memoirs of superannuated country editors. The media grew in the monetized sector because this is the distinctively modern sector of every economy. The media, as index and agent of modernization, *had* to grow in the sector where every other modern pattern of production and consumption was growing or else remain stunted.

The efficient operation of a money economy was made possible only by a great transformation in the thoughtways and life-ways of millions of people. Historically, in any society the "sense of cash" is an acquired trait. It has to be learned, often painfully, by a great many people before their society can negotiate the perilous passage from barter to exchange. Consider, for example, this sentence on the traditional Anatolian peasantry by Professor H. A. R. Gibb: "We may suppose the *re'aya* to have been animated hardly at all by any idea of gain, and to have worked their land with a minimum of effort and very little knowledge."[8]

Gain, effort, knowledge—these are huge categories of discourse. For any adequate comprehension of the personality transformation which accompanied the shift from barter to cash in contemporary Turkey we are obliged to take these large terms in their historical sense. What has been acquired in one generation among a population that had always been ignorant and indifferent is precisely the sense of gain, effort, knowledge which came over centuries to guide personal behavior in the modern participant society of the West.

Cash is an essential solvent in modern life, and the achievement of rising per capita income distribution is a major objective of modern societies. Here the political and sociological problems of the developing countries become intertwined with their economic problems. Economies long caught in the vicious circle of poverty cannot easily break through into the modern industrial system of expanding production of goods and services. This fact reflects no inherent and inevitable distaste for the good things of life among developing peoples. It re-

[8] Hamilton A. R. Gibb and H. Bowen, *Islamic Society and the West*, London, Oxford University Press, 1950, Vol. 1, Part 1, p. 244.

flects rather the difficult communication process—which in the West occurred over several centuries—of stimulating desires and providing means for satisfying them where neither desires nor facilities have previously existed. Westerners engaged in economic development problems have only recently recognized that, once a start is made, the reciprocity between desires and facilities tends to operate in the new nations as elsewhere.

Consumption of media products is thus an economic function, but it performs simultaneously several other functions that are sociological, psychological, and political. Literacy is a technical requirement for media consumption. But literacy, once acquired, becomes a prime mover in the modernization of every aspect of life. Literacy is indeed the basic personal skill that underlies the whole modernizing sequence. With literacy people acquire more than the simple skill of reading. Professor Becker concludes that the written word first equipped men with a "transpersonal memory";[9] Professor Innis writes that historically "man's activities and powers were roughly extended in proportion to the increased use of written records."[10] The very act of achieving distance and control over a formal language gives people access to the world of vicarious experience and trains them to use the complicated mechanism of empathy which is needed to cope with this world. It supplies media consumers, who stimulate media production, thereby activating the reciprocal relationship whose consequences for modernization we have noted. This is why media participation, in every country we have studied, exhibits a centripetal tendency. Those who read newspapers also tend to be the heaviest consumers of movies, broadcasts, and all other media products. Throughout the Middle East illiterate respondents said of their literate compatriots: "They live in another world." Thus literacy becomes the sociological pivot in the activation of psychic mobility, the publicly shared skill which binds modern man's varied daily round into a consistent participant life-style.

Literacy is in this sense also a precondition for motivation. People who can read usually do read—as, indeed, they consume more of all the audio-visual products of the media (the well-known "centripetal effect") and participate more fully in all the modernizing activities of their society. What is required to motivate the isolated and illiterate

[9] Carl L. Becker, *Progress and Power*, Stanford, Stanford University Press, 1936.
[10] Harold Adams Innis, *Empire and Communications*, Oxford, Clarendon Press, 1950, p. 11.

peasants and tribesmen who compose the bulk of the world's population is to provide them with clues as to what the better things of life might be. Needed there is a massive growth of imaginativeness about alternatives to their present life-ways, and a simultaneous growth of institutional means for handling these alternative life-ways. There is no suggestion here that all people should learn to admire precisely the same things as people in the Western society. It is suggested, much more simply, that before any enduring transformation of the vicious circle of poverty can be started, people will have to learn about the life-ways evolved in other societies. What they subsequently accept, adapt, or reject is a matter which each man will in due course decide for himself. Whether he will have the capacity to reach a rational decision hinges, in turn, upon the fullness of his participation in the modernizing process as it works through every sector of his personal and social life. The final test comes in the arena of political participation.

MASS MEDIA AND POLITICAL DEMOCRACY

Democratic governance comes late historically and typically appears as a crowning institution of the participant society. In countries which have achieved stable growth at a high level of modernity the literate individual tends to be the newspaper reader, the cash customer, and the voter.

The media teach people participation of this sort by depicting for them new and strange situations and by familiarizing them with a range of opinions among which they can choose. Some people learn better than others, the variation reflecting their differential skill in empathy. For empathy, in the several aspects it exhibits, is the basic communication skill required of modern men. Empathy endows a person with the capacity to imagine himself as proprietor of a bigger grocery store in a city, to wear nice clothes and live in a nice house, to be interested in "what is going on in the world" and to "get out of his hole." With the spread of curiosity and imagination among a previously quietistic population come the human skills needed for social growth and economic development.

The connection between mass media and political democracy is especially close. Both audiences and constituencies are composed of participant individuals. People participate in the public life of their country mainly by having opinions about many matters which in the isolation of traditional society did not concern them. Participant persons have opinions on a variety of issues and situations which they may never have experienced directly—such as what the government should do about irrigation, how the Algerian revolt could be settled, whether money should be sent to Jordan or armies to Israel, and so on. By having and expressing opinions on such matters a person participates in the network of public communication as well as in political decision.

The mechanism which links public opinion so intimately with political democracy is reciprocal expectation. The governed develop the habit of having opinions, and expressing them, because they expect to be heeded by their governors. The governors, who had been shaped by this expectation and share it, in turn expect the expression of *vox populi* on current issues of public policy. In this idealized formulation of the relationship, then, the spread of mass media cannot impede but can only facilitate democratic development.

But ideal types do not always match perfectly with their empirical instances. In the developed democracy of the United States, for example, the capacity to produce information via mass media is virtually unlimited. The capacity to consume media products—thanks to an abundant supply and widespread distribution of cash, literacy, motivation—is unparalleled anywhere in human history. The production-consumption reciprocal has operated efficiently on a very high level over many decades. Yet as American society presented the world with its most developed model of modernity, certain flaws in the operation of the system became apparent. I do not speak of the Great Crash of 1929—which exhibited a merely technical flaw in management of the economic sub-system. I speak of a much deeper flaw in the participant system as a whole, i.e., the emergence of non-voting as a political phenomenon. A generation ago Harold Gosnell called our attention to this danger. In recent years an alarmed David Riesman has generalized this phenomenon to the larger menace of political apathy. If Americans were really suffering from widespread apathy about their public life, then a cornerstone of our media-opinion system would be crumbling—namely, in our terms, the cornerstone of motivation. (We note in passing that in the developed democracy of France only a short while ago leading thinkers and scholars convened for solemn discussion of political apathy in France—of all places!)

If one danger to developed democracies comes from literate non-voters, the parallel danger to developing democracies comes from the reverse configuration, i.e., *non-literate voters!* Can universal suffrage operate efficiently in a country like India or Egypt which is 90 per cent illiterate? Can the wise Jeffersonian concept of a literacy test for voters be completely ignored nowadays because we have radio? President Nasser has proffered a counter-doctrine for the developing countries, to wit: "It is true that most of our people are still illiterate. But politically that counts far less than it did twenty years ago. . . . Radio has changed everything. . . . Today people in the most remote villages hear of what is happening everywhere and form their opinions. Leaders cannot govern as they once did. We live in a new world."[11]

But has radio really changed everything? When illiterate "people in the most remote villages hear of what is happening everywhere," what do they really hear? They hear, usually via the communal receiver at the village square in the presence of the local elite, the news and views selected for their ears by Egyptian State Broadcasting (ESB). Their receivers bring no alternative news from other radio stations. Being illiterate, they can receive no alternative news and views from newspapers and magazines and books published anywhere.

In terms of personal achievement almost nothing happens to these "people in the most remote villages" by way of Radio Cairo: broadcasting now supplies them with the kind of rote learning each acquired by memorizing the Koran (which he could not read) in childhood. But in terms of personal aspiration nearly everything happened to these people when radio came to their remote villages. For the first time in their experience—both the experience of centuries inherited through their parents and their own lives—these isolated villagers were invited (and by none less than their rulers!) to participate in the public affairs of their nation.

The invitation carried with it, however, none of the enabling legislation needed to make radio-listening an integrative agent of modernization. In a modern society the radio listener is also the cash customer and the voter. In the remote villages of Egypt, when the government inserted radio into the community, nothing else changed in the daily round of life—except the structure of expectations. This is the typical situation that over the past decade has been producing the revolution of rising frustrations. The mass media have been used to stimulate people in some sense. It does so by raising their levels of aspiration—for the good things of the world, for a better life. No adequate provision is made, however, for raising the levels of achievement. Thus

[11] Gamal Abdul Nasser, *Egypt's Liberation*, Washington, D.C., Public Affairs Press, 1955.

people are encouraged to want more than they can possibly get, aspirations rapidly outrun achievements, and frustrations spread. This is how the vicious circle of poverty operates in the psychological dimension.

The impact of this psychic disequilibrium—its force as a positive impediment to modernization—has been disclosed by Major Salah Salem, the youthful Minister of National Guidance who tried to run the Egyptian mass media during the contest for power between Naguib and Nasser. Major Salem, finding his problems of national guidance insoluble, finally solved them by voluntarily locking himself in jail. There he prepared a memoir of his own frustration in the impossible task of converting an inert and isolated peasantry into an informed and participant citizenry by the mass media alone. Major Salem concludes: "Personally I am convinced that the public was wrong."[12]

In similar vein, Nasser has written retrospectively: "Before July 23rd I had imagined that the whole nation was ready and prepared, waiting for nothing but a vanguard to lead the charge. . . . I thought this role would never take more than a few hours . . .—but how different is the reality from the dream! The masses that came were disunited, divided groups of stragglers. . . . There was a confirmed individual egotism. The word 'I' was on every tongue. It was the solution to every difficulty, the cure for every ill."[13]

These judgments by leaders who were frustrated in their aspiration for quick and easy modernization reveal why transitional Egypt—in the dozen years since its liberation—has been so deeply frustrated. Can "the people," in Salem's sense, ever really be "wrong"? Can a social revolution ever really be accomplished in "a few hours"—or its failure attributed, in Nasser's sense, to "egotism"? Or is it, rather, that these young enthusiasts had never learned Lasswell's lesson—that political life is largely a question of "who gets what"? When people get involved in politics, it is natural that they should expect to get more of whatever it is they want. Instead of rebuffing such aspirations as egotism, the statesman of an enlarging polity and modernizing society will rather seek to expand opportunities for people to get what they want. He will seek above all to maintain a tolerable balance between levels of aspiration and achievement. In guiding the society out of the vicious circle toward a growth cycle his conception of the role of public communication is likely to be crucial.

[12] This memoir is quoted in D. Lerner, *The Passing of Traditional Society*, pp. 244-245.

[13] Gamal Abdul Nasser, *op.cit.*, pp. 244-245.

IV. From Vicious Circle to Growth Cycle

"The vicious circle of poverty" is a phrase used to characterize the situation in which no sustained economic growth is possible because each specific advance is rapidly checked by some counter-tendency in the social system. The most important of sucn counter-tendencies is excessive population growth. Any significant economic progress tends to prolong life by reducing famine and pestilence. When death rates decrease more rapidly than birth rates—often, indeed, while birth rates are increasing—then rapid population growth occurs. In poor countries population growth tends to "lead" economic growth by setting rates of increase that must be attained so that the society can stay at its existing levels of poverty. No surpluses can be generated, hence no "leap forward" is possible. Singer has succinctly summarized "the dominant vicious circle of low production—no surpluses for economic investment—no tools and equipment—low standards of production. An underdeveloped country is poor because it has no industry; and it has no industry because it is poor."[14]

The picture looks quite different in a society which has broken out of the vicious circle and set its course toward the achievement of a growth cycle. The new situation is vividly illustrated by the following diagram:[15]

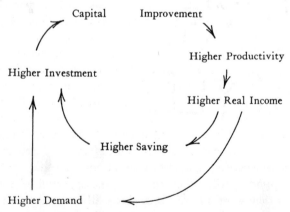

The story told by this diagram reaches its climax with the achievement of a significant rise in real income. Such a rise becomes significant

[14] Hans W. Singer "Economic Progress in Underdeveloped Countries," *Social Research*, XVI, 1, March 1949, p. 5.

[15] Gerald M. Meier and Robert E. Baldwin, *Economic Development: Theory, History, Policy*, New York, Wiley, 1957, pp. 319-320.

when it enables the society simultaneously to raise both demand and saving. We have seen that otherwise, in a poor society, small increases of income tend to be consumed promptly—with nothing left over for saving, hence investment. But when income rises rapidly enough to permit higher consumption and also higher saving, then the growth cycle is initiated. Higher investment leads to capital improvement and rising productivity, which in turn raise real income enough to encourage both higher saving and demand. Thereby higher investment is again stimulated—and the growth cycle becomes self-sustaining.

Specialists on economic development appear to be generally agreed on some version of this picture of the break-out from the vicious circle. There is less consensus, however, on the economic policies that will lead most efficiently from the break-out to the self-sustaining growth cycle. Contemporary economic thinking has tended to emphasize two quite different sets of theoretical analyses—which we may characterize as "disequilibria" and "balanced growth" theories—leading to different policies and programs.

It is difficult to resolve the issues between disequilibria and balanced growth on a theoretical level. The arguments rest in both cases on factors extraneous to the economy—i.e., on the values, beliefs, and institutions of a country and, especially, on its capacity to change these psychosocial factors as may be required for sustained economic growth. For example: higher income, even if rapid and substantial, will not necessarily lead to commensurate increases of saving and investment. There are numerous cases where higher income has led only to conspicuous consumption of imported products or to savings that were invested only abroad—hence with no effect on production and growth at home.

The growth cycle, which stipulates that higher income must be coupled with both higher consumption and investment, is likely to occur only in a society where effort is associated with reward—where saving is likely to compound interest, where investment at home is likely to conjoin personal with patriotic satisfactions (rather than exploit the latter and deny the former). The association of effort with reward comes from the matrix of social institutions, psychological beliefs, political efficiency (in managing public adaptation to innovation) within which economic programs are obliged to operate.

The association of effort with reward, of aspiration with achievement, is a communication process. People must learn to make this association in their own daily lives—linking what they see with what they hear, what they want with what they do, what they do with what they get. Communication is, in this sense, the main instrument of socialization, as socialization is, in turn, the main agency of social change. To parallel the economist's model of the growth cycle, we may represent the conditions for an expanding polity and modernizing society as follows (adapting the input functions proposed by Gabriel Almond).[16]

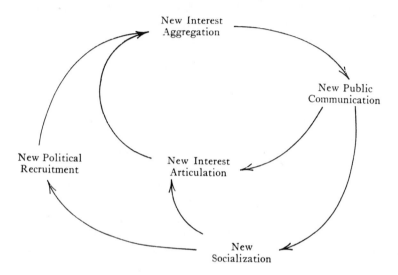

The modernization process begins with new public communication— the diffusion of new ideas and new information which stimulate people to want to behave in new ways. It stimulates the peasant to want to be a freeholding farmer, the farmer's son to want to learn reading so that he can work in the town, the farmer's wife to want to stop bearing children, the farmer's daughter to want to wear a dress and do her hair. In this way new public communication leads directly to new articulation of private interests.

Simultaneously—by analogy with the significant increase of real income that enables both saving and demand to rise simultaneously— new public communication activates new modes of socialization. If new interest-articulation parallels demand, then new socialization parallels saving—the factor that will make possible new investment and, ultimately, the supply of new satisfactions for the new demands. So, while new communication is promoting new articulation of in-

[16] Gabriel A. Almond and James S. Coleman, *op.cit.*, p. 17.

terests among the existing generation, it is also preparing a new generation who will incorporate these interests and go beyond them. The farmer's daughter who wants to show her face is likely to raise a daughter who wants to speak her mind. The farmer's son who wants literacy and a town job is likely to raise a son who wants a diploma and a white collar. Socialization thus produces, ideally, the new man with new ideas in sufficient quality and quantity to stabilize innovation over time.

In order to incorporate innovation efficiently, a society must translate it from private interests into public institutions. An essential step forward must be made from the articulation to the aggregation of private interests—which, when aggregated and accepted in the polity, become the public institutions of a society. It is also necessary that a new process of political recruitment come into operation. Among the newly socialized generation some must be recruited into political life so that the new aggregation of interests into institutions may be accomplished and sustained. So it is that, starting from a breakthrough in communication, reinforced by new ways of socialization (ideas of what one's children may be and practices designed to achieve these aspirations), a new political class is recruited that aggregates the new interests articulated within the society in such fashion as to create its new institutions—its version of modernity.

V. Looking Ahead

Our set of considerations has been presented tersely. We have merely raised and related considerations that need to be explored in depth. This is a task for social scientists in the decade ahead—a task that will be the better performed in the measure that we improve our understanding of the communication crux of the modernizing process.

Our understanding begins with recognition that the revolution of rising expectations has been a major casualty of the past decade. In its place has risen a potential revolution of rising frustrations. This represents a deep danger to the growth of democratic polity in the world. People who do not aspire do not achieve; people who do not achieve do not prosper. Frustration produces aggression or regression.

Aggression in today's transitional societies expresses itself through violence based on moralistic but often inhumane ideologies. Such doctrines, albeit in prettier euphemisms, authorize fear, greed, and hate to operate as racism, xenophobia, vengeance. Regression in these societies signals the return to apathy and the narcosis of resignation.

Aggression among transitional peoples victimizes others; regression victimizes themselves. Neither process is compatible with the dynamic equilibrium that promotes modernization. Hence the global spread of frustration must be checked and a tolerable ratio of aspirations to achievements must be instigated.

Communication is the crux. In the introduction of this volume it was observed that "the state of politics is a function of the communication process." The communication catastrophe in transitional societies has been their failure to discourage—often, indeed, their effort to encourage—the "insatiable expectations of politics" that lead ultimately only to frustration. Short-sighted politicians have been sowing a storm they may not be able to harvest. The policy of whipping up enthusiasm on short-run issues by creating insatiable expectations has never produced long-run payoffs.

What is needed in the years ahead is a new conception of public communication as the crucial instrument which can promote psychic mobility, political stability under conditions of societal equilibrium. The mass media can be used to mobilize the energies of living persons (without creating insatiable expectations) by the rational articulation of new interests. Flanked by the schools and community leaders, the mass media can simultaneously induce a new process of socialization among the rising generation that will, among other effects, recruit new participants into political life. These two processes—short-run mobilization and long-run socialization—can then converge, a generation later, in new aggregations of private interests which are the stuff of a democratic polity.

What we have sketched here is of course an idealized model. In the measure that it corresponds to reality the model provides clarification and guidance for those who must think and act in the transitional lands. The task for future research is to determine under what conditions the model does or does not work, so that a better model may be developed to shape a more effective communication process where it is most needed. This calls for close and continuous cooperation between men of knowledge and men of action on the most challenging social problem of our time—the modernizing of most of the world.

A SELECTED BIBLIOGRAPHY

Prepared by

Thelma Jean Grossholtz and Richard Hendrickson

~~~~~~~~~~~~~~~~~~~~~~~~~~~~~~~~~

ARTICLES

I. Role of the Mass Media in Political Development

Ashford, Douglas E. "Patterns of Consensus in Developing Countries." *American Behavioral Scientist*, IV (April 1961), pp. 7-10. The major problem of consensus formation in developing countries is to expand the world view of participant individuals to include the national scene. Creation of a "nationalistic fervor" by reference to an outside threat leads to instability and may hinder development.

Bruner, Jerome S. and Jeanette Sayre. "Short-Wave Listening in an Italian Community." *Public Opinion Quarterly*, V (Winter 1941), pp. 640-656. A poll of a group of marginal Americans in Boston's Italian north end furnishes a clue to the motivation and behavior of the recent immigrant short wave listener.

Eldersveld, Samuel J. "Experimental Propaganda Techniques and Voting Behavior." *American Political Science Review*, 50 (March 1956), pp. 154-165. Also in Eulau, et al., *Political Behavior: A Reader in Theory and Research*, Glencoe, Ill., The Free Press, 1956, pp. 210-217. The effectiveness of techniques for getting out the vote varies with other considerations such as the type of campaign, personalities involved, etc. Personal contact seems the most effective technique for getting out the vote.

Eulau, Heinz and Peter Schneider. "Dimensions of Political Involvement." *Public Opinion Quarterly*, XX (Spring 1956), pp. 128-142. Political involvement depends on relatedness to the political process. Sensitivity to politics is related to individual's perception of the role of citizen and his perception of the efficacy of political action.

Hadsel, Fred L. "Propaganda in the Funnies." *Current History*, 1 (December 1941), pp. 365-368. More people are reached by the comics than by any other part of the newspaper. Comics analyzed as to content and function.

Kirchheimer, Otto. "German Democracy in the 1950's." *World Politics*, XIII (January 1961), pp. 254-266. External and internal problems of postwar German development. Good documentation of German political development and role of the mass media in this process.

Klapper, Joseph T. "What We Know about the Effects of Mass Communication: The Brink of Hope." *Public Opinion Quarterly*, XXI (Winter 1957-1958), pp. 453-474. Summary of findings of mass media and mass communications research and discussion of some generalizations about effects.

Noelle-Neumann, Elisabeth. "Mass Communication Media and Public Opinion." *Journalism Quarterly*, 36 (Fall 1959), p. 401. Question of real function of the mass media in Western society analyzed. People seek in the media confirmation for their already existing opinions and philosophies.

Robinton, Madeline B. "The Lynskey Tribunal: The British Method of Dealing with Political Corruption." *Political Science Quarterly*, LXVIII (March 1953), pp. 109-124. The British method of holding open hearings with thorough press coverage, although destructive to some individuals without cause, did tend to rally public support for proceedings and led to a return of public confidence in the public administration. The mass media served as a means of insuring maintenance of the society's values.

Simon, Herbert A. and Frederick Stern. "The Effects of Television upon Voting Behavior in Iowa in the 1952 Presidential Election." *American Political Science Review*, 49 (June 1955), pp. 470-477. Also in *Political Behavior: A Reader in Theory and Research*, pp. 205-210. Television had no discernible effect on total participation or party division of the vote. Mass media has reached a saturation point so that the addition of television makes no substantial difference in terms of evoking high interest in a political campaign.

Stewart, Donald H. "The Press and Political Corruption during The Federalist Administration." *Political Science Quarterly*, LXVII (September 1952), pp. 426-447. The newspapers pioneered in directing popular attention to graft and corruption, pointing out land speculation deals, etc. Faults tended to be associated with individuals rather than with abstract principles or institutions. Emphasis on the corruption of the "ins" did much to foster the growth of an opposition party.

Wright, Charles R. "Functional Analysis and Mass Communication." *Public Opinion Quarterly*, XXIV (Winter 1960), pp. 605-620. Kinds of factors involved in functional analysis of the role of the media and the formulation of hypotheses are discussed in terms of the problems involved in developing theory.

II. Communication Patterns

Alisky, Marvin. "Growth of Newspapers in Mexico's Provinces." *Journalism Quarterly*, 37 (Winter 1960), pp. 75-82. Discusses effect of the amazing growth of readership and influence of newspapers outside the national capital on local and provincial politics. They bring their readers into participation in local events and carry comment and criticism of national officials and policies. At the same time they bring local political events to a wider audience and even to national attention.

Cantwell, Frank V. "Public Opinion and the Legislative Process." *American Political Science Review*, LV (October 1946), pp. 924-935. Also in Berelson, B. and Janowitz (eds.), *Reader in Public Opinion and Communication*, Glencoe, Ill., The Free Press, 1950, pp. 121-131. Legislators wait for public opinion to shape itself before dealing formally with policy questions. Events play a more important role than Congress or the President in shaping public opinion. Public opinion seldom proposes a course of action and it always needs leadership.

Damle, Y. B. "Communication of Modern Ideas and Knowledge in Indian Villages." *Public Opinion Quarterly*, XX (Spring 1956), pp. 257-270. The influence of the social structure on the quality and quantity of the communications which are assimilated in seven villages at different distances and with differing contacts with urban center. Structural constraints whether natural or imposed render certain ideas and knowledge dysfunctional and lead to change.

Davison, W. Phillips. "On the Effects of Communication." *Public Opinion Quarterly*, xxiii (Fall 1959), pp. 343-360. Research must look deeper into the effects of communication on the arousal of human needs and how they are satisfied. In one sense the audience bargains with the message and vice versa.

Deutschmann, Paul J. and Wayne A. Danieson. "Diffusion of Knowledge of the Major News Story." *Journalism Quarterly*, 37 (Summer 1960), pp. 345-355. Analysis of the diffusion process involved in dissemination of three big news stories and the role of the "opinion leader" in relaying additional information. This relay function is supplemental to the media and the reinforcement function.

Glickmann, Harvey. "Viewing Public Opinion in Politics: A Common Sense Approach." *Public Opinion Quarterly*, xxiii (Fall 1959), pp. 495-504. Considers the atomistic character of "public" and the influence of environmental factors and sub-publics on the articulation and aggregation problem.

Horikawa, Naoyoshi. "Television in Everyday Life." *Japanese Journalism Review*, 1960, 10, pp. 148-160. An inquiry into the change caused by television on the lives of women and children.

Husain, Asad. "The Future of English Language Newspapers in India." *Journalism Quarterly*, 33 (Spring 1956), pp. 213-219. The English language papers will maintain their prestige largely because the vernacular press has only a regional standing and the national language has not spread to dimensions necessary for a truly national press. English language speakers constitute only 8 per cent of the population but they are spread all over India and the English papers have national coverage.

Jennings, W. Ivor. "Universities in the Colonies," in Shannon, ed., *Underdeveloped Areas*, New York, Harper, 1957, pp. 114-119. Discusses the problem of education for life in the colonies versus the emphasis on examinations and English education.

Katz, Elihu. "The Two-Step Flow of Communication: An Up to Date Report on An Hypothesis." *Public Opinion Quarterly*, xxi (Spring 1957), pp. 61-78. Discusses character of opinion leader and source of his influence. Function of inter-personal relations.

Lowe, Francis E. and Thomas C. McCormick. "A Study of the Influence of Formal and Informal Leaders in an Election Campaign." *Public Opinion Quarterly*, xx (Winter 1956), pp. 651-662. Qualities of informal leaders and degree of influence relative to formal leaders noted. Finds citizen's political opinions relatively independent of those attributed to leader.

Mardin, Serif. "Some Notes on an Early Phase in the Modernization of Communications in Turkey." *Comparative Studies in Society and History*, iii (April 1961), pp. 250-271. The process of modernization in Turkey discussed in terms of Karl Deutsch's model in *Nationalism and Social Communication*. Concentrates on problem of language diversity and national assimilation.

A SELECTED BIBLIOGRAPHY

The building of national unity among the Turks had no relation to the assimilation of linguistic minorities by a linguistic majority that Deutsch assumed.

Park, Robert E. "Reflections on Communication and Culture." *American Journal of Sociology*, XLIV (1939), pp. 191-205. Also in *Reader in Public Opinion and Communication*, pp. 165-175. Communications "spin a web of custom and mutual expectation which binds together diverse social units." Two forms of organization involved, the familial and the communal.

Pickerell, Albert G. "The Press of Thailand: Conditions and Trends." *Journalism Quarterly*, 37 (Winter 1960), pp. 83-96. Paternalistic government, political apathy, and other influences have shaped newspapers which are colorful but lack accuracy and responsibility. Trend toward more bluntness, more factual accounts, less carefree ways but problem of underdevelopment in media resources is major.

Pye, Lucian W. "Communication Patterns and the Problems of Representative Government in Non-Western Societies." *Public Opinion Quarterly*, xx (Spring 1956), pp. 249-256. Traditional patterns of communication, changes wrought by urbanization and westernization and special problems of political communication inherent in character and culture of non-Western society.

Ragsdale, Wilmott. "A Program for Developing the Media of Southeast Asia." *Journalism Quarterly*, 37 (Spring 1960), pp. 275-279. Report of the UNESCO Conference on Development of Information Media in Southeast Asia, Bangkok, January 18-30, 1960. Statistics on media available.

Smith, Bruce L. "Communications Research on Non-industrial Countries." *Public Opinion Quarterly*, 16 (Winter 1952-1953), pp. 527-538. Also in Shannon, *Underdeveloped Areas*, pp. 360-367. Outlines main characteristics of these societies with emphasis on audience characteristics.

Stycos, J. M. "Patterns of Communication in a rural Greek Village." *Public Opinion Quarterly*, xvi (Spring 1952), pp. 59-70. Investigates question: To what extent does "opinion leader" hypothesis fit the communication pattern of a relatively underdeveloped area? Finds that in an area with low literacy, low access to media, the importance of the opinion leader is enhanced and to some extent formalized. Also points to "the information controllers" who because they own radios or newspapers can control the flow of news.

Warner, Bob. "An Emerging Press: The African Story." *Editor and Publisher*, 93 (August 27, 1960), p. 12. An examination of press conditions in the Congo Republic, Guinea, Somali, and Malagasy.

III. Attitude Change, Socialization and Personality Structure

Baur, E. Jackson. "Public Opinion and the Primary Group." *American Sociological Review*, 25 (April 1960), pp. 208-219. Typical history of a public passes through stages characterized by mass behavior, public controversy between organized factions, and institutionalized decision making. In each stage primary groups perform generative and relay functions within larger structures.

Breed, Warren. "Mass Communication and Socio-Cultural Integration." *Social Forces*, 37 (December 1958), pp. 109-116. Analyses mass media as an independent variable in normative integration in terms of publishing or not publishing material which may injure popular faith in the society or important parts of it. Power and class as structural strata are protected by media and the media do not reveal flaws in working of institutions or deviance from norms.

Deutsch, Karl W. "The Growth of Nations: Some Recurrent Patterns of Political and Social Integration." *World Politics*, v (January 1953), pp. 168-195. Defines community and people in terms of communications. Lists possible specific uniform ties in nation-building including the growth of basic communication grids. Concept of self-interest and the experience of self-awareness is part of the problem of social integration.

Eisenstadt, S. N. "Communication Systems and Social Structure: An Exploratory Comparative Study." *Public Opinion Quarterly*, xix (Summer 1955), pp. 153-167. Compares communication system of underdeveloped countries with more urban-modern systems. Draws hypothesis as to how development takes place.

————. "Conditions of Communicative Receptivity." *Public Opinion Quarterly*, 17 (Fall 1953), pp. 363-374. Study of communication process of new immigrants in Israel. Investigates characteristics of "low communicants" and conditions which give rise to this. Finds that individuals need organization in a system and this organization determines his communication receptivity.

Gampertz, K. "The Relation of Empathy to Effective Communication." *Journalism Quarterly*, xxxvii (Autumn 1960), pp. 533-546. Summarizes all writings on empathy: its nature, meaning and role in personality development. Draws some hypothesis about meaning in terms of communication.

Geiger, Kurt. "Changing Political Attitudes in Totalitarian Society: A Case Study of the Role of the Family." *World Politics*, viii (January 1956), pp. 187-205. Interviews with refugees on parent-child relations vis-à-vis Soviets and religion. Conflict of values weakens family as unit of opposition.

Golden, H. H. "Literacy and Social Change in Underdeveloped Countries." *Rural Society*, 20 (1955), pp. 1-7. Finds literacy correlates with industrialization at .87 and at .84 with per capita income.

Greenstein, Fred I. "Sex Related Political Differences in Childhood." *Journal of Politics*, 23 (May 1961), p. 353. Review of findings on children's social development and report on New Haven study showing continuing sex differences in direction and degree of political attention and participation. Differences appear as early as 9-10 years.

————. "Children's Images of Political Authority." *American Political Science Review*, liv (December 1960), p. 934. New Haven study indicates grade 4 to 8 children have some perceptions of political leaders and their roles and importance. Absence of political cynicism or skepticism at this age.

Gulick, John. "Conservatiyism and Change in a Lebanese Village." *Middle East Journal*, 8 (Summer 1954), pp. 295-307. Changes which have taken place as a result of contact with the West. What has changed: occupational roles, economics, religion, kinship structure, social behavior, localism.

Guttman, Louis and Urill G. Foa. "Social Contact and an Inter-Group Attitude." *Public Opinion Quarterly*, xv (Spring 1951), pp. 43-53. Survey of cross-section of Israeli population on attitude toward government civil servants.

A SELECTED BIBLIOGRAPHY

Amount of contact was not related to direction of intergroup attitude but was related to the intensity of that attitude.

Katz, Daniel. "The Functional Approach to the Study of Attitudes." *Public Opinion Quarterly*, XXIV (Summer 1960), pp. 163-204. Reasons for holding or changing attitudes are found in the functions they perform for the individual, specifically the functions of adjustment, ego defense, value expression and knowledge. Motivational impact of other groups of variables considered.

Klapp, Orrin E. "Social Types: Process and Structure." *American Sociological Review*, 23 (December 1958), pp. 674-678. Distinguishes between formal role structure and social typing. The latter specifies much of the informal structure and special situations that develop for which no formal role exists. In a changing society social typing defines emerging roles and thus plays a role in the development of social structure. They give informal status, contribute to identity problems solutions in transitional societies.

Meier, Dorothy and Wendell Bell. "Anomie and Differential Access to the Achievement of Life Goals." *American Sociological Review*, 24 (April 1959), pp. 189-202. Dysfunction and communication problems.

Mair, L. P. "Independent Religious Movements in Three Continents." *Comparative Studies in Society and History*, 1 (January 1959), pp. 113-135. Reaction to opposition to established religious institutions appears similar: greater autonomy in achieving benefits or reinterpretation of the dogma and goals. Suggests political party or labor union organization may be similar.

Patai, Raphael. "The Dynamics of Westernization in the Middle East." *Middle East Journal*, 9 (Winter 1955), pp. 1-16. What prevailed, means used by West, why some practices accepted easier than others, etc. See change as the development of mental attitudes in the direction of rational thinking.

Shils, Edward. "The Concentration and Dispersion of Charisma." *World Politics*, XI (October 1958), pp. 1-19. Charisma can be dispersed if individuals can find a way of breaking loose from habits of extended family without losing the basic organizational structure of personal life. By learning to use own capacity the individual gains in self-respect but he must develop a basic structure to organize himself in relation with others, that is, develop a belief in his own charisma as well as charisma of those in authority.

Tumin, Melvin M. "Some Dysfunctions of Institutional Imbalances." *Behavioral Science*, 1 (July 1956), pp. 218-223. How does the economic structure—especially job recruitment, placement, performance, and reward—compare with the structure of kinship-role playing, and how do these structures interact? Ways in which institutions may become and be dominant and effect of imbalance which results particularly the imbalance in value attainment.

Vickers, Geoffrey. "Is Adaptability Enough?" *Behavioral Science*, 4 (July 1959), pp. 219-234. Outlines a conceptual model for the adaptation of a system. Points out essential features of adaptation, problems raised. Society's regulatory process and how it reacts to changes. Control and conflict within the system.

Walter, E. V. "Power, Civilization and Psychology of Conscience." *American Political Science Review*, LIII (September 1959), pp. 641-661. Function of political power is to regulate, direct, coordinate, and control existing social relationships. To function properly it requires certain social and psychological conditions. Traditional societies differ in these conditions and change brings about crisis in political power.

Wurfel, David. "Foreign Aid and Social Reform in Political Development: A Philippine Case Study." *American Political Science Review*, LIII (June 1959), pp. 456-482. American use of foreign aid to effect social reform, minimum wage act and encourage land reform. Social and political problems encountered in the process.

IV. Role of Specific Groups in Development

Almond, Gabriel A. "A Comparative Study of Interest Groups and the Political Process." *American Political Science Review*, LII (March 1958), pp. 270-282. Description of the Committee on Comparative Politics of the SSRC: its membership, orientation, objectives, and initial hypotheses. Rationale of interest group and functional approach.

Ashford, Douglas E. "Labor Politics in a New Nation." *Western Political Quarterly*, XIII (June 1960), pp. 312-331. Study of U.M.T. labor movement in Morocco since independence. Example of a labor union becoming a well-organized and functionally specific interest group during the achievement of independence and then denying its union purposes in order to engage in politics and seek political influence.

Blanksten, George I. "Political Groups in Latin America." *American Political Science Review*, LIII (March 1959), pp. 106-127. Describes and classifies institutional, associational and non-associational groups in Latin American politics. Argues for the "group analysis" approach for an understanding of Latin American politics.

Dubin, Robert. "Industrial Conflict and Social Welfare." *Journal of Conflict Resolution*, I (June 1957), pp. 179-199. Role of conflict and response to same in social integration and social change. Social change is "hammered out" in the daily lives of citizens and their reference groups. The interplay and conflict over the ends of power-seeking groups is the fundamental social process and the outcome of this conflict settles social policy questions.

Eisenstadt, S. N. "Internal Contradictions in Bureaucratic Politics." *Comparative Studies of Society and History*, I (October 1958), pp. 58-75. Functional analysis of bureaucracies in pre-modern cultures. Shows that goals institutionalized by ruling elites who established centralized bureaucracies were eventually undermined by those recruited into the supporting institutions.

————. "Political Struggle in Bureaucratic Societies." *World Politics*, IX (October 1956), pp. 15-36. Political sphere of bureaucracies is strongly goal-oriented with goals distinct from those of other institutions or sub-groups in the society. Description of these societies and social conditions which give rise to them.

Freedman, Maurice. "Immigrants and Associations: Chinese in 19th Century Singapore," *Comparative Studies in Society and History*, III (October 1960), pp. 25 ff. Societies organized by Chinese created a sub-society during the 19th century. Secret societies insulated Chinese from other societies and provided consensus mechanism within the relatively closed society.

Friedmann, J. "Intellectuals in Developing Societies," *Kyklos* (No. 4, 1960), pp. 513-544. Modern intellectual must be ranged alongside the innovator in affairs of business as a principal agent in promoting economic growth. He mediates new values, formulates an effective ideology, etc.

Hoselitz, B. F. "The Recruitment of White-Collar Workers in Underdeveloped Countries," *International Social Science Bulletin*, vi (No. 3, 1954), pp. 3-11. Also appears in Shannon, *Underdeveloped Areas*, pp. 181-189. Character of the white-collar worker and his recruitment on a personal, non-rational basis must be understood in terms of the development needs of underdeveloped countries.

Kozicki, Richard J. "Indian Interest Groups and Indian Foreign Policy," *Indian Journal of Political Science* (July-September 1958), pp. 219-227. Notes general absence of interest groups in India. But Federation of Indian Chambers of Commerce and Industry is active in foreign policy, particularly discusses this group with respect to Indo-Burmese and Indo-Ceylon policies.

Lerner, Daniel and Richard Robinson. "The Turkish Army as a Modernizing Force," *World Politics*, xiii (October 1960), pp. 19-44. Role of military in spread of Westernization and Western values and in pressuring politicians to behave has been of great importance in Turkey. Contacts with West have been more intense historically and through U.S. aid.

Lichtblau, George E. "The Politics of Trade Union Leadership in Southern Asia," *World Politics*, vii (October 1954), pp. 84-101. Unemployed intellectuals took over leadership of the labor movement to achieve social and political mobility otherwise denied them. Workers and leaders interests converged and were identified with nationalism. Political ambitions and personalized character of relationship converts unions into recruitment mechanism for political process and government takes over a protective role toward worker.

Liebman, Charles S. "Electorate Interest Groups and Local Government Policy," *American Behavioral Scientist*, iv (January 1961), pp. 9 ff. Develops a model of policy formulation which assumes a complete separation of policy formulation and electoral activity. Voter decisions are entirely personality oriented and there is no expectation that particular policies will be realized because a particular candidate is elected. Thus elected officials are not bound by constituent demands.

Rangnekar, D. K. "The Nationalist Revolution in Ceylon," *Pacific Affairs*, xxxiii (December 1960), pp. 361-374. Peaceful transfer of power in Ceylon prevented the development of mass movement which might have served to unify the people. Bandaranaike aroused first nationalist spirit with appeals to politically alienated using socialism and nationalism.

Reed, Howard. "A New Force at Work in Democratic Turkey," *Middle East Journal*, 7 (Winter 1953), pp. 33-44. Peasant has become target of political appeals and as prosperity and communication increase his demands become wider and more detailed. Example of broadening base of political power.

Rudolph, Lloyd I. and Susanne H. Rudolph. "The Political Role of India's Caste Associations," *Pacific Affairs*, xxxiii (March 1960), pp. 5-22. Caste associations as an example of indigenous forms of associations providing channels of communication and bases of leadership and organization to overcome "technical political illiteracy" handicaps of traditional elements and thus allow them participation in politics.

Sakata, Yoshio and John Whitney Hall. "The Motivation of Political Leadership in the Meiji Restoration," *Journal of Asian Studies*, xvi (November 1956), pp. 31-50. Analyzes restoration in terms of the political agents who brought it about. Breakdown of equilibrium of three distinct political institutions and the development of a potential bargaining process as quid pro quo's fluctuated. Significant in terms of imbalances created during development and changes brought about through response to these imbalances.

Sayeed, Khalid B. "Political Role of Pakistan's Civil Service," *Pacific Affairs*, xxx (June 1958), pp. 131-146. Civil servant's distrust of the politician and his ways and the strength of the civil service gives that group unnatural weight in political affairs. They are not responsive to needs and very slow to act.

Shils, Edward. "Intellectuals, Public Opinion and Economic Development." *World Politics*, x (January 1958), pp. 232-255. Finds that the intellectuals need to contact masses with their vision, and sees the press as the chief organ of instructured public opinion. General discussion of press problems in underdeveloped countries.

————. "The Intellectuals in the Political Development of the New States." *World Politics*, xii (April 1960), pp. 329-368. Changing roles of intellectuals in the process of political development.

Szigliano, Robert C. "Political Parties in South Vietnam Under the Republic." *Pacific Affairs*, xxxiii (December 1960), pp. 327-346. Development of Vietnamese political parties as instruments for dealing with foreign rulers. Seek accommodation and a wider range of participation but mostly aimed at independence.

Wickwar, W. Hardy. "Patterns and Problems of Local Administration in the Middle East." *Middle East Journal*, 12 (Summer 1958), pp. 249-260. Problem of decentralization of administration and creation of viable political and administrative units at the local level. Use of Western institutions and the results. Socio-cultural factors inhibiting and enhancing development.

Wright, Gordon. "Peasant Politics in the Third French Republic." *Political Science Quarterly*, lxx (March 1955), pp. 75-86. Role of peasants in development. They have tended to back reactionary forces and slow down social reform.

V. Cultural Factors that Enhance or Impede Democratic Development

Bernstein, Marver. "Israel's Capacity to Govern." *World Politics*, xi (April 1959), pp. 399-417. Analyzes the achievements and problems the nation-building elite of Israel experienced in their development of a modern state. Deals with orientations toward government, development of legitimacy, etc.

Brzezinski, Zbigniew. "The Politics of Underdevelopment." *World Politics*, ix (October 1956), pp. 55-75. Economic development requires totalitarian regimes. Foreign aid programs therefore can not continue to political and social change in the direction of democratic development.

Cook, Thomas I. "Democratic Psychology and Democratic World Order." *World Politics,* 1 (July 1949), pp. 553-564. Need to re-evaluate assumptions about political theory and psychology with a view to developing useful theoretical base for functional theory.

Cowan, C. D. "Indonesia and the Commonwealth in Southeast Asia: A Reappraisal." *International Affairs,* 34 (October 1958), pp. 454-468. Description of events in Indonesia arising out the 1949 decision to change the constitution from a federal to a central unitary state. Notes the biggest problem in Indonesia is the failure to grasp the fundamental principle of Western parliamentary practice: that governments succeed one another modifying each other's programs as the pendulum swings from one to another.

Einaudi, Mario. "The Crisis of Politics and Government in France." *World Politics,* IV (October 1951), pp. 64-84. Problems of parliamentary system in multi-party state. Does not generate spirit of compromise or acceptance of majority rule. Finding the dividing line between party politics and government is the basic problem.

Elkins, Stanley and Eric McKettrick. "A Meaning for Turner's Frontier." *Political Science Quarterly,* LXIX (September 1954), pp. 321-353 and also LXIX (December 1954), pp. 565-602. Political democracy is most obvious where there is a necessity to act, that is, in the initial stages of setting up a new community where there is no structure of natural leadership. Implies no clear distinction between rulers and ruled in this setting.

Emerson, Rupert. "The Erosion of Democracy." *The Journal of Asian Studies,* XX (November 1960), pp. 1 ff. Military take-overs in South East Asia raise the question of the suitability of Western evolved democracy for Asian environments.

Griffith, Ernest S., John Plamenatz and J. Roland Pennock. "Cultural Prerequisites for Democracy." *American Political Science Review,* 50 (March 1956), pp. 101-137. A philosophical essay by each author on the requirements for democracy restricted to five highly industrialized countries.

Hauser, Philip M. "Cultural and Personal Obstacles to Economic Development in the Less Developed Areas." *Human Organization,* 18 (Summer 1959), pp. 78 ff. Elements of colonialism which impede economic development: truncated social orders, pluralistic societies, over-urbanization, resurgent nationalism, mass disillusionment with respect to the timing of economic development. Elements of indigenous culture which impede development: value systems which conflict with material aspirations, highly stratified societies with a relatively small but powerful elite, etc.

Hughes, Colin A. "Semi-Representative Government in the British West Indies." *Political Science Quarterly,* LXVIII (September 1953), pp. 338-353. Two main tendencies in West Indian politics—lone-wolf tradition of personality politics and over-organization on paper which is ineffective in terms of political organization. Transitional societies tend to have loosely organized politics at the same time that many opportunities exist to avoid accountability. This is crucial.

Lane, Robert. "The Fear of Equality." *American Political Science Review,* LIII (March 1959), pp. 35-51. Finds that working-class Americans do not promote or hold to the ideal of equality. This value is promoted largely by intellectuals.

Lipset, Seymour. "Some Social Requisites of Democracy: Economic Development and Political Legitimacy." *American Political Science Review*, LIII (March 1959), pp. 69-105. Compares "democracies" more or less democratic in terms of wealth, industrialization, education, and urbanization. Compares in terms of legitimacy and effectiveness of government. Finds development problems of new states inherent in the requirements mentioned—level of economic development and level of political effectiveness and legitimacy.

Marshall, James. "The Nature of Democracy." *Political Science Quarterly*, LXV (March 1950), pp. 38-54. The measure of a people's democracy is the extent of its freedom from dependence. This is a sign of a political maturity. All modern societies embody a degree of dependence; those which try to decrease the level of dependence are democratic. If citizen is dependent he cannot release the aggressions and anxieties which society creates but must rely on leaders. Democracy is a complex series of human relationships and a comparative cultural relationship.

Rosenberg, Morris. "The Meaning of Politics in Mass Society." *Public Opinion Quarterly*, XV (Spring 1951), pp. 5-15. Lists three positive motivations to political action and three obstructions to political action. Politics gives no immediate concrete gratification and thus rouses apathy but this allows people to accept political defeat of their candidates.

Sayeed, Khalid Ben. "Collapse of Parliamentary Democracy in Pakistan." *Middle East Journal*, 13 (Autumn 1959), pp. 389-406. Background of the situation, the division in leadership, and the problems of the martial law regime in meeting demands of public opinion. Overall view of the problem of democratic development and social reform and difficulties of finding political solutions to social problems.

Tambeah, S. J. and Bryce Ryan. "Secularization of Family Values in Ceylon." *American Sociological Review*, 22 (June 1957), pp. 292-299. Examines traditional family values and mores on fertility in three rural Sinhalese communities. Different levels of urban contact, isolation, and other variables point out that harsh environmental conditions are not sufficient condition for modification of value principles.

van der Kroef, Justus M. "Indonesia's Economic Future." *Pacific Affairs*, XXXII (March 1959), pp. 46-72. The politics of economic development and the problem of need for capital versus the attitude toward foreign capital. Traditional ways of complete representation and unanimity not conducive to development problem solving. Mutual cooperation value places more concern on ideology than on reconstruction.

VI. Theories and Models of Political Systems

Almond, Gabriel A., Taylor Cole and Roy C. Macridis. "A Suggested Research Strategy in Western European Government and Politics." *American Political Science Review*, 49 (December 1955), pp. 1,042-1,049. Review of U.S. and European political theory and research and a suggested strategy for consensus among researchers as to the most urgent needs of the field, the best approaches and suitable methodology.

Almond, Gabriel. "Comparative Political Systems." *Journal of Politics*, xviii (August 1956), also in Eulau, et al. *Political Behavior: A Reader in Theory and Research.* Formulation of the political culture model and the functional analysis of interest groups used in *Politics of the Developing Areas.*

Apter, David. "A Comparative Method for the Study of Politics." *The American Journal of Sociology*, lxiv (November 1958), pp. 221-237. Sets up three main dimensions—social stratification, political groups and government—in order to produce a manipulative theory out of comparative research. Outlines main components of each dimension and purports to show how each dimension interacts with the other two.

————. "The Role of Traditionalism in the Political Modernization of Ghana and Uganda." *World Politics*, xiii (October 1960), pp. 45-68. Compares Ghana and Uganda to show how their modern existence has been and is being shaped by the nature of their traditions. Defines in terms of instrumental versus consummatory systems and the possibilities of innovation in each system.

Berelson, Bernard. "Democratic Theory and Public Opinion." *Public Opinion Quarterly*, 16 (Fall 1952), pp. 313-330. Also appears in Eulau, et al., *Political Behavior: A Reader in Theory and Research.* Discussion of the prerequisites of democracy as outlined by theorists and compared to what public opinion studies have shown to be the actual case about political behavior. Suggests points where theory is too gross and needs refinement. Sets up guidelines as to requirements of "democracy."

Bretton, Henry L. "Current Political Thought and Practice in Ghana." *American Political Science Review*, 52 (March 1958), pp. 47 ff. Attempts to isolate some of the problem areas and political characteristics implicit in behavior patterns of contemporary and future political systems in developing areas. Looks at practices and behavior of party organization and the conduct of elections, parliamentary and administrative affairs.

Easton, David. "An Approach to the Analysis of Political Systems." *World Politics*, ix (April 1957), pp. 383-400. Input-output systems model of political process. Discusses the dynamic character of the process and the kinds of demands, channels, supports and outputs required to keep it operating.

Eisenstadt, S. "Primitive Political Systems: A Preliminary Comparative Analysis." *American Anthropologist*, lxi (April 1959), pp. 200-220. Good description of the basic elements of a political system.

Emerson, Rupert. "Nationalism and Political Development." *Journal of Politics*, 22 (February 1960), pp. 3-28. Nationalism answers none of the practical problems of development or independence. Its contribution is of the spirit and psychology and it may even impede development if used as a screen for domestic failures.

Gyr, John W. "An Investigation Into and Speculations About the Formal Nature of the Problem Solving Process." *Behavioral Science*, 5 (January 1960), pp. 39-59. The process of a person fitting "guesses" about the environment to his experience in it. Need to consider such things as the succession of trials made by the subject in solving problems, information available to him prior to each trial, mechanism inside individual which might account for the specific linkages between information and trial and the control system within the process.

Kahin, George McT., Guy Pauker, Lucian W. Pye. "Comparative Politics of Non-Western Countries." *American Political Science Review,* 49 (December 1955), pp. 1022-1041. A preliminary review and forecast of studies in comparative politics concentrating on problems of non-Western countries: the political process, groups and media of influence, dynamic factors to be considered by students in the field.

Kahl, Joseph A. "Some Social Concomitants of Industrialization and Urbanization." *Human Organization,* 18 (Summer 1959), pp. 53 ff. Good review of literature on urbanization and its effects on family structure, personal choices, attitudes toward life, etc.

Rudolph, Susanne. "Consensus and Conflict in India." *World Politics,* XIII (April 1961), pp. 383-399. Indian politics does not legitimize power or men who "live off" politics. Discusses reasons for and results of this phenomenon.

Rustow, Dankwart A. "New Horizons for Comparative Politics." *World Politics,* IX (July 1957), pp. 530-549. Differences between comparative politics of Western and non-Western world emphasize need for new concepts. Broad view of the situation shows similarities in experience. The constants have become variables and we need a more historical touch.

Weiner, Myron. "Struggle Against Power: Notes on Indian Political Behavior" *World Politics,* VIII (April 1956), pp. 392 ff. One prerequisite of a democratic system is a willingness of political groups to make political calculations (e.g. compromises and coalitions) to increase their strength. This is lacking in India and leaders are not concerned for the political consequences of their acts. Indian attitudes toward power tend to place leaders outside of formal power in their own organization.

BOOKS

I. The Communications Process

Bent, Silas. *Newspaper Crusaders: A Neglected Story.* New York: McGraw-Hill, 1939.

Bruce, John. *Gaudy Century: The Story of San Francisco's Hundred Years of Robust Journalism.* New York: Random House, 1948.

Cater, Douglass. *The Fourth Branch of Government.* Boston: Houghton Mifflin, 1959.

De Fleur, Melvin and Otto N. Larsen. *The Flow of Information: An Experiment in Mass Communications.* New York: Harper, 1958.

Hovland, Carl I. "Effects of Mass Media of Communication," *Handbook of Social Psychology,* II, G. Lindzey (editor). Cambridge: Addison-Wesley, 1954, pp. 1062-1103.

Hovland, Carl I., Irving I. Janis, and Harold H. Kelley. *Communication and Persuasion.* New Haven: Yale University Press, 1953.

Hughes, Helen McGill. *News and the Human Interest Story.* Chicago: University of Chicago Press, 1939.

Janowitz, M. *The Community Press in an Urban Setting.* Glencoe, Ill.: The Free Press, 1952.

A SELECTED BIBLIOGRAPHY

Katz, Elihu and Paul Lazarsfeld. "Personal Influence," in Eulau, et al., *Political Behavior*, Glencoe, Ill.: The Free Press, 1956, pp. 149-159.

Lang, Kurt and Gladys E. "Mass Media and Voting," in Eugene Burdick and Arthur J. Brodbeck (editors), *American Voting Behavior*. Glencoe, Ill.: The Free Press, 1959.

Lasswell, Harold D. "The Structure and Function of Communications in Society," in L. Bryson, *The Communication of Ideas*. New York: Institute of Religion and Social Studies, 1948.

Lazarsfeld, Paul F., Bernard Berelson, and Hazel Gaudet. *The People's Choice: How the Voter Makes Up His Mind in a Presidential Campaign*. New York: Duell, Sloan and Pearce, 1944.

Lazarsfeld, Paul F. and Robert K. Merton. "Mass Communication, Popular Taste and Organized Social Action," in L. Bryson, *The Communication of Ideas*. New York: Institute of Religion and Social Studies, 1948.

Lazarsfeld, Paul F. and Frank Stanton. *Radio Research 1942-1943*. New York: Duell, Sloan and Pearce, 1944.

Lee, Alfred McClung. *The Daily Newspaper in America: The Evolution of a Social Instrument*. New York: Macmillan, 1937.

Merton, Robert K. "Patterns of Influence: A Study of Interpersonal Influence and of Communication Behavior in a Local Community," in Lazarsfeld, Paul F. and Frank Stanton, *Communications Research 1948-1949*. New York: Harper and Brothers, 1949, pp. 180-220.

Merton, Robert K. "The Sociology of Knowledge and Mass Communication," Part III of *Social Theory and Structure*. Glencoe, Ill.: The Free Press, 1959.

Pool, Ithiel de Sola. *Trends in Content Analysis*. Urbana, Ill.: University of Illinois Press, 1959.

Riley, John W., Jr. and M. W. Riley. "Mass Communication and the Social Structure" in Merton, Broom and Cottrell, *Sociology Today*. New York: Basic Books, 1959, pp. 537-578.

Rosten, Leo. *The Washington Correspondents*. New York: Harcourt, Brace Company, 1937.

Schramm, Wilbur. *Responsibility in Mass Communications*. New York: Harper and Brothers, 1957.

Schramm, Wilbur (editor). *Mass Communications*. Urbana, Ill.: University of Illinois Press, 1944.

Schramm, Wilbur (editor). *The Process and Effects of Mass Communications*. Urbana, Ill.: University of Illinois Press, 1954.

Science Research Associates. *The Sunday Comics*. January 1956.

Siebert, Fred S., T. B. Peterson, and Wilbur Schramm. *Four Theories of the Press*. Urbana, Ill.: University of Illinois Press, 1956.

Sinclair, Upton. *The Brass Check*. Pasadena, Cal.: The Author, 1919.

Waples, Douglas, Bernard Berelson, and F. R. Bradshaw. *What Reading Does to People: A Summary of Evidence on the Social Effects of Reading and a Statement of Problems for Research*. Chicago: University of Chicago Press, 1940.

Williams, J. G. *Radio in Fundamental Education in Undeveloped Areas*. Paris: UNESCO, 1950.

Wright, Charles R. *Mass Communication: A Sociological Perspective.* New York: Random House (Paperback), 1960.

II. Attitude Change, Socialization and Personality

Child, Irvin L. "Socialization," in G. Lindzey, *Handbook of Social Psychology,* ii. Cambridge: Addison-Wesley, 1954, pp. 655-89.

Daedalus, 89 (Spring 1960), "Mass Culture and Mass Media."

Doob, Leonard W. *Becoming More Civilized: A Psychological Explanation.* New Haven: Yale University Press, 1960.

Handlin, Oscar. *The Uprooted.* New York: Grosset and Dunlap Publishers, 1951 (paperback).

Hays, Samuel P. *The Response to Industrialism 1885-1914.* Chicago: University of Chicago Press, 1957.

Heberle, Rudolf. *Social Movements: An Introduction to Political Sociology.* New York: Appleton-Century-Crofts, 1951.

Hoselitz, Bert F. (editor). *Sociological Aspects of Economic Development.* Glencoe, Ill.: The Free Press, 1960.

Hyman, Herbert. *Political Socialization: A Study in the Psychology of Political Behavior.* Glencoe, Ill.: The Free Press, 1960.

Inkeles, Alex and David J. Levinson. "National Character: The Study of Modal Personality and Sociocultural Systems," in G. Lindzey, *Handbook of Social Psychology,* ii. Cambridge: Addison-Wesley, 1954, pp. 977-1016.

Kerr, Clark, John T. Dunlap, et al. *Industrialism and Industrial Man.* Cambridge: Harvard University Press, 1960.

Kluckhohn, Clyde. "Culture and Behavior," in G. Lindzey, *Handbook of Social Psychology,* ii. Cambridge: Addison-Wesley, 1954, pp. 921-976.

Lipset, S. M., Paul F. Lazarsfeld, A. H. Barton, and J. Linz. "The Psychology of Voting: An Analysis of Political Behavior," in G. Lindzey, *Handbook of Social Psychology,* ii. Cambridge: Addison-Wesley, 1954, pp. 1144-1148.

Mannoni, O. *Prospero and Caliban: The Psychology of Colonization.* Translated by Pamela Powesland, New York: Praeger, 1956.

Public Opinion Quarterly, xxii, Fall 1958, Daniel Lerner (editor). "Attitude Research in Modernizing Areas."

Public Opinion Quarterly, xxiv, Summer 1960, Daniel Katz (editor). "Attitude Change."

Pye, Lucian W. *Politics, Personality, and Nation Building,* New Haven, Yale University Press, 1962.

Shils, Edward. "The Study of the Primary Group," in Lerner and Lasswell (editors), *The Policy Sciences: Recent Development in Scope and Method.* Stanford: Stanford University Press, 1951.

Slotkin, James S. *From Field to Factory: New Industrial Employees.* (Research Center in Economic Development and Cultural Change, University of Chicago) Glencoe, Ill.: The Free Press, 1960.

Smith, M. Brewster, Jerome S. Bruner and Robert W. White. *Opinions and Personality.* New York: John Wiley and Sons, Inc., 1956.

Spindler, G. D. *Socio-Cultural and Psychological Processes in Menomini Accul-turation.* Berkeley: University of California Press, 1955.

Thomas, William F. and Florian Znanieki. *The Polish Peasant in Europe and America.* New York: Knopf, 1927.

III. Studies of Specific Groups and Case Studies of Development

Apter, David. *The Gold Coast in Transition.* Princeton: Princeton University Press, 1955.

Ashford, Douglas. *Political Change in Morocco.* Princeton: Princeton University Press, 1961.

Bailey, F. G. *Caste and the Economic Frontier: A Village in Highland Orissa.* Manchester: Manchester University Press, 1958.

Bascom, William R. and Melville J. Herskovits (editors). *Continuity and Change in African Cultures.* Chicago: Chicago University Press, 1958.

Coleman, James S. *Nigeria: Background to Nationalism.* Berkeley: University of California Press, 1958.

Dore, R. P. *City Life in Japan: A Study of a Tokyo Ward.* Berkeley: University of California Press, 1958.

Dore, R. P. *Land Reform in Japan.* London: Royal Institute of International Affairs, Oxford University Press, 1959.

Ehrmann, Henry W. (editor). *Interest Groups on Four Continents.* Pittsburgh: University of Pittsburgh Press, 1958.

Emerson, Rupert. *From Empire to Nation: The Rise to Self-Assertion of Asian and African Peoples.* Cambridge: Harvard University Press, 1960.

Fallers, L. B. *Bantu Bureaucracy: A Study of Integration and Conflict in the Political Institutions of East African People.* Cambridge: W. Heffer and Sons, 1956.

Fisher, Margaret and Joan V. Bondurant. *The Indian Experience with Democratic Elections.* Berkeley: University of California, 1956.

Ginsburg, N. and Chester Roberts. *Malaya.* Seattle: University of Washington Press, 1958.

Karpat, Kemal H. *Turkey's Politics: The Transition to a Multi-Party System.* Princeton: Princeton University Press, 1959.

Kawai, Kazuo. *Japan's American Interlude.* Chicago: University of Chicago Press, 1960.

Kobre, Sidney. *The Development of the Colonial Newspaper.* Pittsburgh: Colonial Press, 1944.

Lynd, Robert S. and Helen Merrill Lynd. *Middletown in Transition: A Study in Cultural Conflicts.* New York: Harcourt, Brace and Company, 1937.

MacKenzie, W. J. M. and Kenneth Robinson (editors). *Five Elections in Africa: A Group of Electoral Studies.* Oxford: Clarendon Press, 1960.

Marriott, McKim (editor). *Village India: Studies in the Little Community.* Chicago: University of Chicago Press, 1955.

Marvick, D. (editor). *Political Decision-Makers.* Glencoe, Ill.: The Free Press, 1960.

Park, R. and Irene Tinker (editors). *Leadership and Political Institutions in India.* (Some papers from seminar at Berkeley 1956) Princeton: Princeton University Press, 1959.

Redfield, Robert. *The Little Community and Peasant Society and Culture.* Chicago: University of Chicago Press, 1960.

Rose, Saul. *Socialism in Southern Asia.* New York: Oxford University Press, 1959.

Scott, Robert. *Mexican Government in Transition.* Urbana, Ill.: University of Illinois Press, 1959.

Shannon, Lyle (editor). *Underdeveloped Areas.* New York: Harper, 1957.

Smith, Thomas C. *Political Change and Industrial Development in Japan: Government Enterprise, 1868-1880.* Stanford: Stanford University Press, 1955.

Smythe, Hugh H. and Mabel M. *The New Nigerian Elite.* Stanford: Stanford University Press, 1960.

Social Change in Latin America Today: Its Implications for United States Policy. (Published for the Council on Foreign Relations) New York: Harper, 1960.

Van Niel, Robert. *The Emergence of Modern Indonesian Elite.* Chicago: Quadrangle Books, 1960.

Weiner, Myron. *Party Politics in India.* Princeton: Princeton University Press, 1957.

Wolf, Charles, Jr. *Foreign Aid: Theory and Practice in Southern Asia.* Princeton: Princeton University Press, 1960.

Wriggins, W. H. *Ceylon: Dilemma of a New Nation.* Princeton: Princeton University Press, 1960.

Zinkin, Maurice. *Development for Free Asia.* New York: Institute of Pacific Relations, 1956.

IV. Theories and Models of Political Systems

Almond, Gabriel and James S. Coleman, et al. *The Politics of the Developing Areas.* Princeton: Princeton University Press, 1960.

Banfield, Edward C. and Laura F. *The Moral Basis of a Backward Society.* Glencoe, Ill.: The Free Press, 1958.

Barnes, J. A. *Politics in a Changing Society.* New York: Humanities Press, 1954.

Dahl, Robert. "Hierarchy, Democracy and Bargaining in Politics and Economics," in *Research Frontiers in Politics and Government.* Washington: Brookings Institute, 1955, pp. 47-55. Also appears in Eulau, et al. *Political Behavior,* pp. 83-90.

Dahl, Robert and Charles E. Lindblom. *Politics, Economics and Welfare.* New York: Harper, 1953.

De Grazia, Sebastian. *The Political Community: A Study of Anomie.* Chicago: University of Chicago Press, 1948.

Eulau, H. et al. *Political Behavior.* Glencoe, Ill.: The Free Press, 1956.

Johnson, John J. *Political Change in Latin America: The Emergence of the Middle Sectors.* Stanford: Stanford University Press, 1958.

Key, V. O. *Politics, Parties and Pressure Groups.* New York: Crowell Publishers, 1958.

Lasswell, Harold D. *The Analysis of Political Behavior: An Empirical Approach.* New York: Oxford University Press, 1947.

Lasswell, Harold D. *Power and Personality*. New York: W. W. Norton Company, 1948.

Latham, Earl. *The Group Basis of Politics: A Study in Basing Point Legislation*. Ithaca: Cornell University Press, 1952.

Lerner, Daniel. *The Passing of Traditional Society: Modernizing the Middle East*. Glencoe, Ill.: The Free Press, 1958.

Lipset, Seymour M. *Political Man: Where, How and Why Democracy Works in the Modern World*. New York: Doubleday and Company, Inc., 1960.

Michels, Robert. *Political Parties: A Sociological Study of the Oligarchical Tendencies of Modern Democracy*. New York: Dover Publishers, Inc., 1959.

Riesman, David et al. *The Lonely Crowd*. New Haven: Yale University Press, 1950.

Schapera, I. *Government and Politics in Tribal Societies*. London: Oxford University Press, 1956.

Tocqueville, Alexis de. *Democracy in America*. New York: Oxford University Press, 1947.

Truman, David B. *The Governmental Process*. New York: Knopf, 1953.

Weber, Max. *From Max Weber: Essays in Sociology*. Translated and edited by H. H. Gerth and C. Wright Mills, New York: Oxford University Press, 1958.

Wittfogel, Karl A. *Oriental Despotism: A Comparative Study of Total Power*. New Haven: Yale University Press, 1957.

CONTRIBUTORS

FREDERICK W. FREY, born in Cleveland, Ohio, in 1929, is Assistant Professor of Political Science at the Massachusetts Institute of Technology. He did his graduate work at Balliol College, Oxford, on a Rhodes Scholarship, and at Princeton. From 1957 to 1959 and again in 1961 he was in Turkey, engaged in research on the social backgrounds of Turkish political leaders, on the value-systems of Turkish high-school and college students, and on Turkish voting behavior, and he has helped direct a national attitudinal survey of Turkish villagers. He has published articles on Turkey in the *Public Opinion Quarterly* (jointly), *The Atlantic, The Nation, Land Reborn,* and in Turkish journals.

HERBERT HYMAN, born in New York City in 1918, is Professor of Sociology and Associate Director of the Bureau of Applied Social Research at Columbia University. He is Chairman of the Methodology Section of the American Sociological Association and a past President of the American Association for Public Opinion Research. He has been a Visiting Professor at the University of Ankara, Turkey, and the University of Oslo, Norway. His publications include: *Political Socialization, Survey Design and Analysis, Interviewing in Social Research,* and *Applications of Methods of Evaluation.*

DANIEL LERNER, born in New York City in 1917, is Ford Professor of Sociology and International Communication at the Massachusetts Institute of Technology, and a Senior Research Associate of its Center for International Studies. During World War II he served as Chief Editor of the intelligence branch of the Psychological Warfare Division, SHAEF, and as Chief of Intelligence in the Information Control Division of the Office of Military Government, U.S.A. His books include: *Sykewar, Propaganda in War and Crisis, The Nazi Elite, The Policy Sciences* (with H. D. Lasswell), and *The Passing of Traditional Society.*

DAVID C. MC CLELLAND, born in Mount Vernon, New York, in 1917, is Professor of Psychology and Chairman of the Department of Social Relations at Harvard University. He has served in various administrative capacities on governmental and foundation projects studying the motivation for achievement and the early identification of talent. His most recent publications are: *Talent and Society* (with others), three chapters in *Motives in Fantasy, Action, and Society* (edited by John W. Atkinson), and *The Achieving Society.*

JAMES N. MOSEL, born in Steubenville, Ohio, in 1918, is Associate Professor of Psychology at The George Washington University. In 1954-1955 he conducted a study of communications behavior in Thailand, and in 1958-1959 he studied the Thai elite. Later he served as Visiting Professor in the Institute of Public Administration of Thammasart University, Bangkok, and also taught at Chulalongkorn University and the Buddhist University in Bangkok. He is the author of *Thai Administrative Behavior* and numerous research articles in psychological journals, as well as articles on Thai literature, including *A Survey of Classical Thai Poetry* and *Trends and Structure in Contemporary Thai Poetry*.

HERBERT PASSIN, born in Chicago in 1916, is Professor of Sociology in the East Asian Institute of Columbia University. He has lived and travelled for long periods in Asia, Africa, and Mexico. His major publications are: *In Search of Identity* (with John W. Bennett), and *The Japanese Village in Transition* (with Arthur Raper and others).

ITHIEL DE SOLA POOL, born in New York City in 1917, is Professor of Political Science at the Massachusetts Institute of Technology and has been director of the international communication program of the Center for International Studies at this institution. His main field of research has been public opinion and communcations, with special reference to political movements. Among his publications are: *Symbols of Democracy*, *Trends in Content Analysis* (ed.), and *American Business and Public Policy*.

LUCIAN W. PYE, born in China in 1921, is Chairman of Political Science at the Massachusetts Institute of Technology, and a Senior Staff member of its Center for International Studies. He has done field work in Southeast Asia, and has served in various capacities in the organizations of scholarly associations and of governmental agencies. He is the author of *Politics, Personality, and Nation Building*, *Guerrilla Communism in Malaya*, and co-author of *The Politics of the Developing Areas*, and *The Emerging Nations*.

WILBUR SCHRAMM, born in Marietta, Ohio, in 1907, is Director of the Institute for Communication Research, and Janet M. Peck Professor of International Communication, at Stanford University. He has done research in many countries, is chairman of the social psychology section of the International Association for Mass Communication Research, and is the author of *Process and Effects of Mass Communication*, *One Day in the World's Press*, *Responsibility in Mass Communication*, *Television in the Lives of Our Children*, and other books.

EDWARD A. SHILS, born in Philadelphia in 1915, is Professor of Sociology and Social Thought in the Committee on Social Thought at the University of Chicago, and a Fellow of King's College, Cambridge. He has also taught at Harvard University and at the Universities of Paris, London, and Manchester. Professor Shils is the translator of works by Max Weber and Karl Mannheim, co-editor of *Toward a General Theory of Action* and *Theories of Society*, and the author of *The Torment of Secrecy: The Background and Consequences of American Security Policies* and of numerous articles in sociology and on the politics of underdevelopment.

FREDERICK T. C. YU, Visiting Professor of Journalism at Columbia University, was born in 1921 in China, where he received his college education and worked as a journalist. He came to the United States in 1947, received his doctorate from the State University of Iowa in 1951, and was at one time a Ford Foundation Postdoctoral Fellow at the MIT Center for International Studies and Harvard University. He has taught at the University of Iowa, University of Southern California, Stetson University, and Montana State University; he has also been on the editorial staff of several newspapers, including the *Springfield* (Ohio) *News-Sun* and the *Washington Post*.

INDEX

communications: cultural restraints to, 138-39; and destruction of traditional societies, 3; and development policies, 12-14; and disruption of tradition, 36-38; and economic development, 43-52; general theory of, 20, 329-50; and instilling skills, 39-40; and international relations, 42; and marketing, 41; and national action, 53-54; and national planning, 39; and political control, 52-53; and political development, 298-305; and sense of nation-ness, 38; and social behavior, 4, 242; and social status, 53; and social structure, 34-36; as web of society, 4

communications approach: as method of social analysis, 5-6; and political behavior, 6

communications channels and social structure, 4

communications network, 205

communications policy, 229-33

communications process: and amplifying action, 6; comparison of modern and traditional, 24-29; and political rationality, 6; and political realism, 6-7; and the polity, 8; and prediction, 7

communications systems: fragmented kinds, 27; modern forms of, 25-26; traditional forms of, 24; traditional modes, 241-47; transitional forms of, 26-29

communications theory, 20

communicators: emergence of, 78-81; ethos of profession, 78-81; neutral role of, 78-79; professional, 25-26

Communism: appeal to writers in underdeveloped countries, 118; approach compared to traditional, 241-44; approach to gap between elite and mass, 255-57; approach to mass media, 234-36, 238-41; and communications theory, 261. See also Communist China

Communist China: and class consciousness, 261-62; communications in communes, 266-69, 271-77; communications systems in, 266-90 passim; communications techniques, 254-57; control of press, 104-05; criticism and self-criticism, 277, 292-93; language reform, 96; and mass line, 263-64; organization of communications, 269-71; propaganda directive of Central Committee, 273; script changes, 96; thought reform, 290-95; unity of

theory and practice, 264-66; use of communications, 37; use of literature, 283-88; use of motion pictures, 281-83; use of oral communicators, 288-90; use of press, 274-75; use of radio, 277-79

Congo, 83, 97

consensus, political, 10; lack of in transitional societies, 124-25

Coombs, Clyde H., 190

Cumberland, William W., 306

cybernetics and communications theory, 20

Dahl, Robert A., 302

Daily Mirror, 99

Daily Telegraph, 104

Damle, Y. B., 247

D'Arboussier, Gabriel, 89

demagogues and demagogy, 9, 64-68, 75-76

democratic development, 54-55

demonstration effect, 237

Denny, R., 165

deutero learning, 184, 225-26

Deutsch, Karl W., 20

development and democracy, 54-55; policies for, 11-14

Dewey, John, 34

Disraeli, 83

Domanach, Jean-Marie, 262

Dumazedier, J., 248

East Africa, 130, 134, 143, 144

economic development, 15, 42, 43-52

education: foreign experience in, 74-75; humanistic, 76; and political development, 71-73; and specialization, 70-73; technological, 76

educational system: and children's textbooks, 170-71; requirements for, 44-45

Egypt, 234, 344-45

Egyptian State Broadcasting (ESB), 344

Eisenstadt, S. N., 138, 139, 145

Eliot, Charles William, 34

Ellson, Douglas, 227

Embree, John F., 187

empathy, 226, 332, 341-42

fairy tales, 168

Fang Han-chi, 279

Farber, I. E., 290

Federation of Leftist Writers (Shanghai), 284

feedback mechanisms, 26